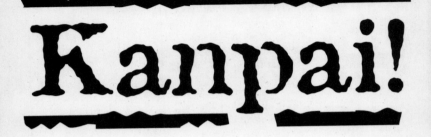

Kanpai!

VOLUME TWO

by Maki Murakami

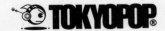

HAMBURG // LONDON // LOS ANGELES // TOKYO

CONTENTS

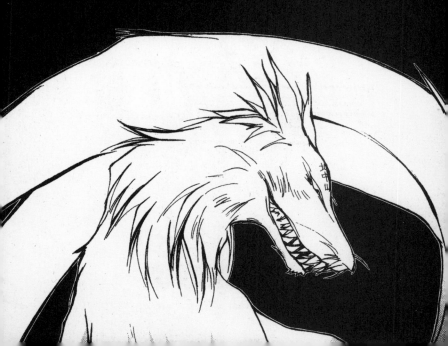

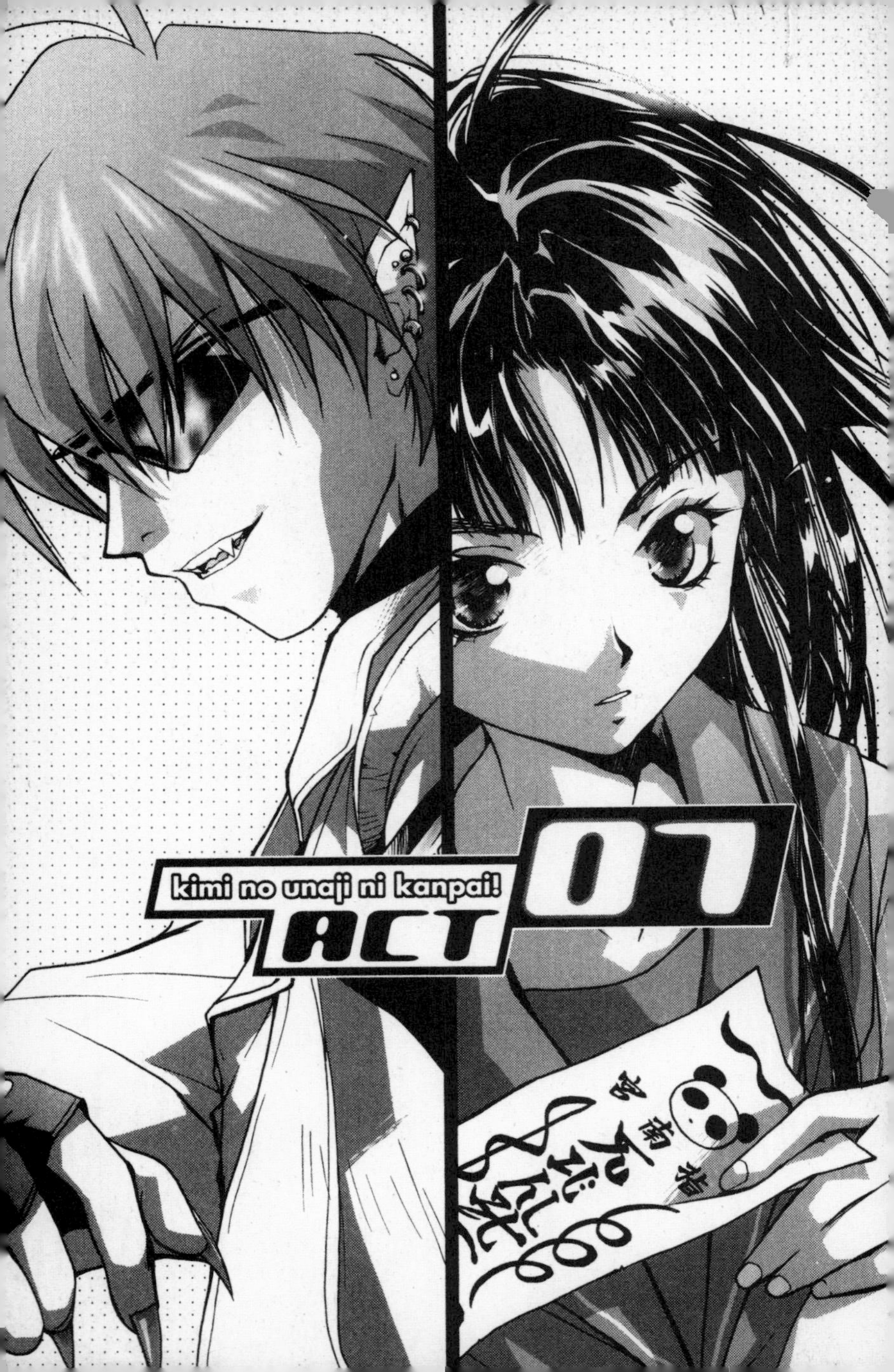

kimi no unaji ni kanpai!
ACT 07

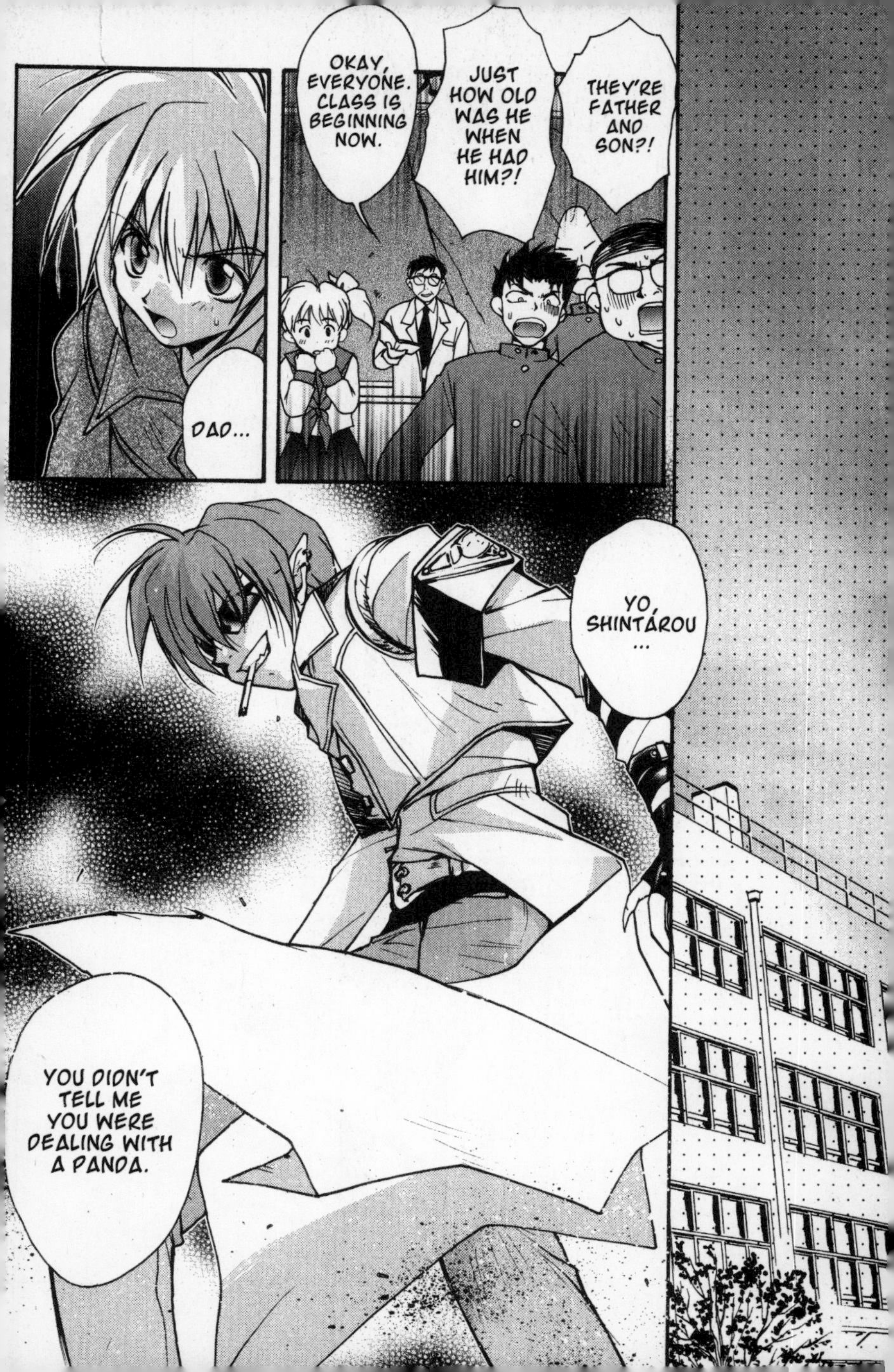
THEY'RE FATHER AND SON?!
JUST HOW OLD WAS HE WHEN HE HAD HIM?!
OKAY, EVERYONE. CLASS IS BEGINNING NOW.
DAD...
YO, SHINTÁROU ...
YOU DIDN'T TELL ME YOU WERE DEALING WITH A PANDA.

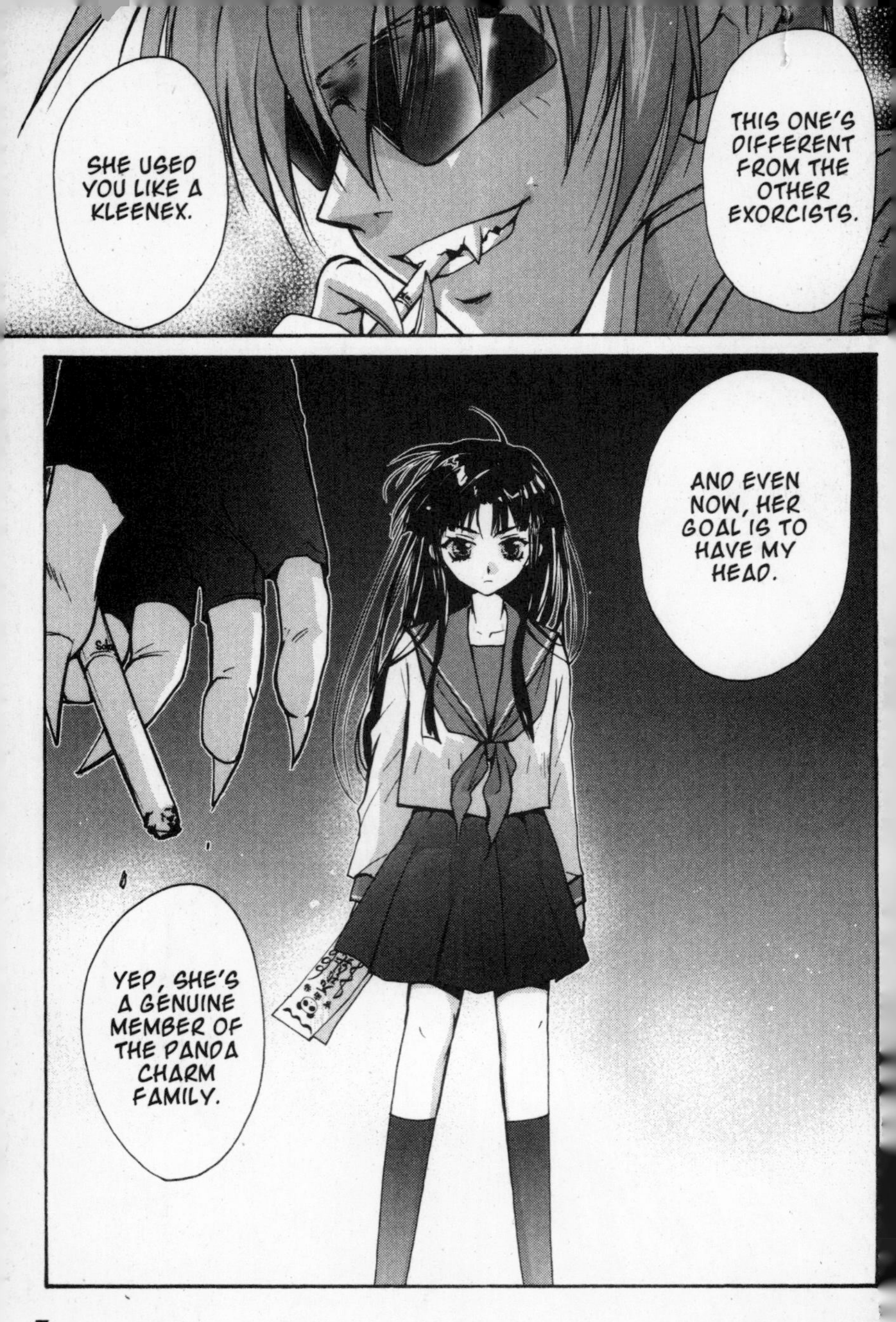
THIS ONE'S DIFFERENT FROM THE OTHER EXORCISTS.
SHE USED YOU LIKE A KLEENEX.
AND EVEN NOW, HER GOAL IS TO HAVE MY HEAD.
YEP, SHE'S A GENUINE MEMBER OF THE PANDA CHARM FAMILY.

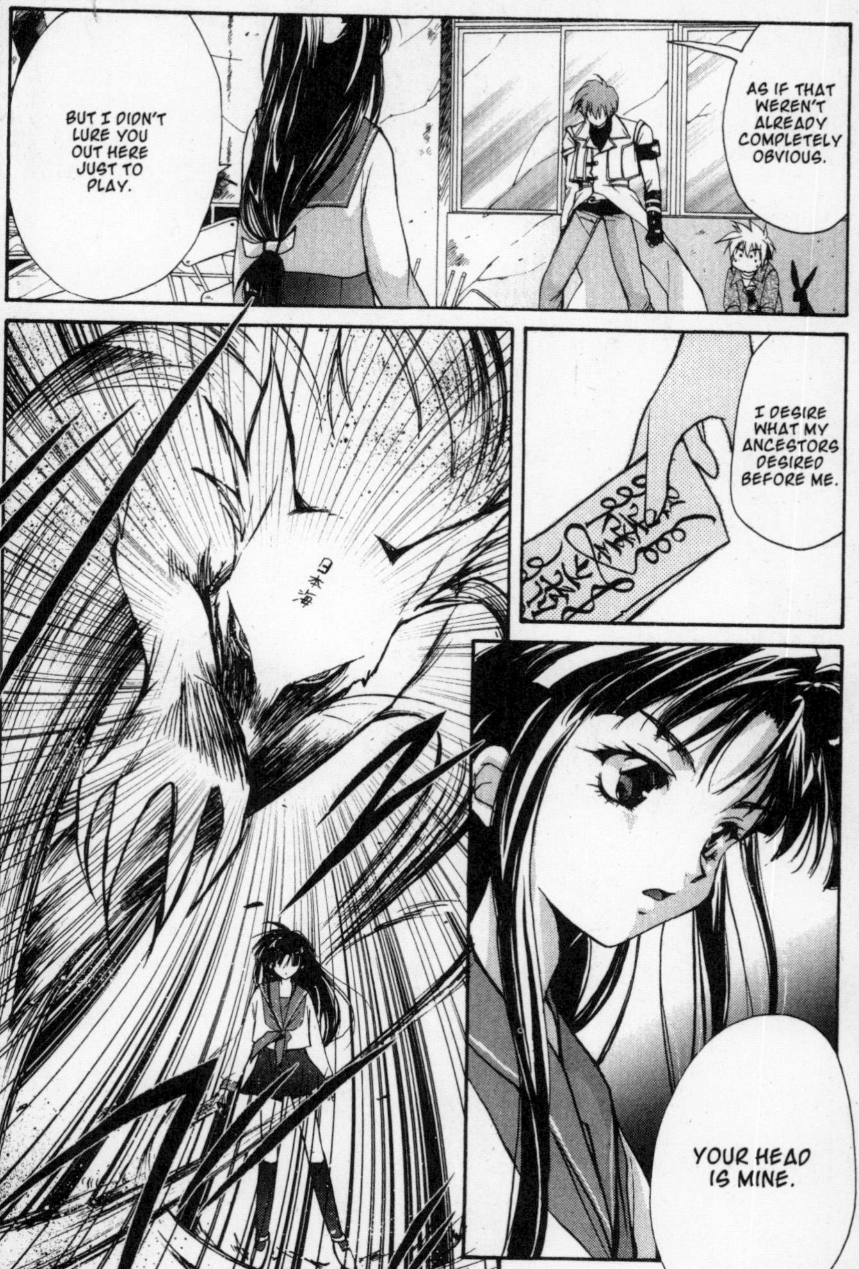
AS IF THAT WEREN'T ALREADY COMPLETELY OBVIOUS.
BUT I DIDN'T LURE YOU OUT HERE JUST TO PLAY.
I DESIRE WHAT MY ANCESTORS DESIRED BEFORE ME.
YOUR HEAD IS MINE.
日本海

Forehead:
Sea of Japan

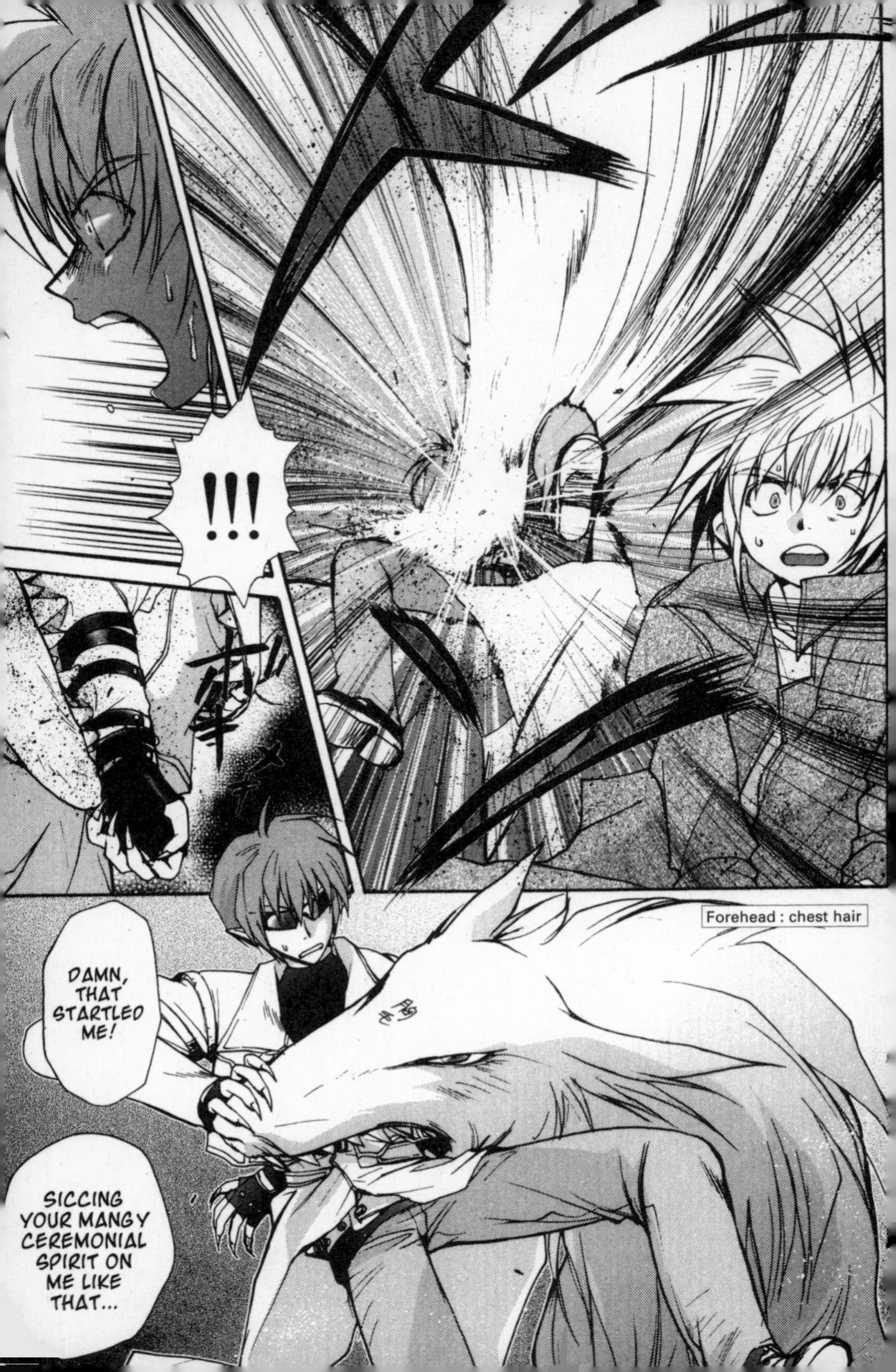
!!!
Forehead : chest hair
DAMN, THAT STARTLED ME!
SICCING YOUR MANGY CEREMONIAL SPIRIT ON ME LIKE THAT...

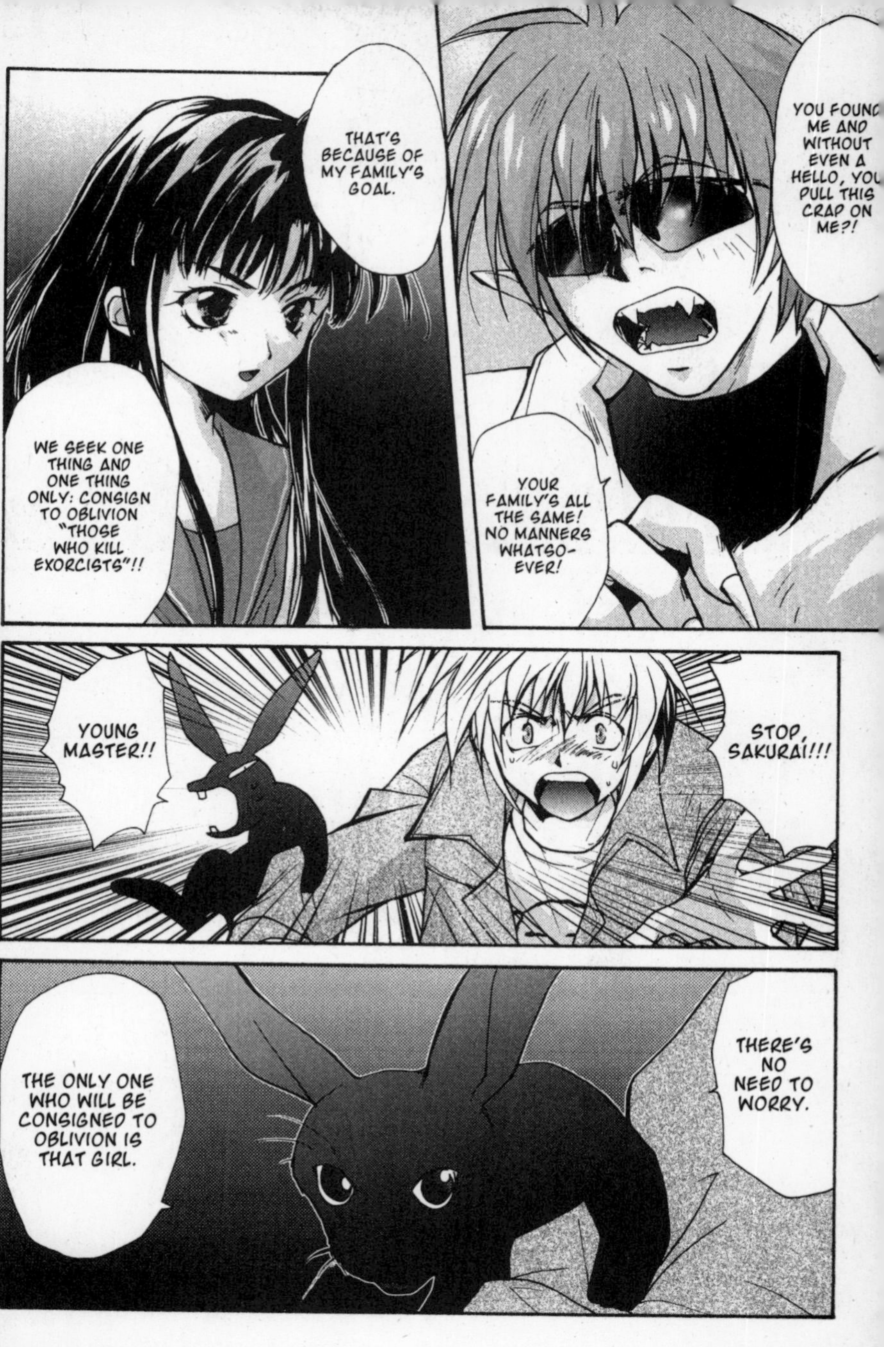

YOU FOUND ME AND WITHOUT EVEN A HELLO, YOU PULL THIS CRAP ON ME?!
YOUR FAMILY'S ALL THE SAME! NO MANNERS WHATSO-EVER!
THAT'S BECAUSE OF MY FAMILY'S GOAL.
WE SEEK ONE THING AND ONE THING ONLY: CONSIGN TO OBLIVION "THOSE WHO KILL EXORCISTS"!!
STOP, SAKURAI!!!
YOUNG MASTER!!
THERE'S NO NEED TO WORRY.
THE ONLY ONE WHO WILL BE CONSIGNED TO OBLIVION IS THAT GIRL.

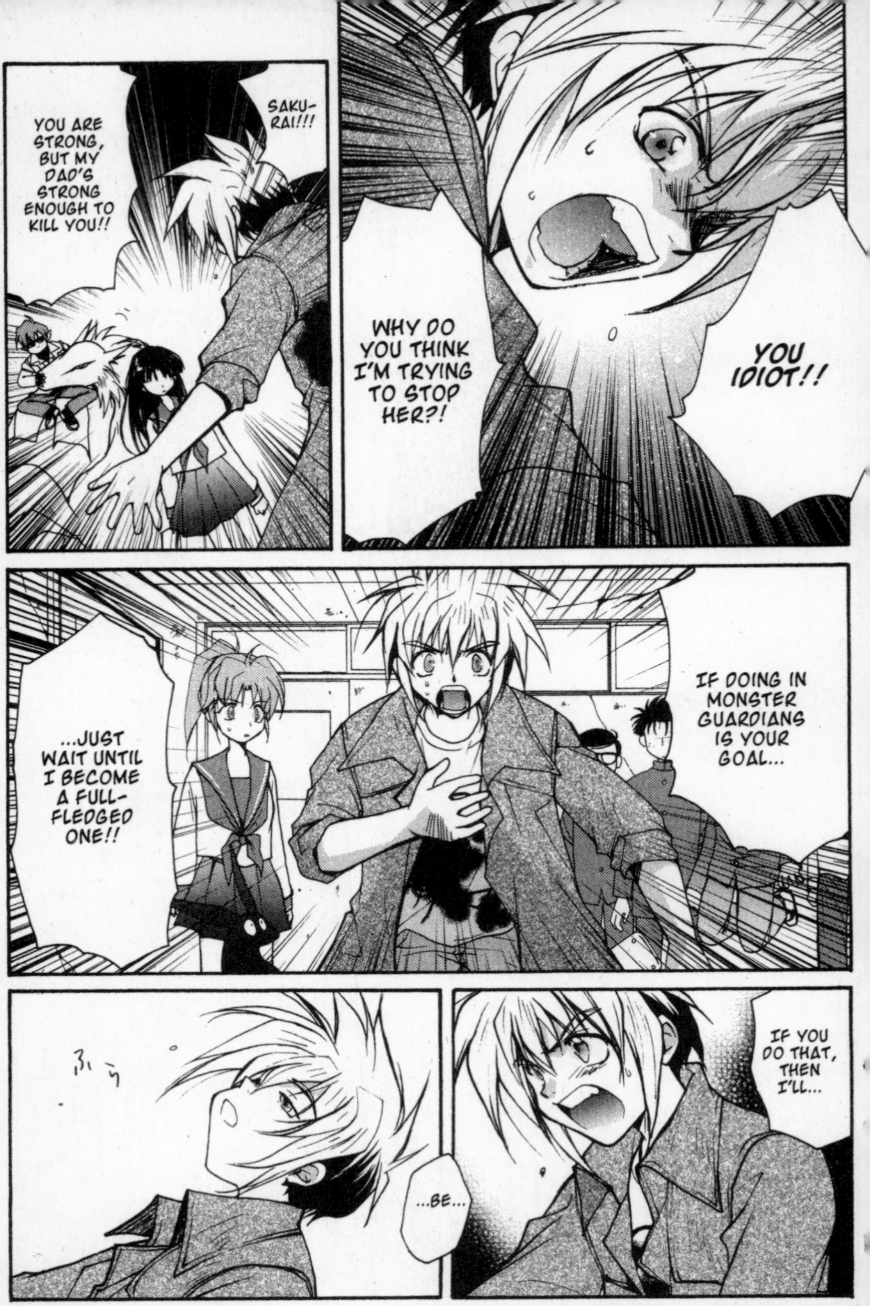
YOU IDIOT!!
WHY DO YOU THINK I'M TRYING TO STOP HER?!
SAKU-RAI!!!
YOU ARE STRONG, BUT MY DAD'S STRONG ENOUGH TO KILL YOU!!
IF DOING IN MONSTER GUARDIANS IS YOUR GOAL...
...JUST WAIT UNTIL I BECOME A FULL-FLEDGED ONE!!
IF YOU DO THAT, THEN I'LL...
...BE...

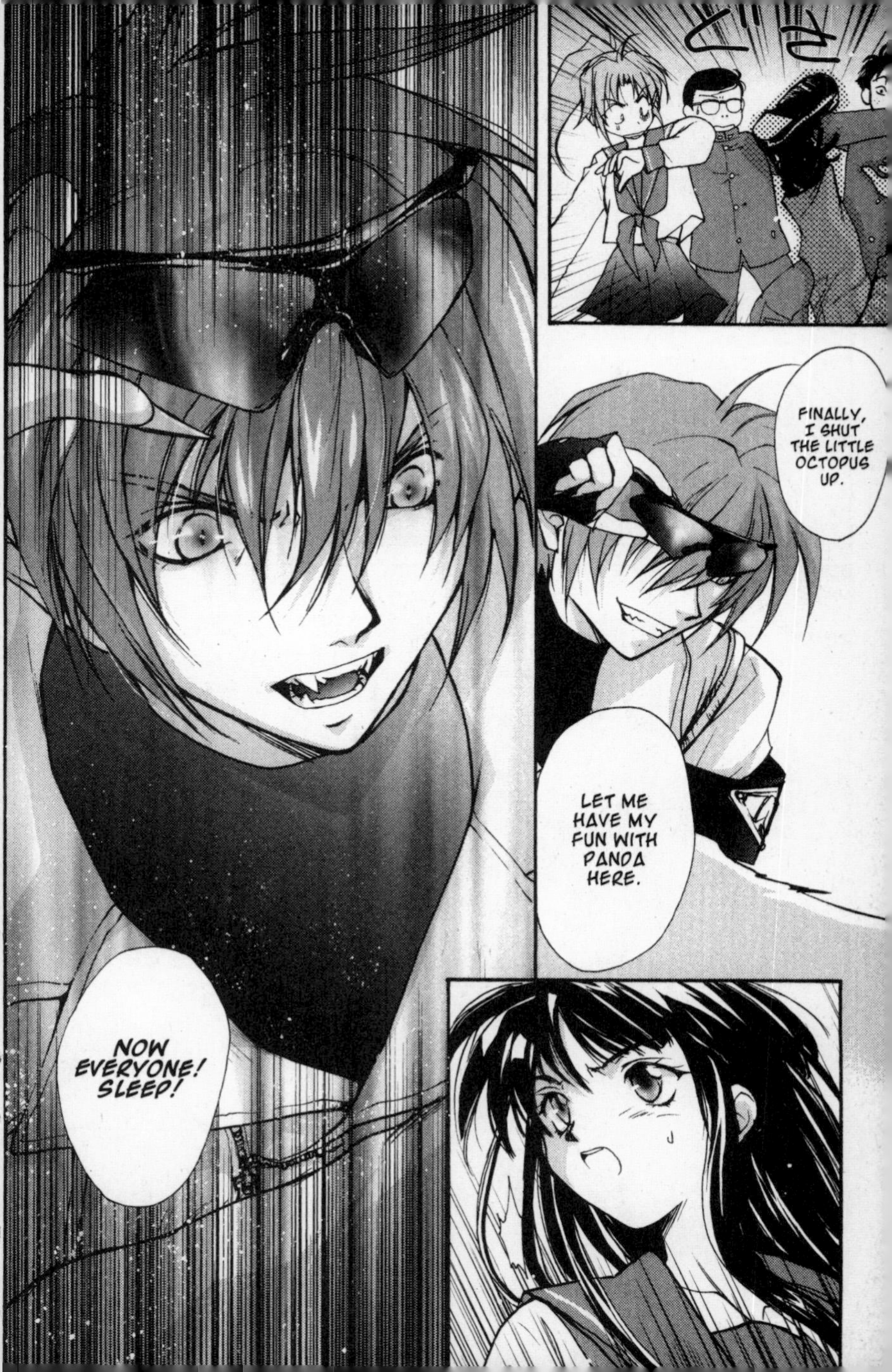
FINALLY, I SHUT THE LITTLE OCTOPUS UP.
LET ME HAVE MY FUN WITH PANDA HERE.
NOW EVERYONE! SLEEP!

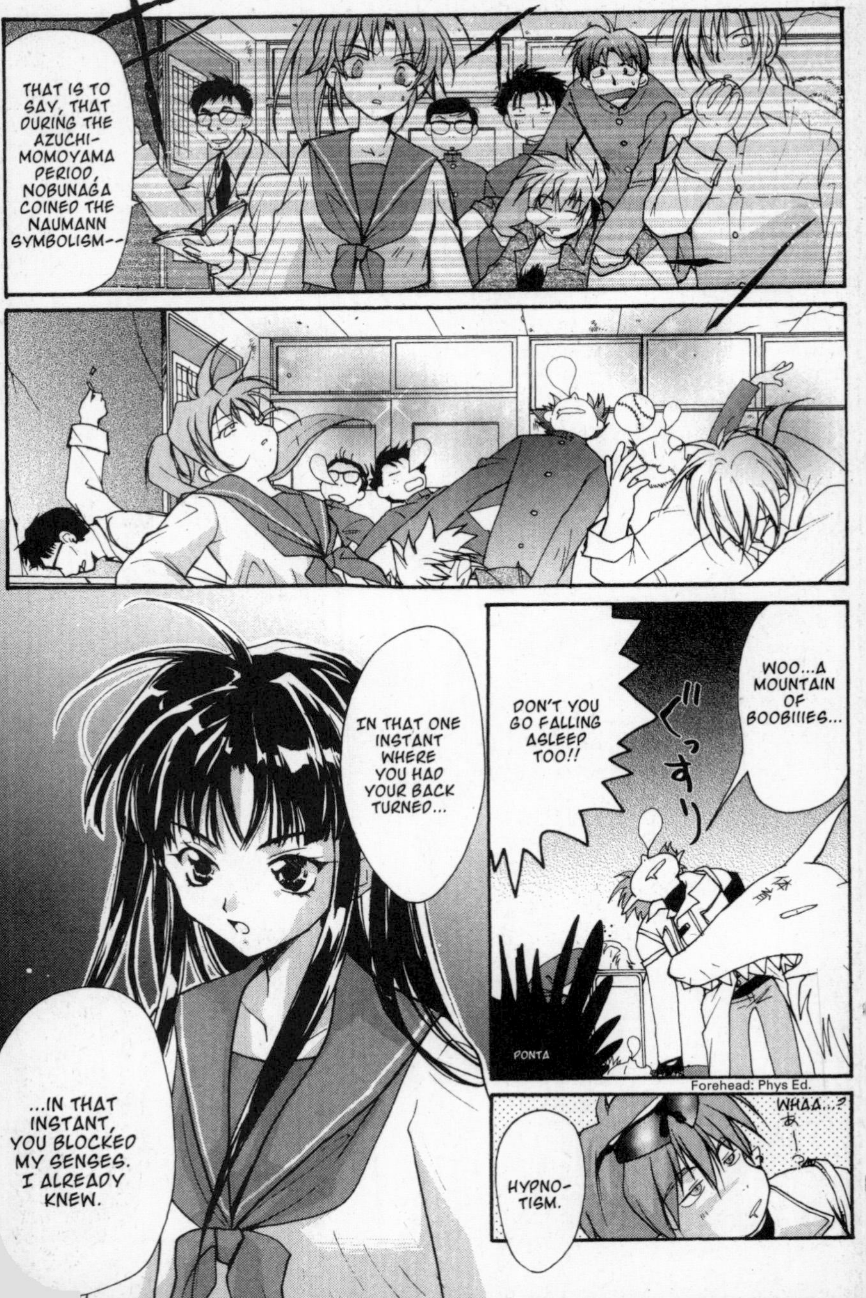
THAT IS TO SAY, THAT DURING THE AZUCHI-MOMOYAMA PERIOD, NOBUNAGA COINED THE NAUMANN SYMBOLISM--
WOO...A MOUNTAIN OF BOOBIIIES...
DON'T YOU GO FALLING ASLEEP TOO!!
ぐっすり
PONTA
Forehead: Phys Ed.
WHAA...?
あー
HYPNO-TISM.
IN THAT ONE INSTANT WHERE YOU HAD YOUR BACK TURNED...
...IN THAT INSTANT, YOU BLOCKED MY SENSES. I ALREADY KNEW.

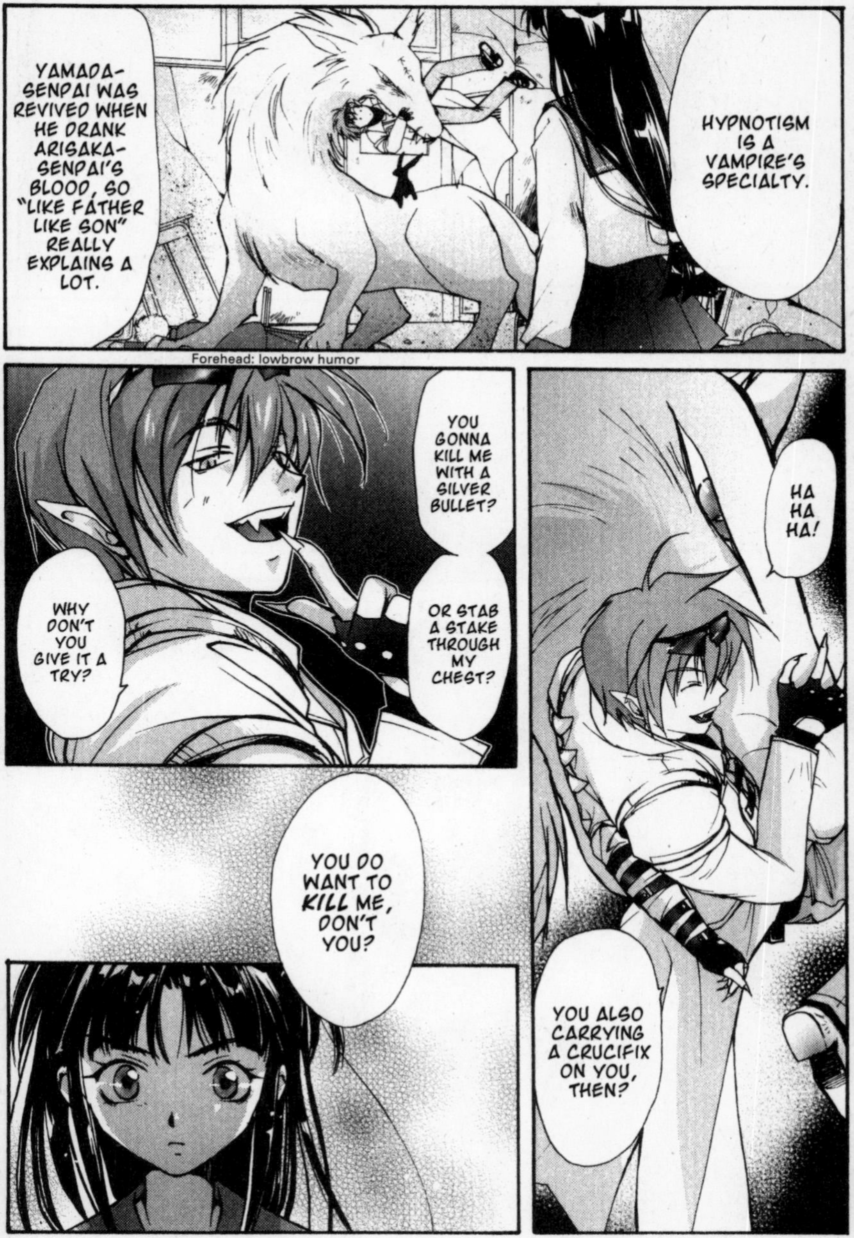
HYPNOTISM IS A VAMPIRE'S SPECIALTY.
YAMADA-SENPAI WAS REVIVED WHEN HE DRANK ARISAKA-SENPAI'S BLOOD, SO "LIKE FATHER LIKE SON" REALLY EXPLAINS A LOT.
Forehead: lowbrow humor
HA HA HA!
YOU ALSO CARRYING A CRUCIFIX ON YOU, THEN?
YOU GONNA KILL ME WITH A SILVER BULLET?
OR STAB A STAKE THROUGH MY CHEST?
WHY DON'T YOU GIVE IT A TRY?
YOU DO WANT TO *KILL* ME, DON'T YOU?

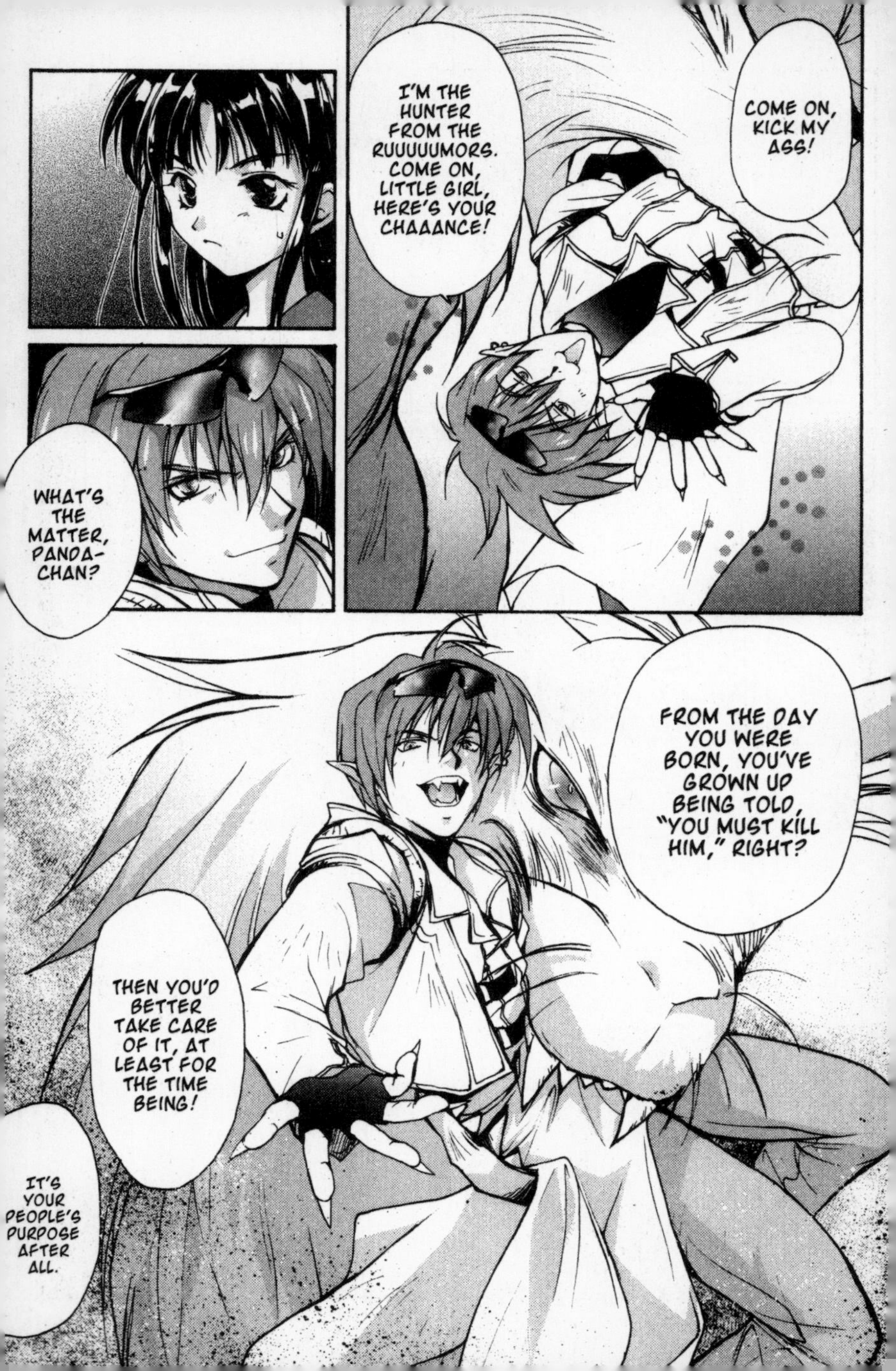
COME ON, KICK MY ASS!
I'M THE HUNTER FROM THE RUUUUUMORS. COME ON, LITTLE GIRL, HERE'S YOUR CHAAANCE!
WHAT'S THE MATTER, PANDA-CHAN?
FROM THE DAY YOU WERE BORN, YOU'VE GROWN UP BEING TOLD, "YOU MUST KILL HIM," RIGHT?
THEN YOU'D BETTER TAKE CARE OF IT, AT LEAST FOR THE TIME BEING!
IT'S YOUR PEOPLE'S PURPOSE AFTER ALL.

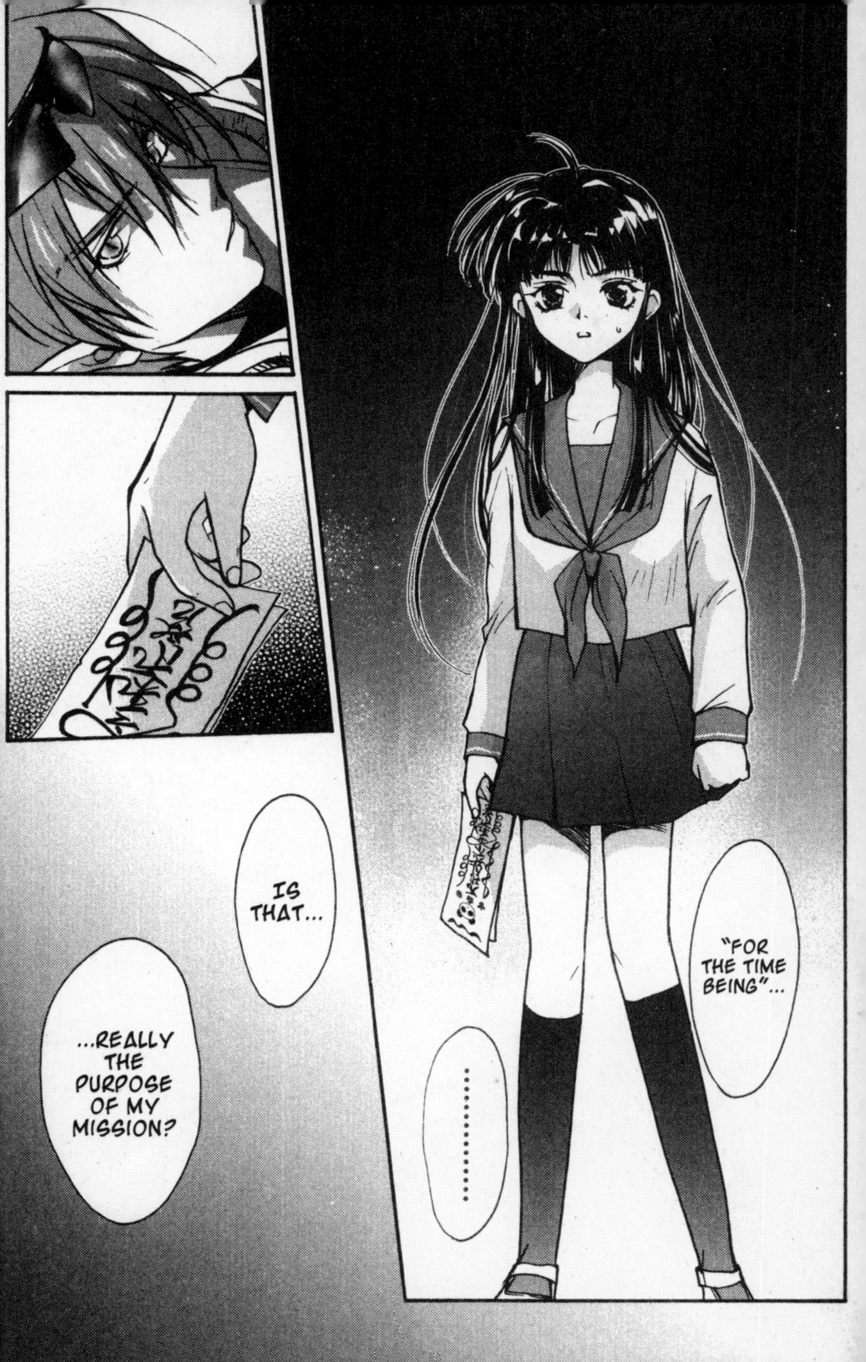
"FOR THE TIME BEING"...
....
IS THAT...
...REALLY THE PURPOSE OF MY MISSION?

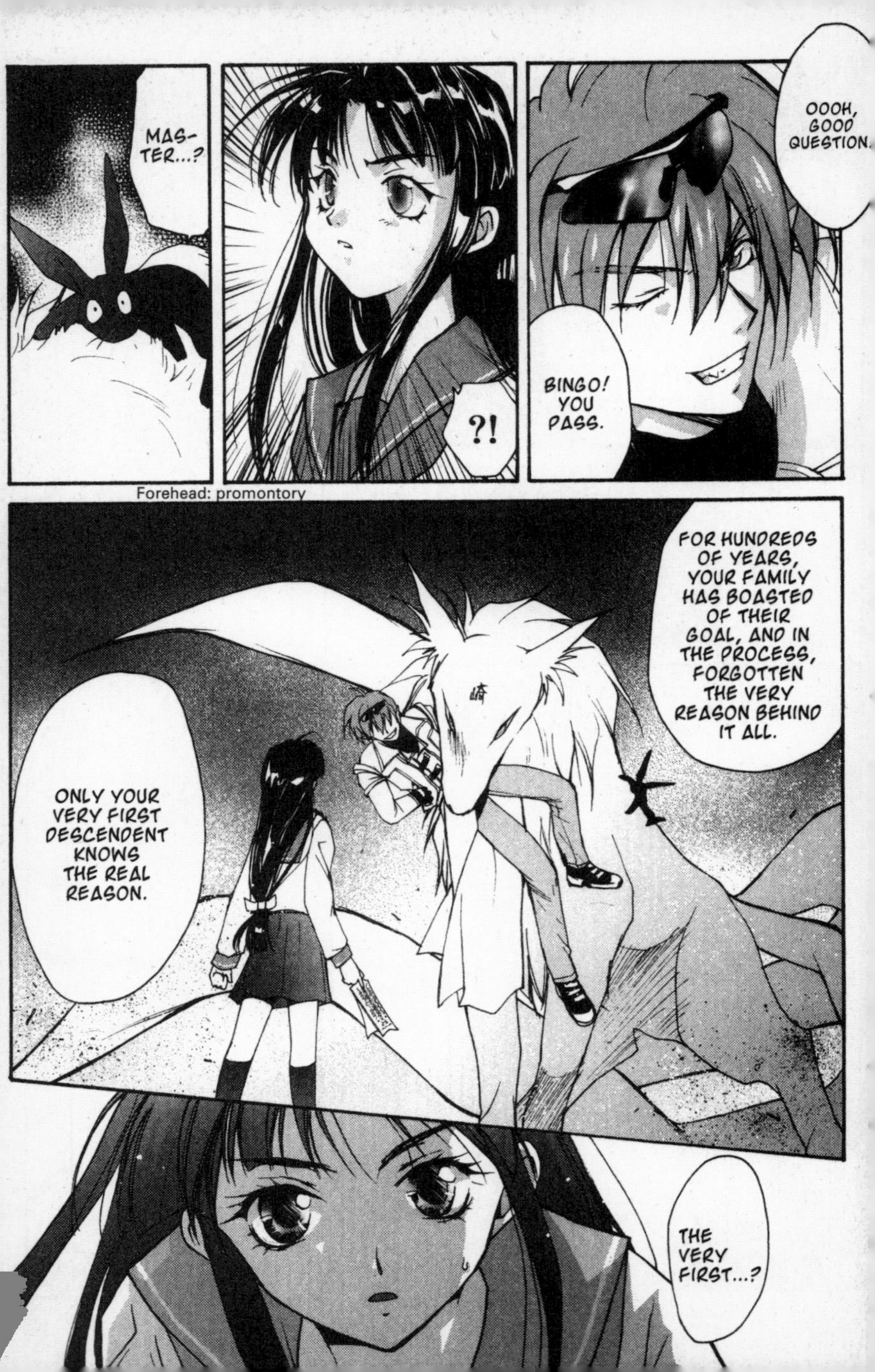
OOOH, GOOD QUESTION.
BINGO! YOU PASS.
?!
MAS-TER...?
Forehead: promontory
FOR HUNDREDS OF YEARS, YOUR FAMILY HAS BOASTED OF THEIR GOAL, AND IN THE PROCESS, FORGOTTEN THE VERY REASON BEHIND IT ALL.
ONLY YOUR VERY FIRST DESCENDENT KNOWS THE REAL REASON.
THE VERY FIRST...?

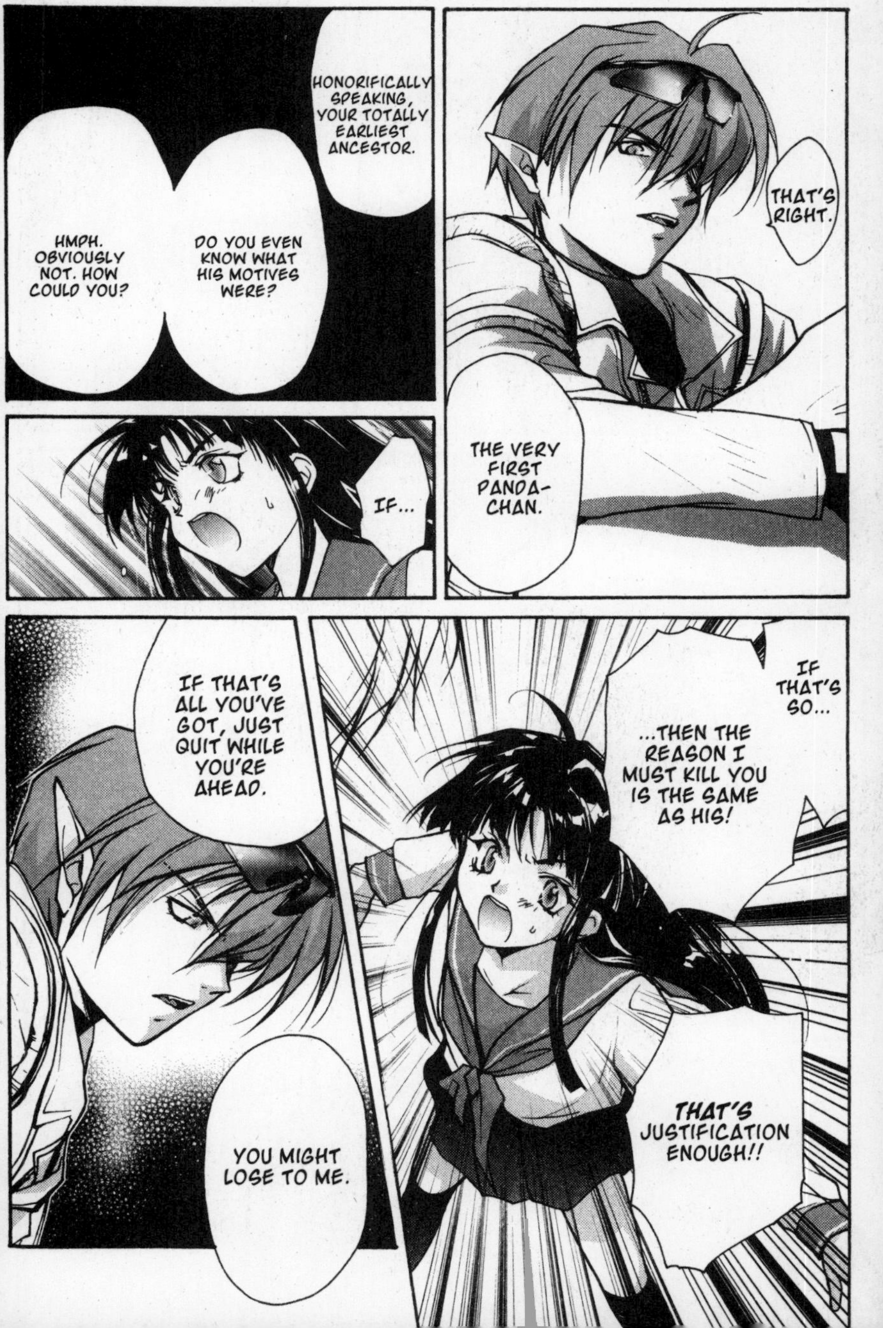
THAT'S RIGHT.
THE VERY FIRST PANDA-CHAN.
HONORIFICALLY SPEAKING, YOUR TOTALLY EARLIEST ANCESTOR.
DO YOU EVEN KNOW WHAT HIS MOTIVES WERE?
HMPH. OBVIOUSLY NOT. HOW COULD YOU?
IF...
IF THAT'S SO...
...THEN THE REASON I MUST KILL YOU IS THE SAME AS HIS!
THAT'S JUSTIFICATION ENOUGH!!
IF THAT'S ALL YOU'VE GOT, JUST QUIT WHILE YOU'RE AHEAD.
YOU MIGHT LOSE TO ME.

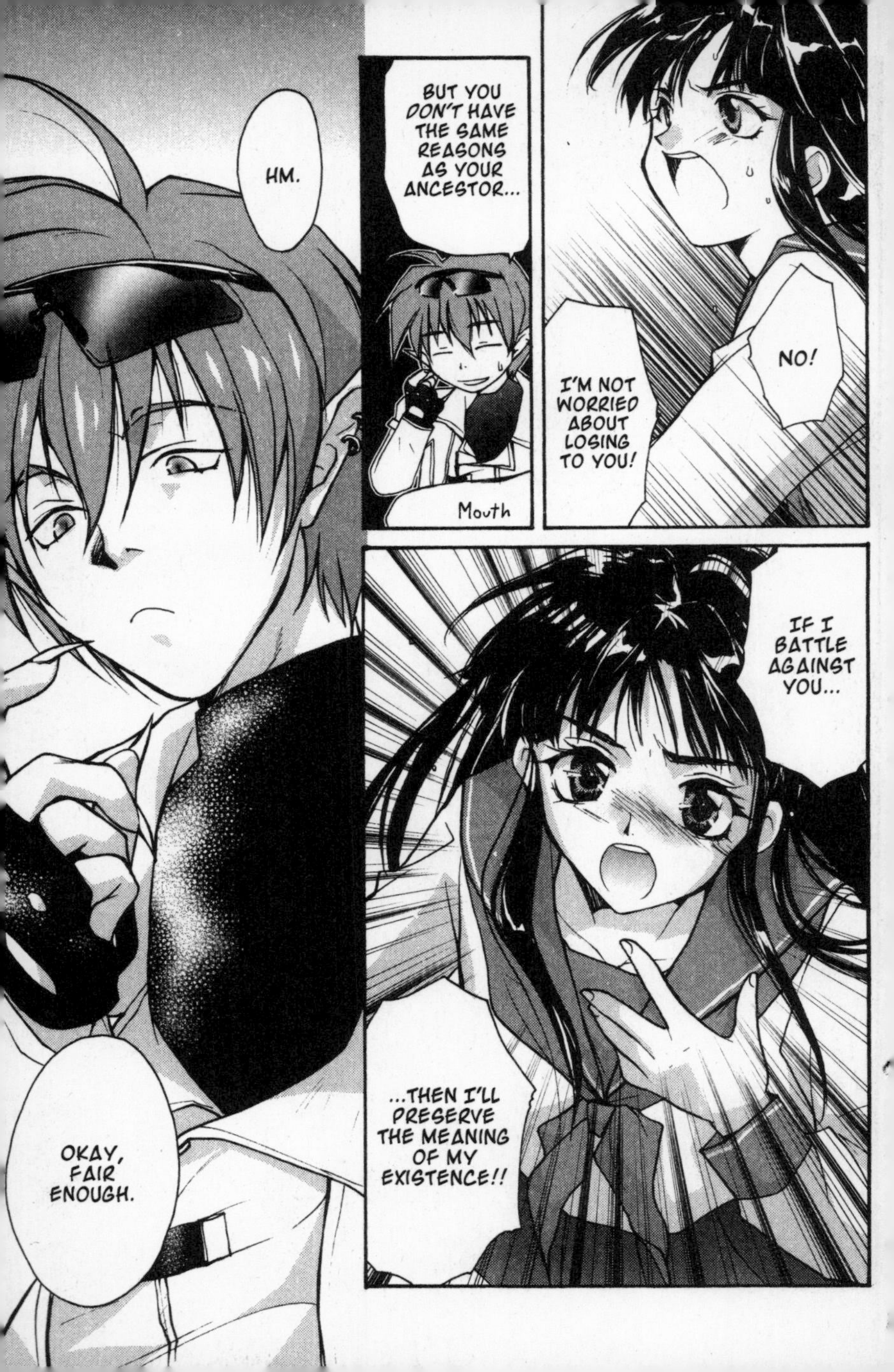
NO!
I'M NOT WORRIED ABOUT LOSING TO YOU!
BUT YOU DON'T HAVE THE SAME REASONS AS YOUR ANCESTOR...
Mouth
IF I BATTLE AGAINST YOU...
...THEN I'LL PRESERVE THE MEANING OF MY EXISTENCE!!
HM.
OKAY, FAIR ENOUGH.

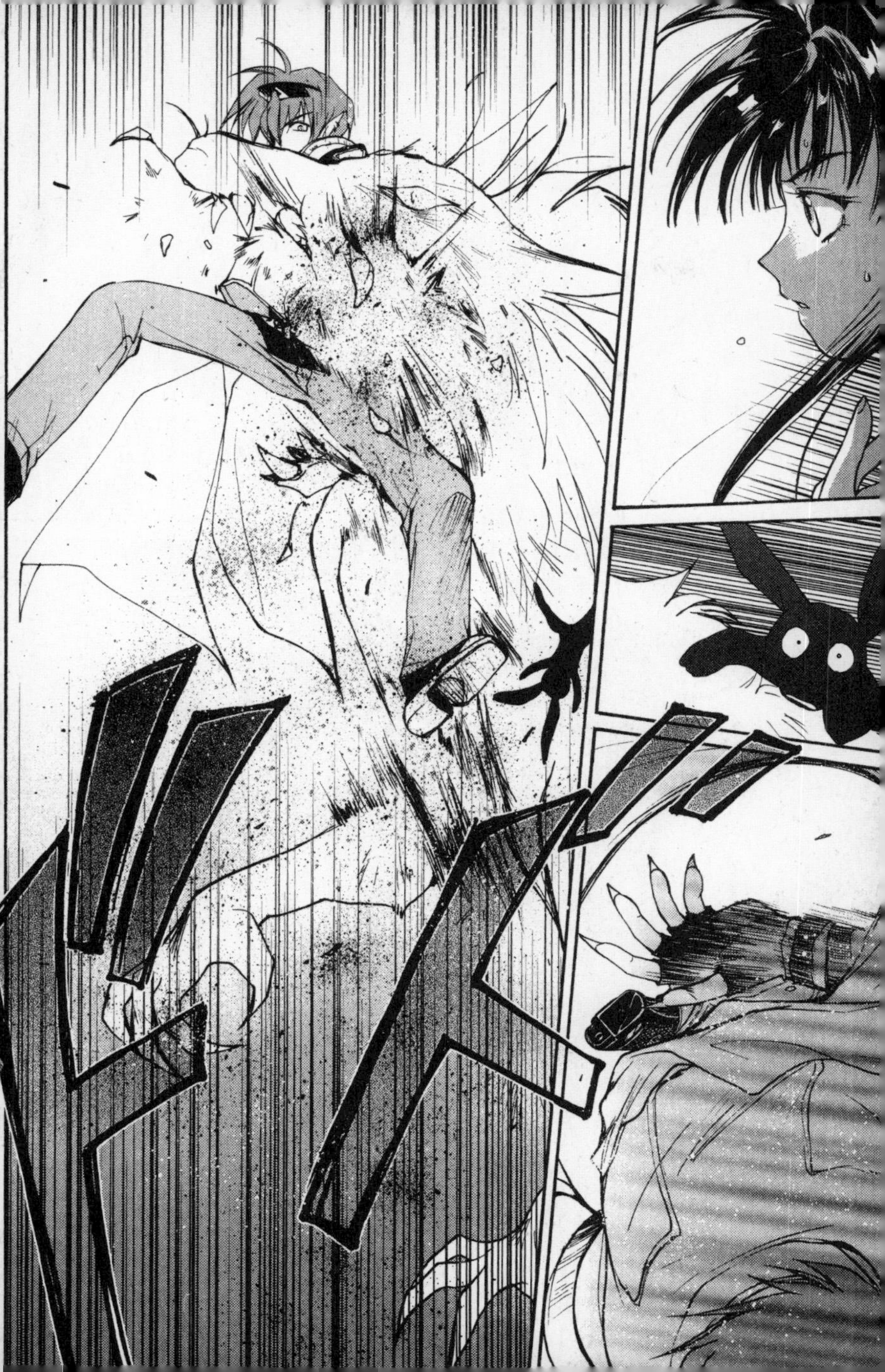

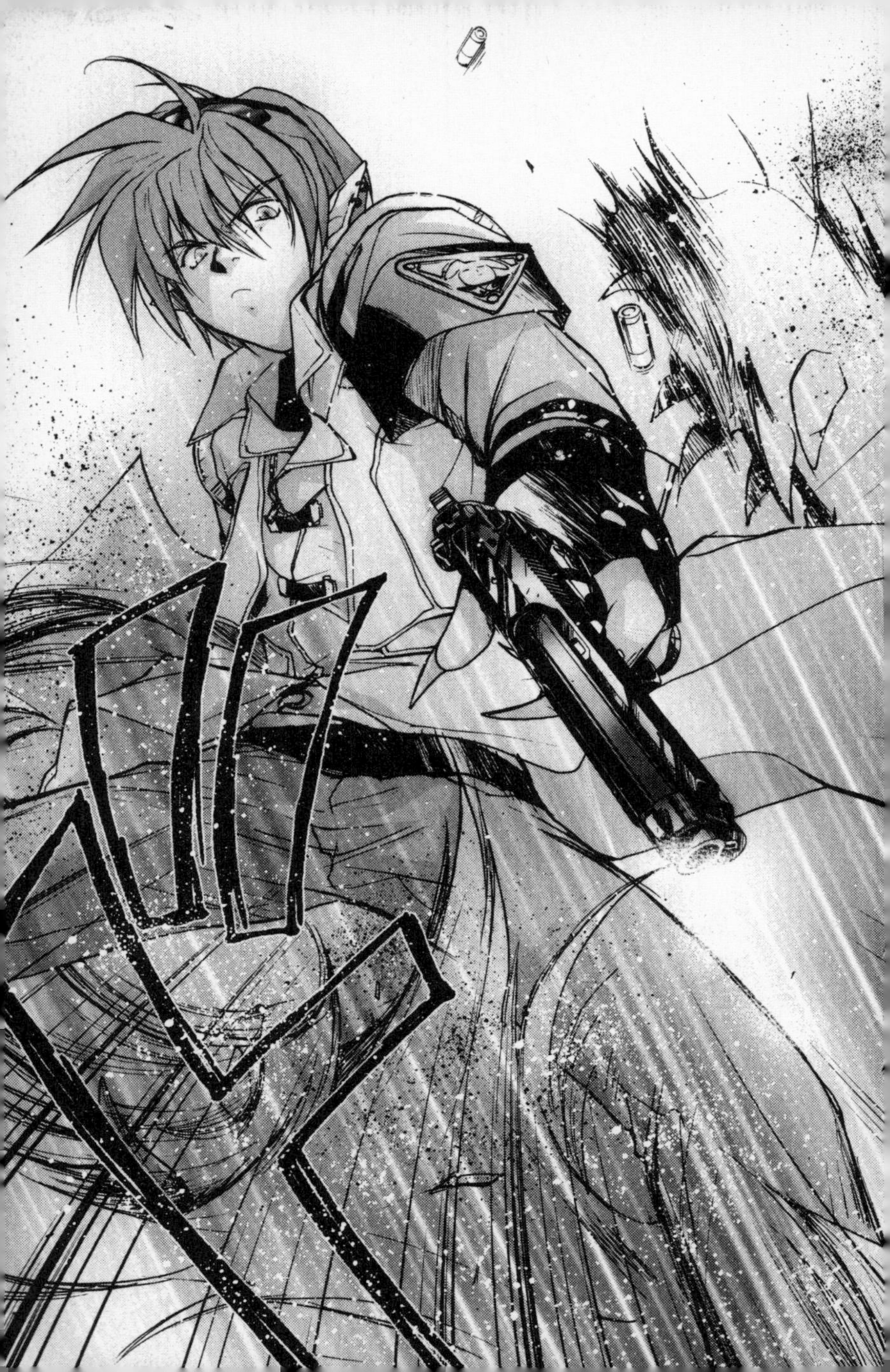

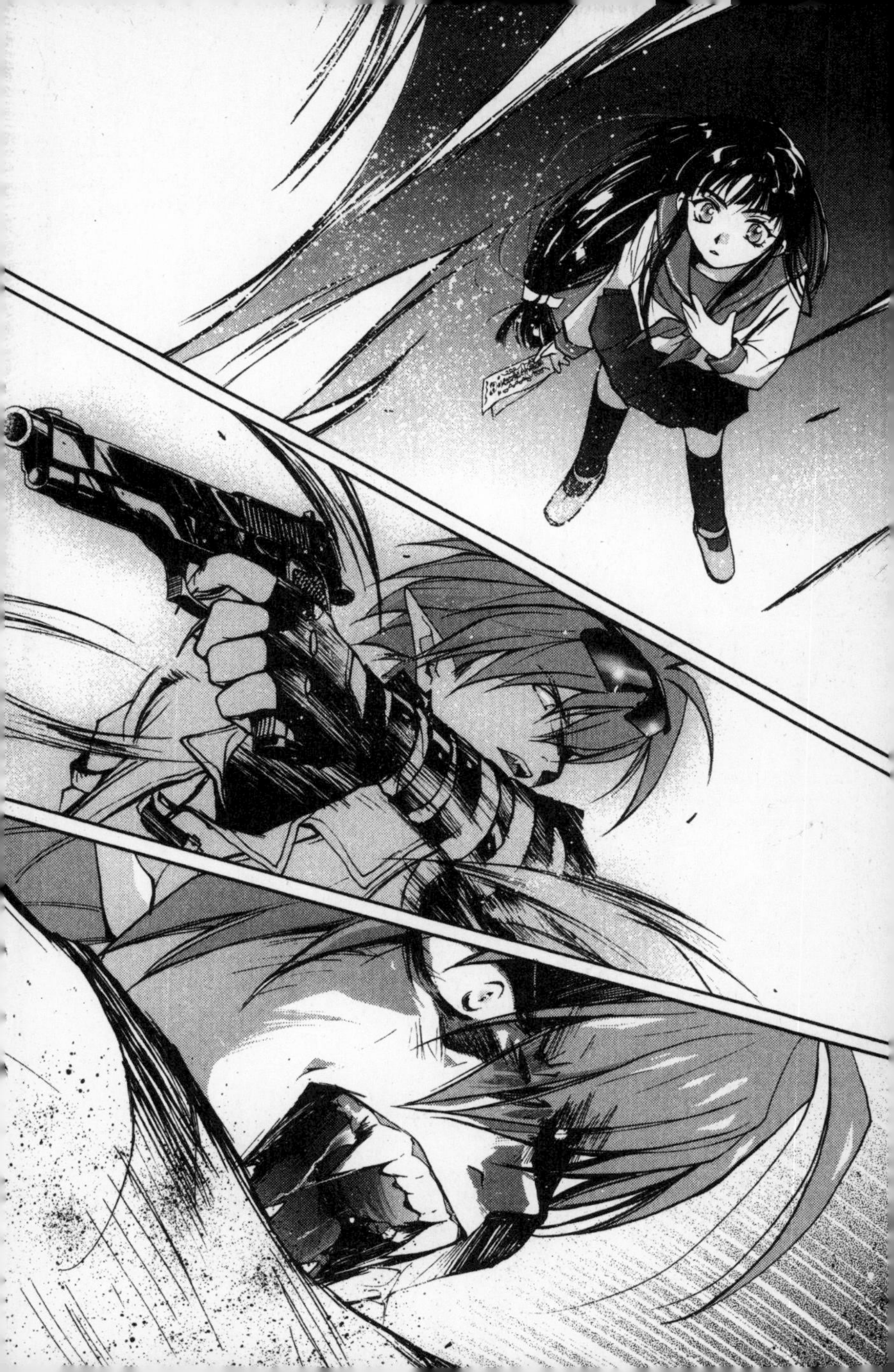

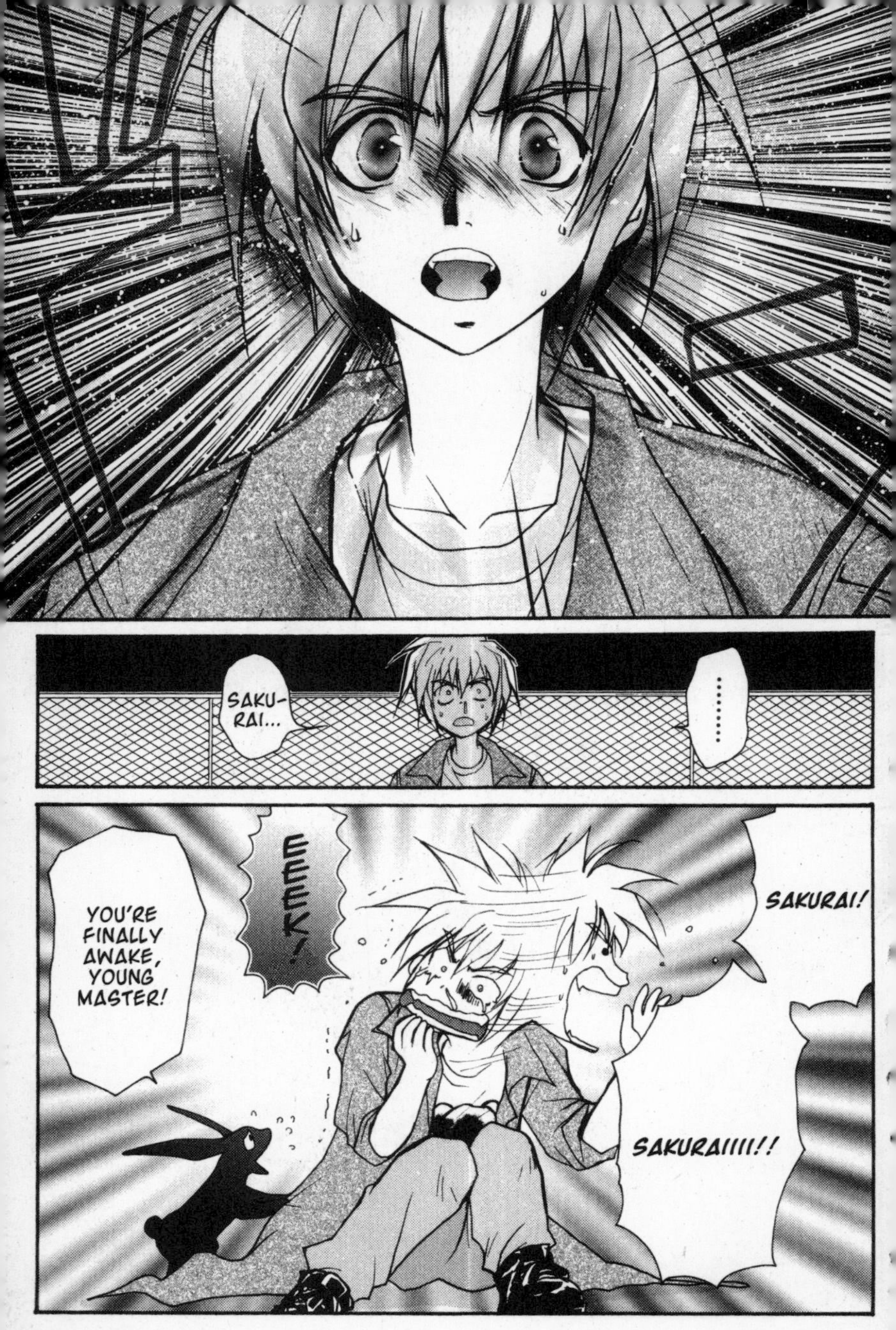
....
SAKURAI...
SAKURAI!
EEEK!
YOU'RE FINALLY AWAKE, YOUNG MASTER!
SAKURAIIII!!

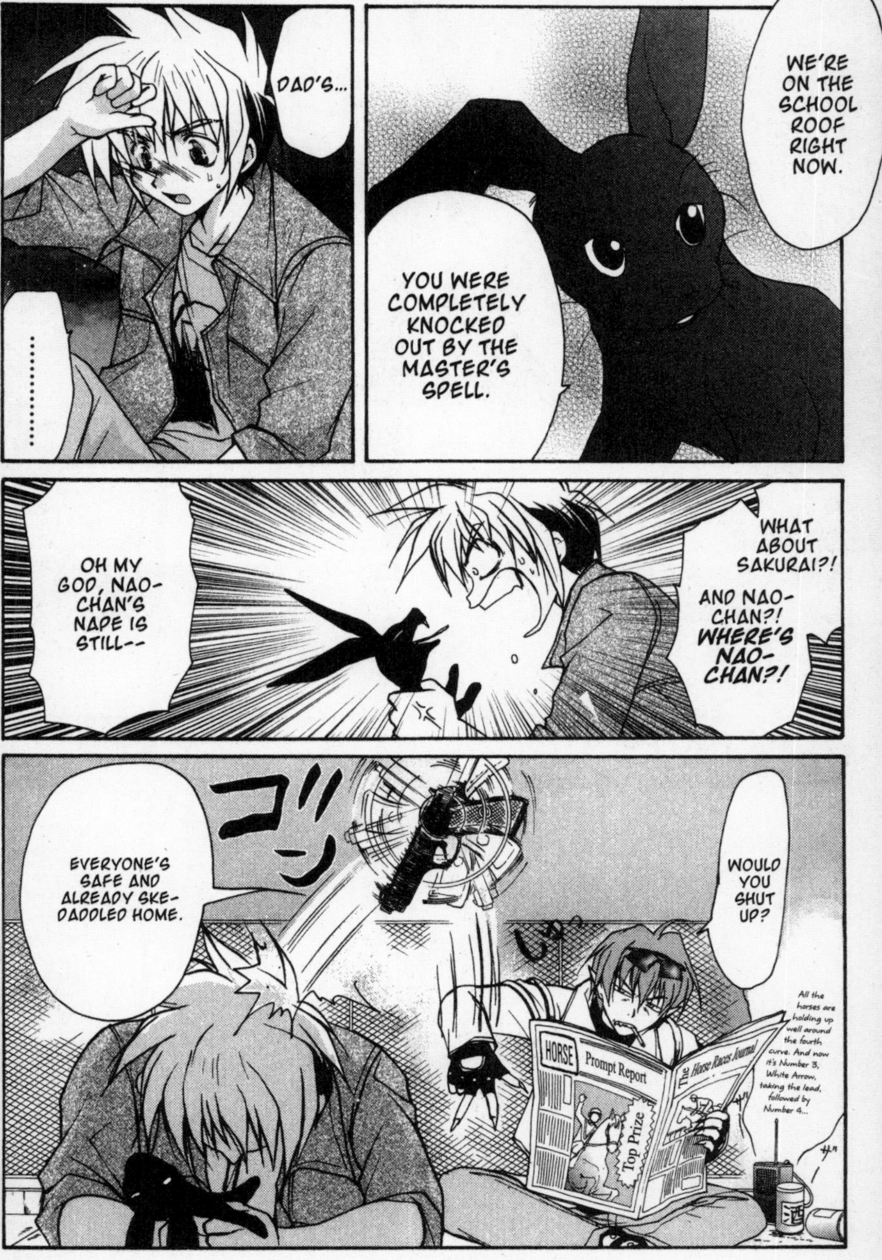
WE'RE ON THE SCHOOL ROOF RIGHT NOW.
YOU WERE COMPLETELY KNOCKED OUT BY THE MASTER'S SPELL.
DAD'S...
......
WHAT ABOUT SAKURAI?!
AND NAO-CHAN?! WHERE'S NAO-CHAN?!
OH MY GOD, NAO-CHAN'S NAPE IS STILL--
WOULD YOU SHUT UP?
All the horses are holding up well around the fourth curve. And now it's Number 3, White Arrow, taking the lead, followed by Number 4...
HORSE
Prompt Report
The Horse Races Journal
Top Prize
EVERYONE'S SAFE AND ALREADY SKE-DADDLED HOME.

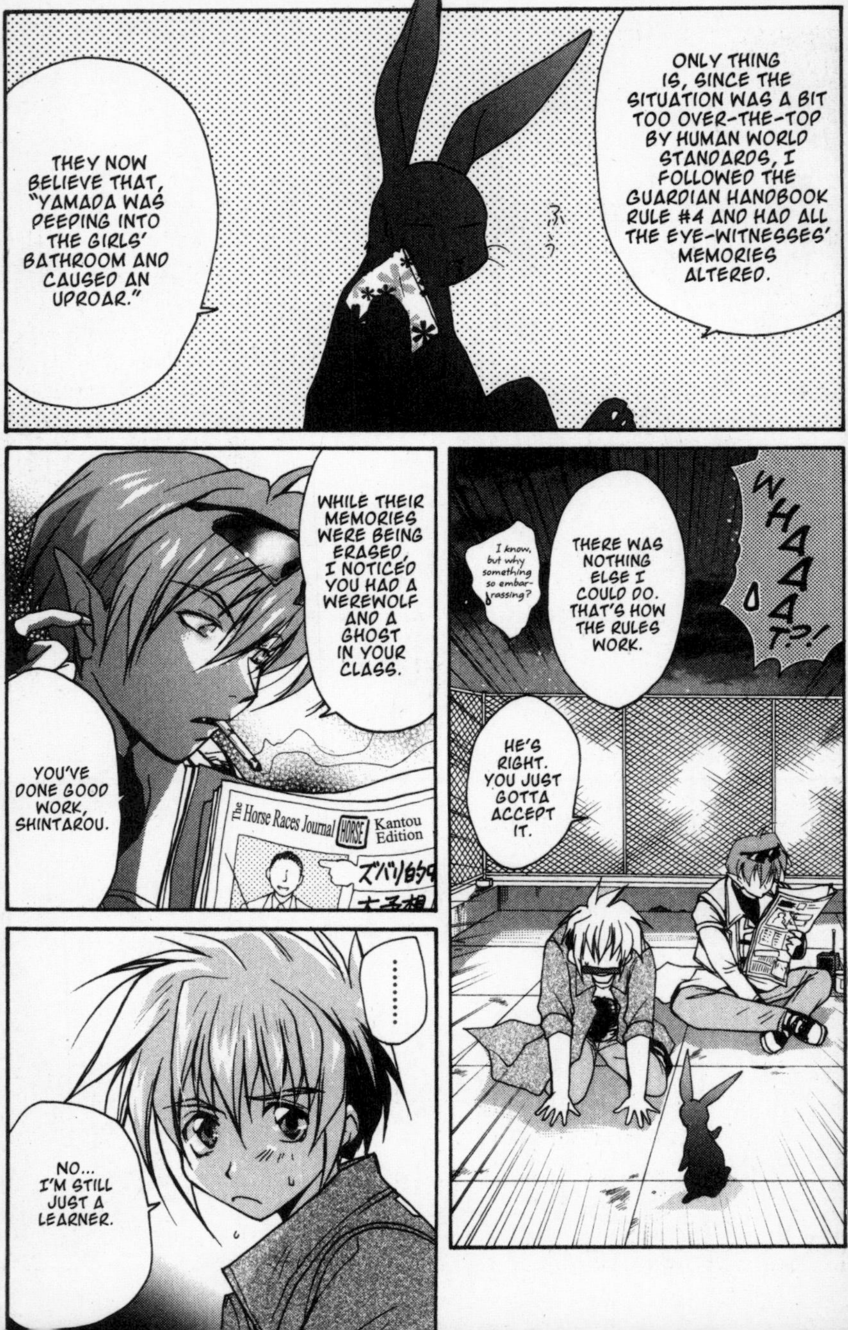
ONLY THING IS, SINCE THE SITUATION WAS A BIT TOO OVER-THE-TOP BY HUMAN WORLD STANDARDS, I FOLLOWED THE GUARDIAN HANDBOOK RULE #4 AND HAD ALL THE EYE-WITNESSES' MEMORIES ALTERED.
ふぅ
THEY NOW BELIEVE THAT, "YAMADA WAS PEEPING INTO THE GIRLS' BATHROOM AND CAUSED AN UPROAR."
WHAAAAT?!
THERE WAS NOTHING ELSE I COULD DO. THAT'S HOW THE RULES WORK.
I know, but why something so embarrassing?
HE'S RIGHT. YOU JUST GOTTA ACCEPT IT.
WHILE THEIR MEMORIES WERE BEING ERASED, I NOTICED YOU HAD A WEREWOLF AND A GHOST IN YOUR CLASS.
YOU'VE DONE GOOD WORK, SHINTAROU.
The Horse Races Journal HORSE Kantou Edition
......
NO... I'M STILL JUST A LEARNER.

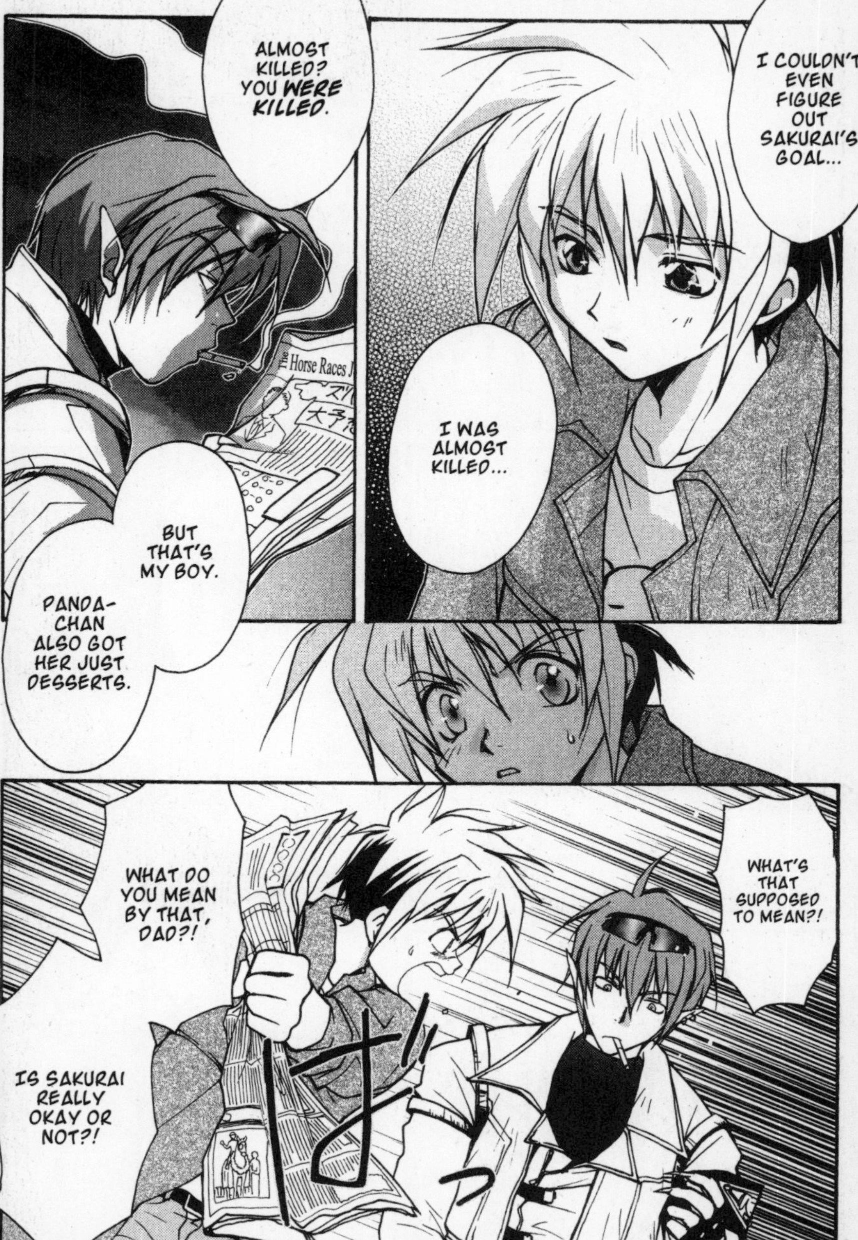
I COULDN'T EVEN FIGURE OUT SAKURAI'S GOAL...
I WAS ALMOST KILLED...
ALMOST KILLED? YOU **WERE KILLED**.
The Horse Races
BUT THAT'S MY BOY.
PANDA-CHAN ALSO GOT HER JUST DESSERTS.
WHAT'S THAT SUPPOSED TO MEAN?!
WHAT DO YOU MEAN BY THAT, DAD?!
IS SAKURAI REALLY OKAY OR NOT?!

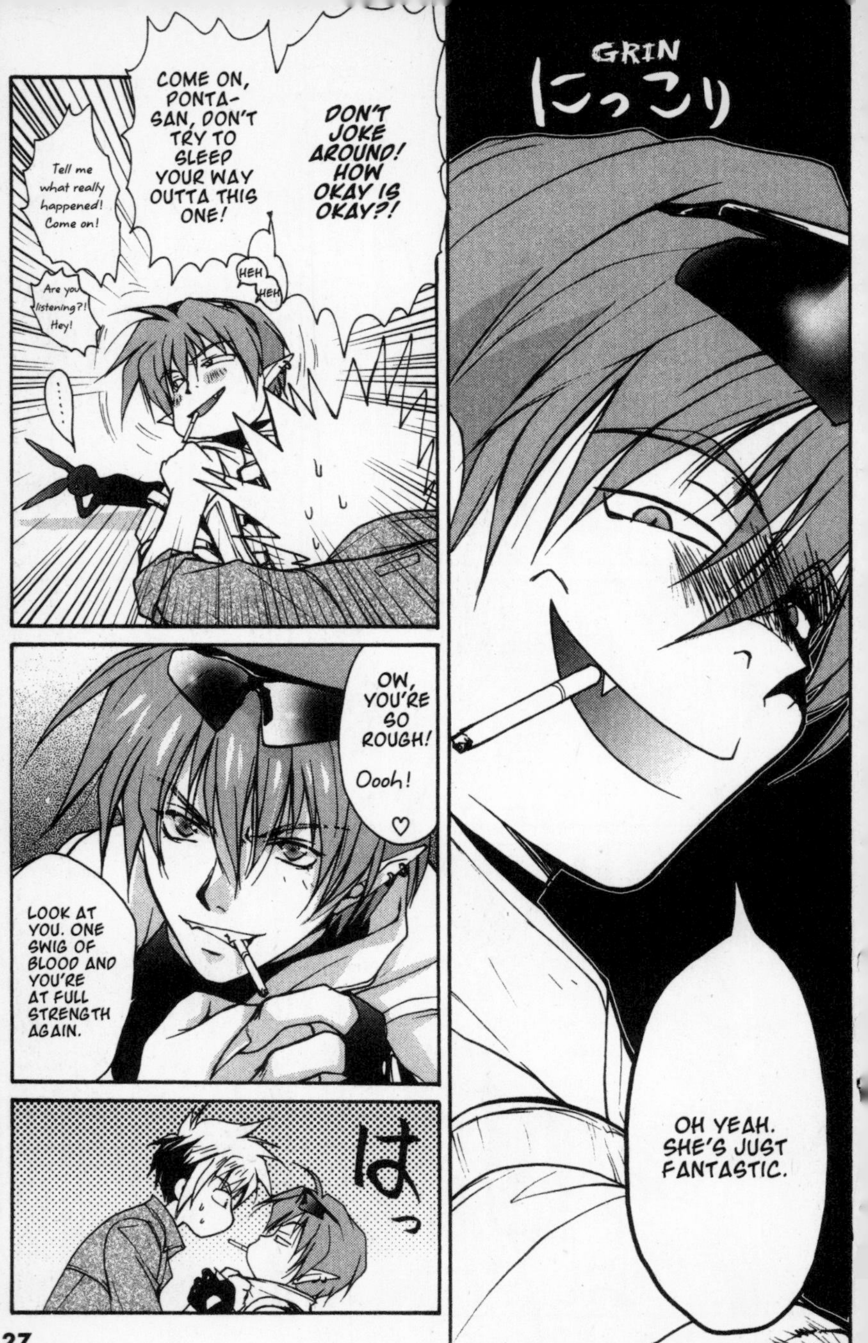
GRIN
にっこり
OH YEAH. SHE'S JUST FANTASTIC.
DON'T JOKE AROUND! HOW OKAY IS OKAY?!
COME ON, PONTA-SAN, DON'T TRY TO SLEEP YOUR WAY OUTTA THIS ONE!
Tell me what really happened! Come on!
HEH HEH
Are you listening?! Hey!
......
OW, YOU'RE SO ROUGH!
Oooh! ♥
LOOK AT YOU. ONE SWIG OF BLOOD AND YOU'RE AT FULL STRENGTH AGAIN.
はっ

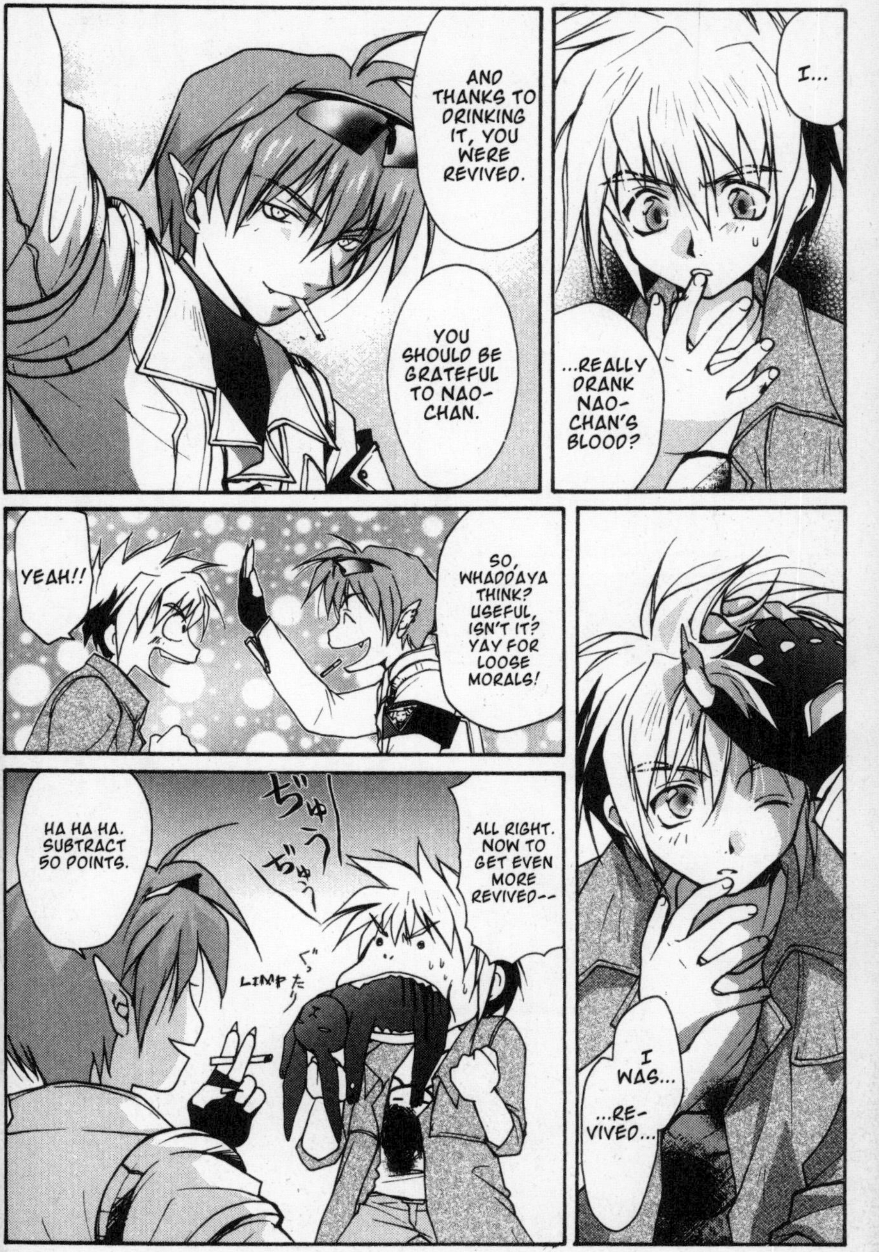
I...
...REALLY DRANK NAO-CHAN'S BLOOD?
AND THANKS TO DRINKING IT, YOU WERE REVIVED.
YOU SHOULD BE GRATEFUL TO NAO-CHAN.
I WAS...
...RE-VIVED...
SO, WHADDAYA THINK? USEFUL, ISN'T IT? YAY FOR LOOSE MORALS!
YEAH!!
ALL RIGHT. NOW TO GET EVEN MORE REVIVED--
ぢゅ～
ぢゅ～
HA HA HA. SUBTRACT 50 POINTS.
ぐ
LIMP たり

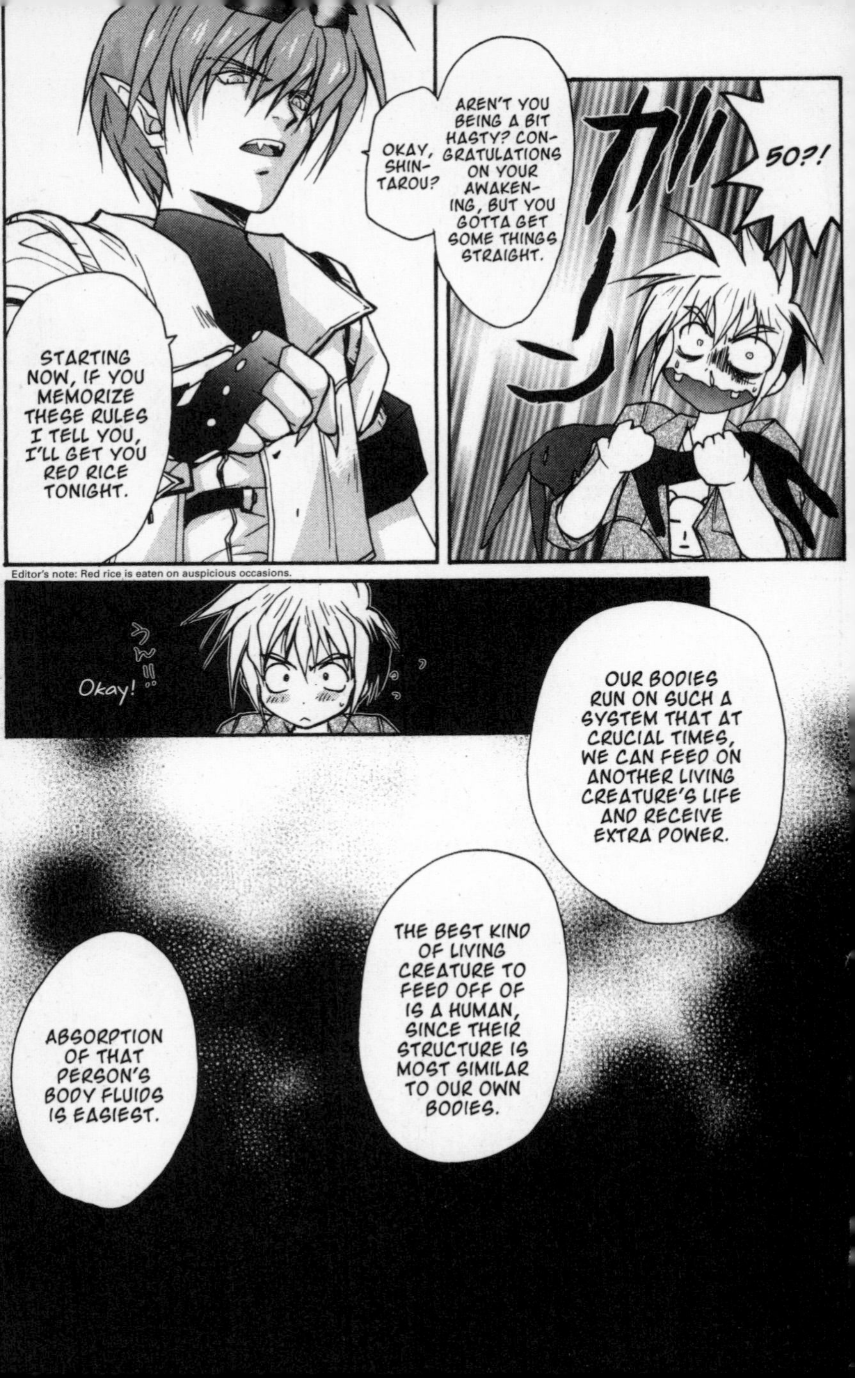
AREN'T YOU BEING A BIT HASTY? CONGRATULATIONS ON YOUR AWAKENING, BUT YOU GOTTA GET SOME THINGS STRAIGHT.
STARTING NOW, IF YOU MEMORIZE THESE RULES I TELL YOU, I'LL GET YOU RED RICE TONIGHT.
OKAY, SHINTAROU?
SO?!
Okay!
OUR BODIES RUN ON SUCH A SYSTEM THAT AT CRUCIAL TIMES, WE CAN FEED ON ANOTHER LIVING CREATURE'S LIFE AND RECEIVE EXTRA POWER.
THE BEST KIND OF LIVING CREATURE TO FEED OFF OF IS A HUMAN, SINCE THEIR STRUCTURE IS MOST SIMILAR TO OUR OWN BODIES.
ABSORPTION OF THAT PERSON'S BODY FLUIDS IS EASIEST.

Editor's note: Red rice is eaten on auspicious occasions.

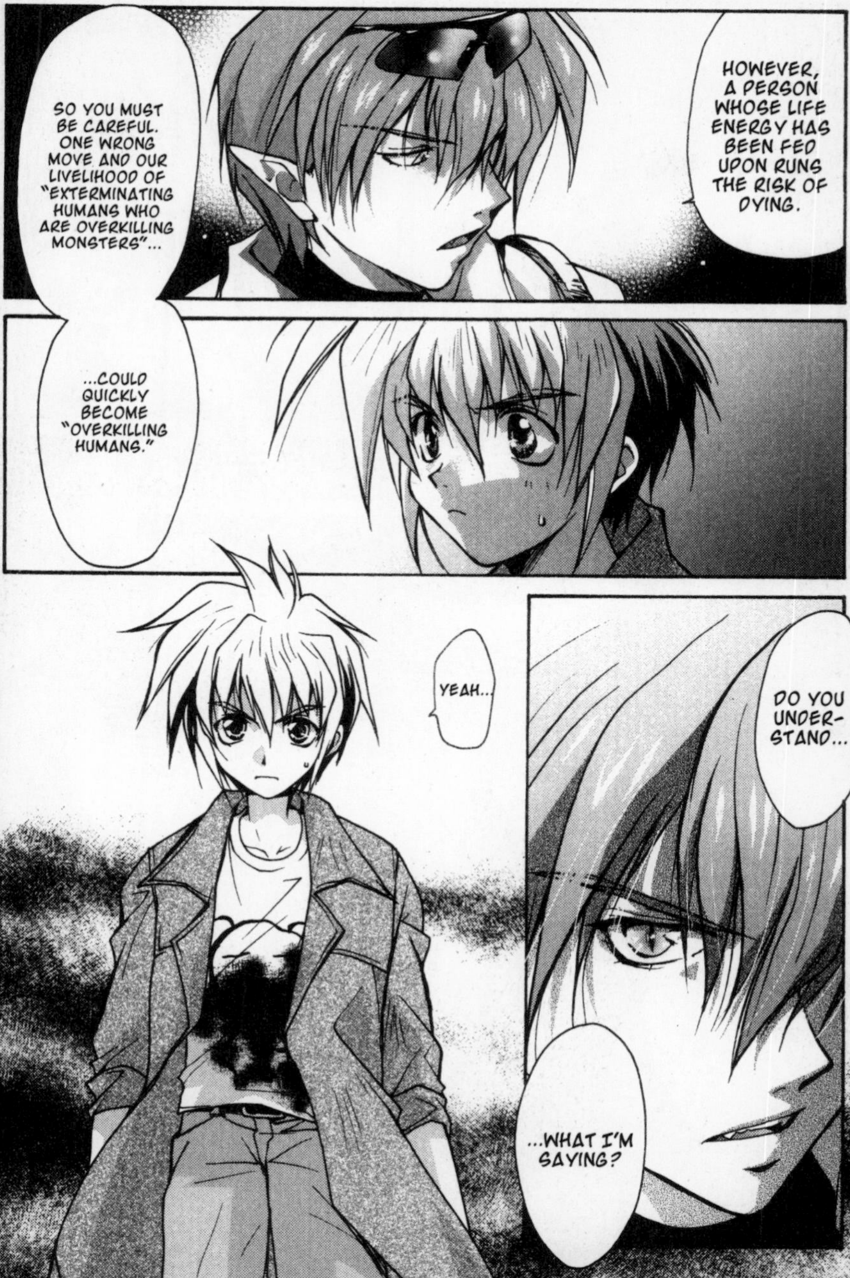
HOWEVER, A PERSON WHOSE LIFE ENERGY HAS BEEN FED UPON RUNS THE RISK OF DYING.
SO YOU MUST BE CAREFUL. ONE WRONG MOVE AND OUR LIVELIHOOD OF "EXTERMINATING HUMANS WHO ARE OVERKILLING MONSTERS"...
...COULD QUICKLY BECOME "OVERKILLING HUMANS."
DO YOU UNDER-STAND...
...WHAT I'M SAYING?
YEAH...

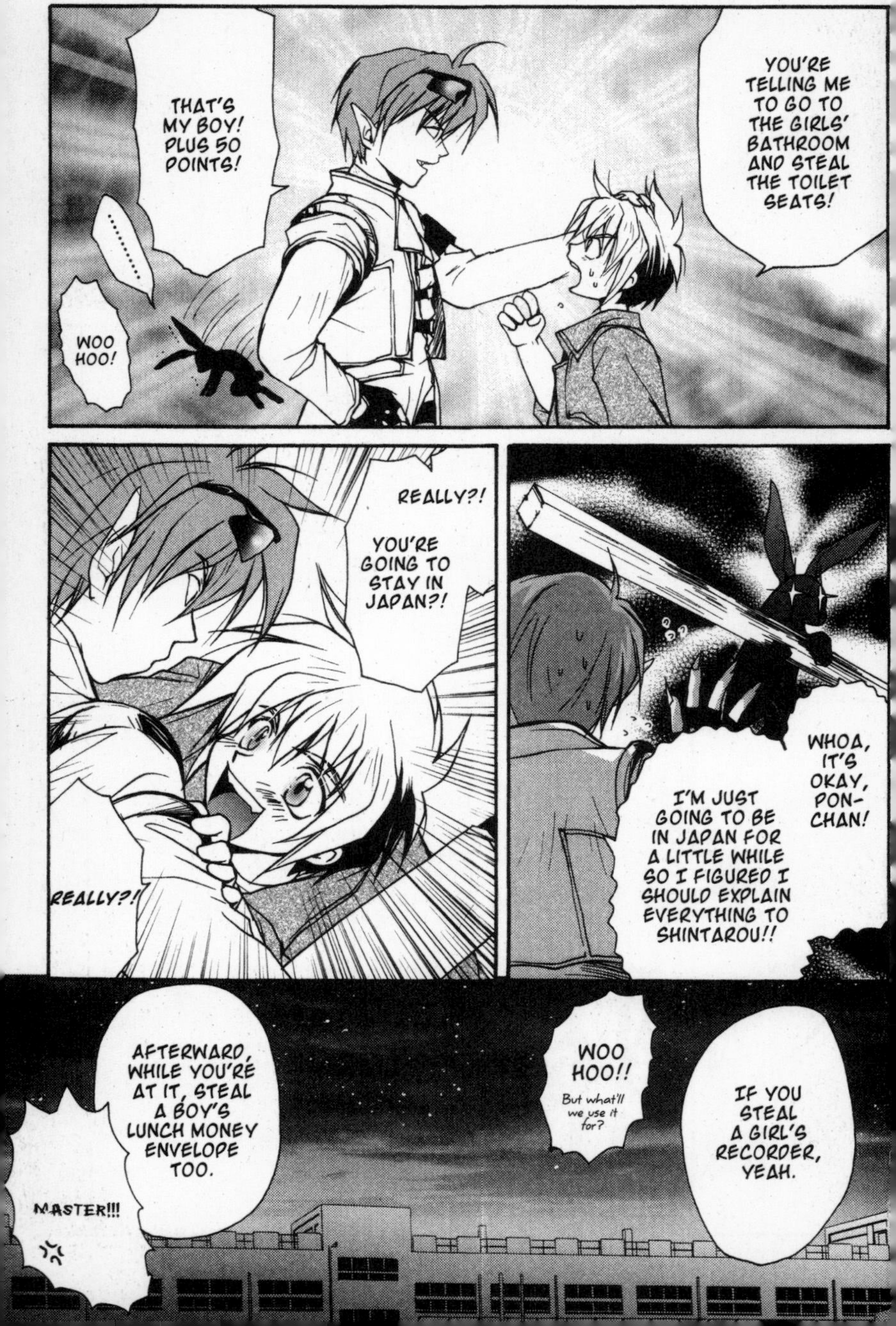
YOU'RE TELLING ME TO GO TO THE GIRLS' BATHROOM AND STEAL THE TOILET SEATS!
THAT'S MY BOY! PLUS 50 POINTS!
......
WOO HOO!
WHOA, IT'S OKAY, PON-CHAN!
I'M JUST GOING TO BE IN JAPAN FOR A LITTLE WHILE SO I FIGURED I SHOULD EXPLAIN EVERYTHING TO SHINTAROU!!
REALLY?!
YOU'RE GOING TO STAY IN JAPAN?!
REALLY?!
IF YOU STEAL A GIRL'S RECORDER, YEAH.
WOO HOO!!
But what'll we use it for?
AFTERWARD, WHILE YOU'RE AT IT, STEAL A BOY'S LUNCH MONEY ENVELOPE TOO.
MASTER!!!

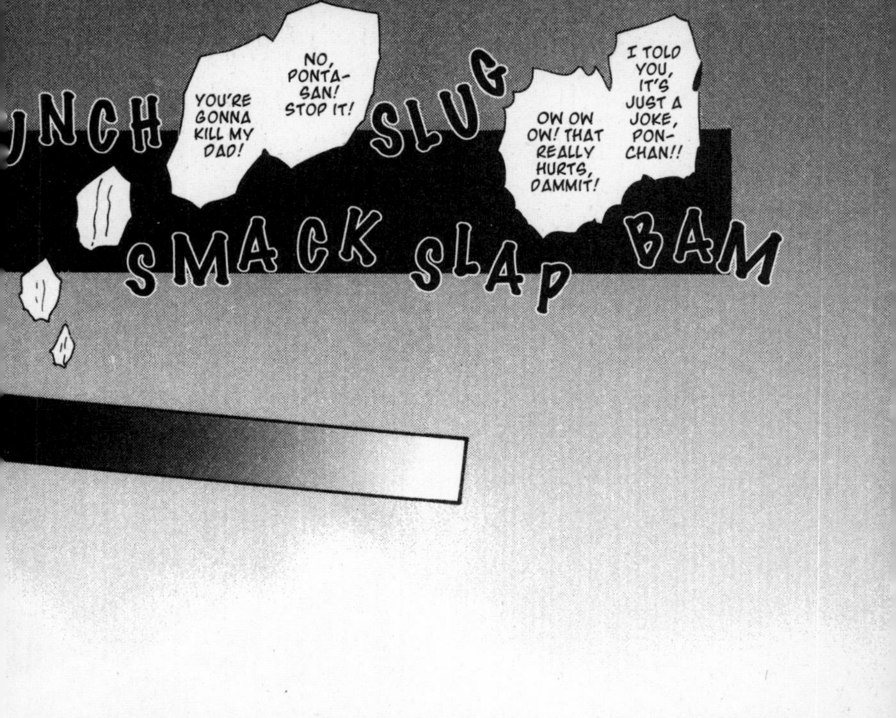
I TOLD YOU, IT'S JUST A JOKE, PON-CHAN!!
OW OW OW! THAT REALLY HURTS, DAMMIT!
SLUG
NO, PONTA-SAN! STOP IT!
YOU'RE GONNA KILL MY DAD!
UNCH
BAM
SLAP
SMACK
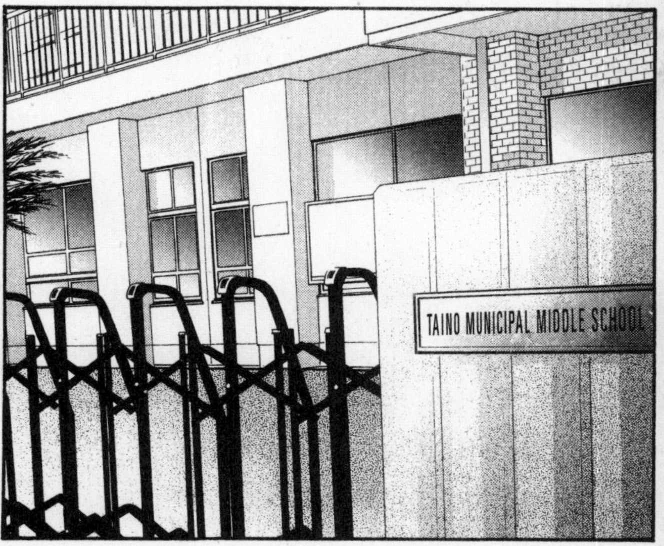
TAINO MUNICIPAL MIDDLE SCHOOL
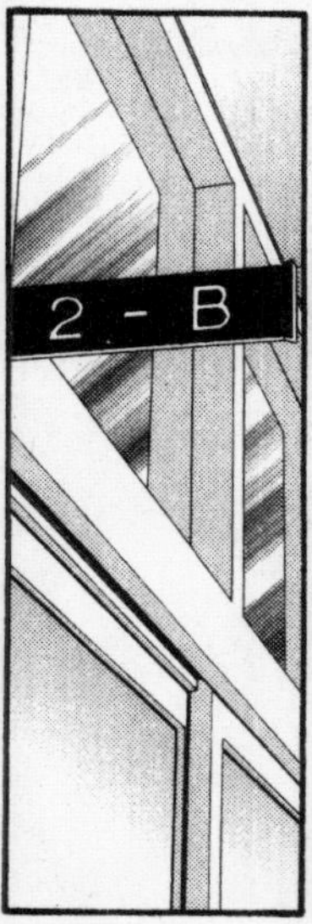
2 - B

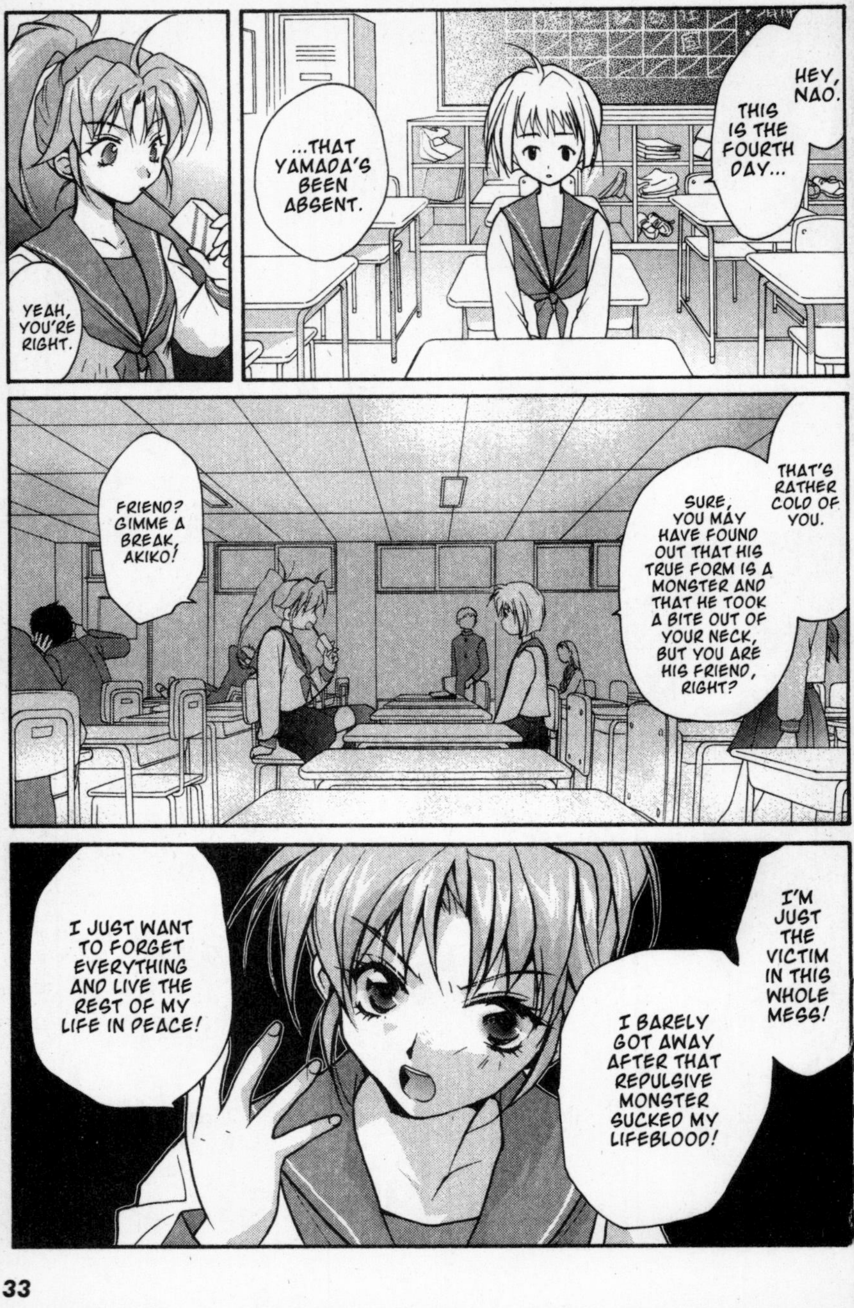
HEY, NAO.
THIS IS THE FOURTH DAY...
...THAT YAMADA'S BEEN ABSENT.
YEAH, YOU'RE RIGHT.
THAT'S RATHER COLD OF YOU.
SURE, YOU MAY HAVE FOUND OUT THAT HIS TRUE FORM IS A MONSTER AND THAT HE TOOK A BITE OUT OF YOUR NECK, BUT YOU ARE HIS FRIEND, RIGHT?
FRIEND? GIMME A BREAK, AKIKO!
I'M JUST THE VICTIM IN THIS WHOLE MESS!
I BARELY GOT AWAY AFTER THAT REPULSIVE MONSTER SUCKED MY LIFEBLOOD!
I JUST WANT TO FORGET EVERYTHING AND LIVE THE REST OF MY LIFE IN PEACE!

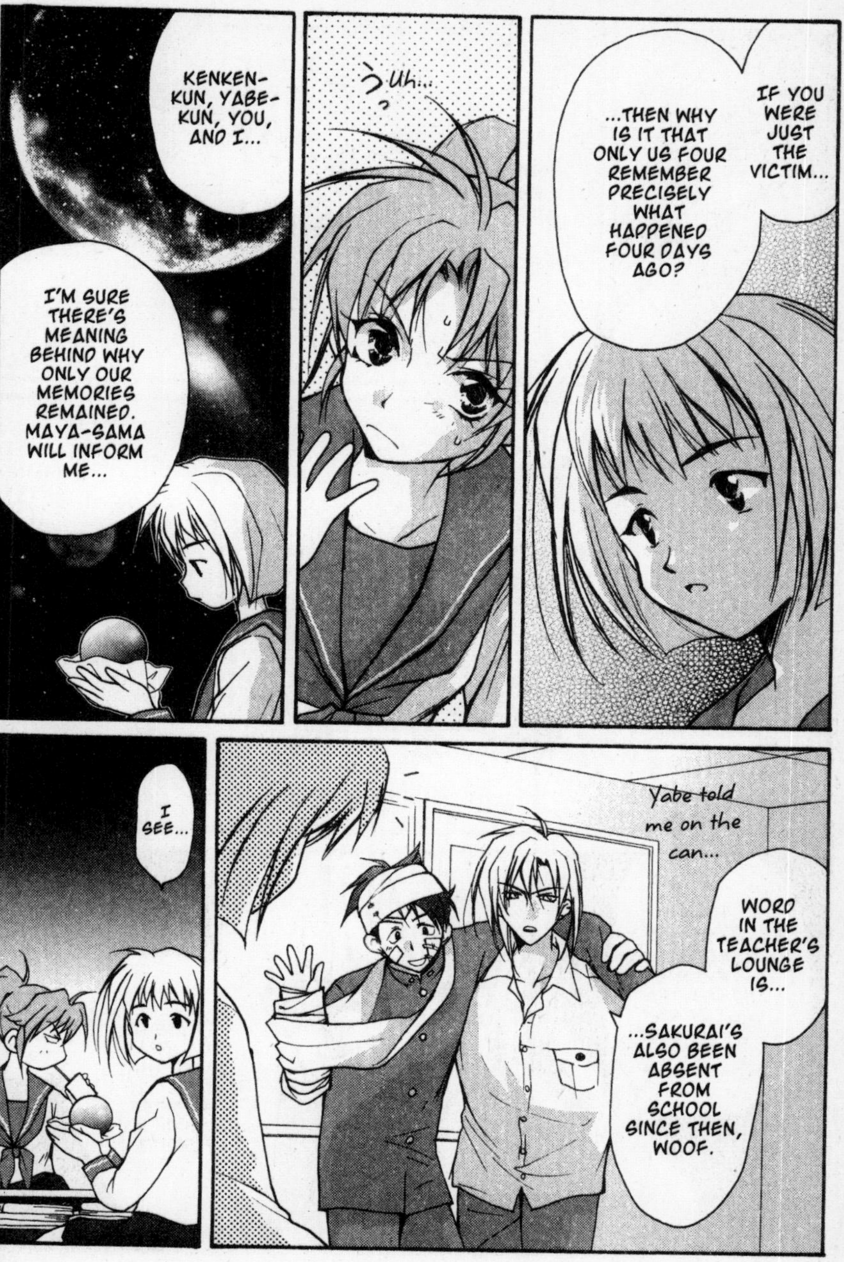
IF YOU WERE JUST THE VICTIM...
...THEN WHY IS IT THAT ONLY US FOUR REMEMBER PRECISELY WHAT HAPPENED FOUR DAYS AGO?
Uh...
KENKEN-KUN, YABE-KUN, YOU, AND I...
I'M SURE THERE'S MEANING BEHIND WHY ONLY OUR MEMORIES REMAINED. MAYA-SAMA WILL INFORM ME...
Yabe told me on the can...
WORD IN THE TEACHER'S LOUNGE IS...
...SAKURAI'S ALSO BEEN ABSENT FROM SCHOOL SINCE THEN, WOOF.
I SEE...

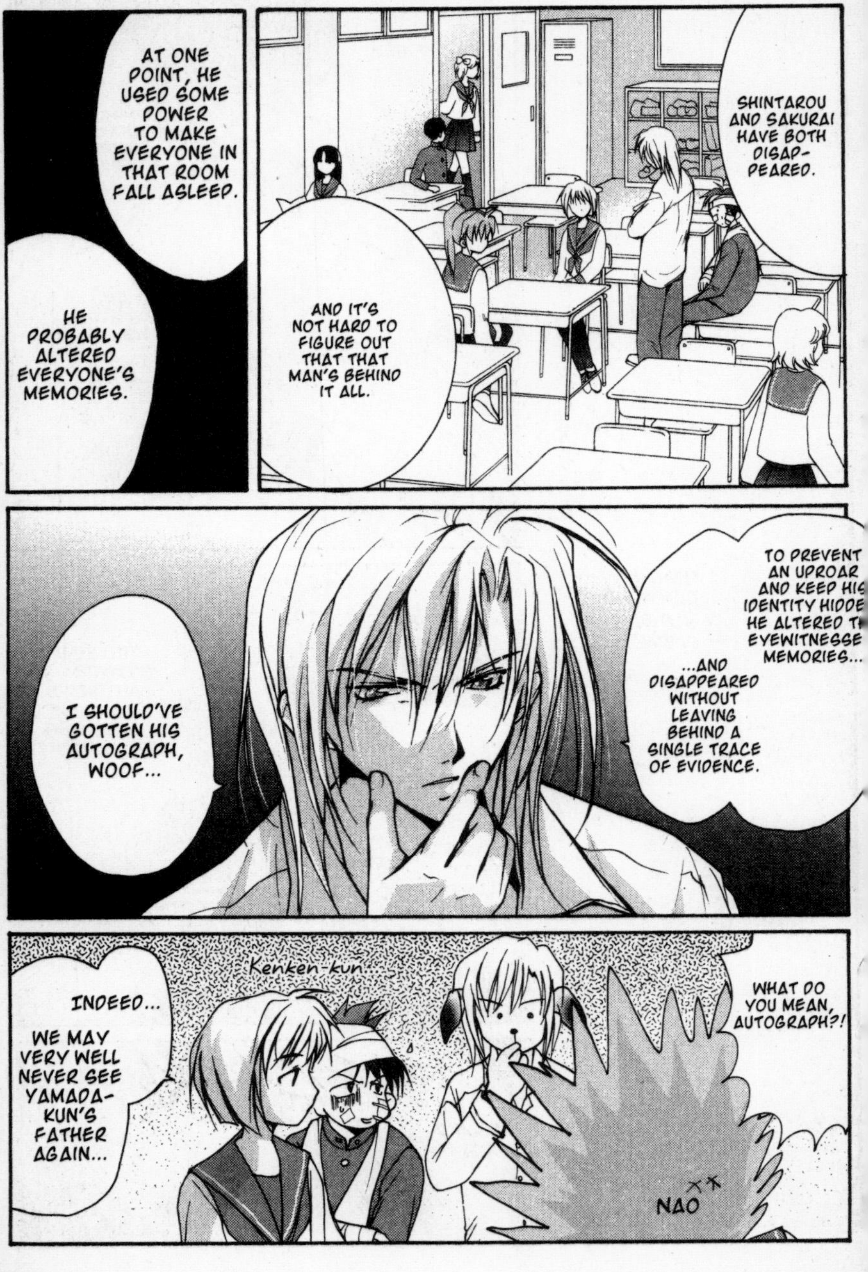
SHINTAROU AND SAKURAI HAVE BOTH DISAPPEARED.
AND IT'S NOT HARD TO FIGURE OUT THAT THAT MAN'S BEHIND IT ALL.
AT ONE POINT, HE USED SOME POWER TO MAKE EVERYONE IN THAT ROOM FALL ASLEEP.
HE PROBABLY ALTERED EVERYONE'S MEMORIES.
TO PREVENT AN UPROAR AND KEEP HIS IDENTITY HIDDE HE ALTERED T EYEWITNESSE MEMORIES...
...AND DISAPPEARED WITHOUT LEAVING BEHIND A SINGLE TRACE OF EVIDENCE.
I SHOULD'VE GOTTEN HIS AUTOGRAPH, WOOF...
WHAT DO YOU MEAN, AUTOGRAPH?!
NAO
Kenken-kun...
INDEED...
WE MAY VERY WELL NEVER SEE YAMADA-KUN'S FATHER AGAIN...

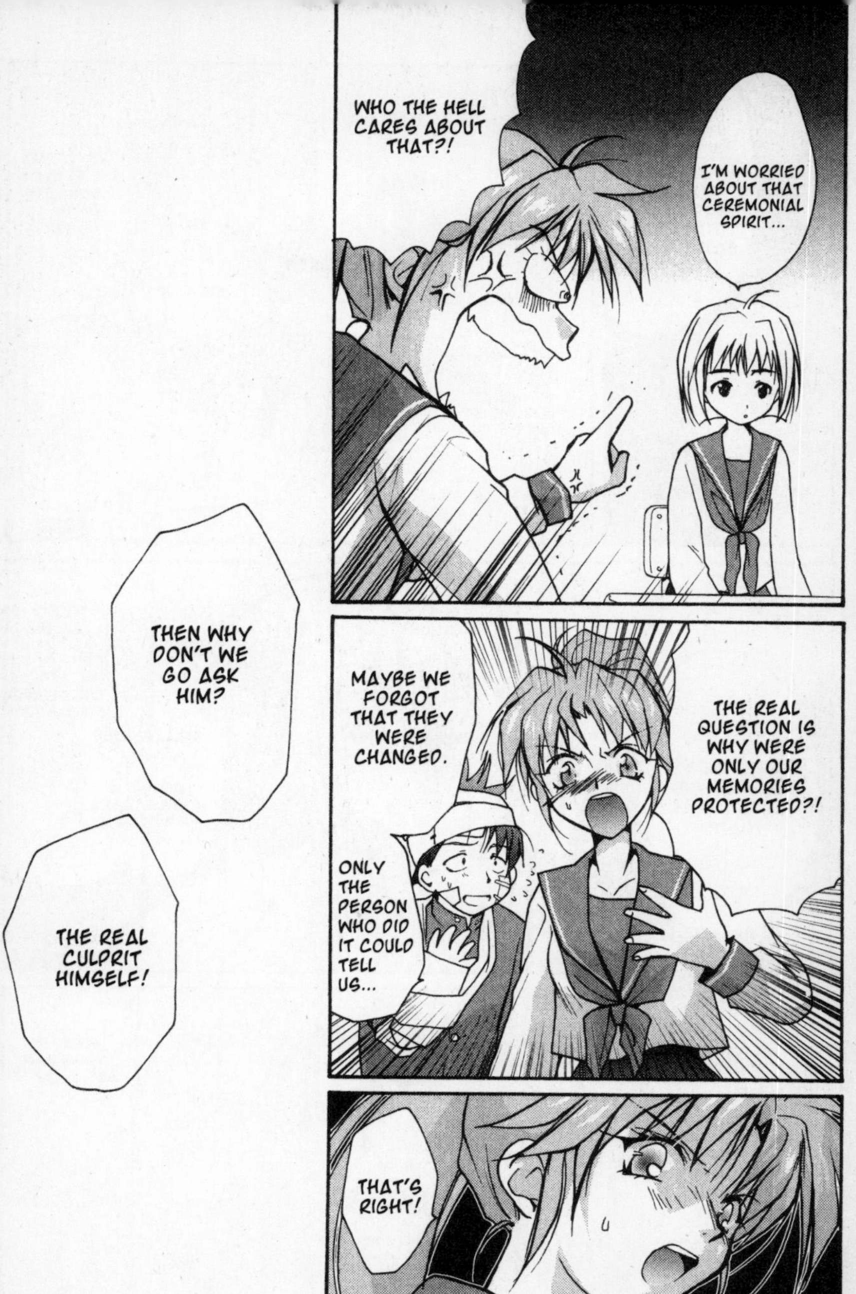
I'M WORRIED ABOUT THAT CEREMONIAL SPIRIT...
WHO THE HELL CARES ABOUT THAT?!
THE REAL QUESTION IS WHY WERE ONLY OUR MEMORIES PROTECTED?!
MAYBE WE FORGOT THAT THEY WERE CHANGED.
ONLY THE PERSON WHO DID IT COULD TELL US...
THAT'S RIGHT!
THEN WHY DON'T WE GO ASK HIM?
THE REAL CULPRIT HIMSELF!

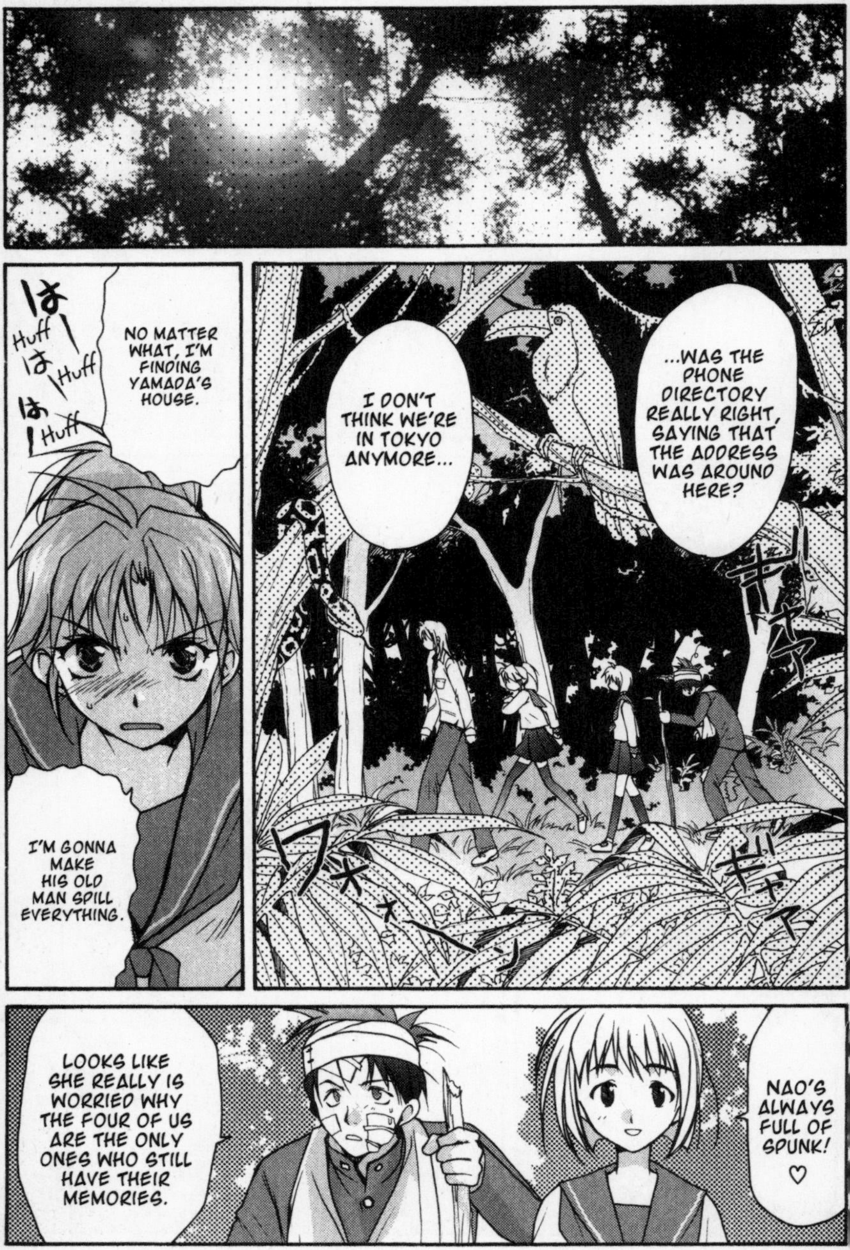
...WAS THE PHONE DIRECTORY REALLY RIGHT, SAYING THAT THE ADDRESS WAS AROUND HERE?
I DON'T THINK WE'RE IN TOKYO ANYMORE...
は! Huff
は! Huff
は! Huff
NO MATTER WHAT, I'M FINDING YAMADA'S HOUSE.
I'M GONNA MAKE HIS OLD MAN SPILL EVERYTHING.
NAO'S ALWAYS FULL OF SPUNK! ♡
LOOKS LIKE SHE REALLY IS WORRIED WHY THE FOUR OF US ARE THE ONLY ONES WHO STILL HAVE THEIR MEMORIES.

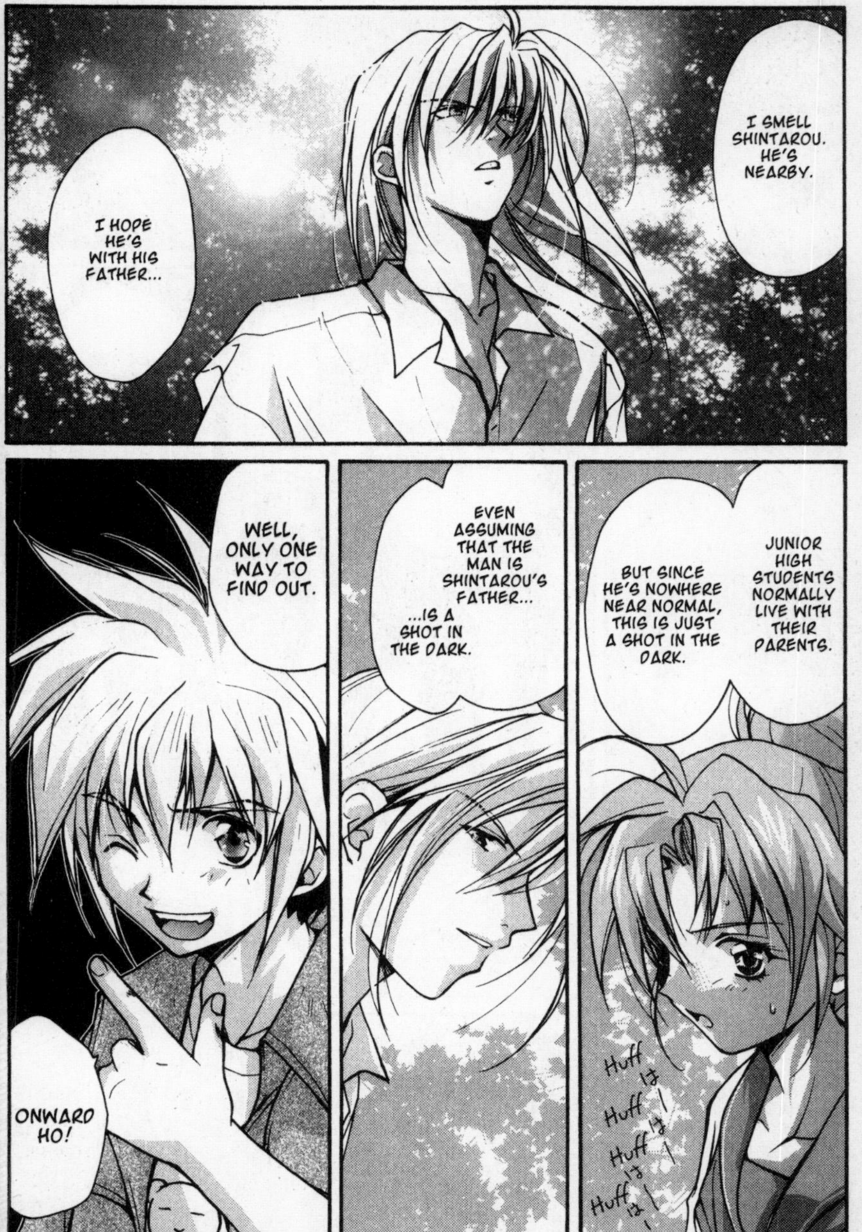
I SMELL SHINTAROU. HE'S NEARBY.
I HOPE HE'S WITH HIS FATHER...
JUNIOR HIGH STUDENTS NORMALLY LIVE WITH THEIR PARENTS.
BUT SINCE HE'S NOWHERE NEAR NORMAL, THIS IS JUST A SHOT IN THE DARK.
Huff Huff Huff Huff
EVEN ASSUMING THAT THE MAN IS SHINTAROU'S FATHER...
...IS A SHOT IN THE DARK.
WELL, ONLY ONE WAY TO FIND OUT.
ONWARD HO!

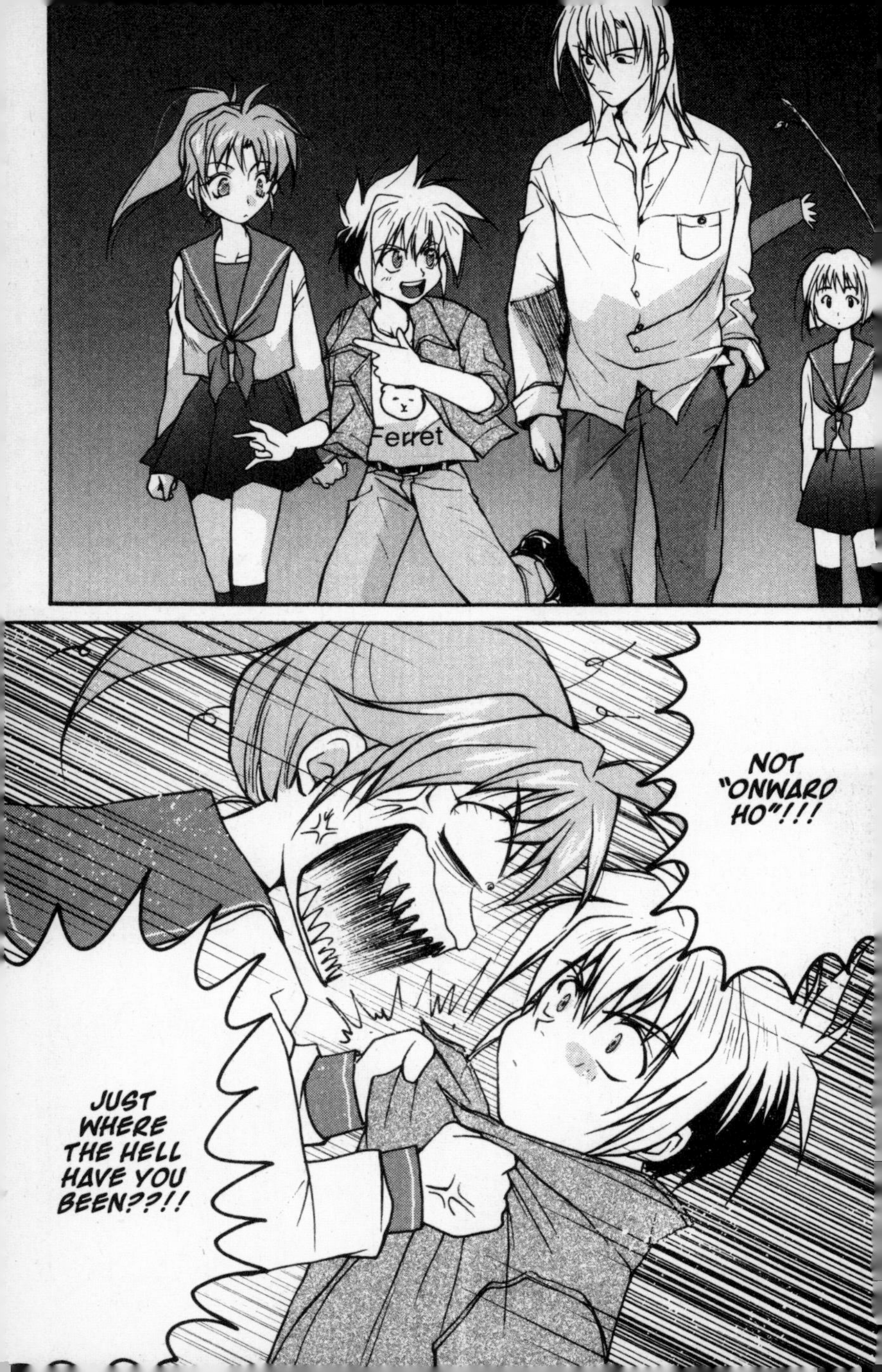
Ferret
NOT "ONWARD HO"!!!
JUST WHERE THE HELL HAVE YOU BEEN??!!

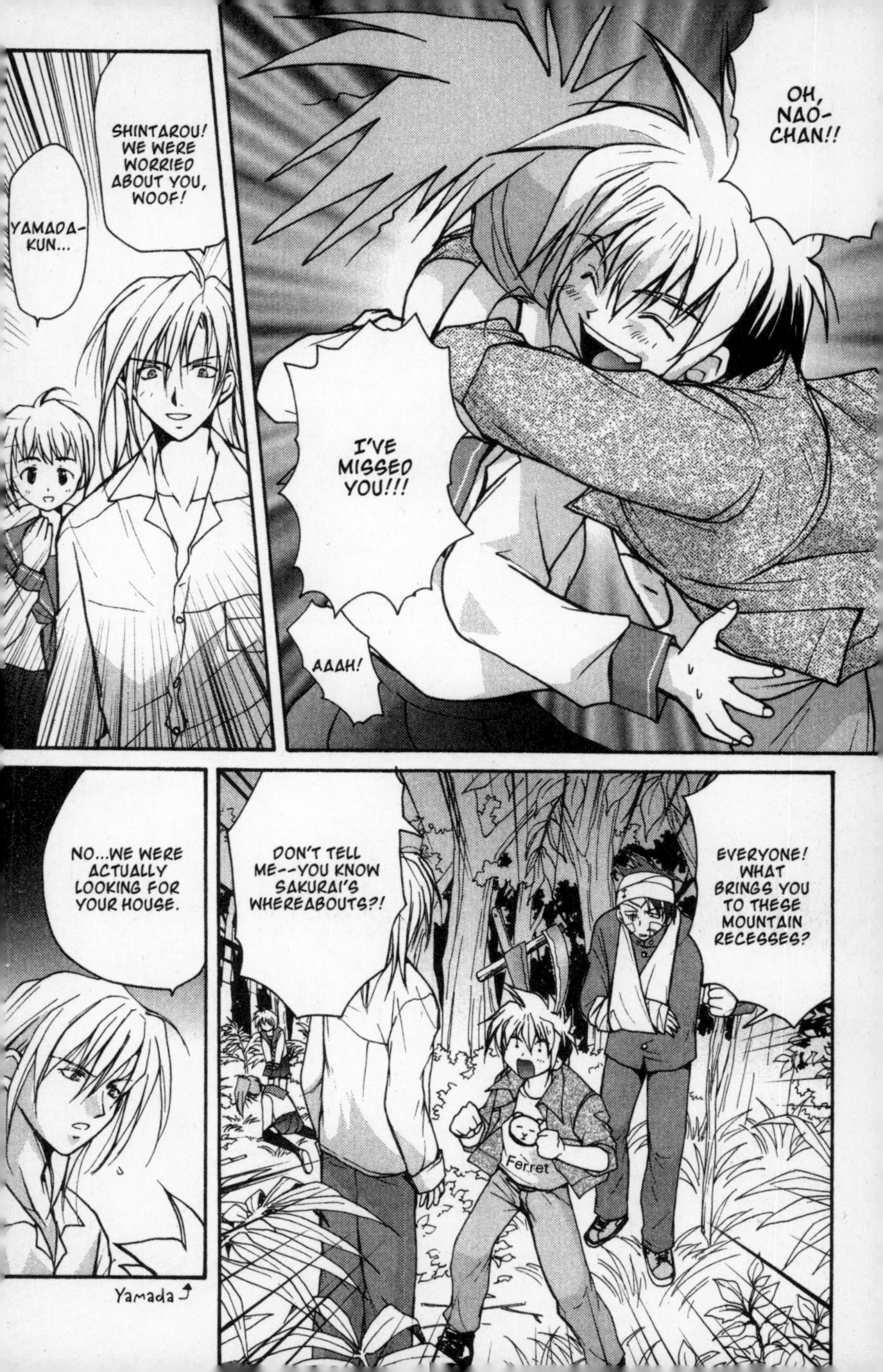

OH, NAO-CHAN!!
I'VE MISSED YOU!!!
AAAH!
SHINTAROU! WE WERE WORRIED ABOUT YOU, WOOF!
YAMADA-KUN...
EVERYONE! WHAT BRINGS YOU TO THESE MOUNTAIN RECESSES?
DON'T TELL ME--YOU KNOW SAKURAI'S WHEREABOUTS?!
Ferret
NO...WE WERE ACTUALLY LOOKING FOR YOUR HOUSE.
Yamada

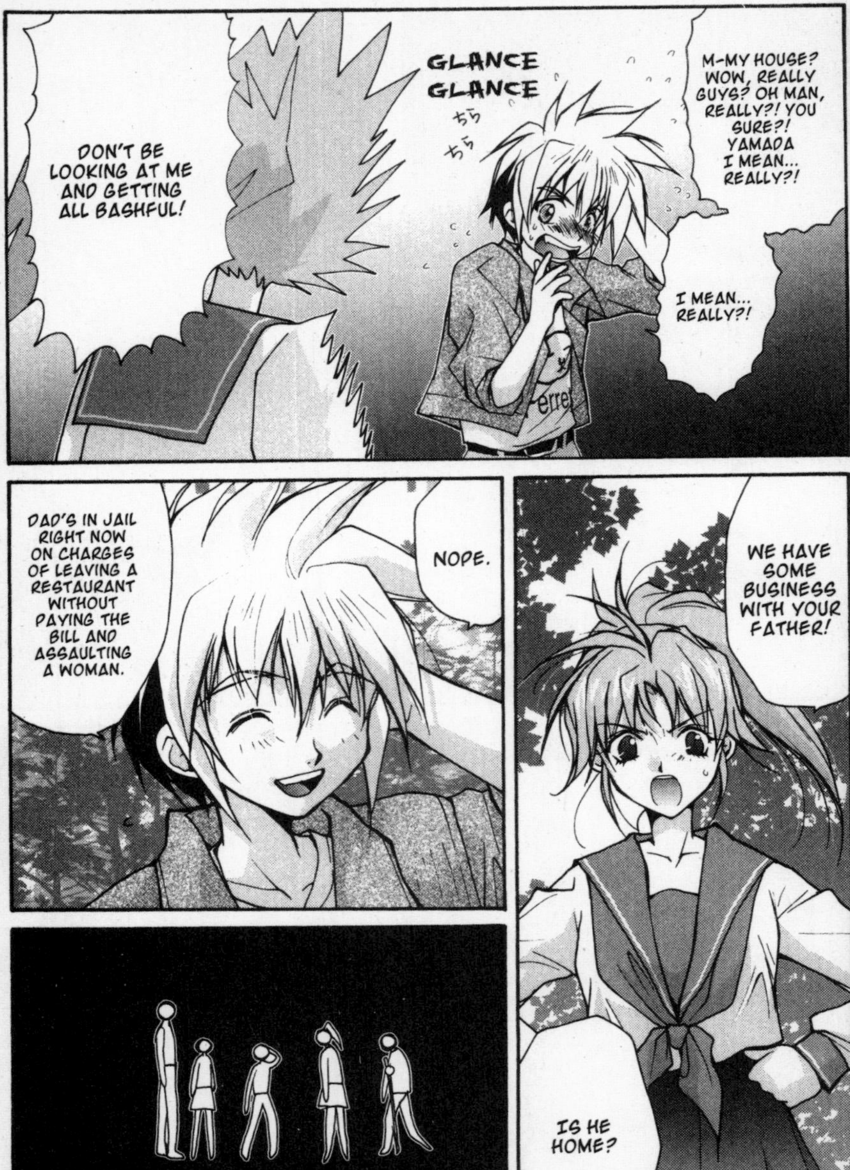
M-MY HOUSE? WOW, REALLY GUYS? OH MAN, REALLY?! YOU SURE?! YAMADA I MEAN... REALLY?!
I MEAN... REALLY?!
GLANCE GLANCE
ちら ちら
DON'T BE LOOKING AT ME AND GETTING ALL BASHFUL!
WE HAVE SOME BUSINESS WITH YOUR FATHER!
IS HE HOME?
NOPE.
DAD'S IN JAIL RIGHT NOW ON CHARGES OF LEAVING A RESTAURANT WITHOUT PAYING THE BILL AND ASSAULTING A WOMAN.

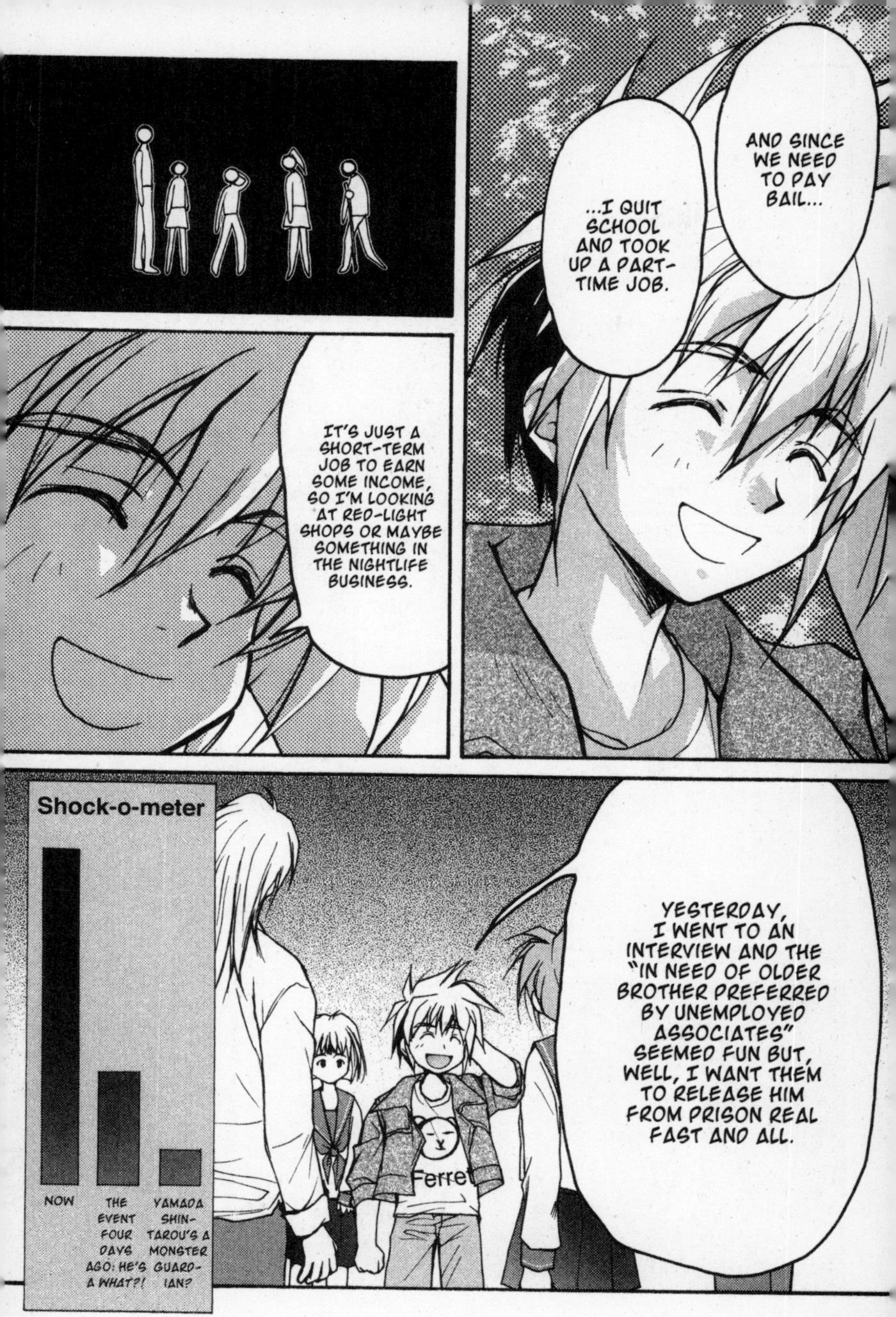
AND SINCE WE NEED TO PAY BAIL...
...I QUIT SCHOOL AND TOOK UP A PART-TIME JOB.
IT'S JUST A SHORT-TERM JOB TO EARN SOME INCOME, SO I'M LOOKING AT RED-LIGHT SHOPS OR MAYBE SOMETHING IN THE NIGHTLIFE BUSINESS.
YESTERDAY, I WENT TO AN INTERVIEW AND THE "IN NEED OF OLDER BROTHER PREFERRED BY UNEMPLOYED ASSOCIATES" SEEMED FUN BUT, WELL, I WANT THEM TO RELEASE HIM FROM PRISON REAL FAST AND ALL.
Shock-o-meter
NOW
THE EVENT FOUR DAYS AGO: HE'S A WHAT?!
YAMADA SHIN-TAROU'S A MONSTER GUARD-IAN?
Ferret

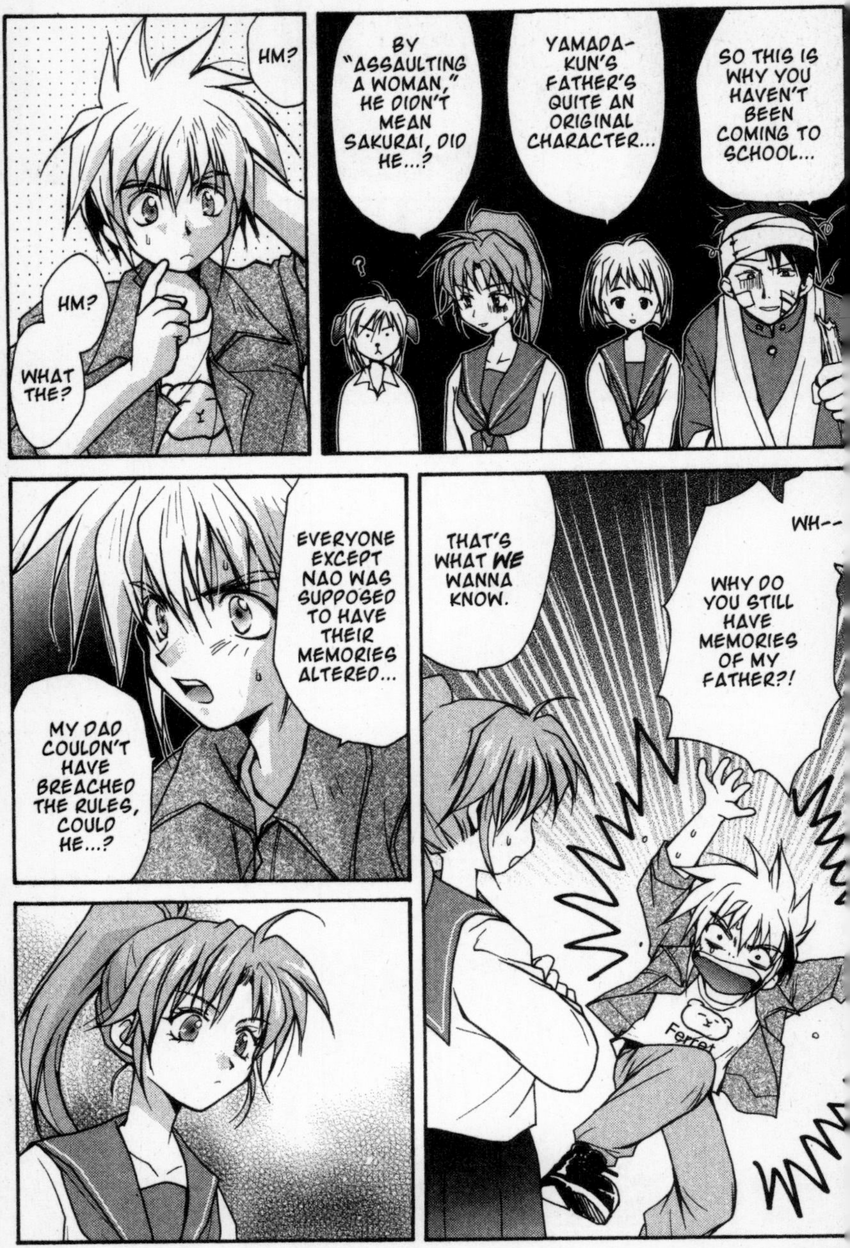
SO THIS IS WHY YOU HAVEN'T BEEN COMING TO SCHOOL...
YAMADA-KUN'S FATHER'S QUITE AN ORIGINAL CHARACTER...
BY "ASSAULTING A WOMAN," HE DIDN'T MEAN SAKURAI, DID HE...?
?
HM?
HM?
WHAT THE?
WH--
WHY DO YOU STILL HAVE MEMORIES OF MY FATHER?!
THAT'S WHAT *WE* WANNA KNOW.
Ferret
EVERYONE EXCEPT NAO WAS SUPPOSED TO HAVE THEIR MEMORIES ALTERED...
MY DAD COULDN'T HAVE BREACHED THE RULES, COULD HE...?

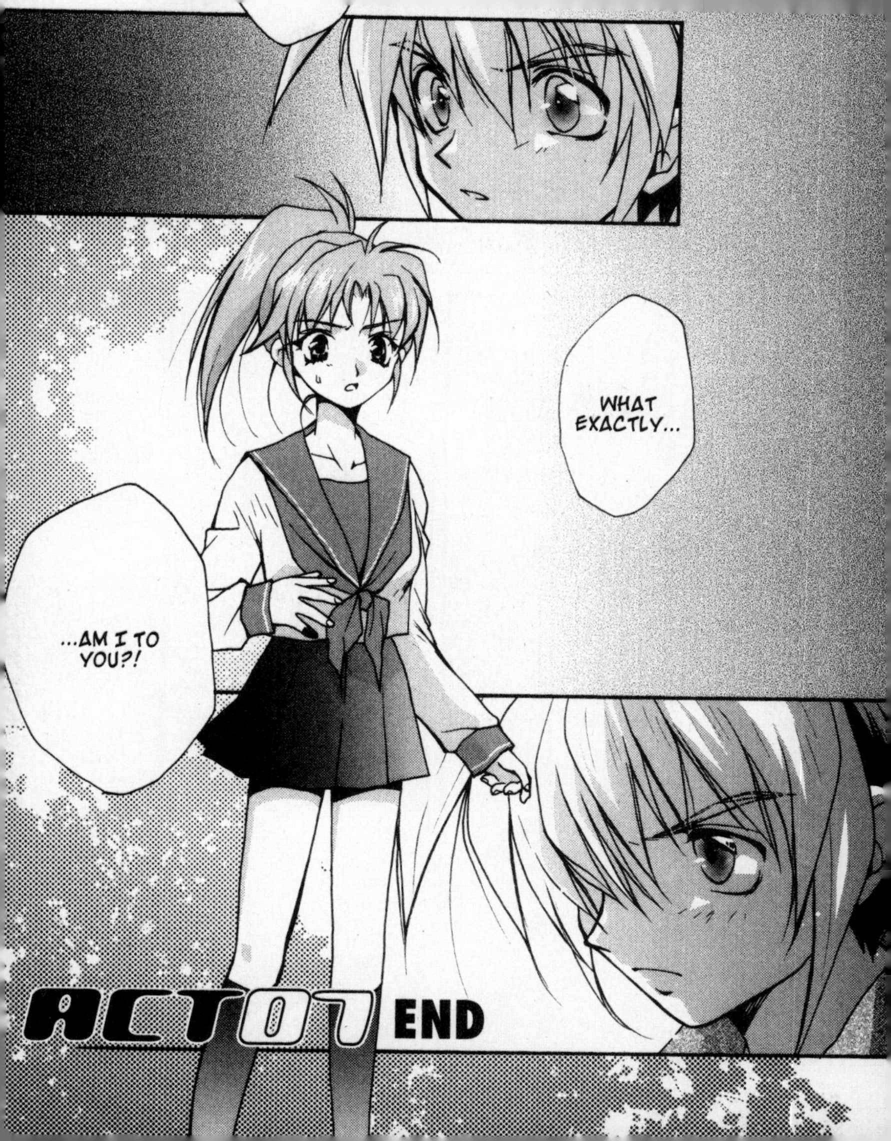
WHAT EXACTLY...
...AM I TO YOU?!
ACT 07 END

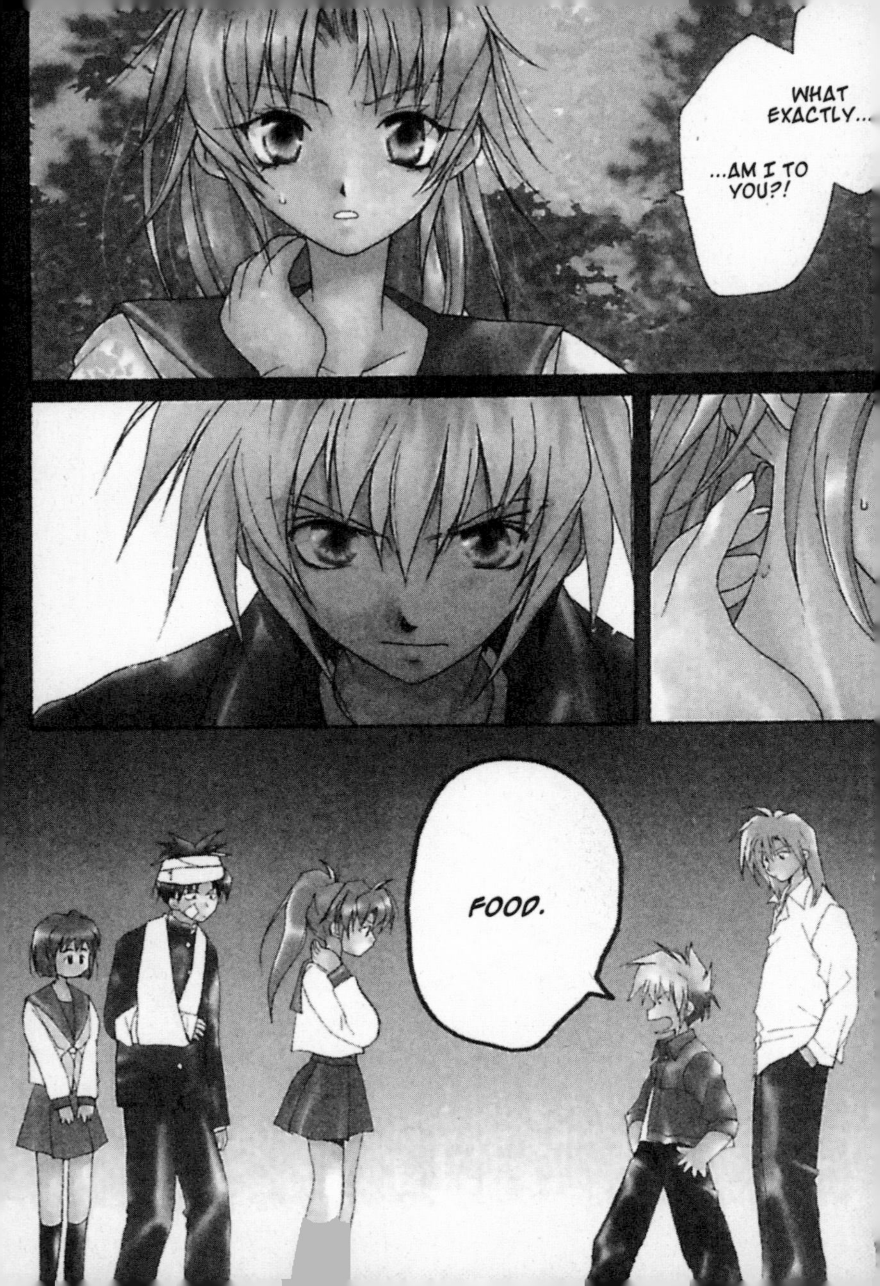
WHAT EXACTLY...
...AM I TO YOU?!
FOOD.

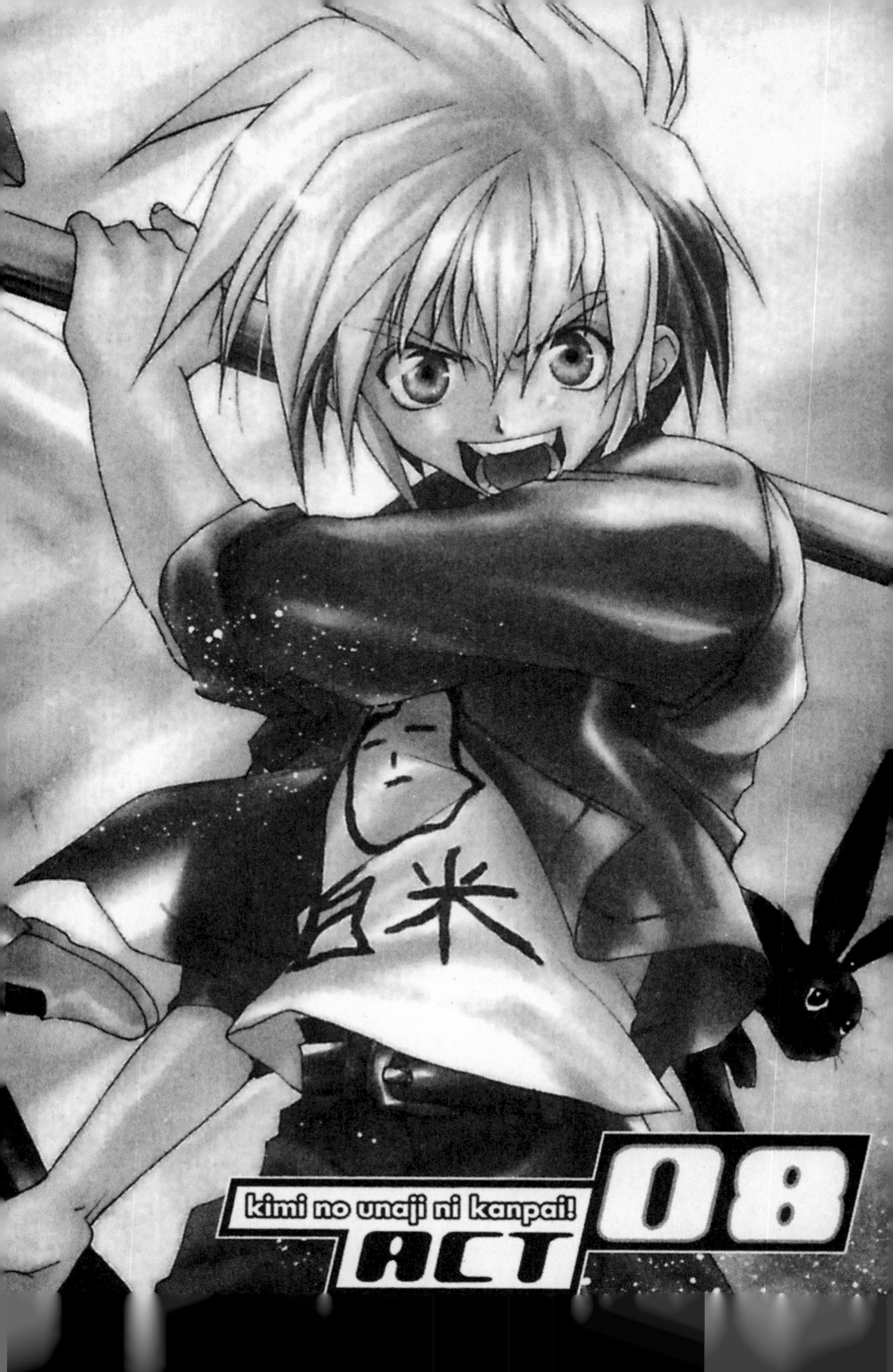
kimi no unaji ni kanpai!
ACT 08

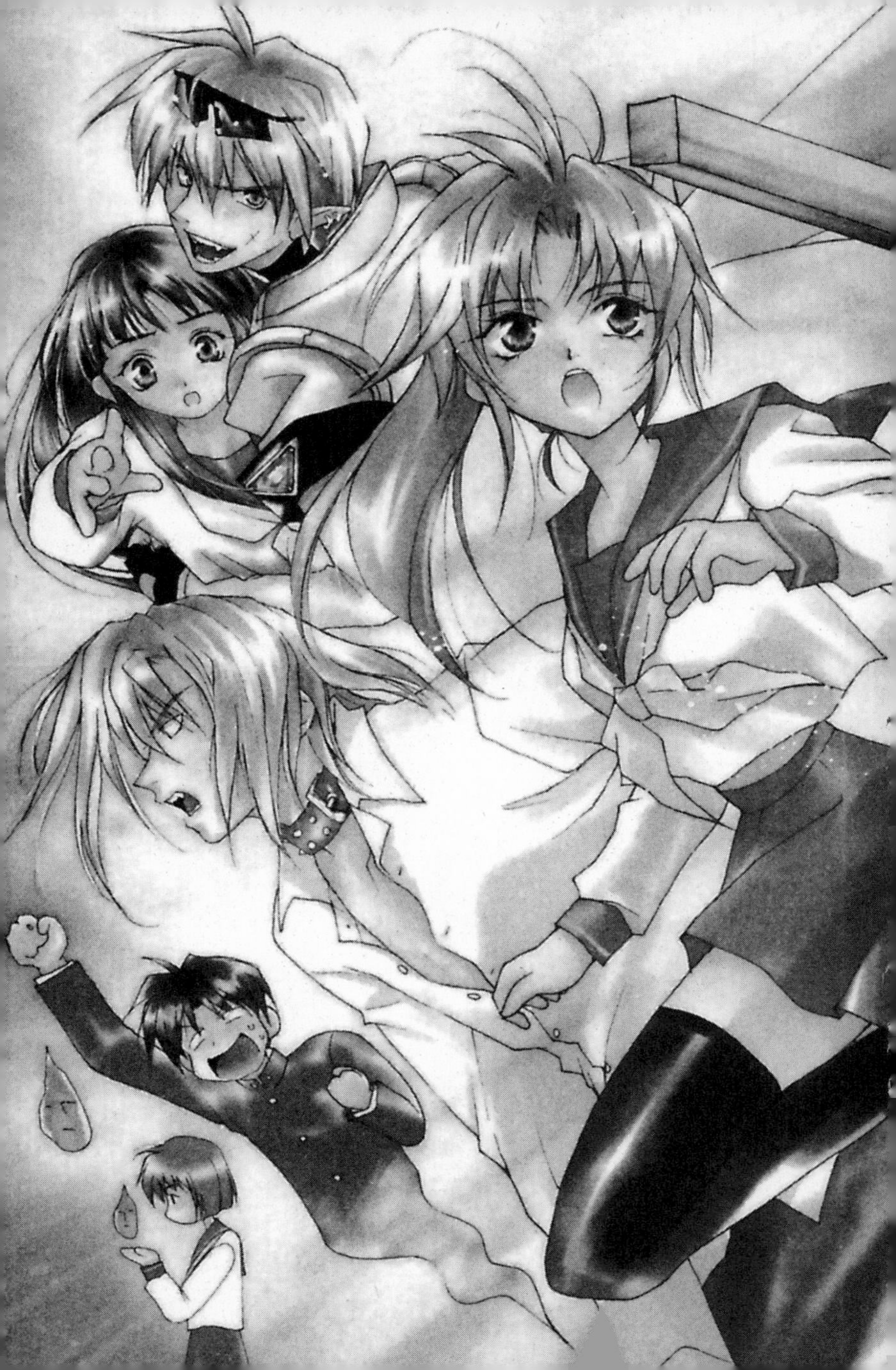

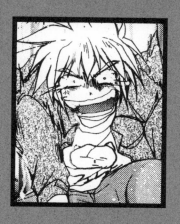

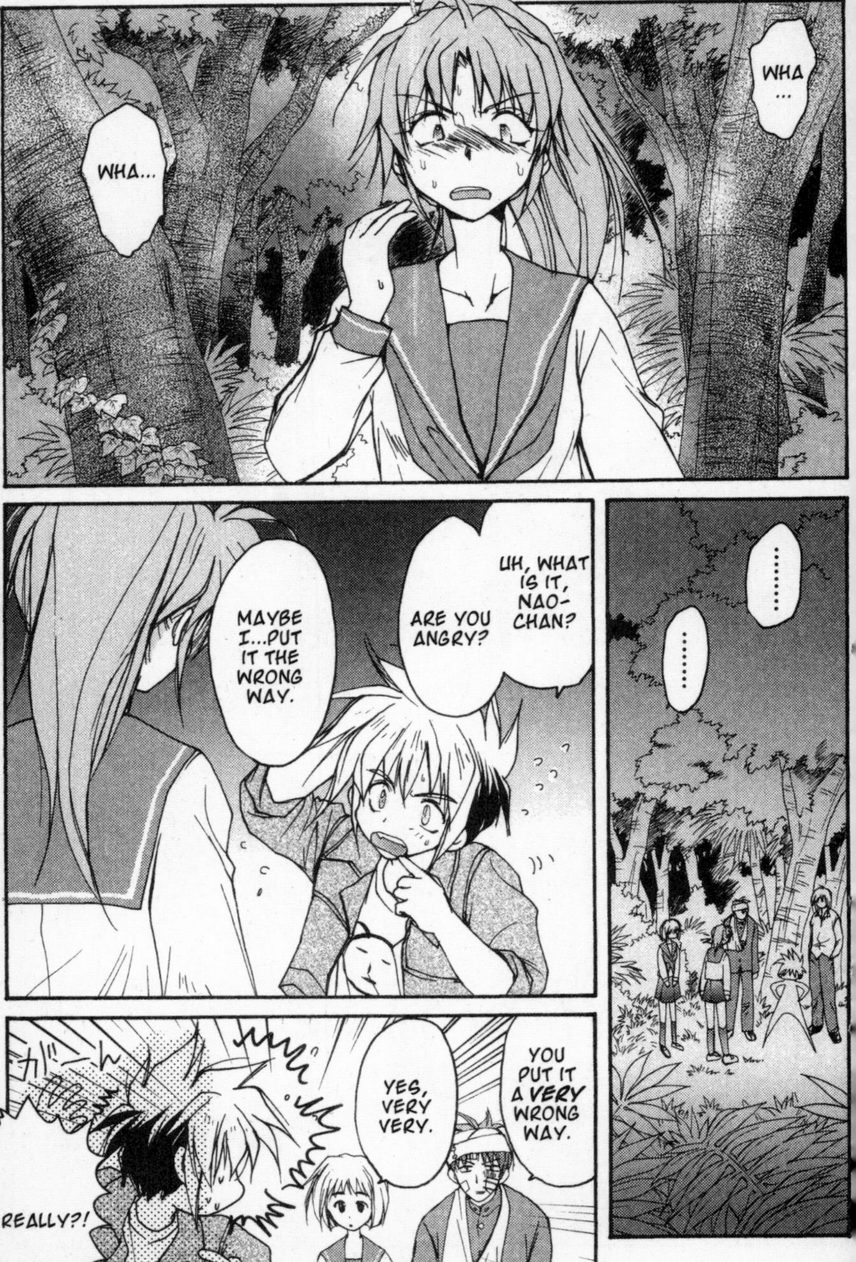
WHA ...
WHA...
....
....
UH, WHAT IS IT, NAO-CHAN?
ARE YOU ANGRY?
MAYBE I...PUT IT THE WRONG WAY.
YOU PUT IT A **VERY** WRONG WAY.
YES, VERY VERY.
REALLY?!

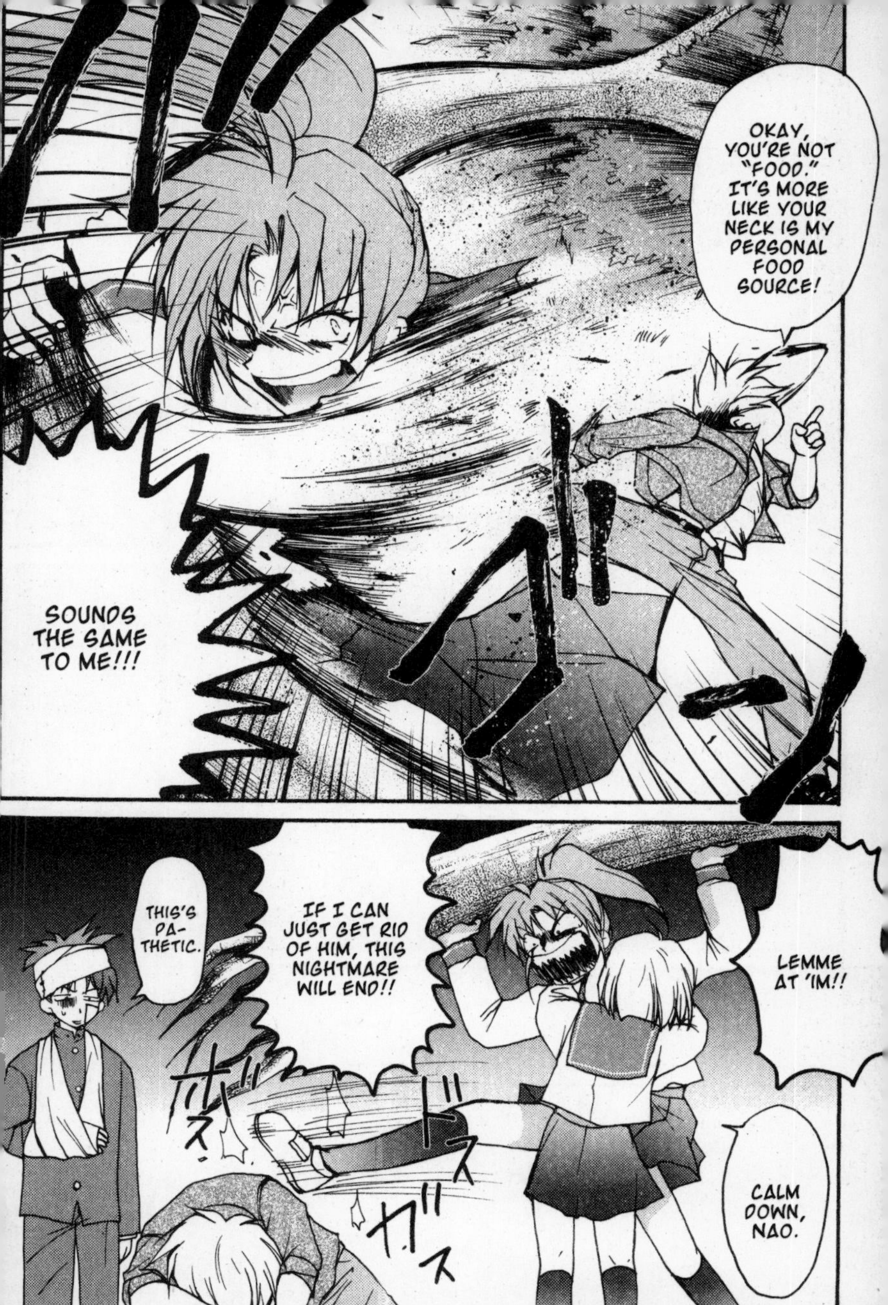
OKAY, YOU'RE NOT "FOOD." IT'S MORE LIKE YOUR NECK IS MY PERSONAL FOOD SOURCE!
SOUNDS THE SAME TO ME!!!
LEMME AT 'IM!!
CALM DOWN, NAO.
IF I CAN JUST GET RID OF HIM, THIS NIGHTMARE WILL END!!
THIS'S PA-THETIC.

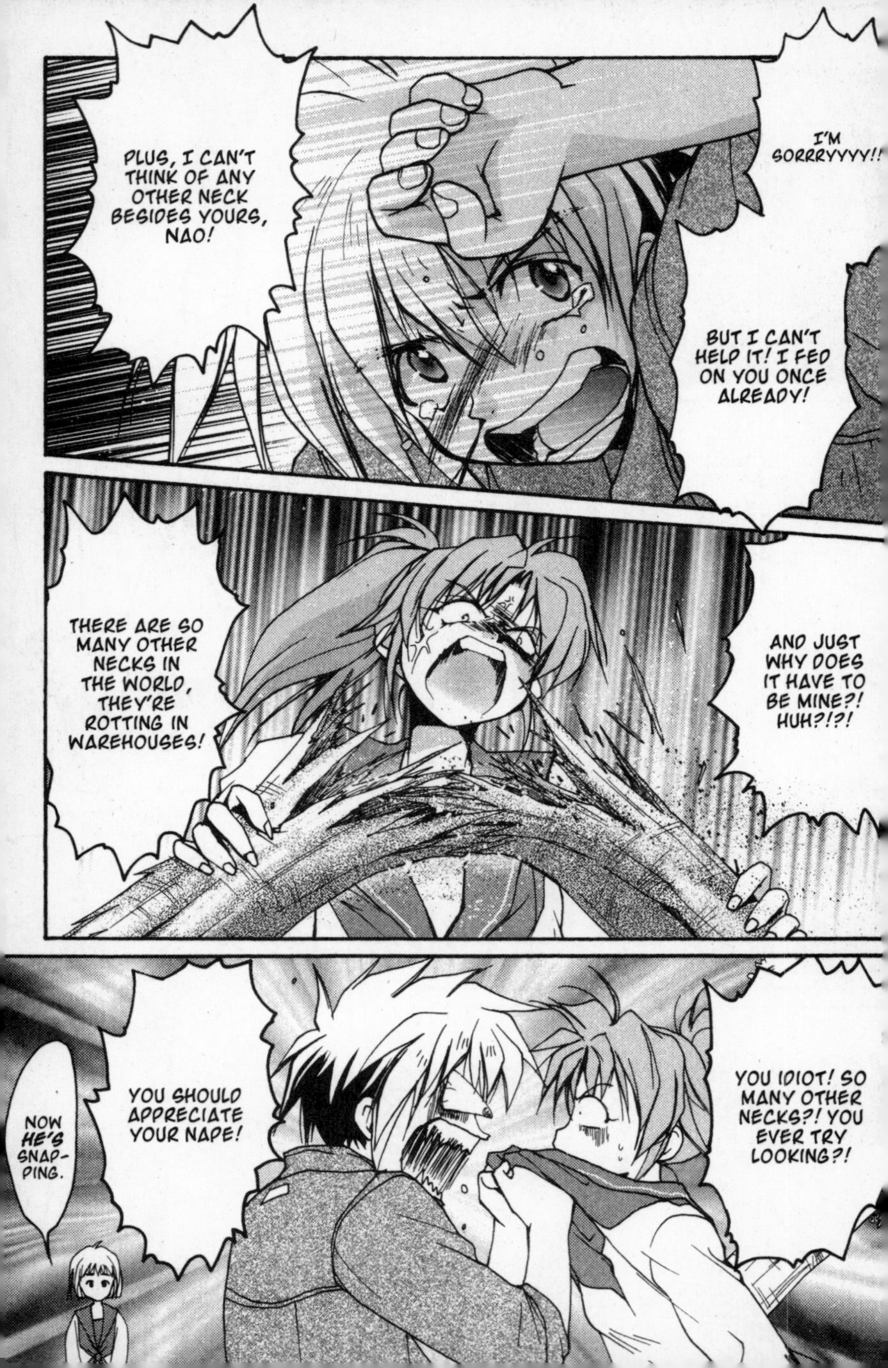
I'M SORRRYYYY!!
BUT I CAN'T HELP IT! I FED ON YOU ONCE ALREADY!
PLUS, I CAN'T THINK OF ANY OTHER NECK BESIDES YOURS, NAO!
AND JUST WHY DOES IT HAVE TO BE MINE?! HUH?!?!
THERE ARE SO MANY OTHER NECKS IN THE WORLD, THEY'RE ROTTING IN WAREHOUSES!
YOU IDIOT! SO MANY OTHER NECKS?! YOU EVER TRY LOOKING?!
YOU SHOULD APPRECIATE YOUR NAPE!
NOW HE'S SNAP-PING.

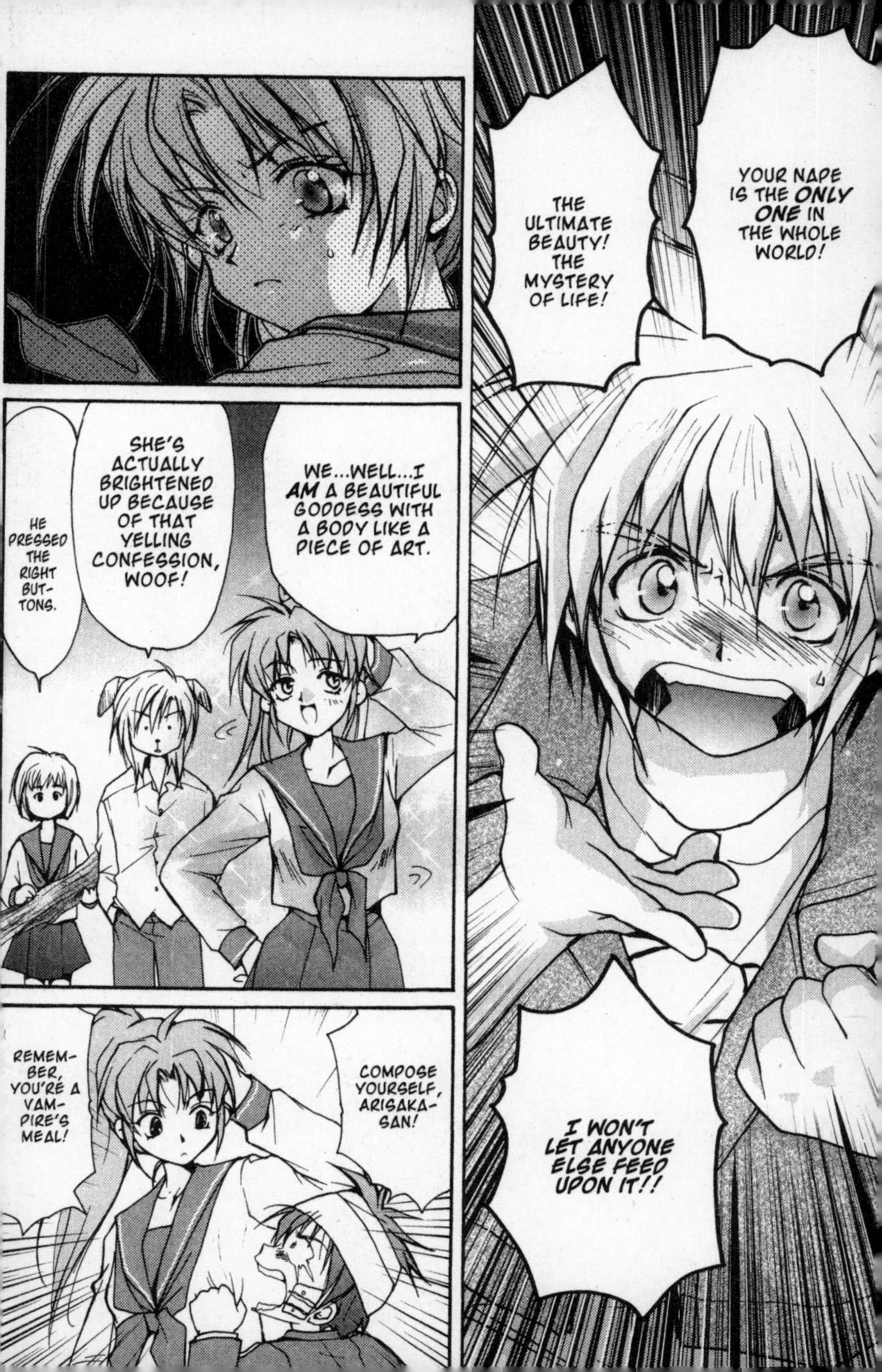
YOUR NAPE IS THE *ONLY ONE* IN THE WHOLE WORLD!
THE ULTIMATE BEAUTY! THE MYSTERY OF LIFE!
I WON'T LET ANYONE ELSE FEED UPON IT!!
WE...WELL...I *AM* A BEAUTIFUL GODDESS WITH A BODY LIKE A PIECE OF ART.
SHE'S ACTUALLY BRIGHTENED UP BECAUSE OF THAT YELLING CONFESSION, WOOF!
HE PRESSED THE RIGHT BUTTONS.
COMPOSE YOURSELF, ARISAKA-SAN!
REMEMBER, YOU'RE A VAMPIRE'S MEAL!

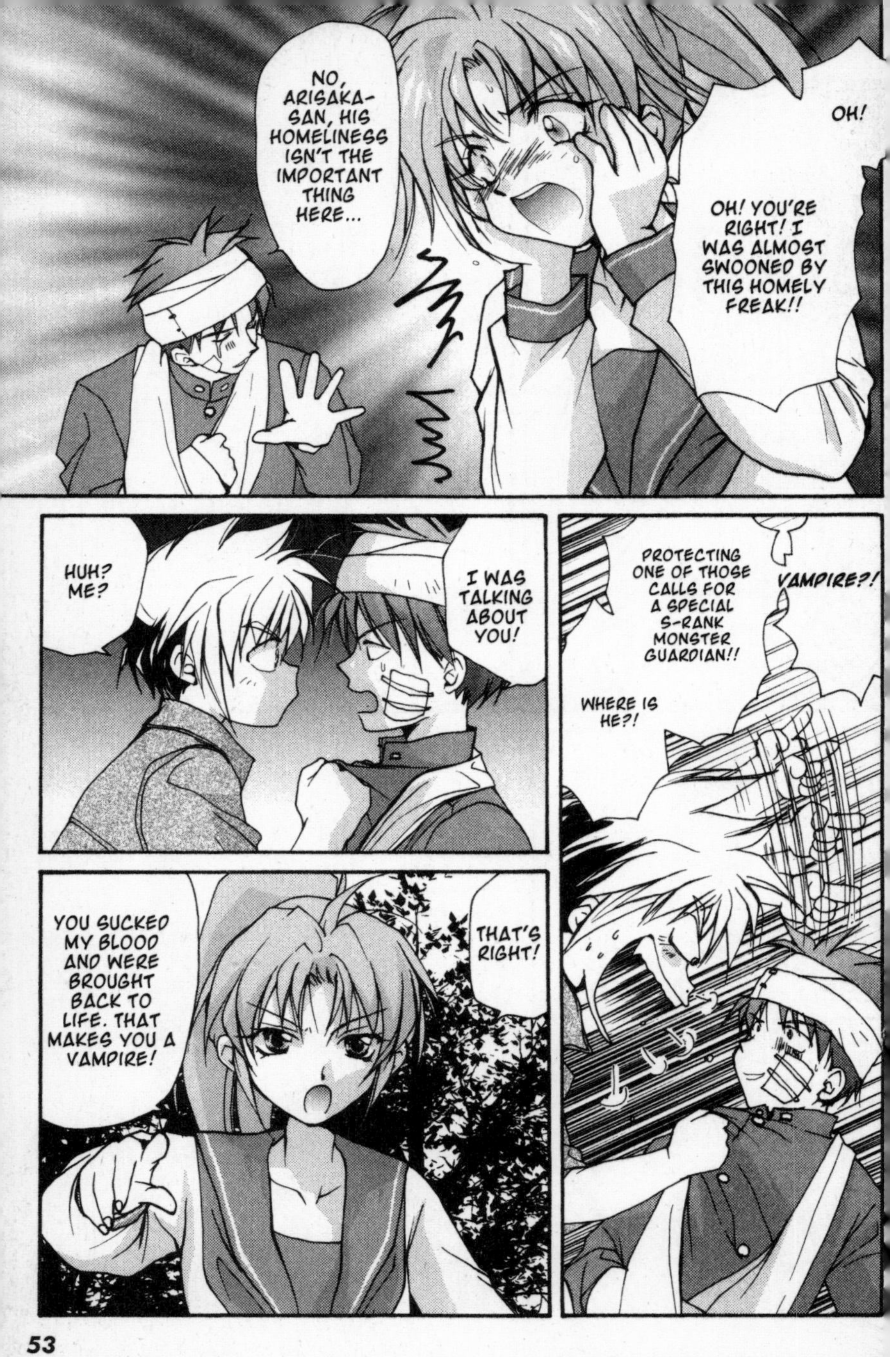
OH!
OH! YOU'RE RIGHT! I WAS ALMOST SWOONED BY THIS HOMELY FREAK!!
NO, ARISAKA-SAN, HIS HOMELINESS ISN'T THE IMPORTANT THING HERE...
VAMPIRE?!
PROTECTING ONE OF THOSE CALLS FOR A SPECIAL S-RANK MONSTER GUARDIAN!!
WHERE IS HE?!
I WAS TALKING ABOUT YOU!
HUH? ME?
THAT'S RIGHT!
YOU SUCKED MY BLOOD AND WERE BROUGHT BACK TO LIFE. THAT MAKES YOU A VAMPIRE!

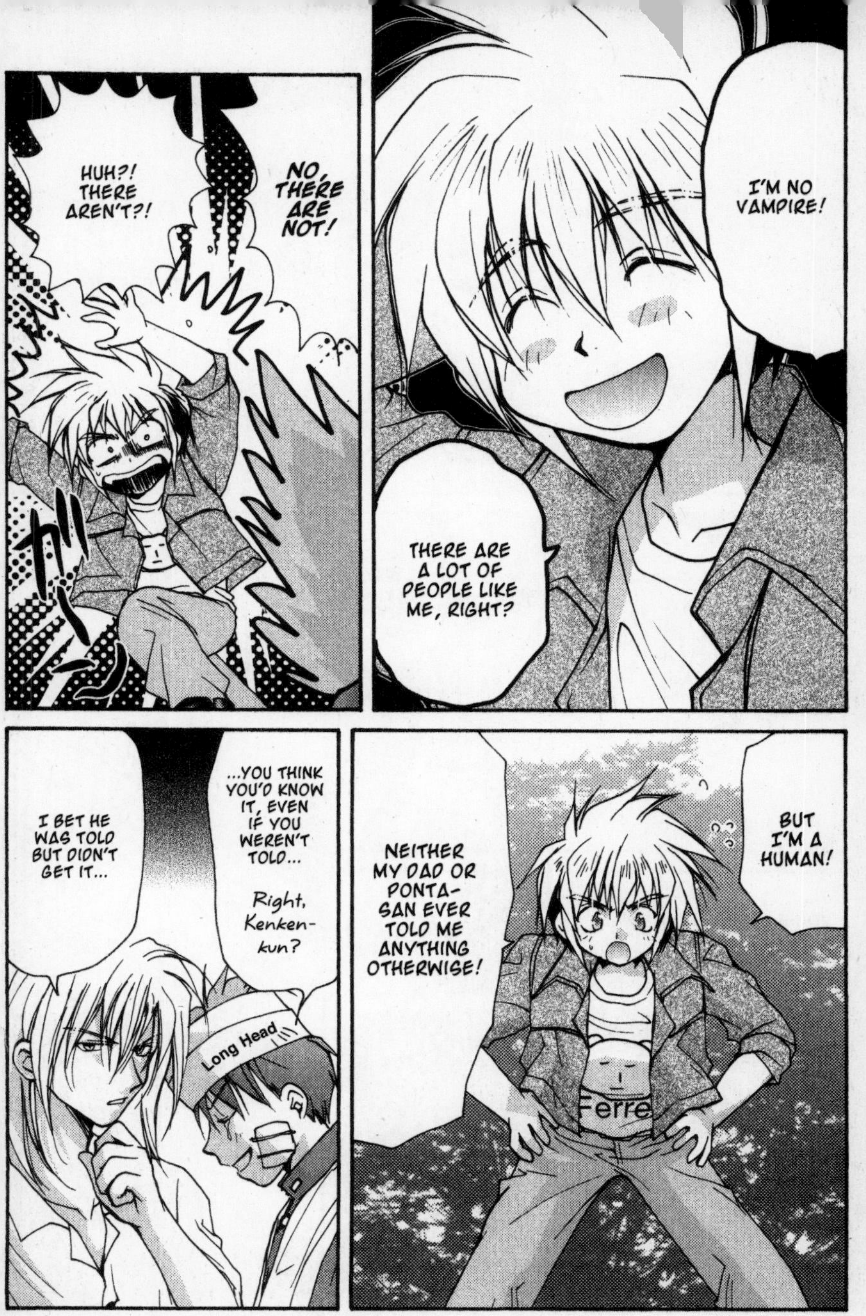
I'M NO VAMPIRE!
THERE ARE A LOT OF PEOPLE LIKE ME, RIGHT?
NO, THERE ARE NOT!
HUH?! THERE AREN'T?!
BUT I'M A HUMAN!
NEITHER MY DAD OR PONTA-SAN EVER TOLD ME ANYTHING OTHERWISE!
Ferre
...YOU THINK YOU'D KNOW IT, EVEN IF YOU WEREN'T TOLD...
Right, Kenken-kun?
I BET HE WAS TOLD BUT DIDN'T GET IT...
Long Head

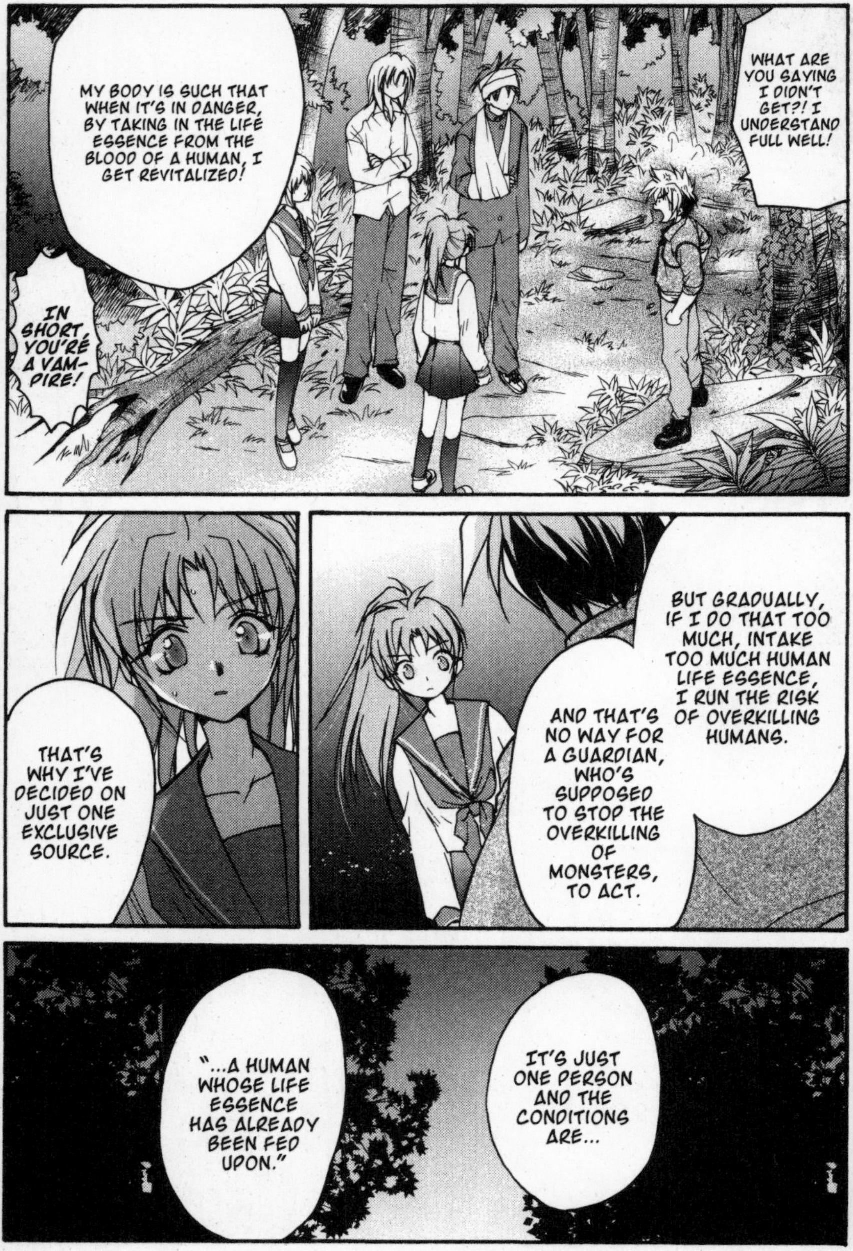
WHAT ARE YOU SAYING I DIDN'T GET?! I UNDERSTAND FULL WELL!
MY BODY IS SUCH THAT WHEN IT'S IN DANGER, BY TAKING IN THE LIFE ESSENCE FROM THE BLOOD OF A HUMAN, I GET REVITALIZED!
IN SHORT, YOU'RE A VAMPIRE!
BUT GRADUALLY, IF I DO THAT TOO MUCH, INTAKE TOO MUCH HUMAN LIFE ESSENCE, I RUN THE RISK OF OVERKILLING HUMANS.
AND THAT'S NO WAY FOR A GUARDIAN, WHO'S SUPPOSED TO STOP THE OVERKILLING OF MONSTERS, TO ACT.
THAT'S WHY I'VE DECIDED ON JUST ONE EXCLUSIVE SOURCE.
IT'S JUST ONE PERSON AND THE CONDITIONS ARE...
"...A HUMAN WHOSE LIFE ESSENCE HAS ALREADY BEEN FED UPON."

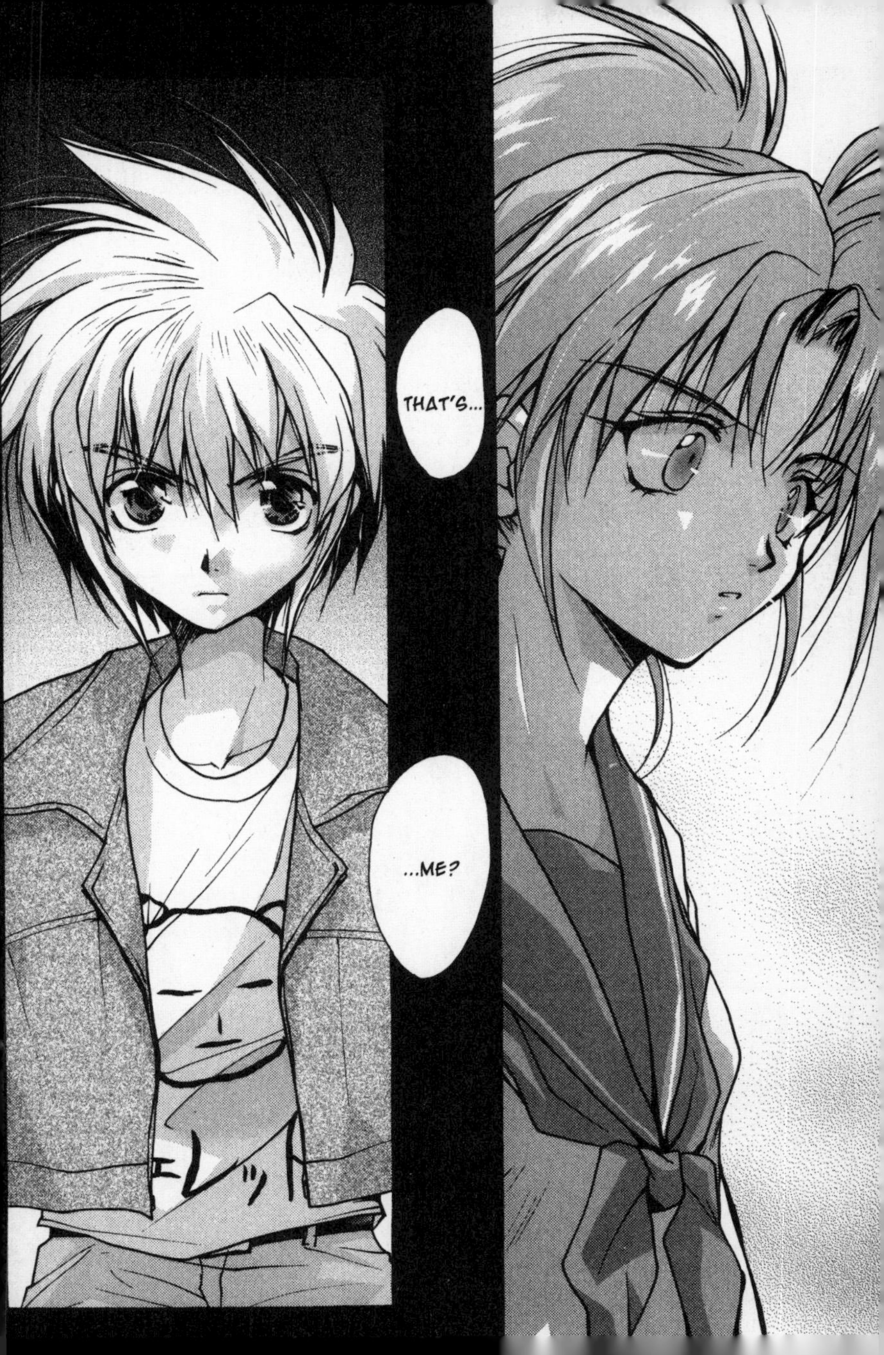
THAT'S...
...ME?

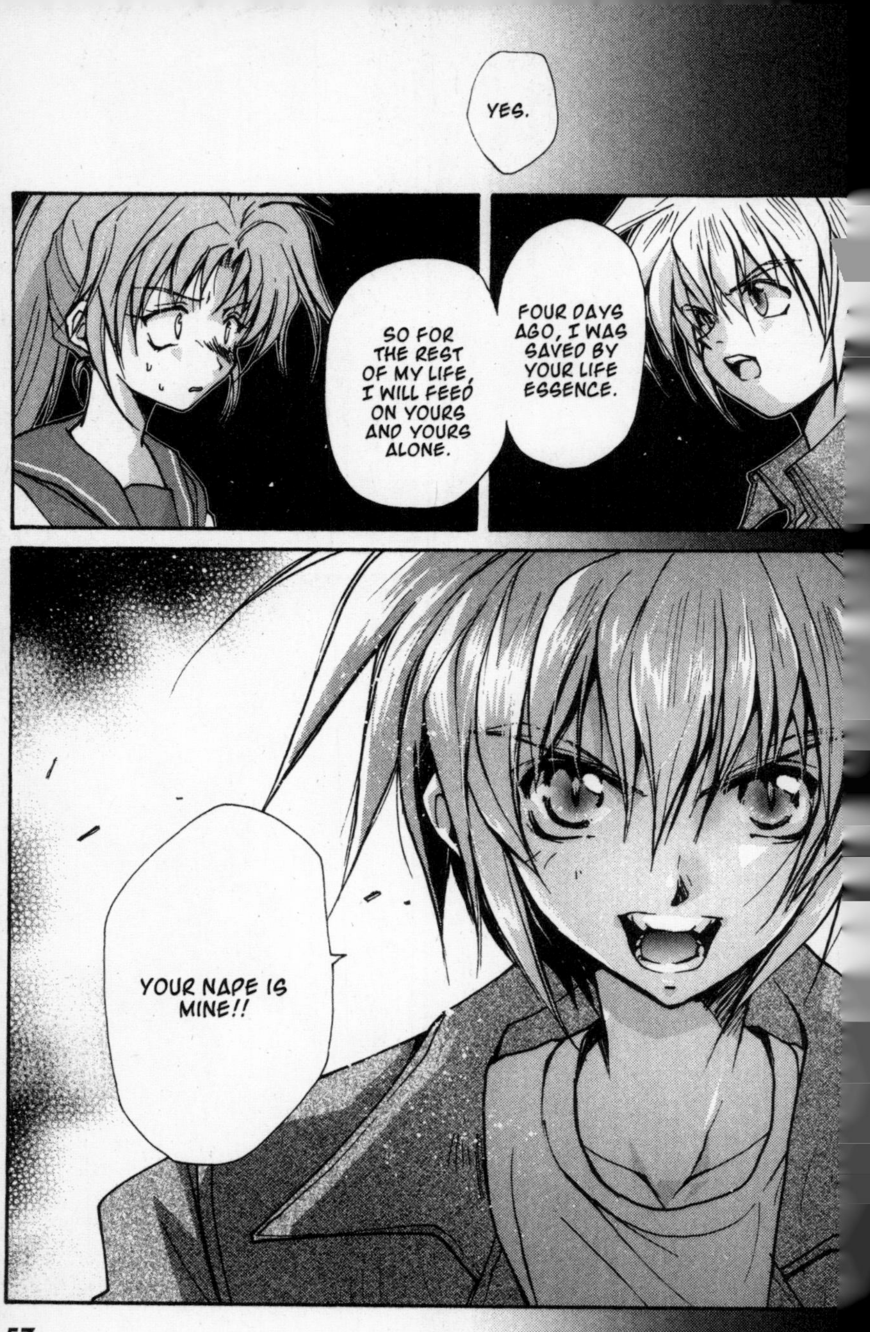
YES.
FOUR DAYS AGO, I WAS SAVED BY YOUR LIFE ESSENCE.
SO FOR THE REST OF MY LIFE, I WILL FEED ON YOURS AND YOURS ALONE.
YOUR NAPE IS MINE!!

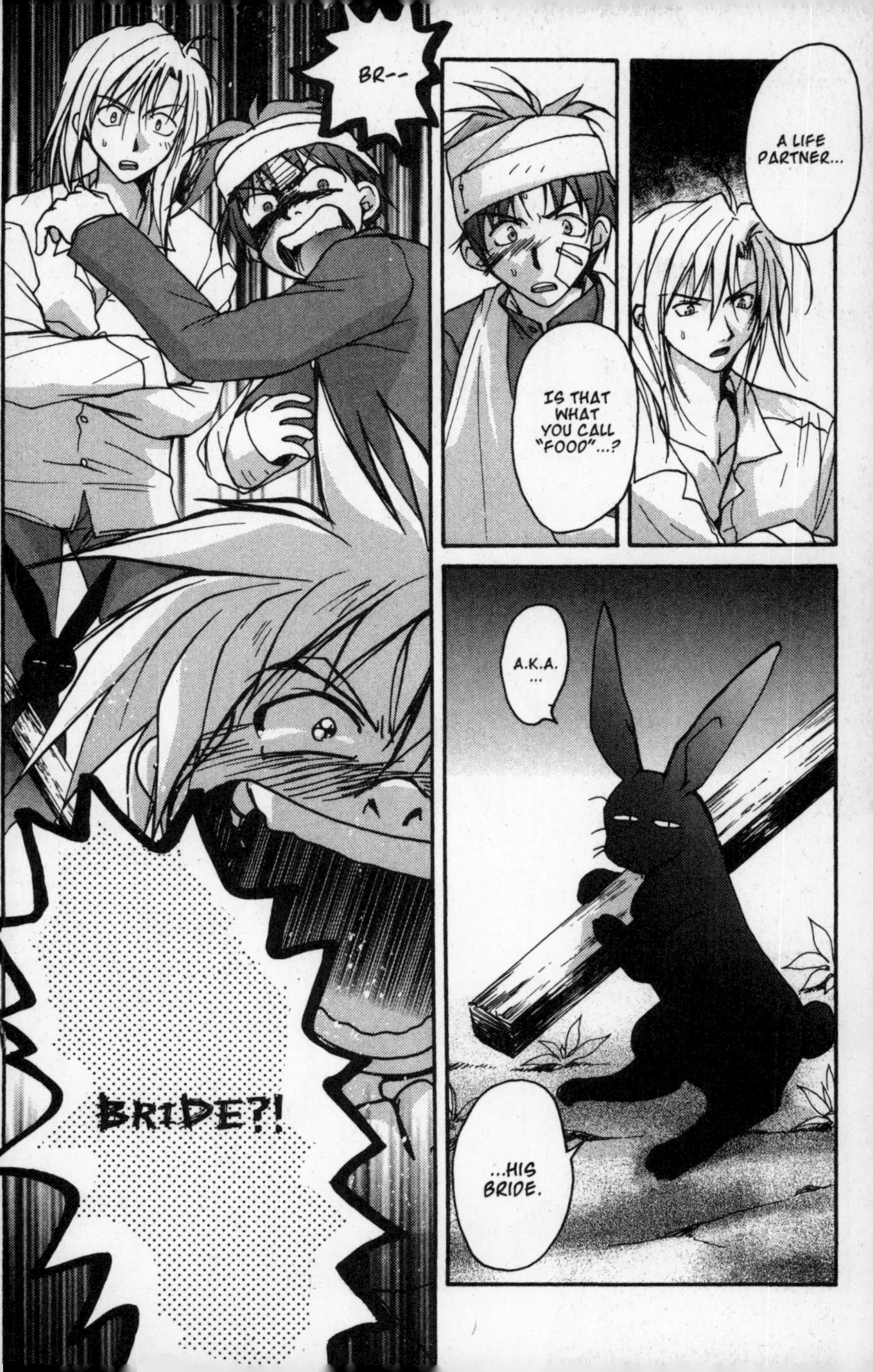
A LIFE PARTNER...
IS THAT WHAT YOU CALL "FOOD"...?
A.K.A. ...
...HIS BRIDE.
BR--
BRIDE?!

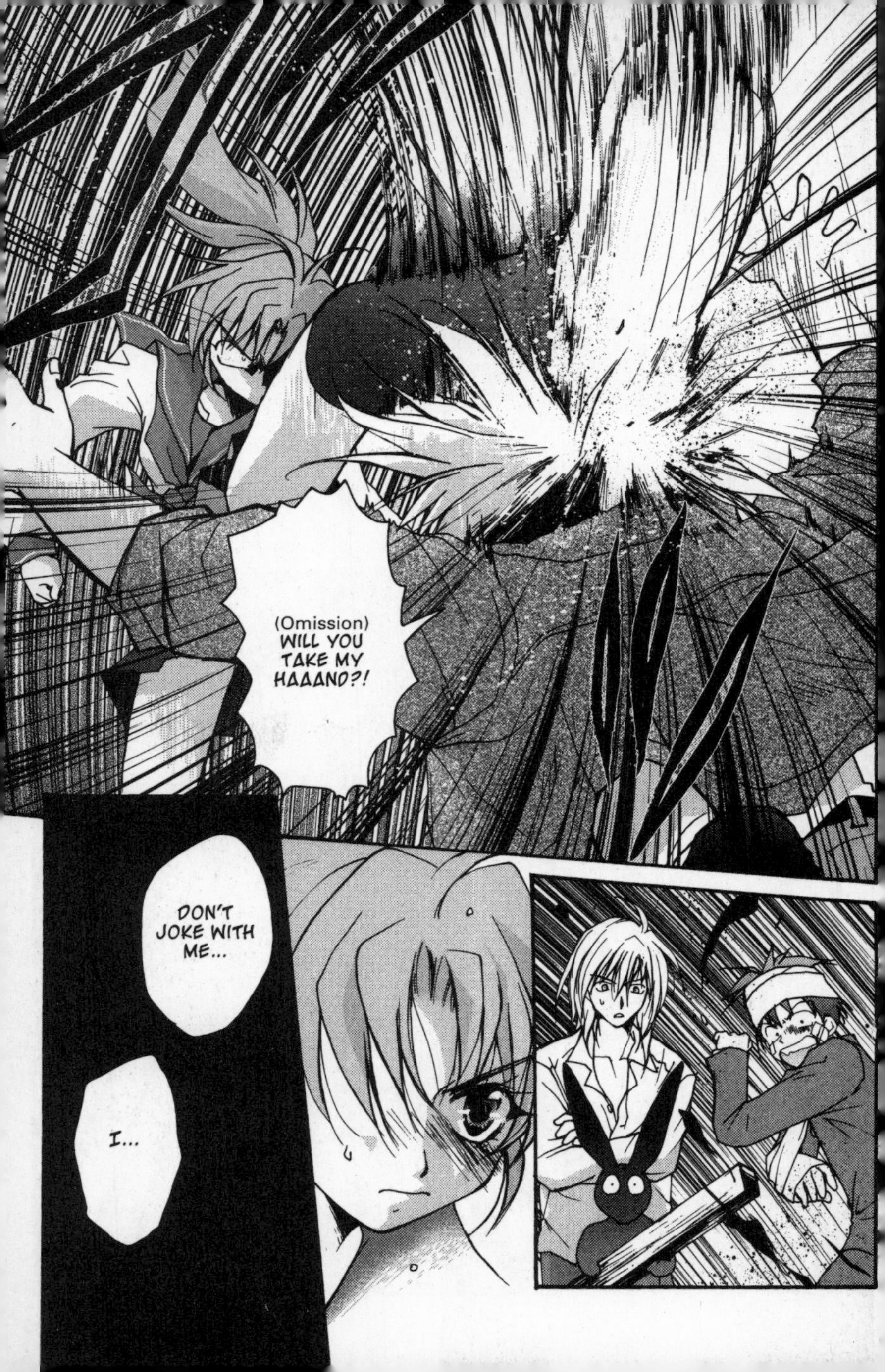
(Omission) WILL YOU TAKE MY HAAAND?!
DON'T JOKE WITH ME...
I...

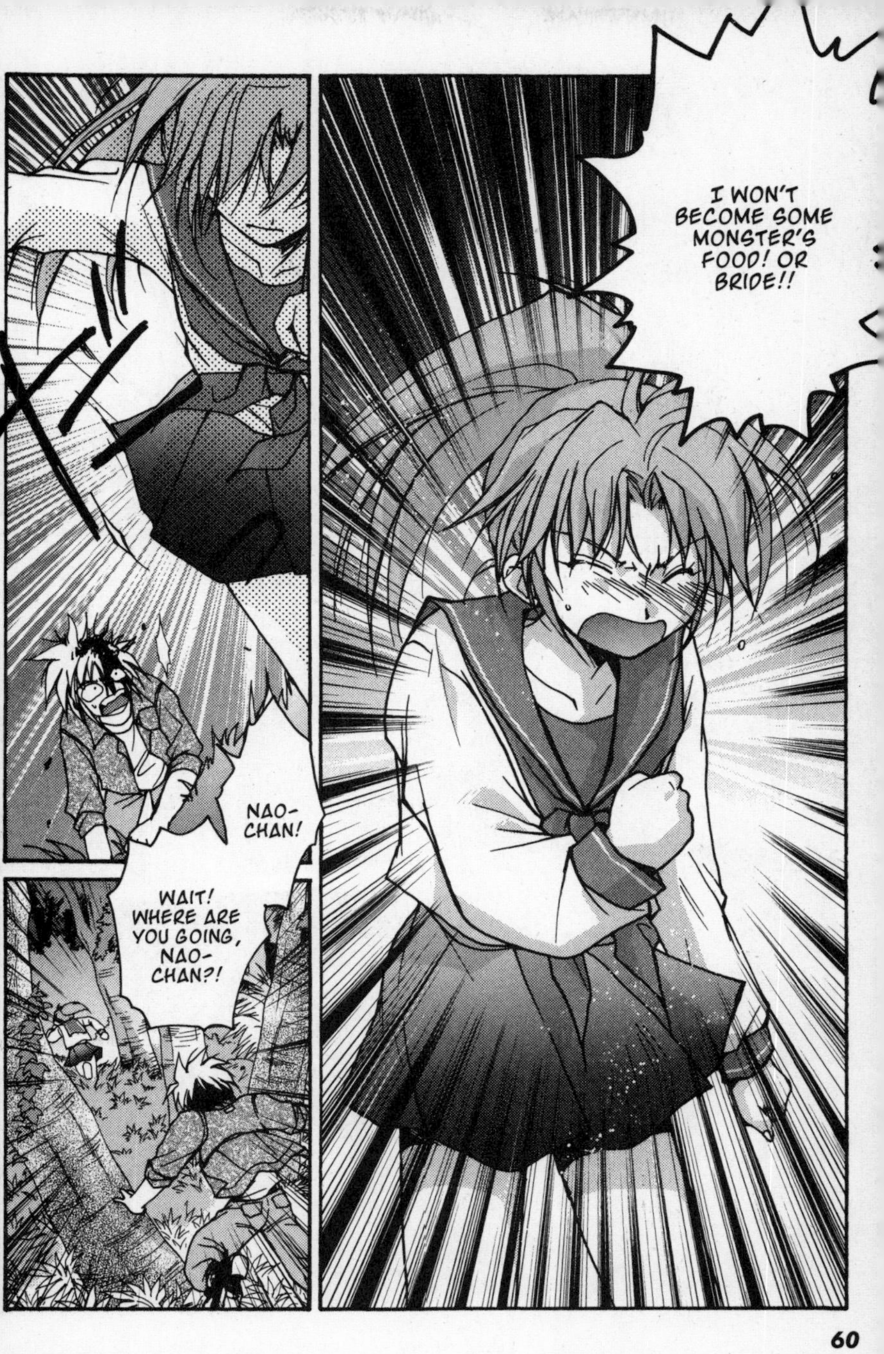
I WON'T BECOME SOME MONSTER'S FOOD! OR BRIDE!!
NAO-CHAN!
WAIT! WHERE ARE YOU GOING, NAO-CHAN?!

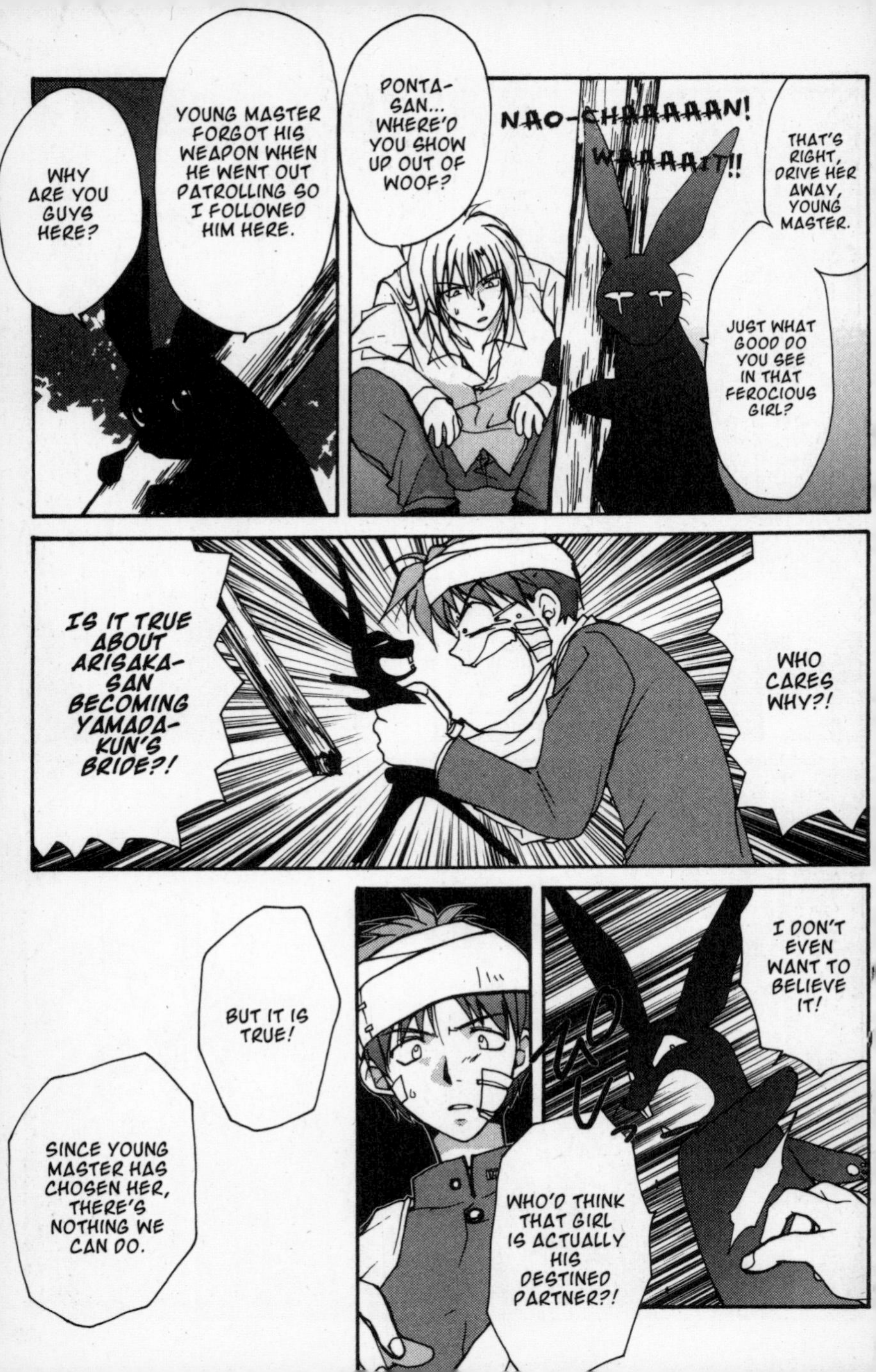
THAT'S RIGHT, DRIVE HER AWAY, YOUNG MASTER.
NAO-CHAAAAAAN! WAAAAAIT!!
JUST WHAT GOOD DO YOU SEE IN THAT FEROCIOUS GIRL?
PONTA-SAN... WHERE'D YOU SHOW UP OUT OF WOOF?
YOUNG MASTER FORGOT HIS WEAPON WHEN HE WENT OUT PATROLLING SO I FOLLOWED HIM HERE.
WHY ARE YOU GUYS HERE?
WHO CARES WHY?!
IS IT TRUE ABOUT ARISAKA-SAN BECOMING YAMADA-KUN'S BRIDE?!
I DON'T EVEN WANT TO BELIEVE IT!
WHO'D THINK THAT GIRL IS ACTUALLY HIS DESTINED PARTNER?!
BUT IT IS TRUE!
SINCE YOUNG MASTER HAS CHOSEN HER, THERE'S NOTHING WE CAN DO.

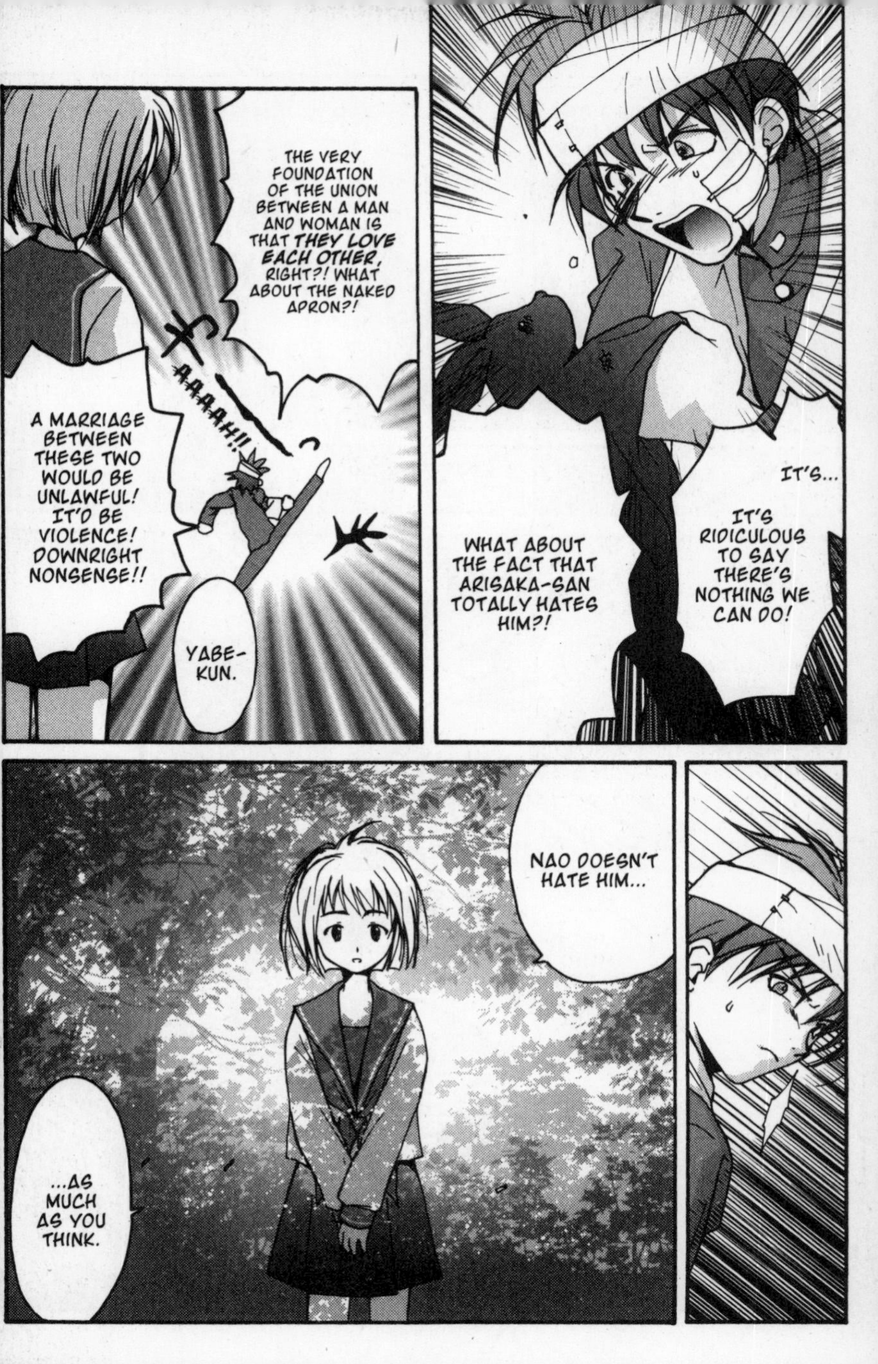
IT'S...
IT'S RIDICULOUS TO SAY THERE'S NOTHING WE CAN DO!
WHAT ABOUT THE FACT THAT ARISAKA-SAN TOTALLY HATES HIM?!
THE VERY FOUNDATION OF THE UNION BETWEEN A MAN AND WOMAN IS THAT ***THEY LOVE EACH OTHER***, RIGHT?! WHAT ABOUT THE NAKED APRON?!
A MARRIAGE BETWEEN THESE TWO WOULD BE UNLAWFUL! IT'D BE VIOLENCE! DOWNRIGHT NONSENSE!!
YABE-KUN.
NAO DOESN'T HATE HIM...
...AS MUCH AS YOU THINK.

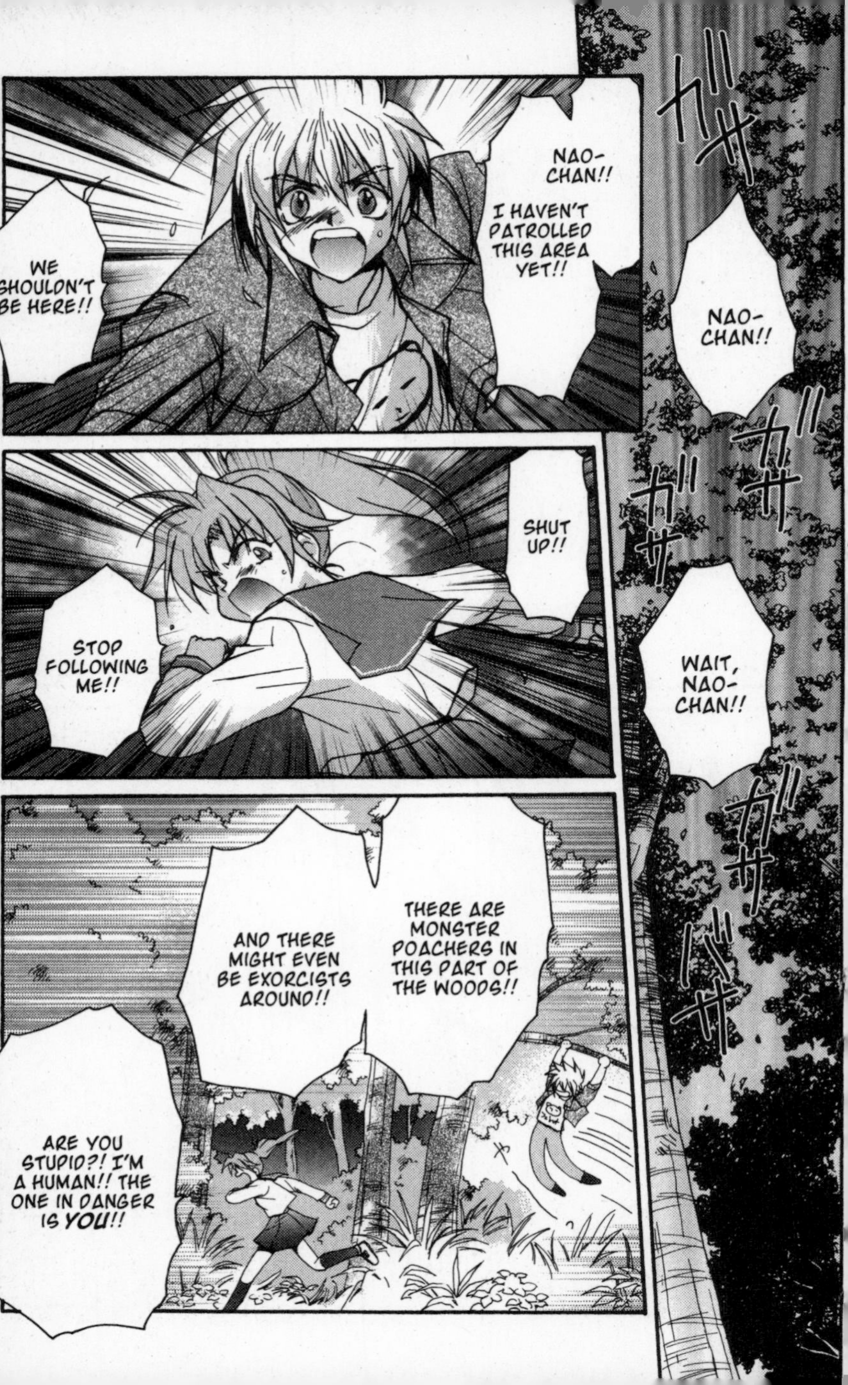
ガサ
NAO-CHAN!!
ガサ
ガサ
WAIT, NAO-CHAN!!
ガサ
ガサ
NAO-CHAN!!
I HAVEN'T PATROLLED THIS AREA YET!!
WE SHOULDN'T BE HERE!!
SHUT UP!!
STOP FOLLOWING ME!!
THERE ARE MONSTER POACHERS IN THIS PART OF THE WOODS!!
AND THERE MIGHT EVEN BE EXORCISTS AROUND!!
ARE YOU STUPID?! I'M A HUMAN!! THE ONE IN DANGER IS ***YOU***!!

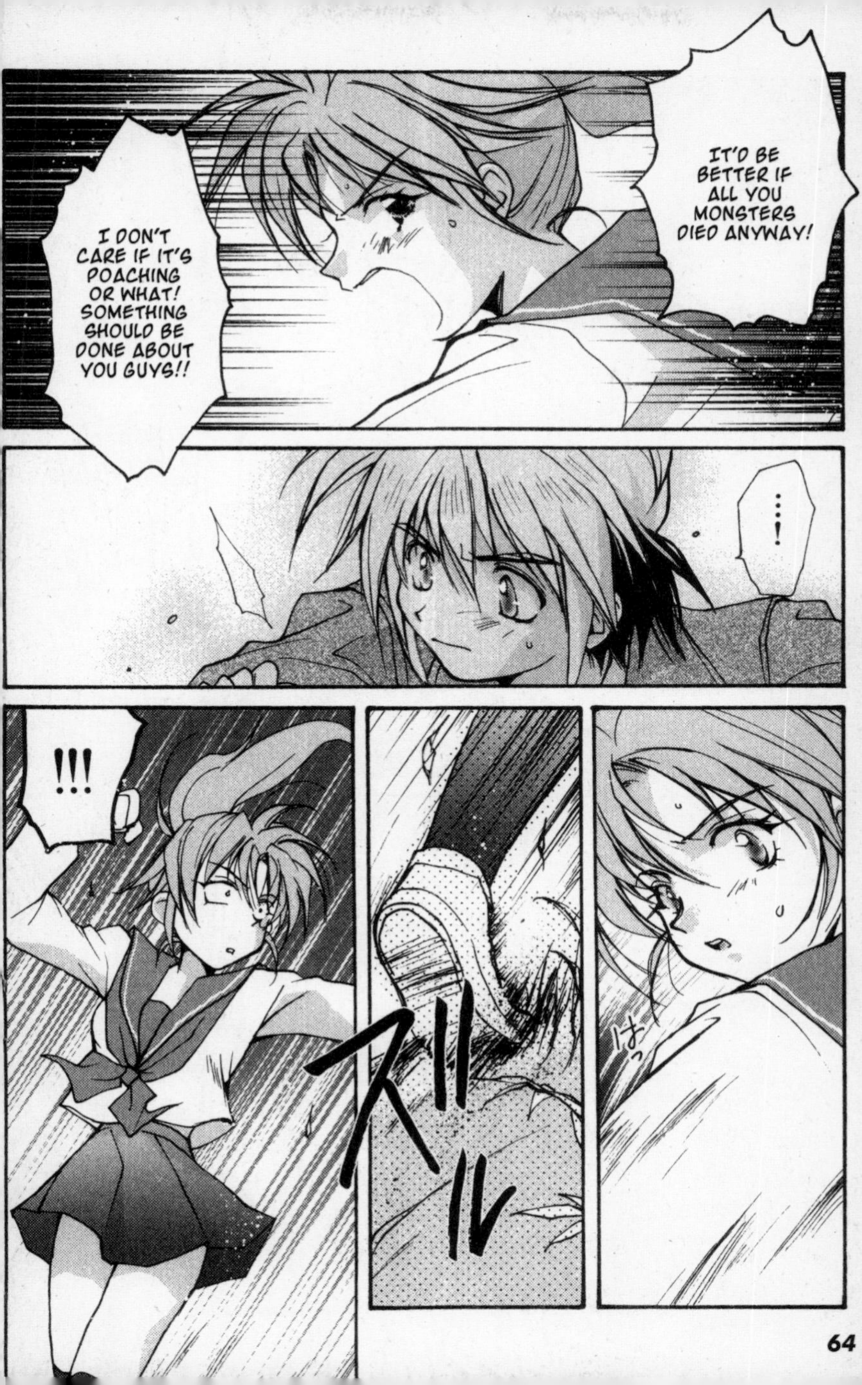
IT'D BE BETTER IF ALL YOU MONSTERS DIED ANYWAY!
I DON'T CARE IF IT'S POACHING OR WHAT! SOMETHING SHOULD BE DONE ABOUT YOU GUYS!!
...!
はっ
スル
!!!

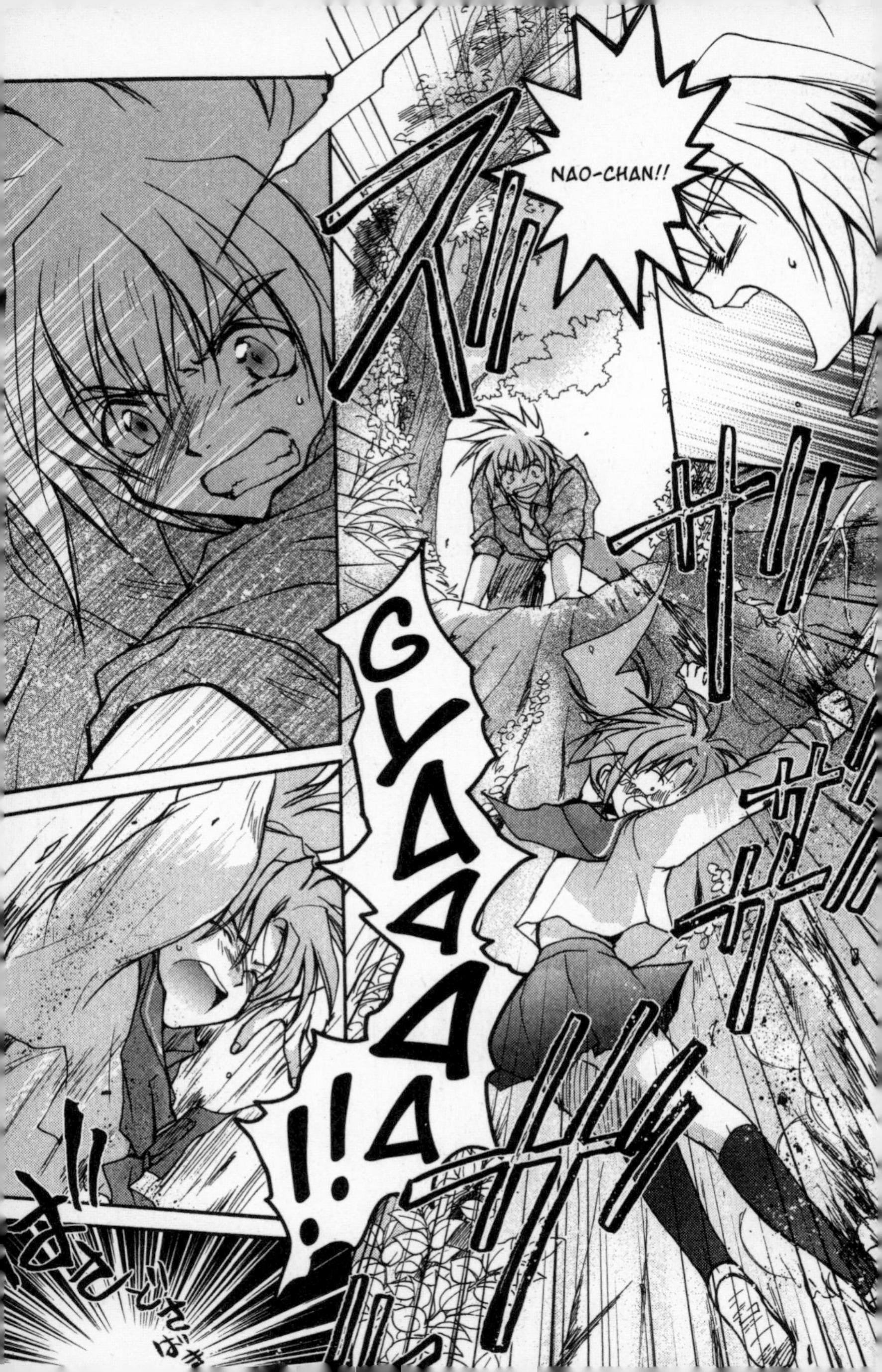
NAO-CHAN!!
GYAAAA!!

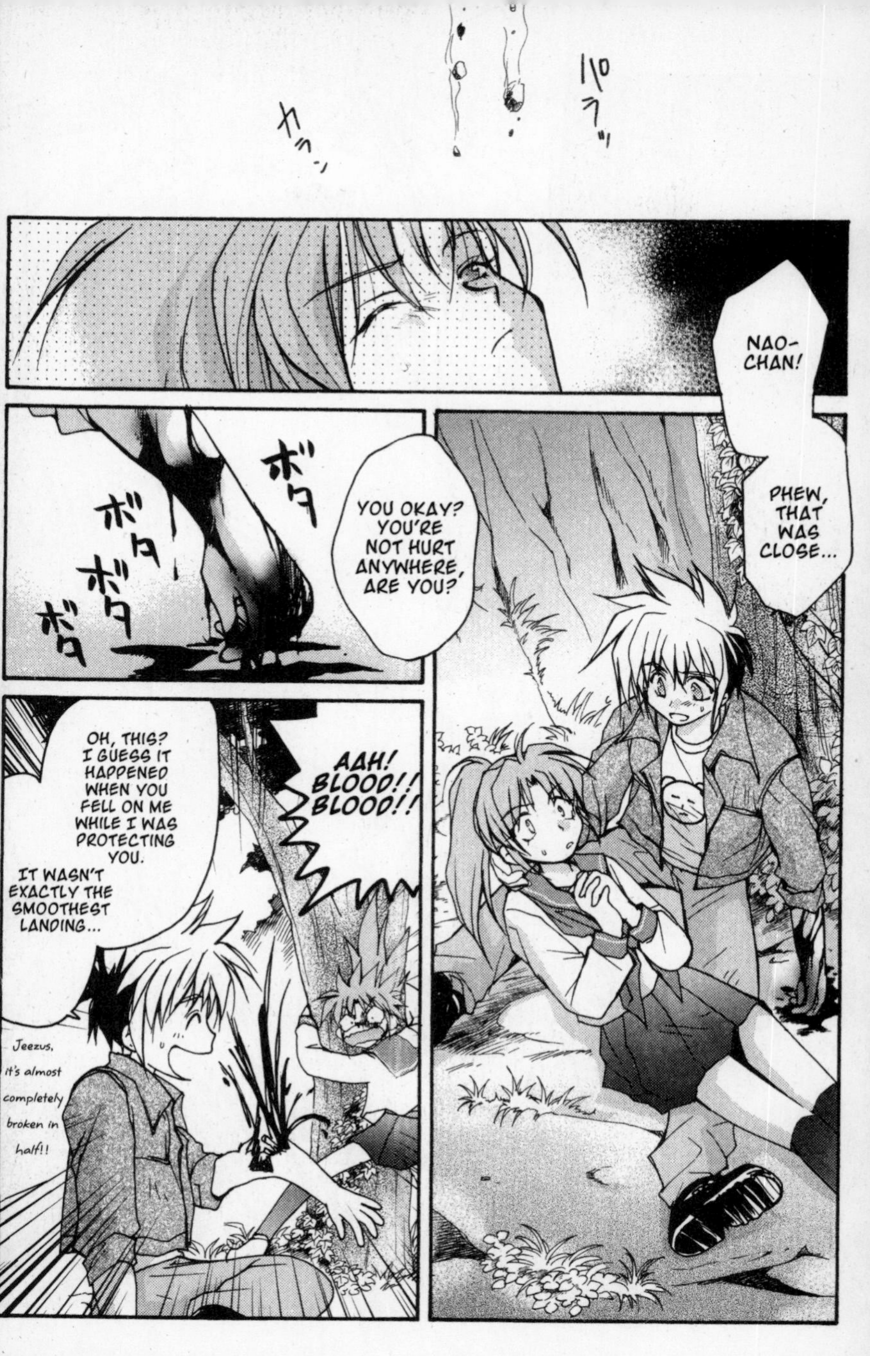
パラッ
NAO-CHAN!
PHEW, THAT WAS CLOSE...
YOU OKAY? YOU'RE NOT HURT ANYWHERE, ARE YOU?
ボタ
ボタ
ボタ
ボタ
AAH! BLOOD!! BLOOD!!
OH, THIS? I GUESS IT HAPPENED WHEN YOU FELL ON ME WHILE I WAS PROTECTING YOU.
IT WASN'T EXACTLY THE SMOOTHEST LANDING...
Jeezus, it's almost completely broken in half!!

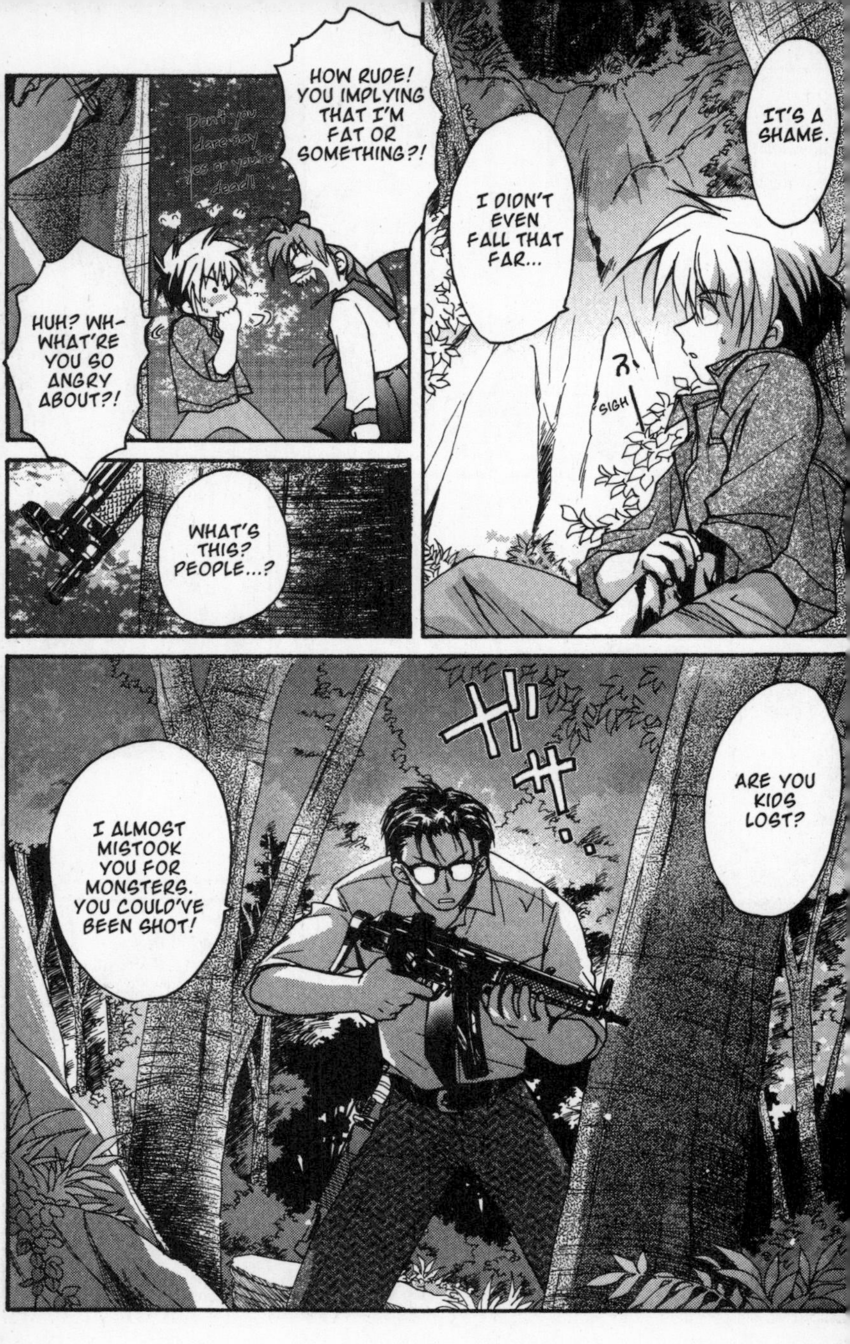
IT'S A SHAME.
I DIDN'T EVEN FALL THAT FAR...
ふ
SIGH
HOW RUDE! YOU IMPLYING THAT I'M FAT OR SOMETHING?!
Don't you dare say yes or you're dead!
HUH? WH-WHAT'RE YOU SO ANGRY ABOUT?!
WHAT'S THIS? PEOPLE...?
ARE YOU KIDS LOST?
I ALMOST MISTOOK YOU FOR MONSTERS. YOU COULD'VE BEEN SHOT!

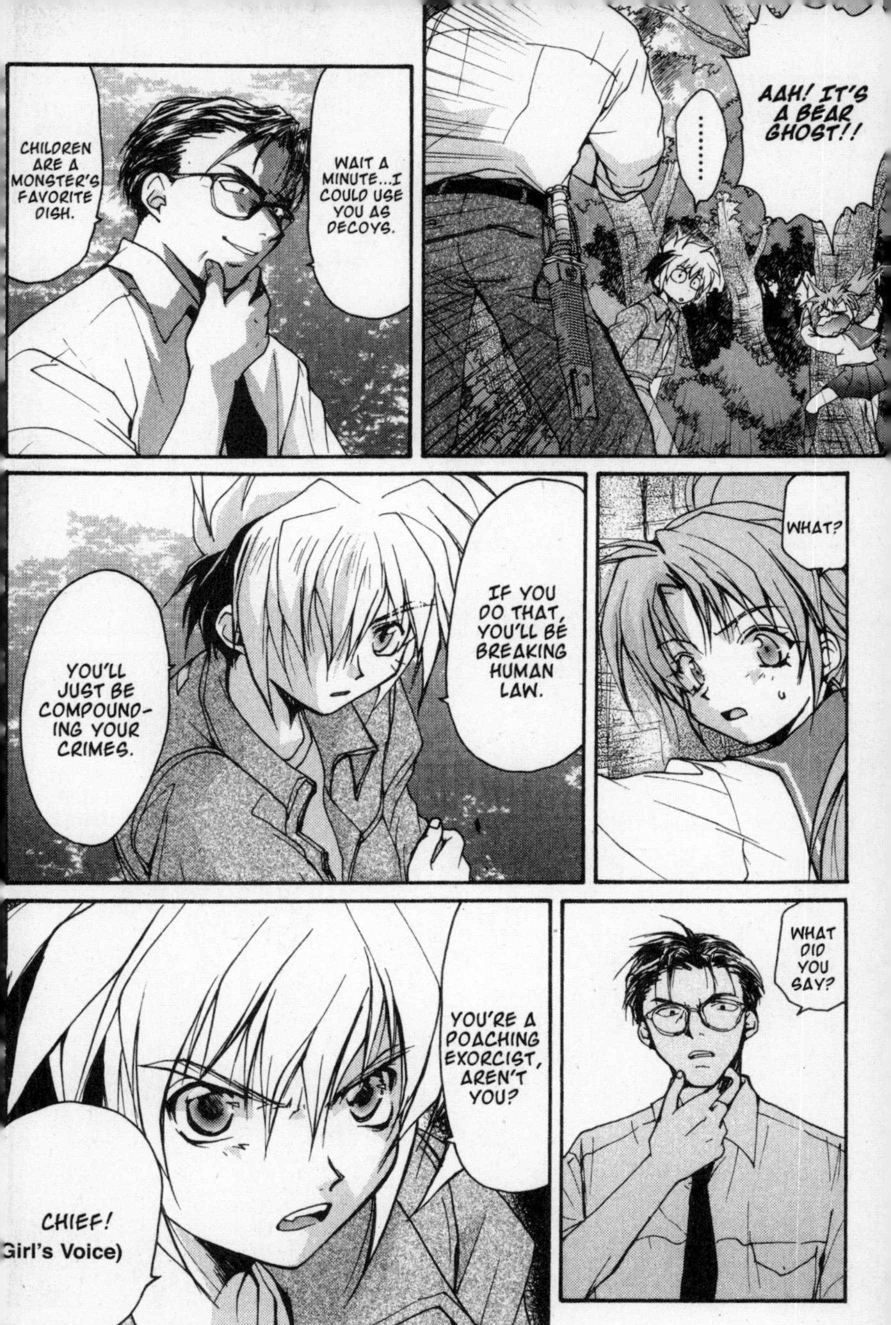
AAH! IT'S A BEAR GHOST!!
......
WAIT A MINUTE...I COULD USE YOU AS DECOYS.
CHILDREN ARE A MONSTER'S FAVORITE DISH.
WHAT?
IF YOU DO THAT, YOU'LL BE BREAKING HUMAN LAW.
YOU'LL JUST BE COMPOUNDING YOUR CRIMES.
WHAT DID YOU SAY?
YOU'RE A POACHING EXORCIST, AREN'T YOU?
CHIEF!
(Girl's Voice)

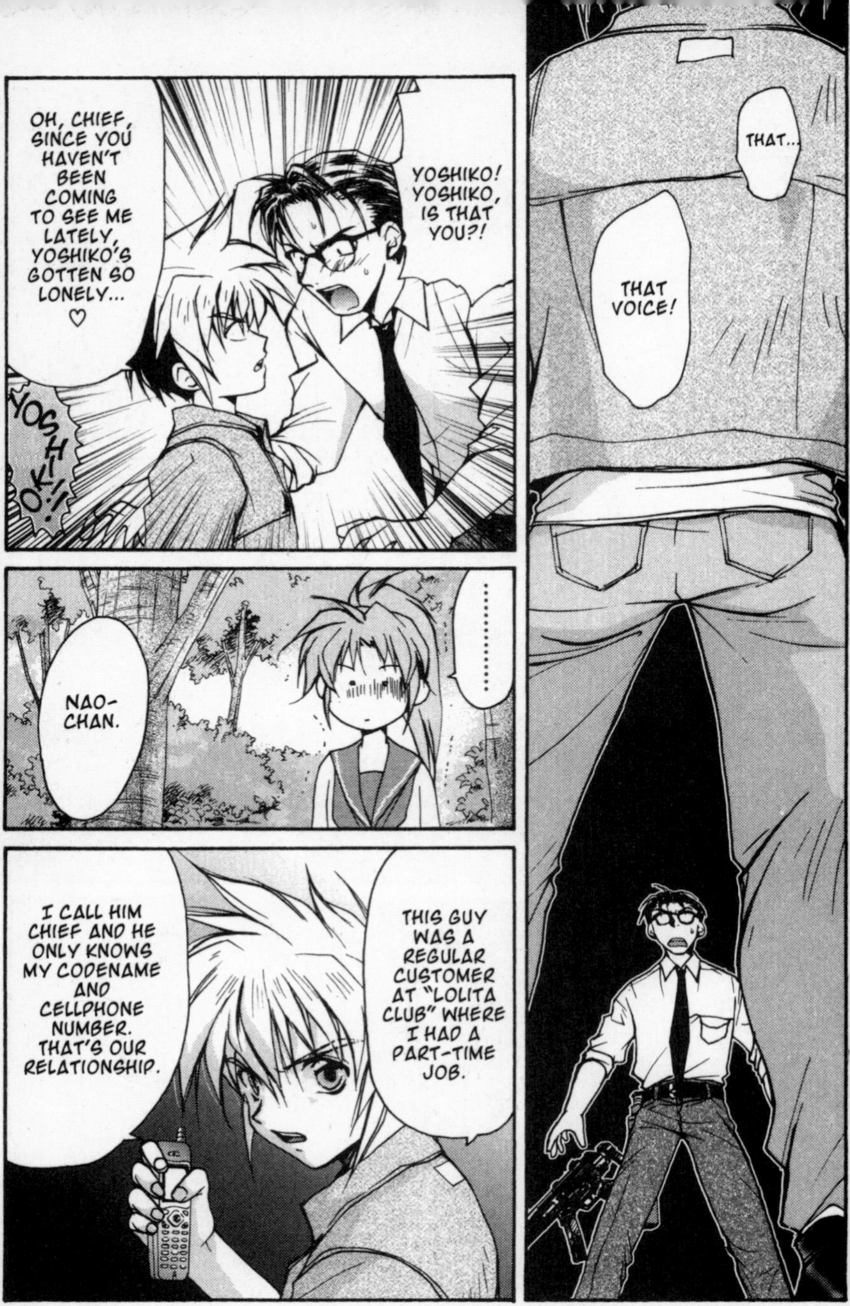
THAT...
THAT VOICE!
YOSHIKO! YOSHIKO, IS THAT YOU?!
OH, CHIEF, SINCE YOU HAVEN'T BEEN COMING TO SEE ME LATELY, YOSHIKO'S GOTTEN SO LONELY... ♡
YOSHIKO!!
......
NAO-CHAN.
THIS GUY WAS A REGULAR CUSTOMER AT "LOLITA CLUB" WHERE I HAD A PART-TIME JOB.
I CALL HIM CHIEF AND HE ONLY KNOWS MY CODENAME AND CELLPHONE NUMBER. THAT'S OUR RELATIONSHIP.

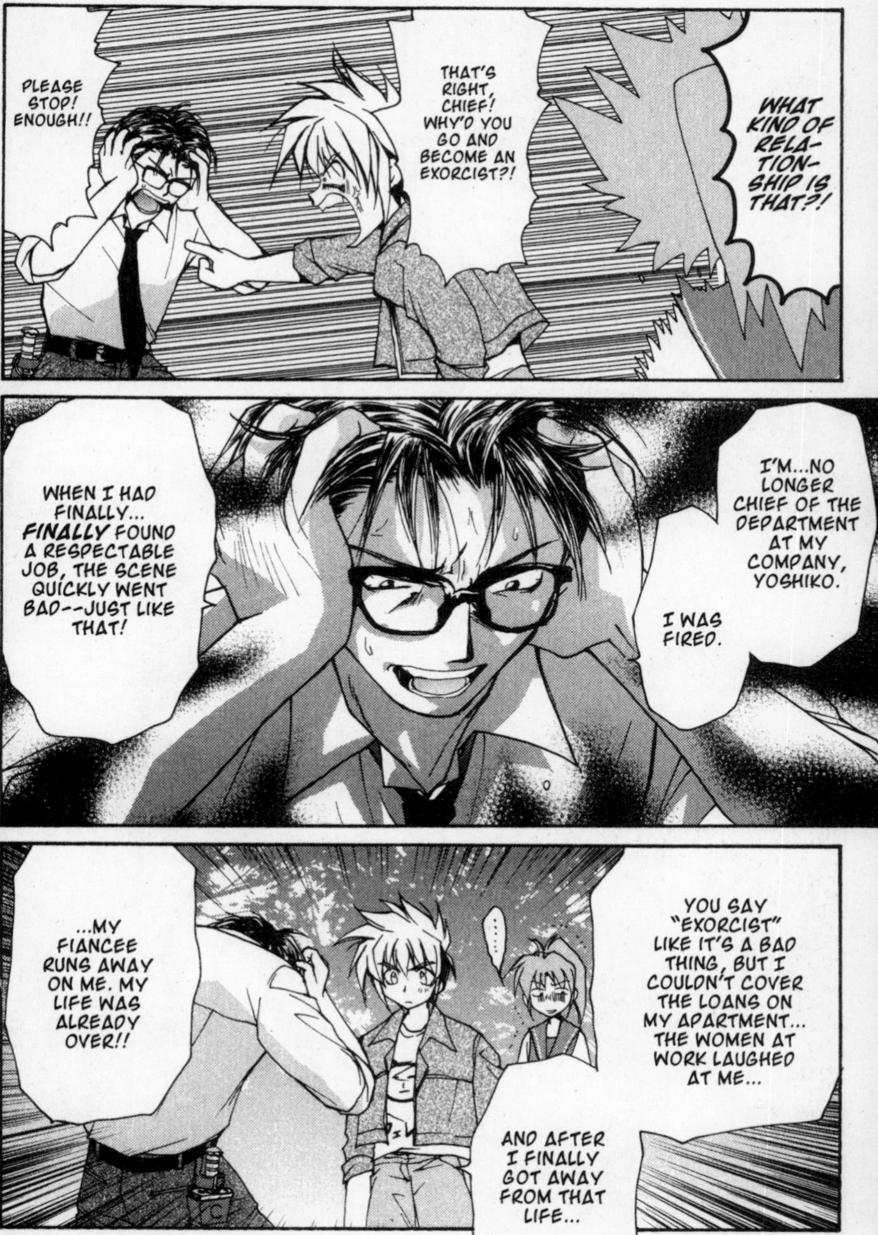
WHAT KIND OF RELATIONSHIP IS THAT?!
THAT'S RIGHT, CHIEF! WHY'D YOU GO AND BECOME AN EXORCIST?!
PLEASE STOP! ENOUGH!!
I'M...NO LONGER CHIEF OF THE DEPARTMENT AT MY COMPANY, YOSHIKO.
I WAS FIRED.
WHEN I HAD FINALLY... FINALLY FOUND A RESPECTABLE JOB, THE SCENE QUICKLY WENT BAD--JUST LIKE THAT!
YOU SAY "EXORCIST" LIKE IT'S A BAD THING, BUT I COULDN'T COVER THE LOANS ON MY APARTMENT... THE WOMEN AT WORK LAUGHED AT ME...
......
AND AFTER I FINALLY GOT AWAY FROM THAT LIFE...
...MY FIANCEE RUNS AWAY ON ME. MY LIFE WAS ALREADY OVER!!

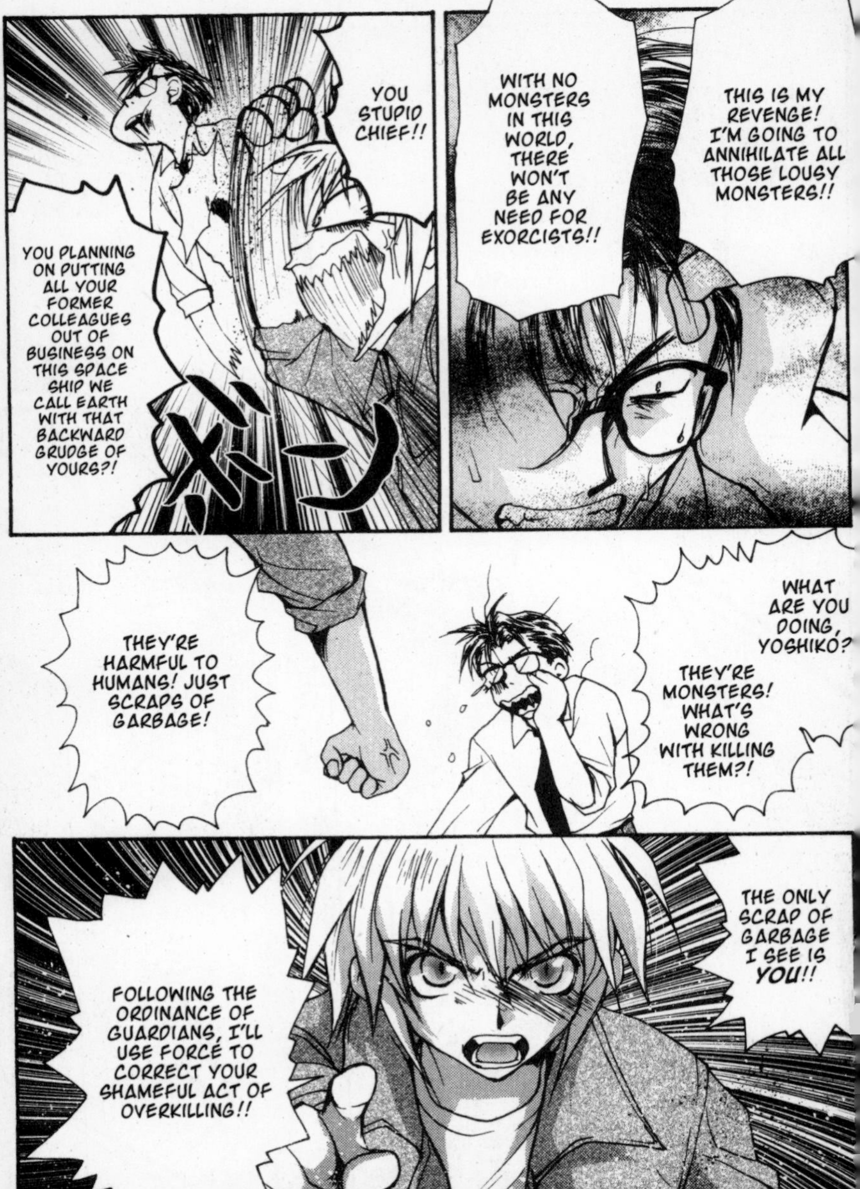
THIS IS MY REVENGE! I'M GOING TO ANNIHILATE ALL THOSE LOUSY MONSTERS!!
WITH NO MONSTERS IN THIS WORLD, THERE WON'T BE ANY NEED FOR EXORCISTS!!
YOU STUPID CHIEF!!
YOU PLANNING ON PUTTING ALL YOUR FORMER COLLEAGUES OUT OF BUSINESS ON THIS SPACE SHIP WE CALL EARTH WITH THAT BACKWARD GRUDGE OF YOURS?!
WHAT ARE YOU DOING, YOSHIKO?
THEY'RE MONSTERS! WHAT'S WRONG WITH KILLING THEM?!
THEY'RE HARMFUL TO HUMANS! JUST SCRAPS OF GARBAGE!
THE ONLY SCRAP OF GARBAGE I SEE IS ***YOU***!!
FOLLOWING THE ORDINANCE OF GUARDIANS, I'LL USE FORCE TO CORRECT YOUR SHAMEFUL ACT OF OVERKILLING!!

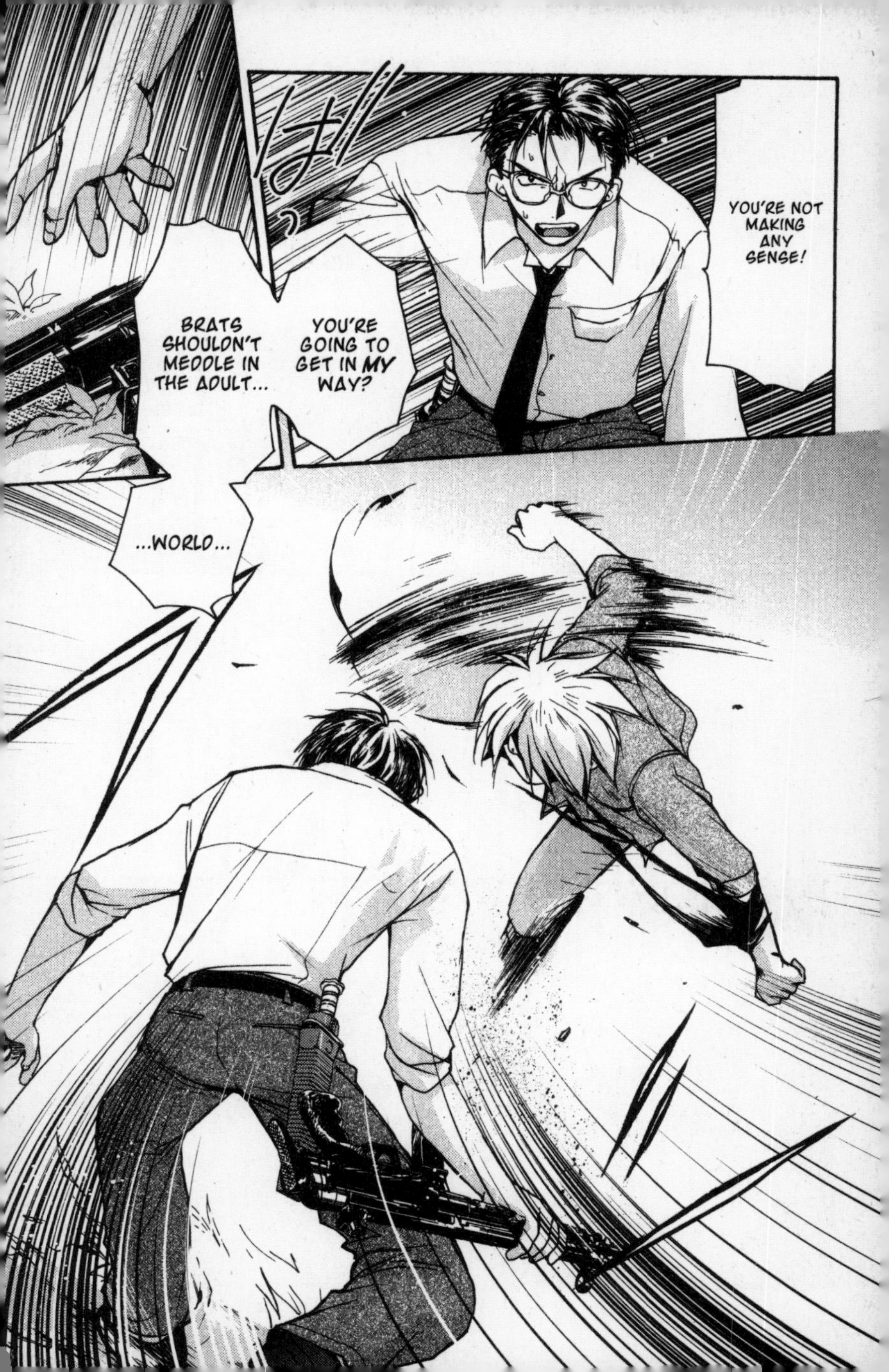
YOU'RE NOT MAKING ANY SENSE!
はっ
YOU'RE GOING TO GET IN MY WAY?
BRATS SHOULDN'T MEDDLE IN THE ADULT...
...WORLD...

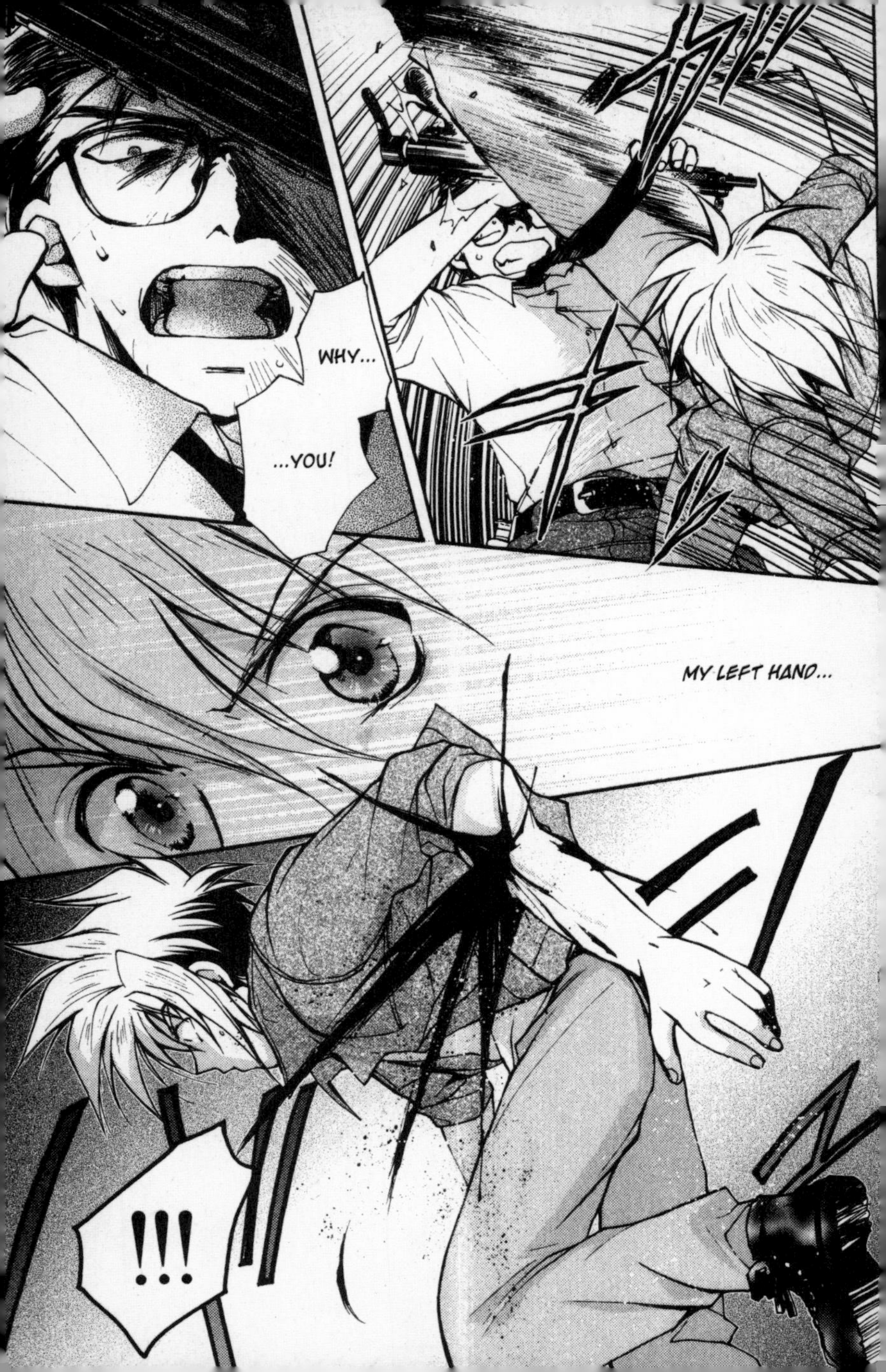
WHY...
...YOU!
MY LEFT HAND...
!!!

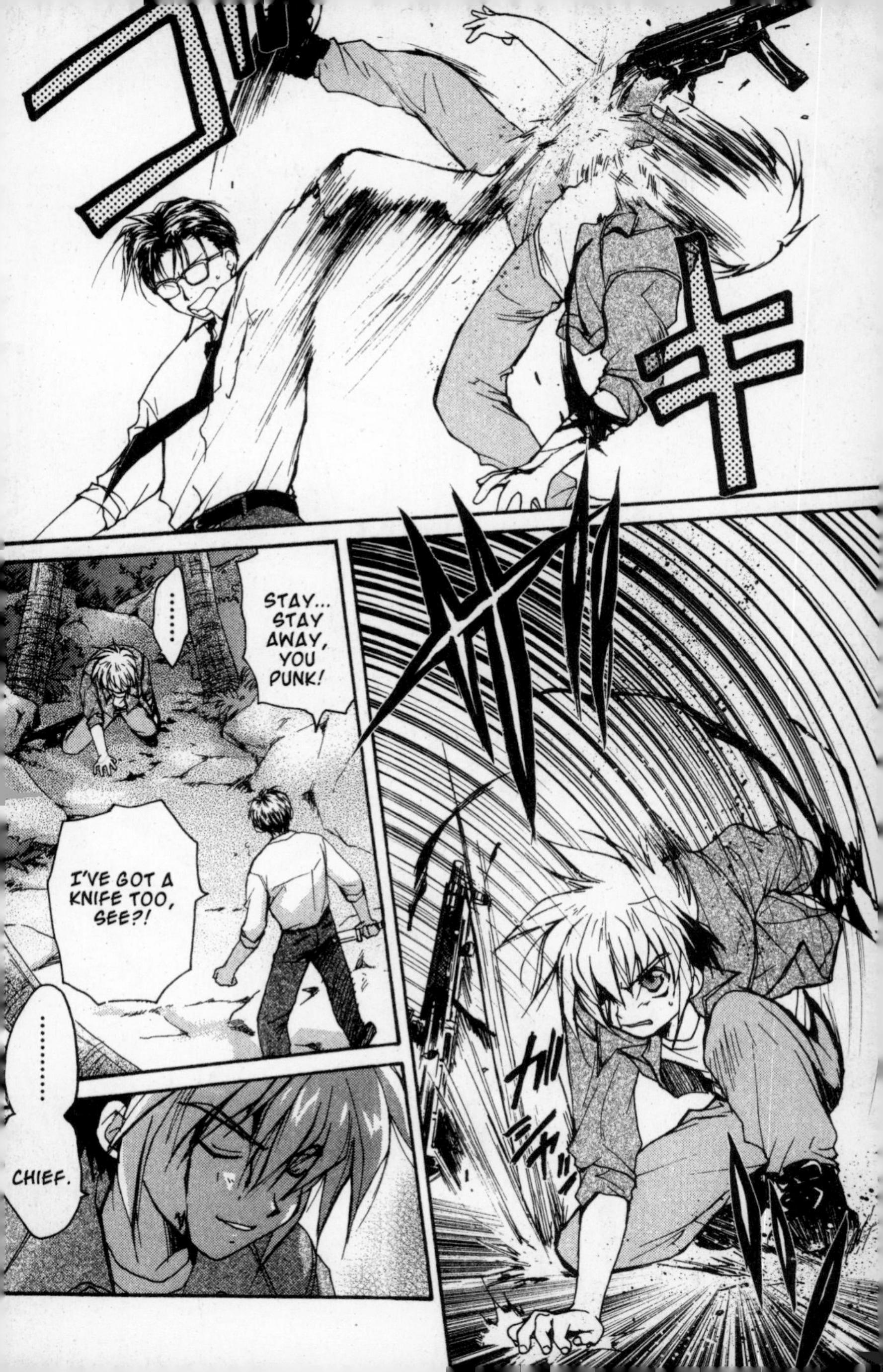
STAY... STAY AWAY, YOU PUNK!
......
I'VE GOT A KNIFE TOO, SEE?!
......
CHIEF.

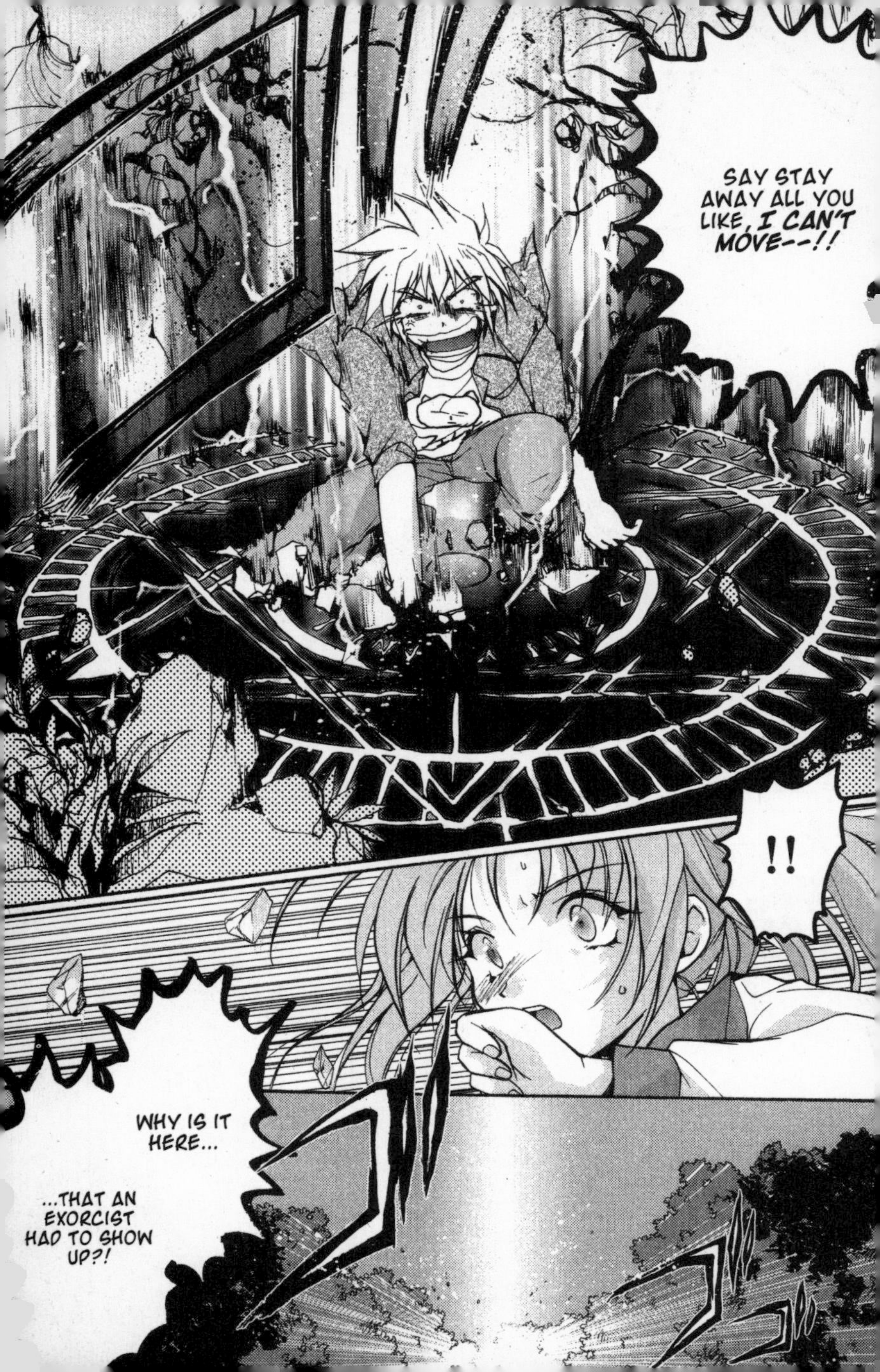
SAY STAY AWAY ALL YOU LIKE, I CAN'T MOVE--!!
!!
WHY IS IT HERE...
...THAT AN EXORCIST HAD TO SHOW UP?!

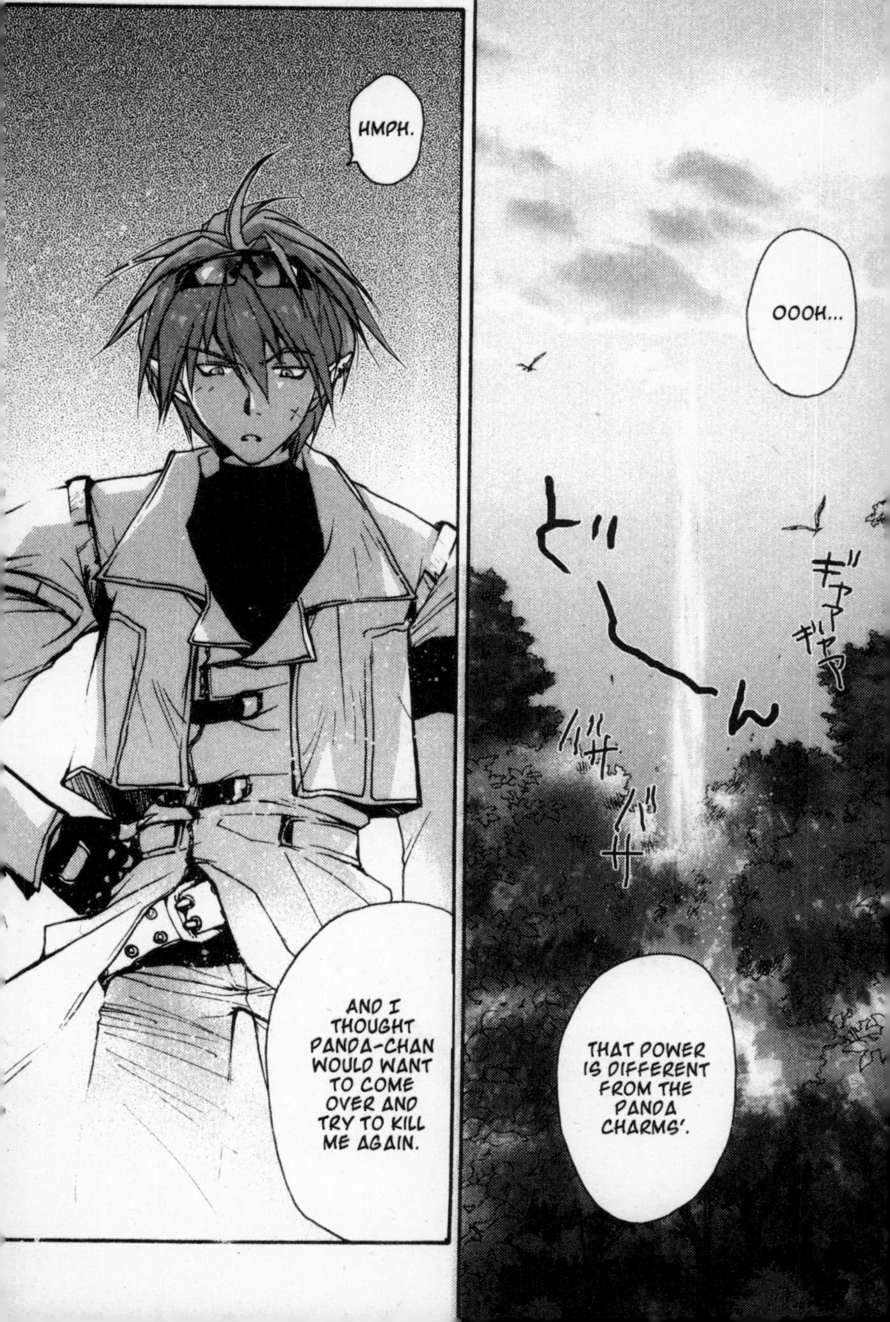
OOOH...
どしーん
ギャアギャア
バサバサ
THAT POWER IS DIFFERENT FROM THE PANDA CHARMS'.
HMPH.
AND I THOUGHT PANDA-CHAN WOULD WANT TO COME OVER AND TRY TO KILL ME AGAIN.

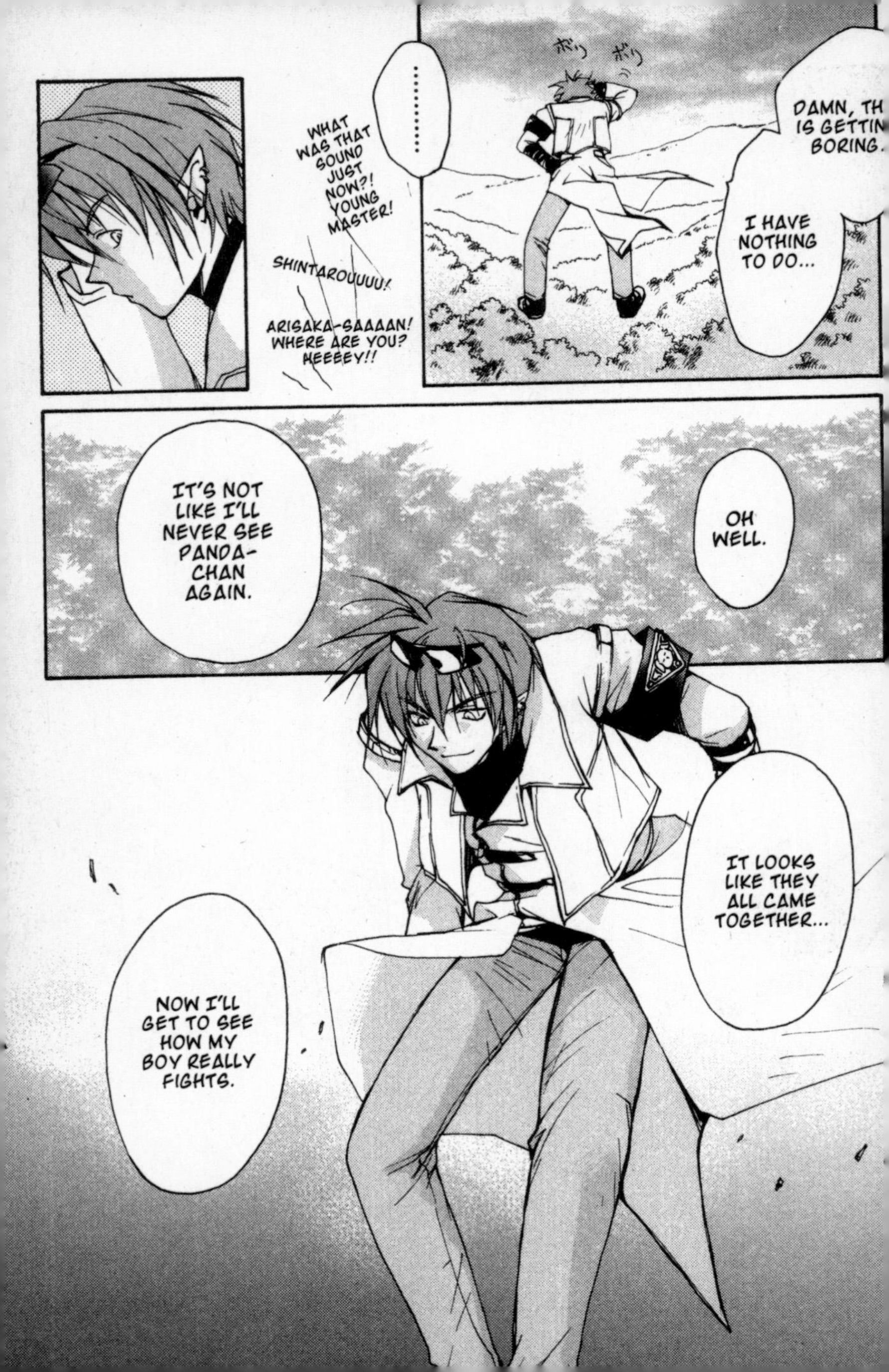
DAMN, TH IS GETTIN BORING.
I HAVE NOTHING TO DO...
......
WHAT WAS THAT SOUND JUST NOW?! YOUNG MASTER!
SHINTAROUUUU!
ARISAKA-SAAAAN! WHERE ARE YOU? HEEEEY!!
OH WELL.
IT'S NOT LIKE I'LL NEVER SEE PANDA-CHAN AGAIN.
IT LOOKS LIKE THEY ALL CAME TOGETHER...
NOW I'LL GET TO SEE HOW MY BOY REALLY FIGHTS.

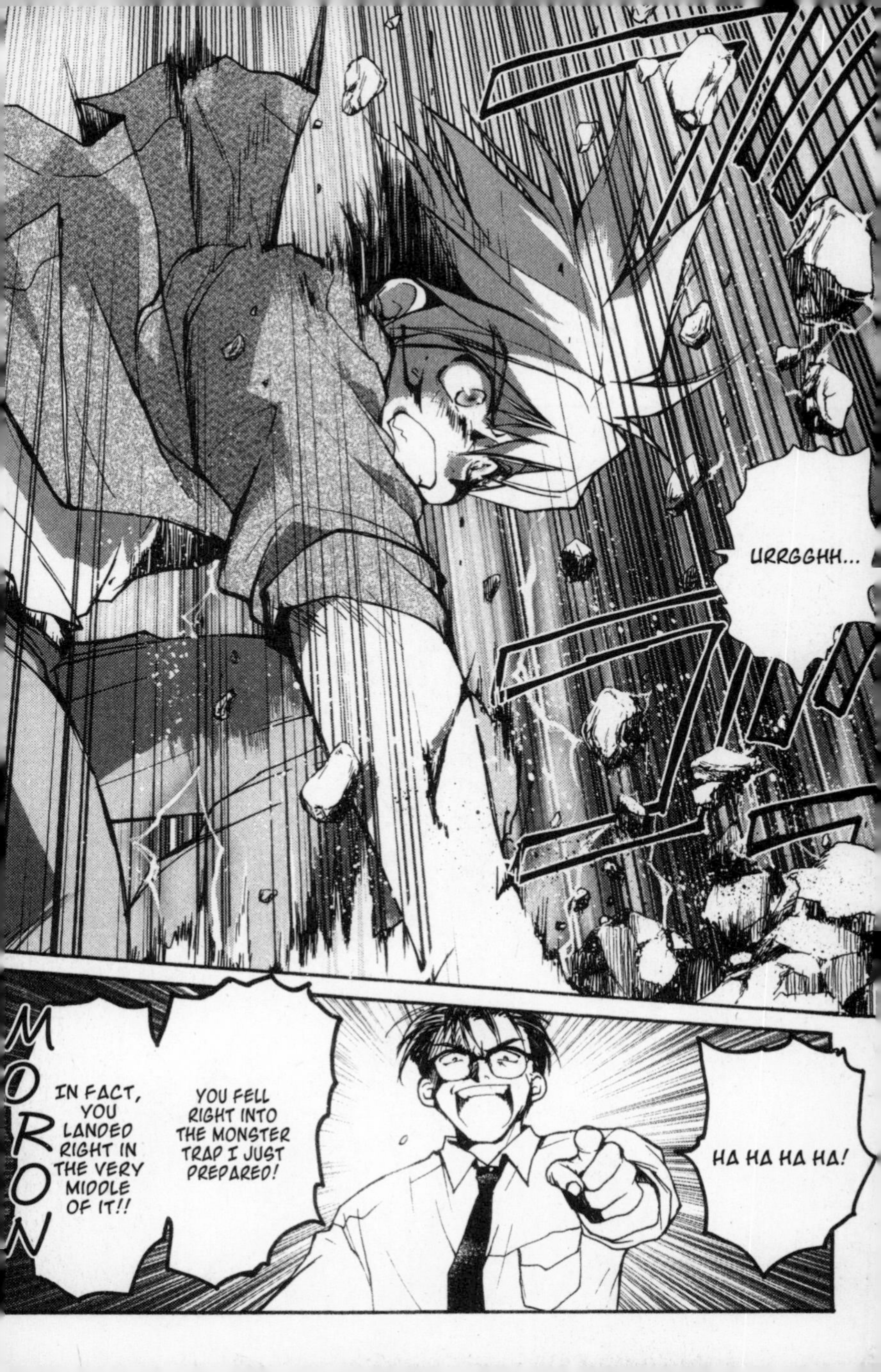
URRGGHH...
HA HA HA HA!
YOU FELL RIGHT INTO THE MONSTER TRAP I JUST PREPARED!
IN FACT, YOU LANDED RIGHT IN THE VERY MIDDLE OF IT!!
MORON

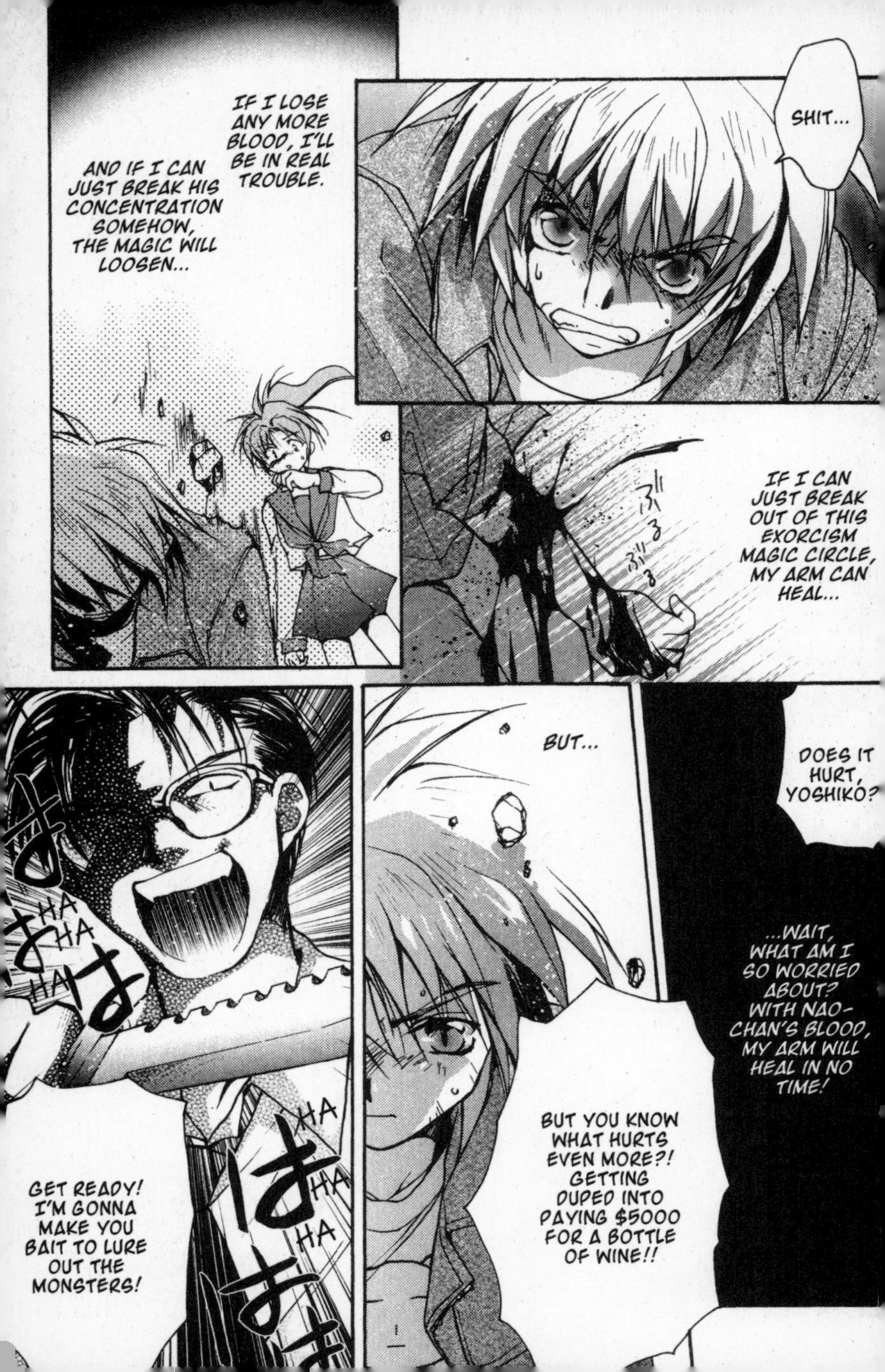
SHIT...
IF I CAN JUST BREAK OUT OF THIS EXORCISM MAGIC CIRCLE, MY ARM CAN HEAL...
IF I LOSE ANY MORE BLOOD, I'LL BE IN REAL TROUBLE.
AND IF I CAN JUST BREAK HIS CONCENTRATION SOMEHOW, THE MAGIC WILL LOOSEN...
DOES IT HURT, YOSHIKO?
BUT...
...WAIT, WHAT AM I SO WORRIED ABOUT? WITH NAO-CHAN'S BLOOD, MY ARM WILL HEAL IN NO TIME!
BUT YOU KNOW WHAT HURTS EVEN MORE?! GETTING DUPED INTO PAYING $5000 FOR A BOTTLE OF WINE!!
HA HA HA
HA HA HA
GET READY! I'M GONNA MAKE YOU BAIT TO LURE OUT THE MONSTERS!

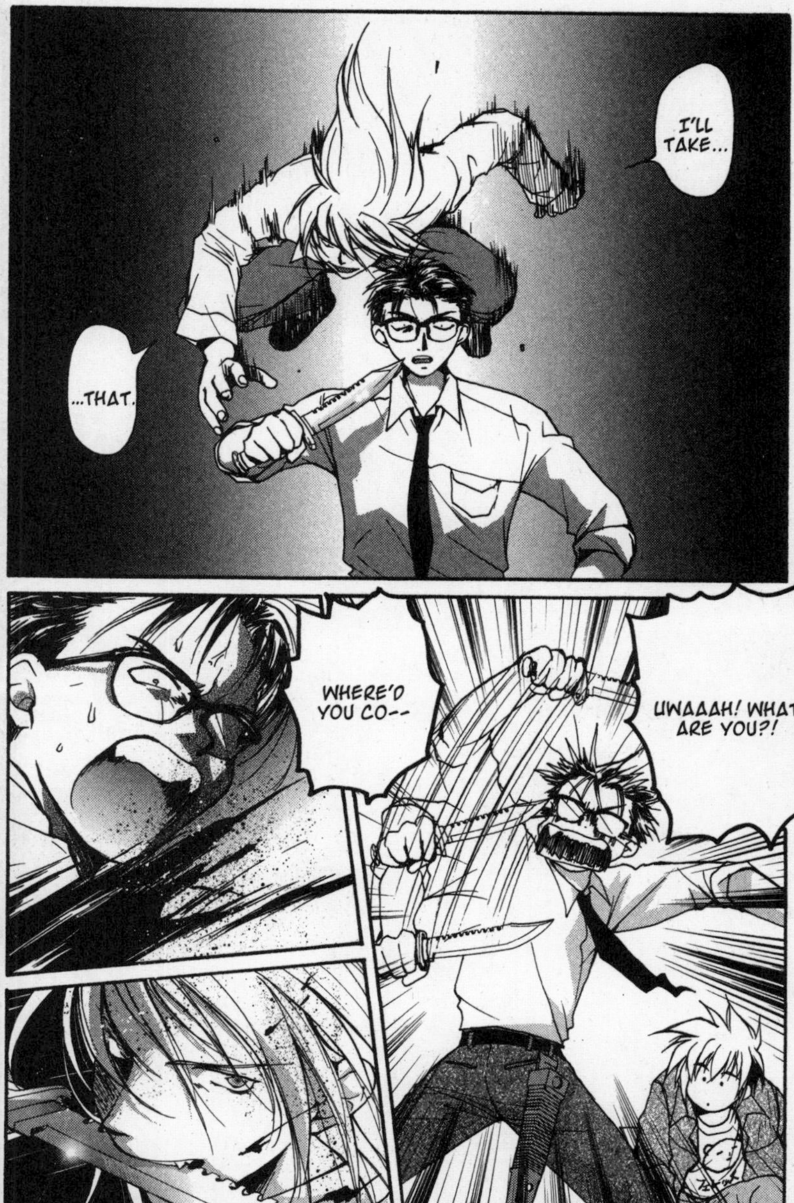
I'LL TAKE...
...THAT.
UWAAAH! WHAT ARE YOU?!
WHERE'D YOU CO--

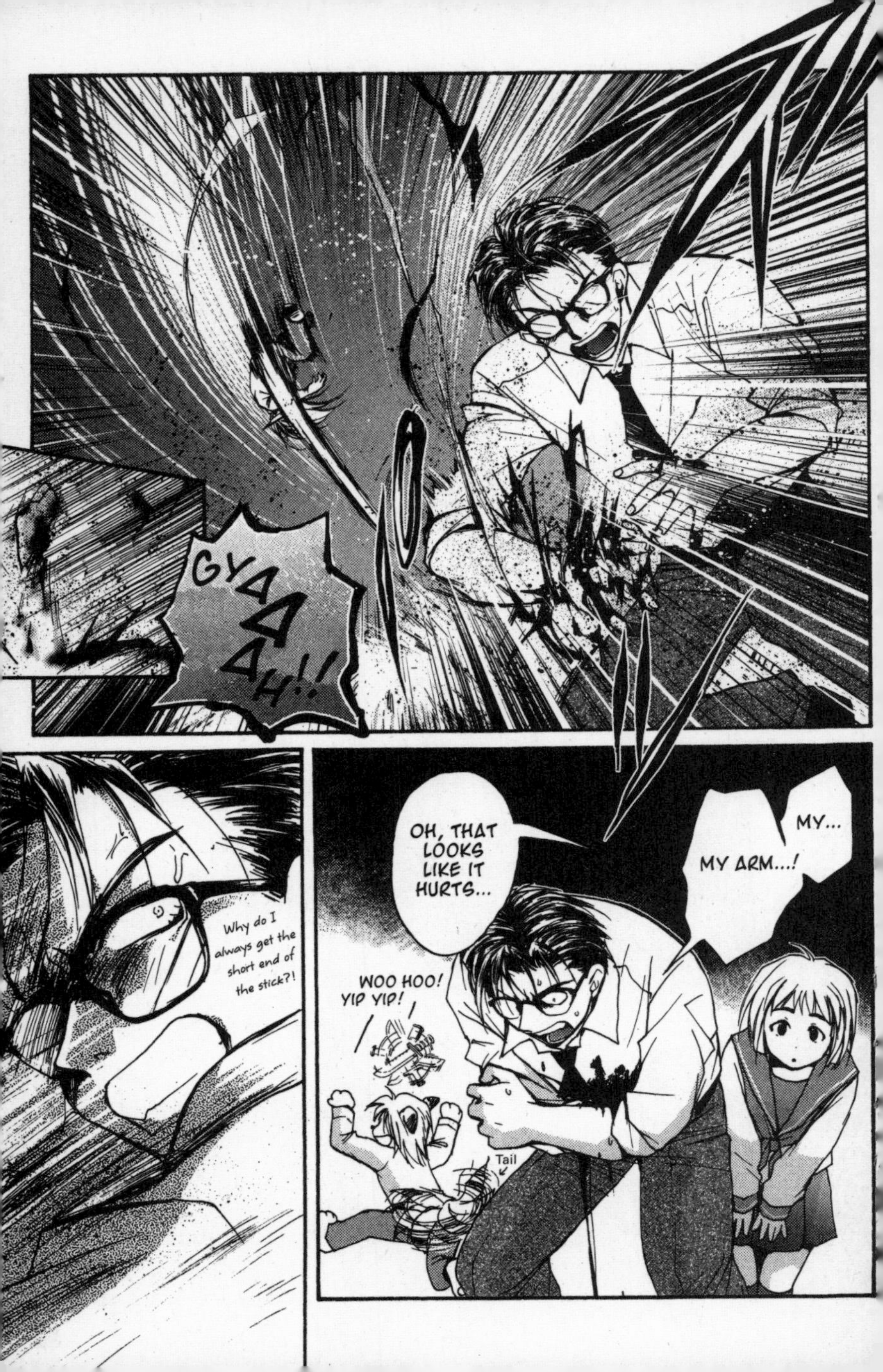
GYAAAAH!!
MY...
MY ARM...!
OH, THAT LOOKS LIKE IT HURTS...
WOO HOO! YIP YIP!
Tail
Why do I always get the short end of the stick?!

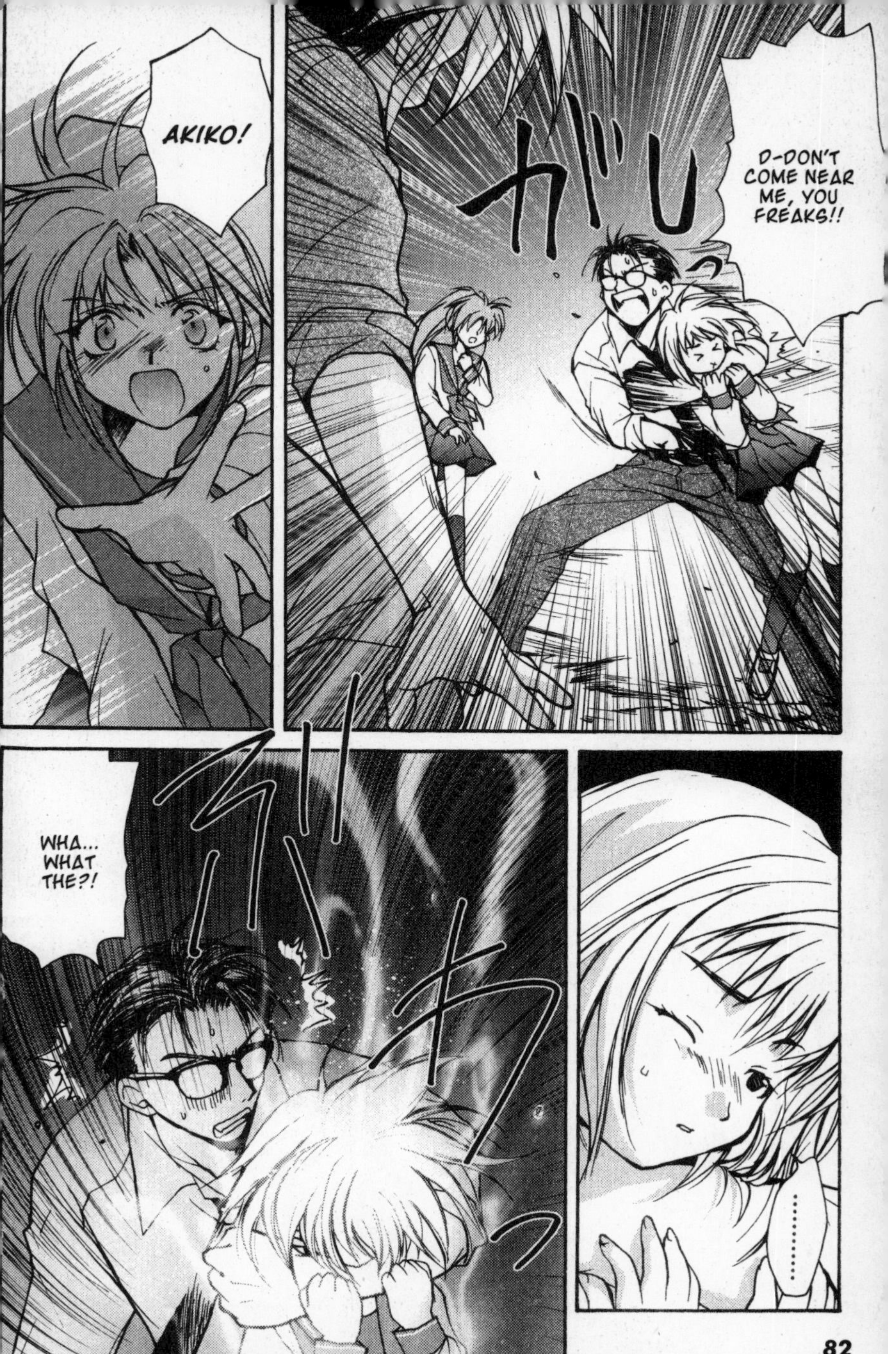
D-DON'T COME NEAR ME, YOU FREAKS!!
AKIKO!
......
WHA... WHAT THE?!

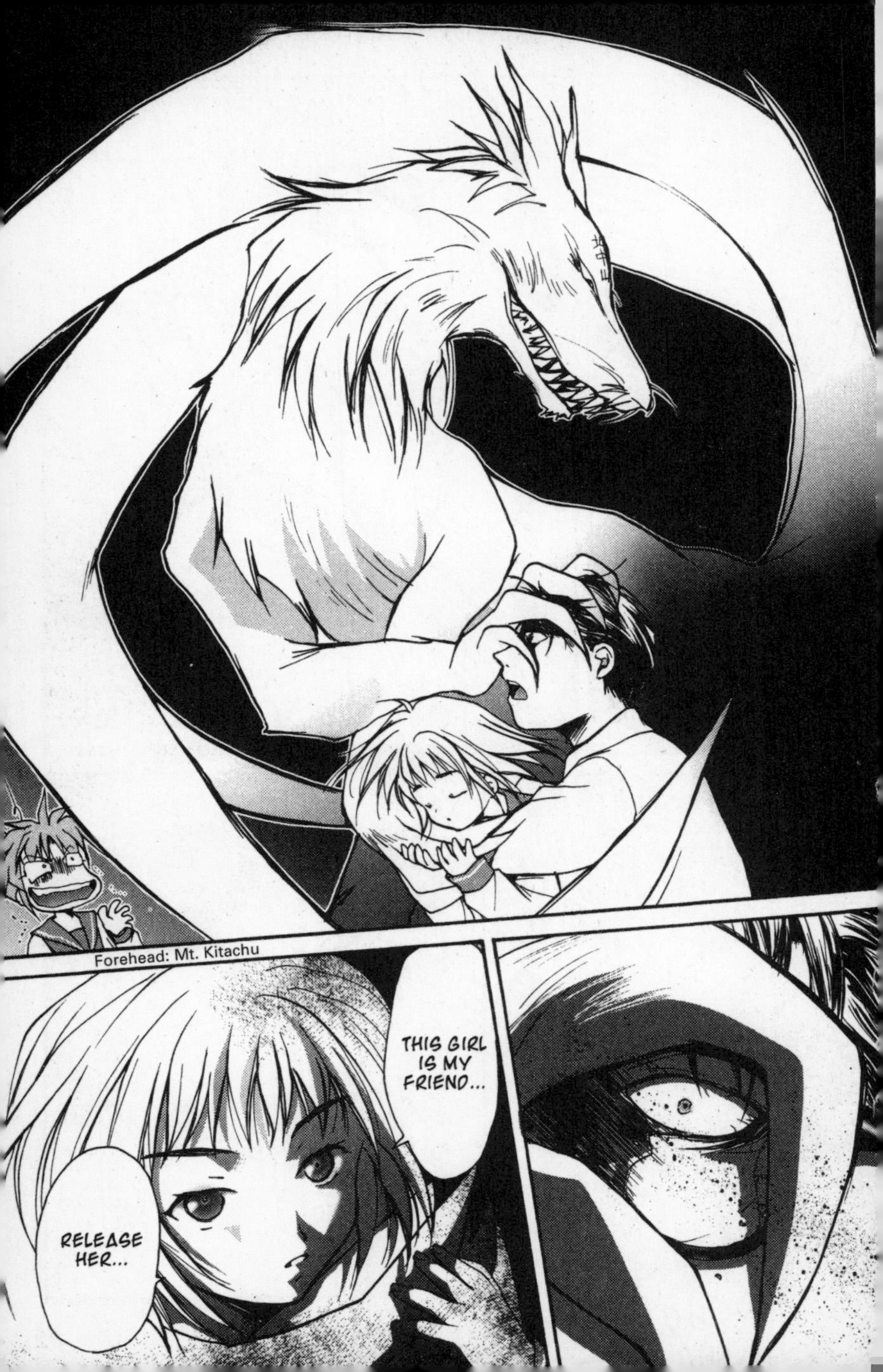
Forehead: Mt. Kitachu
THIS GIRL IS MY FRIEND...
RELEASE HER...

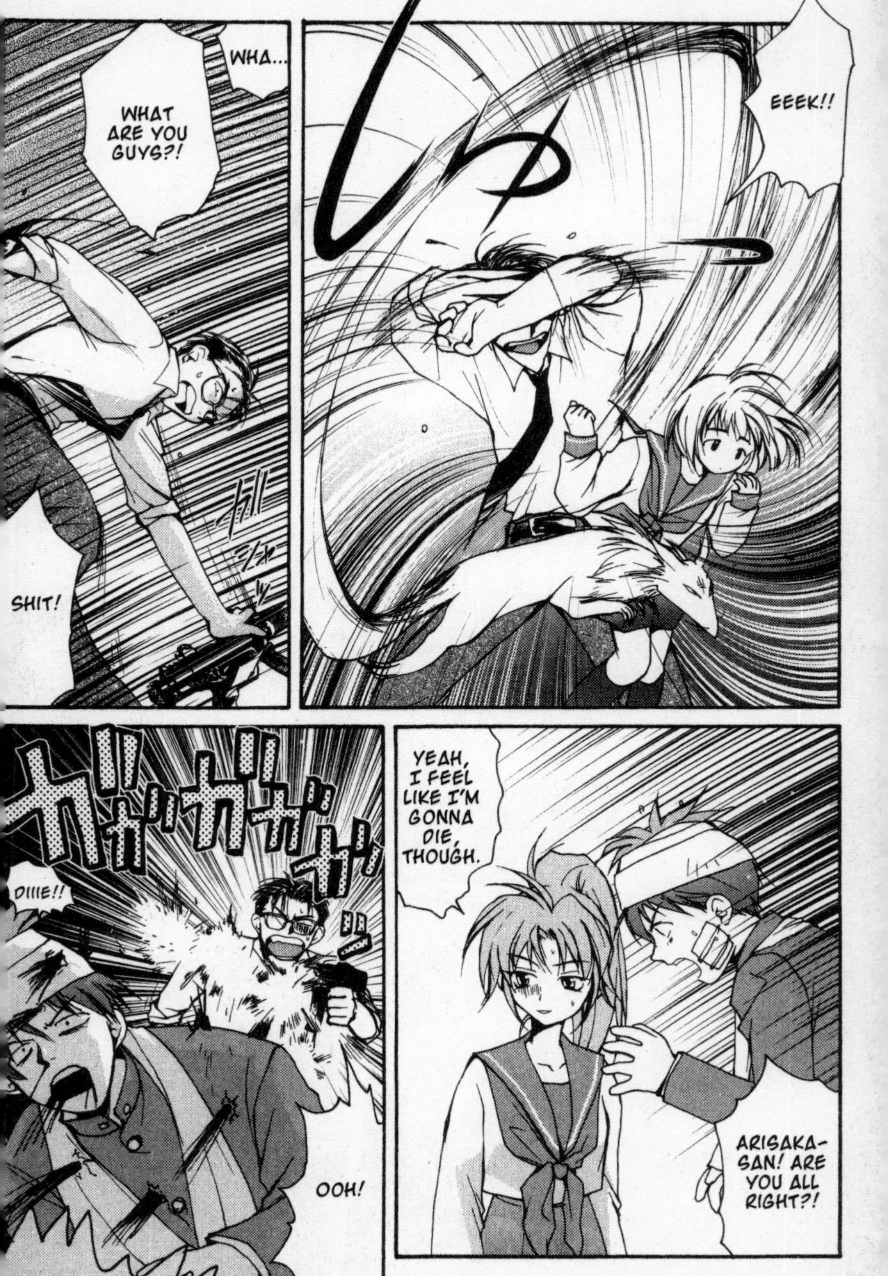
EEEK!!
WHA...
WHAT ARE YOU GUYS?!
SHIT!
ARISAKA-SAN! ARE YOU ALL RIGHT?!
YEAH, I FEEL LIKE I'M GONNA DIE, THOUGH.
DIIIE!!
OOH!

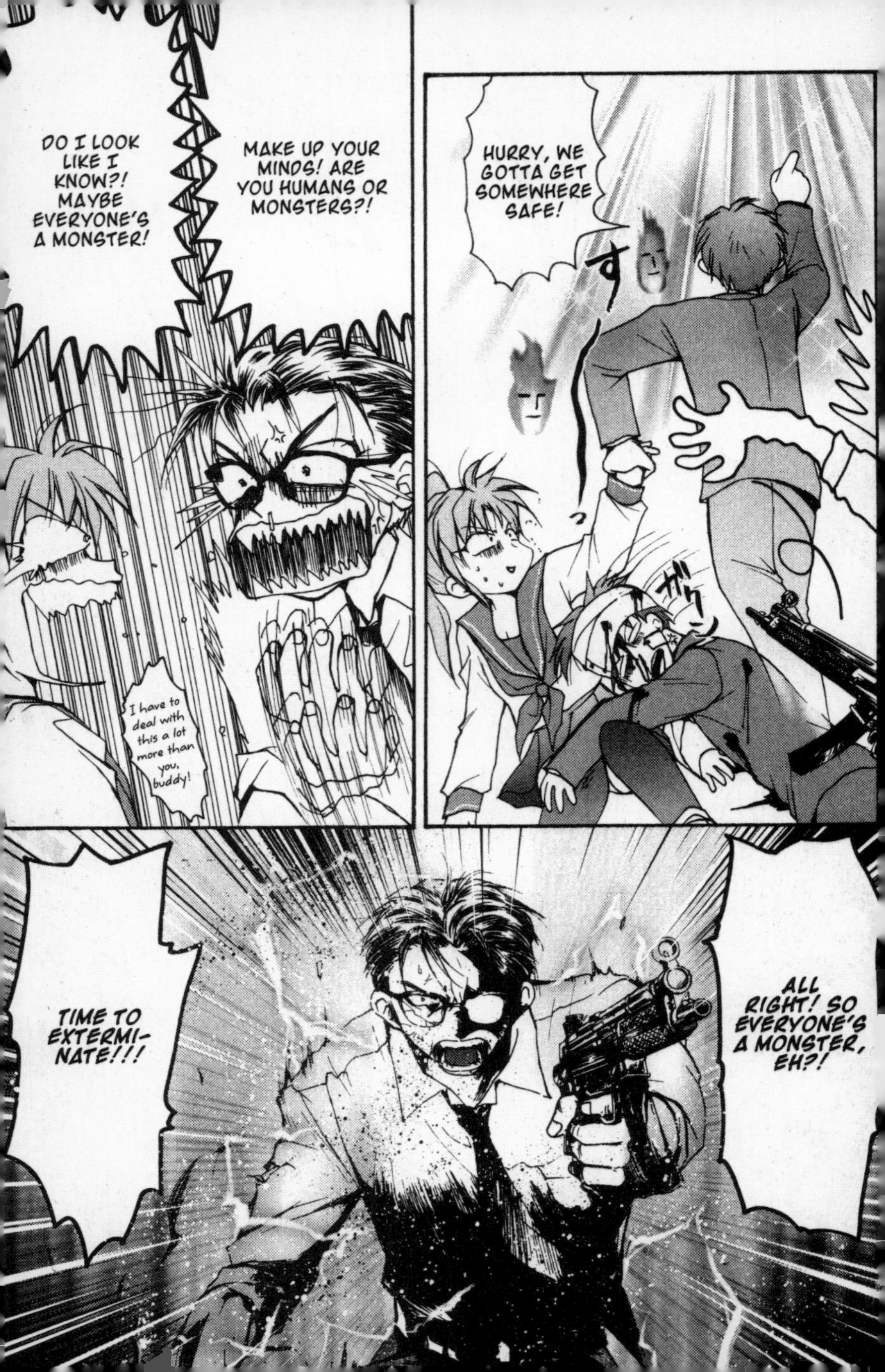
HURRY, WE GOTTA GET SOMEWHERE SAFE!
す
MAKE UP YOUR MINDS! ARE YOU HUMANS OR MONSTERS?!
DO I LOOK LIKE I KNOW?! MAYBE EVERYONE'S A MONSTER!
I have to deal with this a lot more than you, buddy!
ALL RIGHT! SO EVERYONE'S A MONSTER, EH?!
TIME TO EXTERMINATE!!!

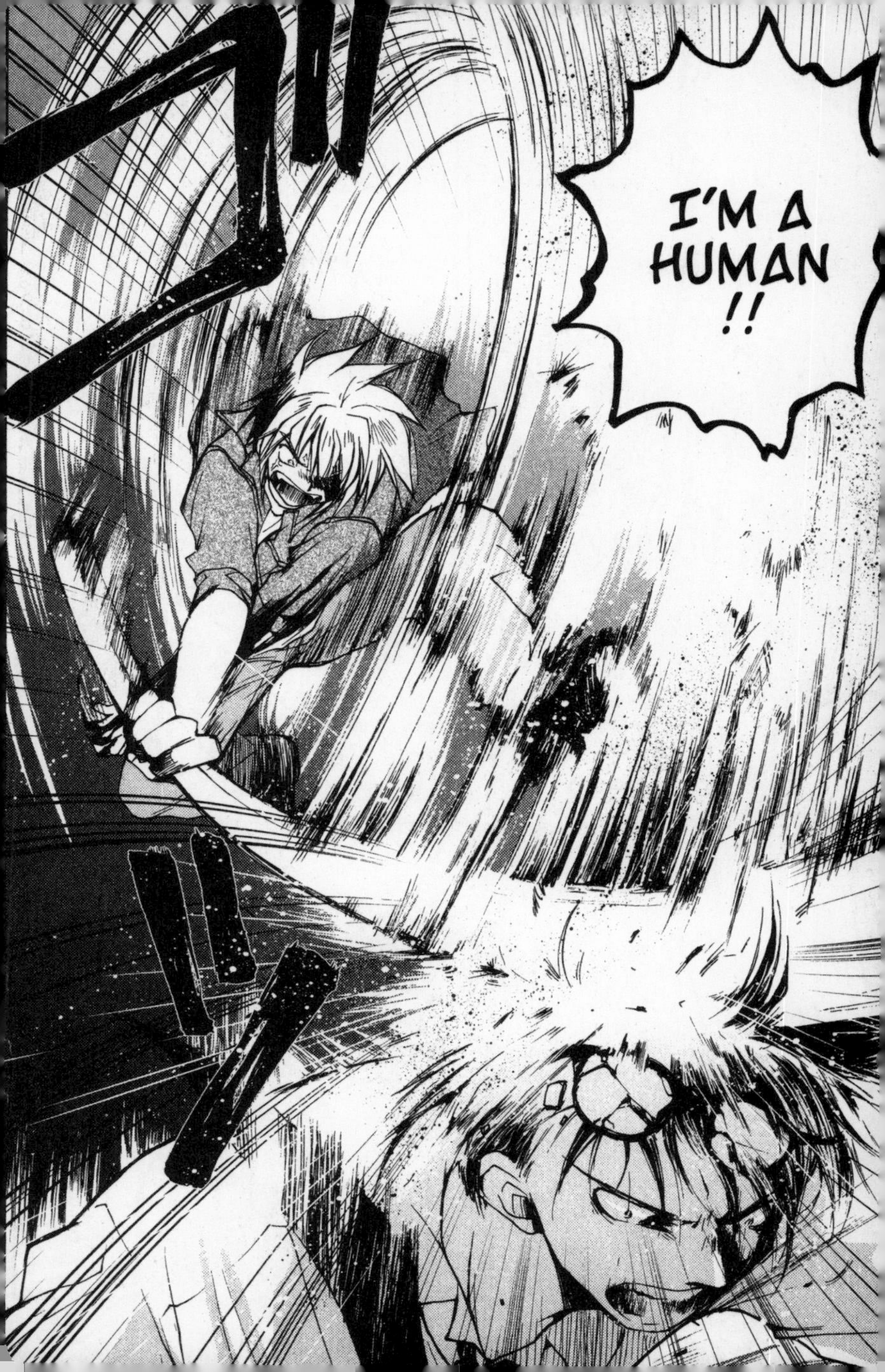
I'M A HUMAN !!

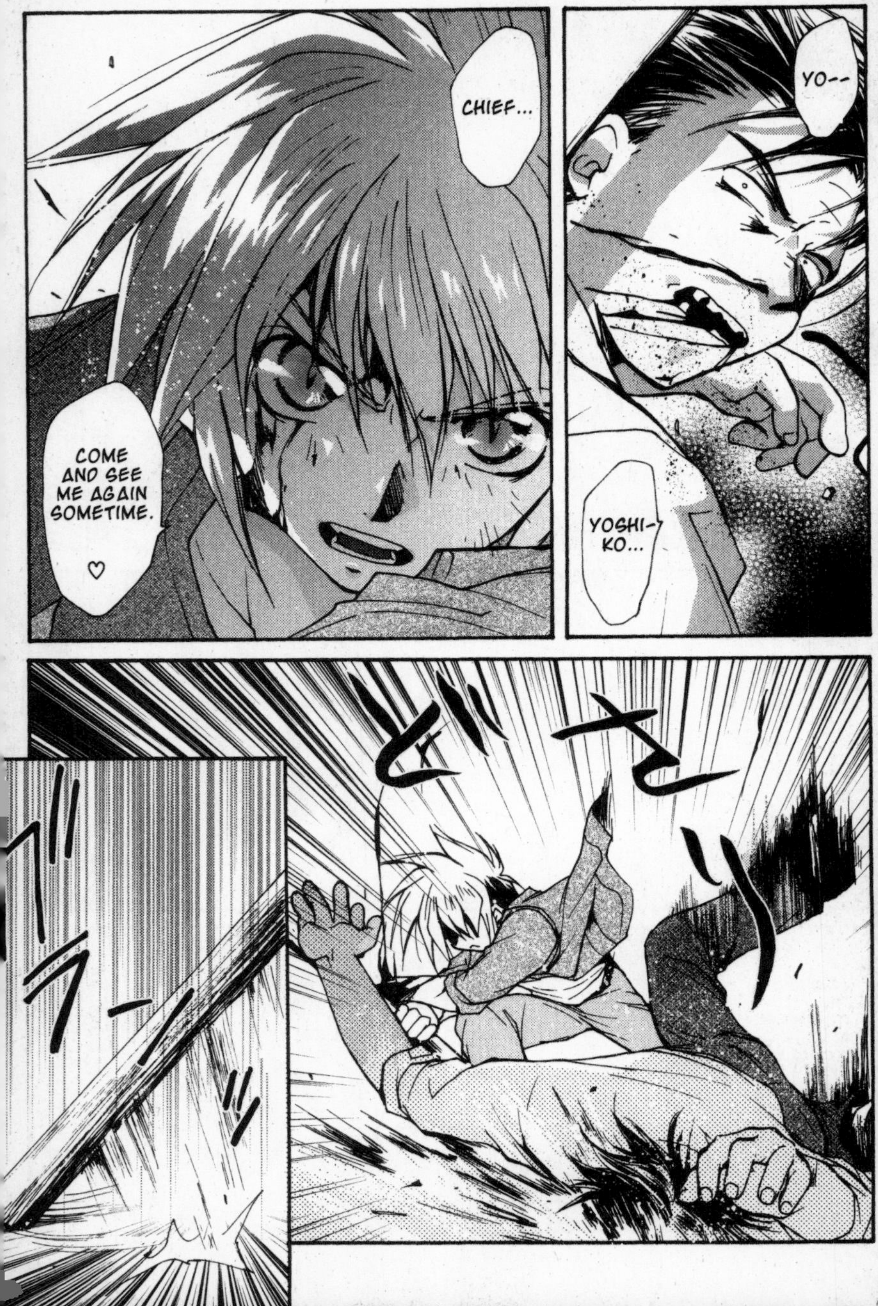
YO--
YOSHI-KO...
CHIEF...
COME AND SEE ME AGAIN SOMETIME. ♡

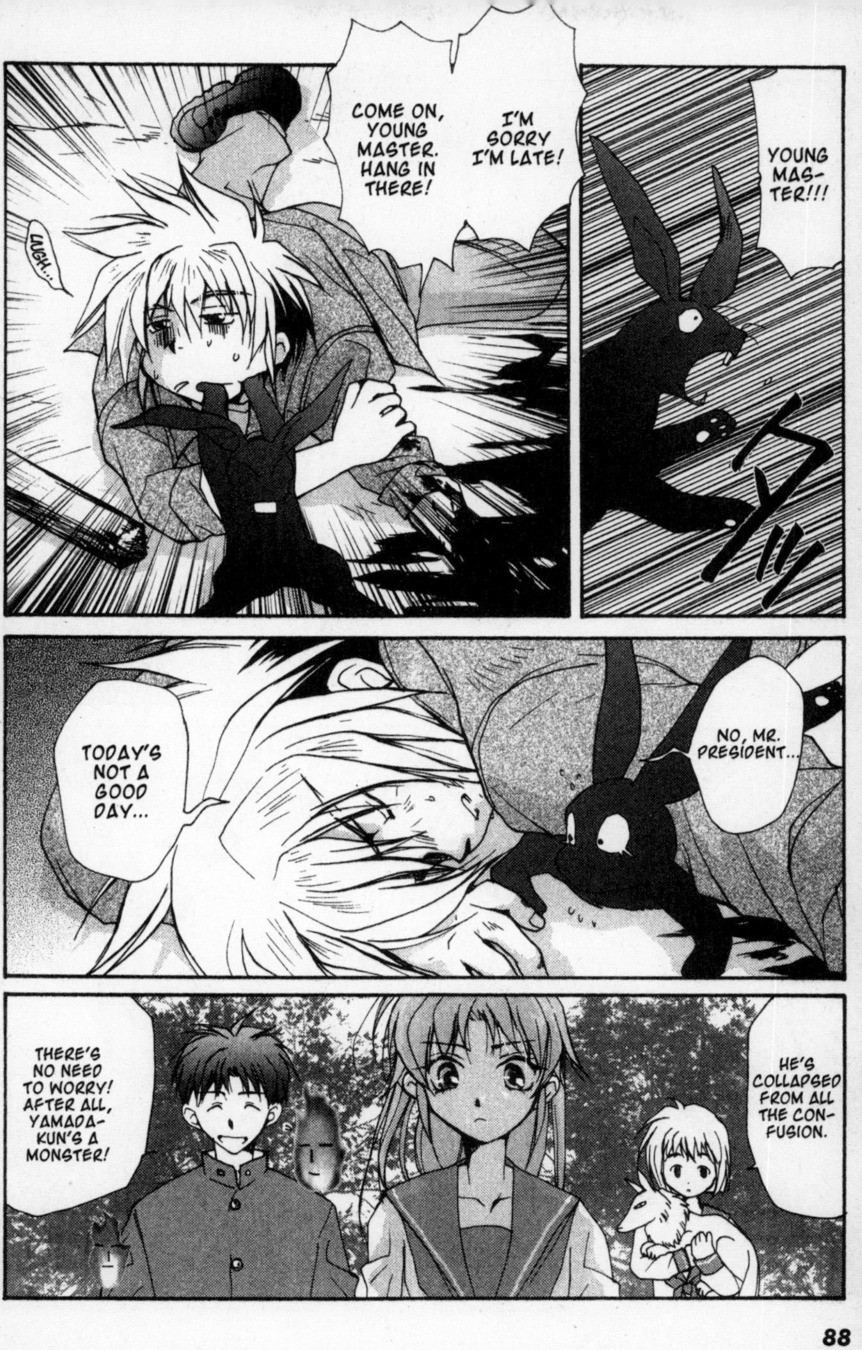
YOUNG MAS-TER!!!
タッ
I'M SORRY I'M LATE!
COME ON, YOUNG MASTER. HANG IN THERE!
UUGH...
NO, MR. PRESIDENT...
TODAY'S NOT A GOOD DAY...
HE'S COLLAPSED FROM ALL THE CON-FUSION.
THERE'S NO NEED TO WORRY! AFTER ALL, YAMADA-KUN'S A MONSTER!

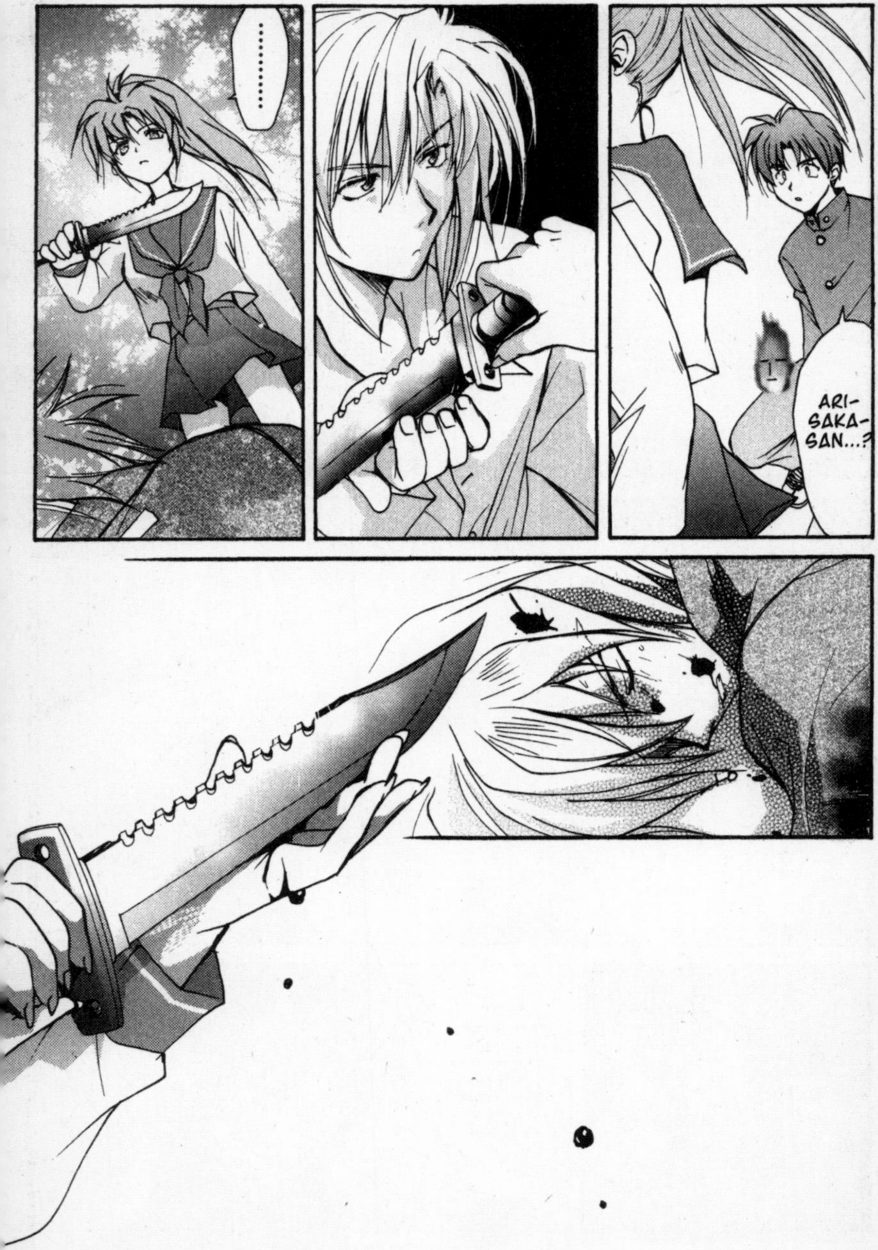
ARI-SAKA-SAN...?
....

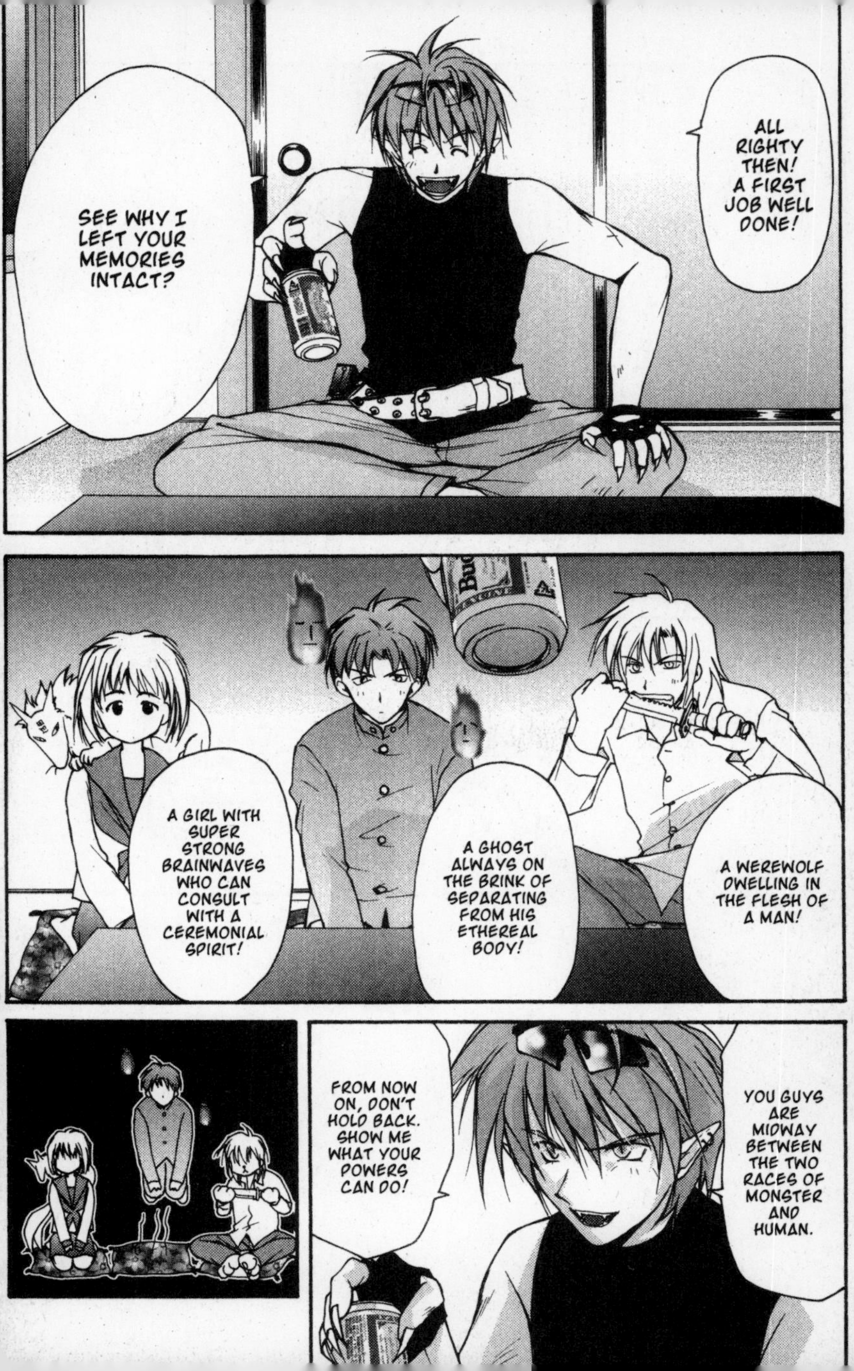
ALL RIGHTY THEN! A FIRST JOB WELL DONE!
SEE WHY I LEFT YOUR MEMORIES INTACT?
A WEREWOLF DWELLING IN THE FLESH OF A MAN!
A GHOST ALWAYS ON THE BRINK OF SEPARATING FROM HIS ETHEREAL BODY!
A GIRL WITH SUPER STRONG BRAINWAVES WHO CAN CONSULT WITH A CEREMONIAL SPIRIT!
YOU GUYS ARE MIDWAY BETWEEN THE TWO RACES OF MONSTER AND HUMAN.
FROM NOW ON, DON'T HOLD BACK. SHOW ME WHAT YOUR POWERS CAN DO!

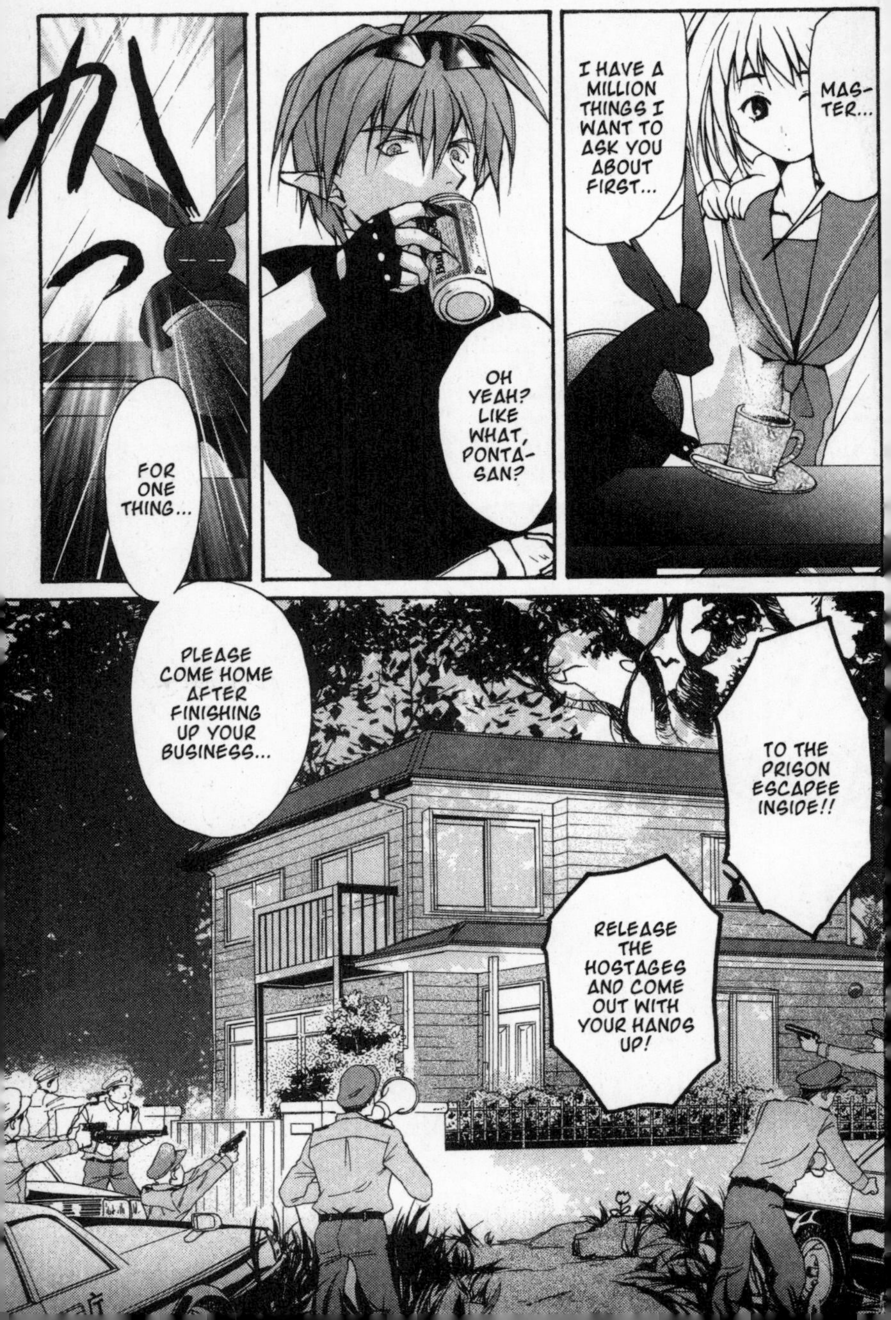
MASTER...
I HAVE A MILLION THINGS I WANT TO ASK YOU ABOUT FIRST...
OH YEAH? LIKE WHAT, PONTA-SAN?
カッ
FOR ONE THING...
PLEASE COME HOME AFTER FINISHING UP YOUR BUSINESS...
TO THE PRISON ESCAPEE INSIDE!!
RELEASE THE HOSTAGES AND COME OUT WITH YOUR HANDS UP!

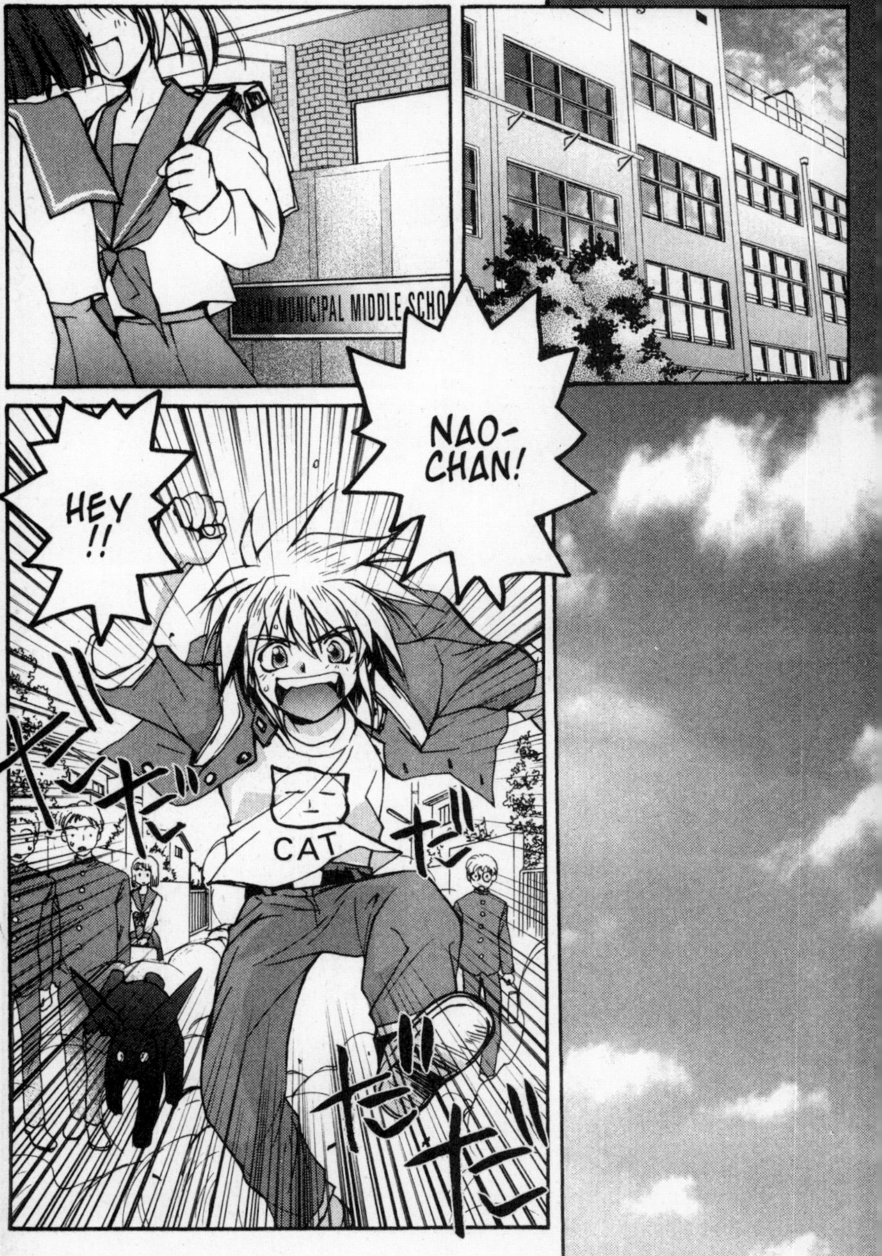
MUNICIPAL MIDDLE SCHO
NAO-CHAN!
HEY !!
CAT

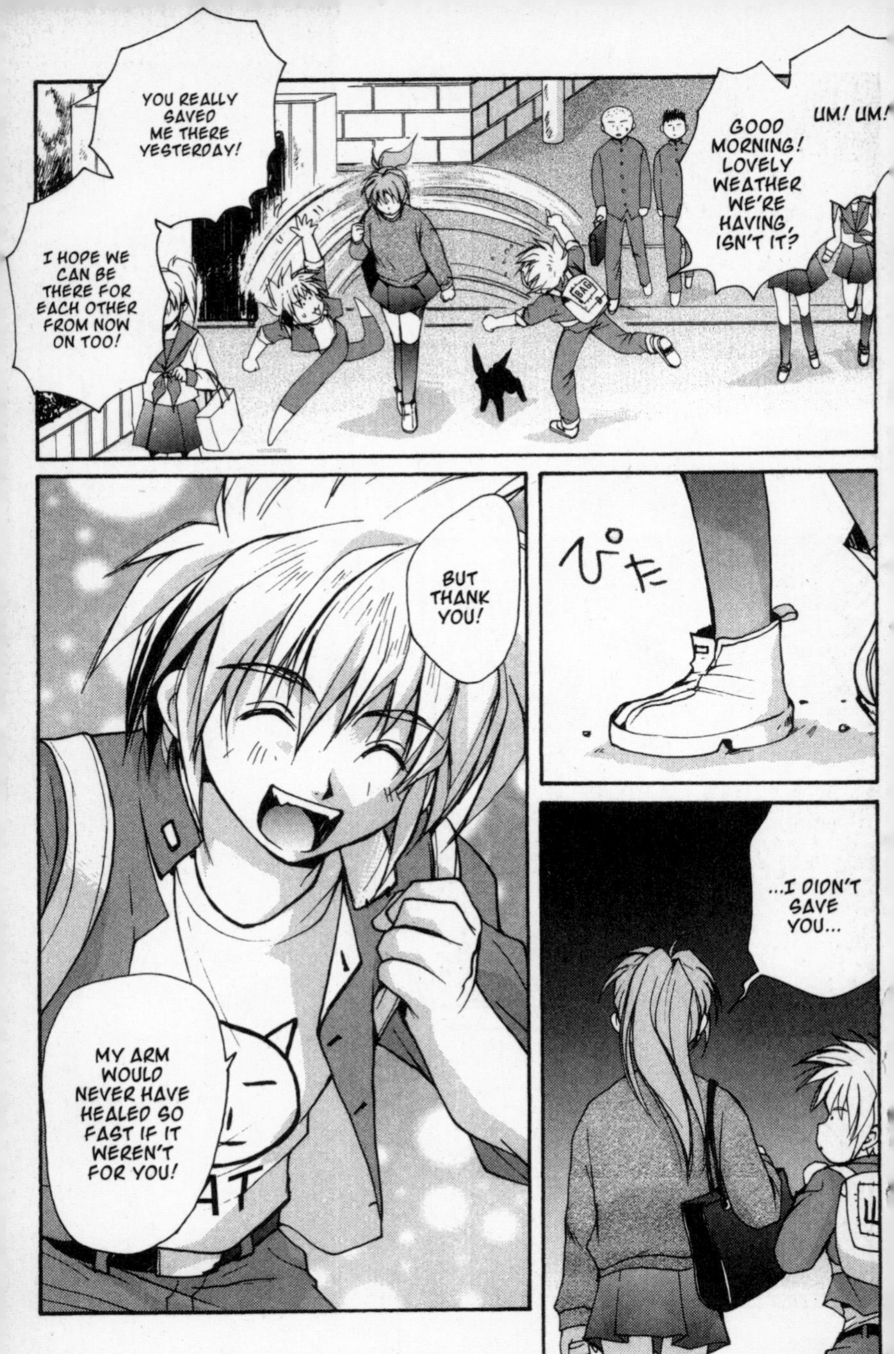
UM! UM!
GOOD MORNING! LOVELY WEATHER WE'RE HAVING, ISN'T IT?
YOU REALLY SAVED ME THERE YESTERDAY!
I HOPE WE CAN BE THERE FOR EACH OTHER FROM NOW ON TOO!
ぴた
...I DIDN'T SAVE YOU...
BUT THANK YOU!
MY ARM WOULD NEVER HAVE HEALED SO FAST IF IT WEREN'T FOR YOU!

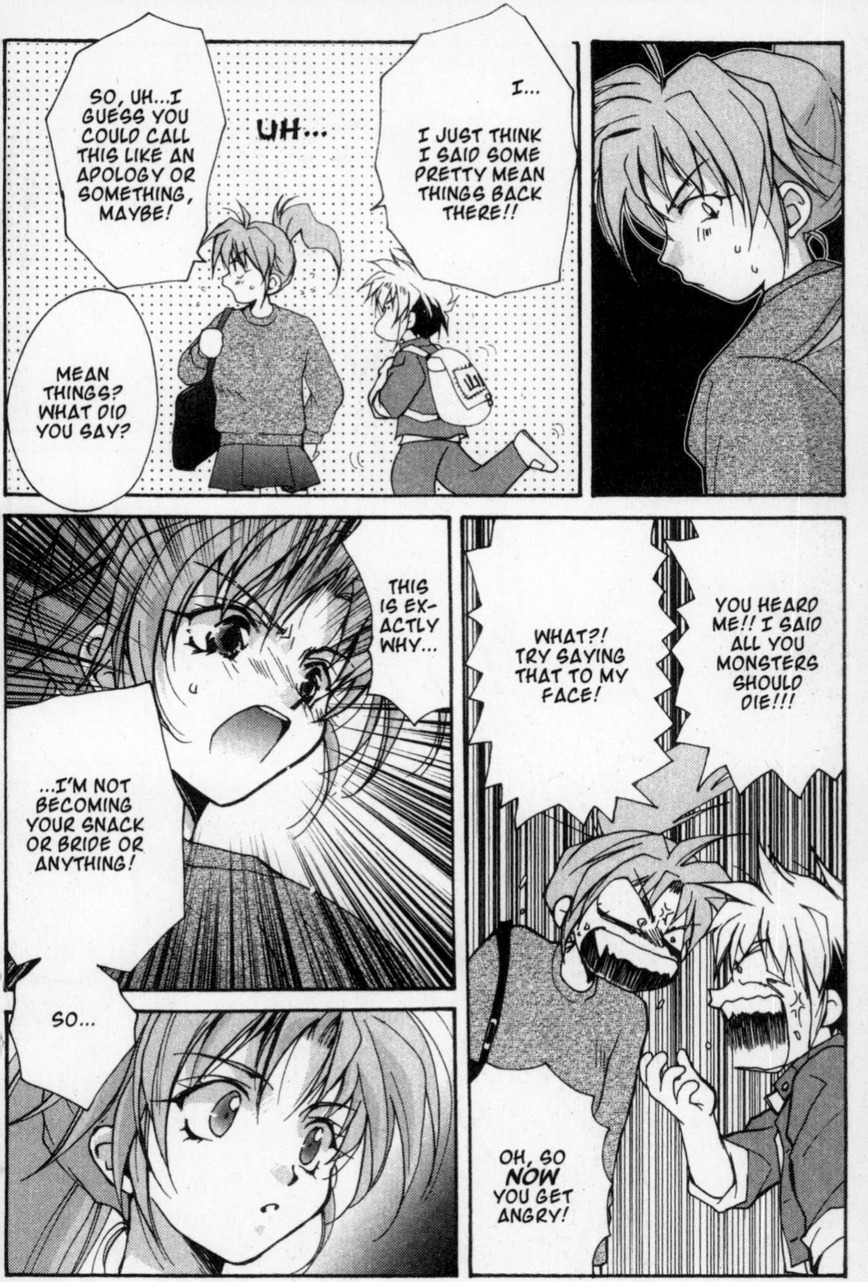
I...
I JUST THINK I SAID SOME PRETTY MEAN THINGS BACK THERE!!
UH...
SO, UH...I GUESS YOU COULD CALL THIS LIKE AN APOLOGY OR SOMETHING, MAYBE!
MEAN THINGS? WHAT DID YOU SAY?
YOU HEARD ME!! I SAID ALL YOU MONSTERS SHOULD DIE!!!
WHAT?! TRY SAYING THAT TO MY FACE!
OH, SO NOW YOU GET ANGRY!
THIS IS EXACTLY WHY...
...I'M NOT BECOMING YOUR SNACK OR BRIDE OR ANYTHING!
SO...

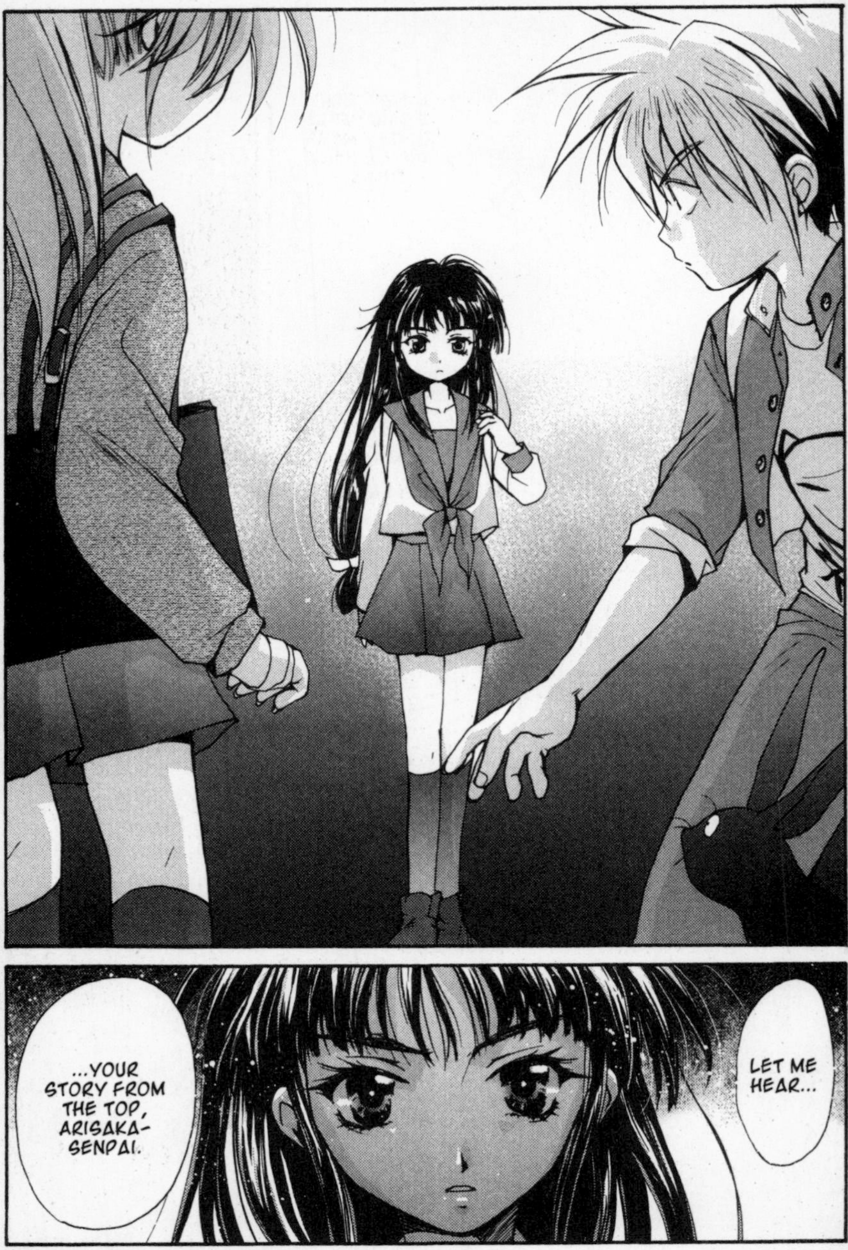
LET ME HEAR...
...YOUR STORY FROM THE TOP, ARISAKA-SENPAI.

ACT 08 END

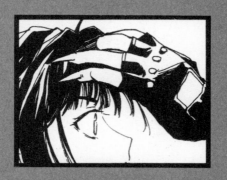

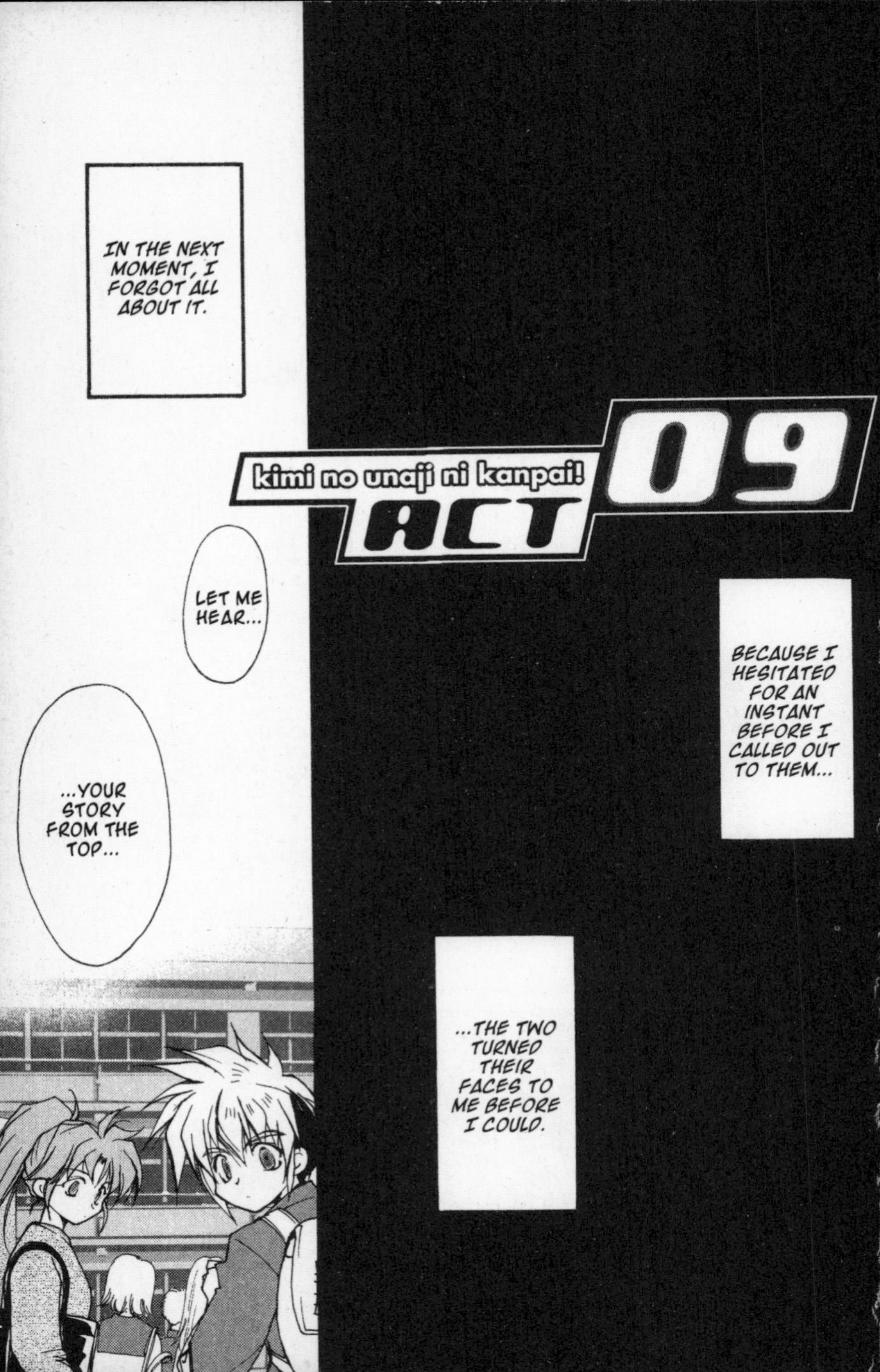
kimi no unaji ni kanpai! ACT 09
BECAUSE I HESITATED FOR AN INSTANT BEFORE I CALLED OUT TO THEM...
...THE TWO TURNED THEIR FACES TO ME BEFORE I COULD.
IN THE NEXT MOMENT, I FORGOT ALL ABOUT IT.
LET ME HEAR...
...YOUR STORY FROM THE TOP...

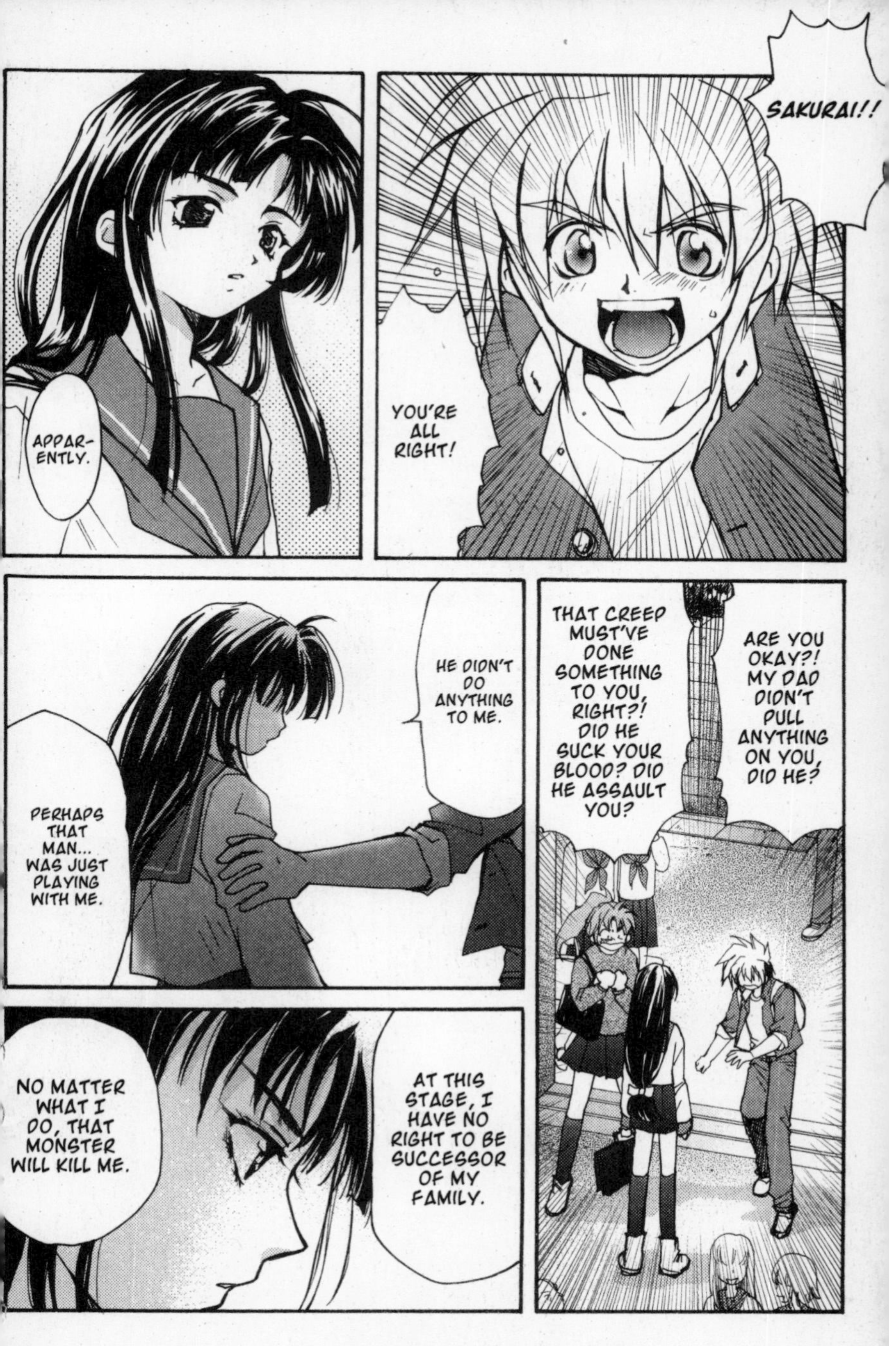
SAKURAI!!
YOU'RE ALL RIGHT!
APPAR-ENTLY.
ARE YOU OKAY?! MY DAD DIDN'T PULL ANYTHING ON YOU, DID HE?
THAT CREEP MUST'VE DONE SOMETHING TO YOU, RIGHT?! DID HE SUCK YOUR BLOOD? DID HE ASSAULT YOU?
HE DIDN'T DO ANYTHING TO ME.
PERHAPS THAT MAN... WAS JUST PLAYING WITH ME.
AT THIS STAGE, I HAVE NO RIGHT TO BE SUCCESSOR OF MY FAMILY.
NO MATTER WHAT I DO, THAT MONSTER WILL KILL ME.

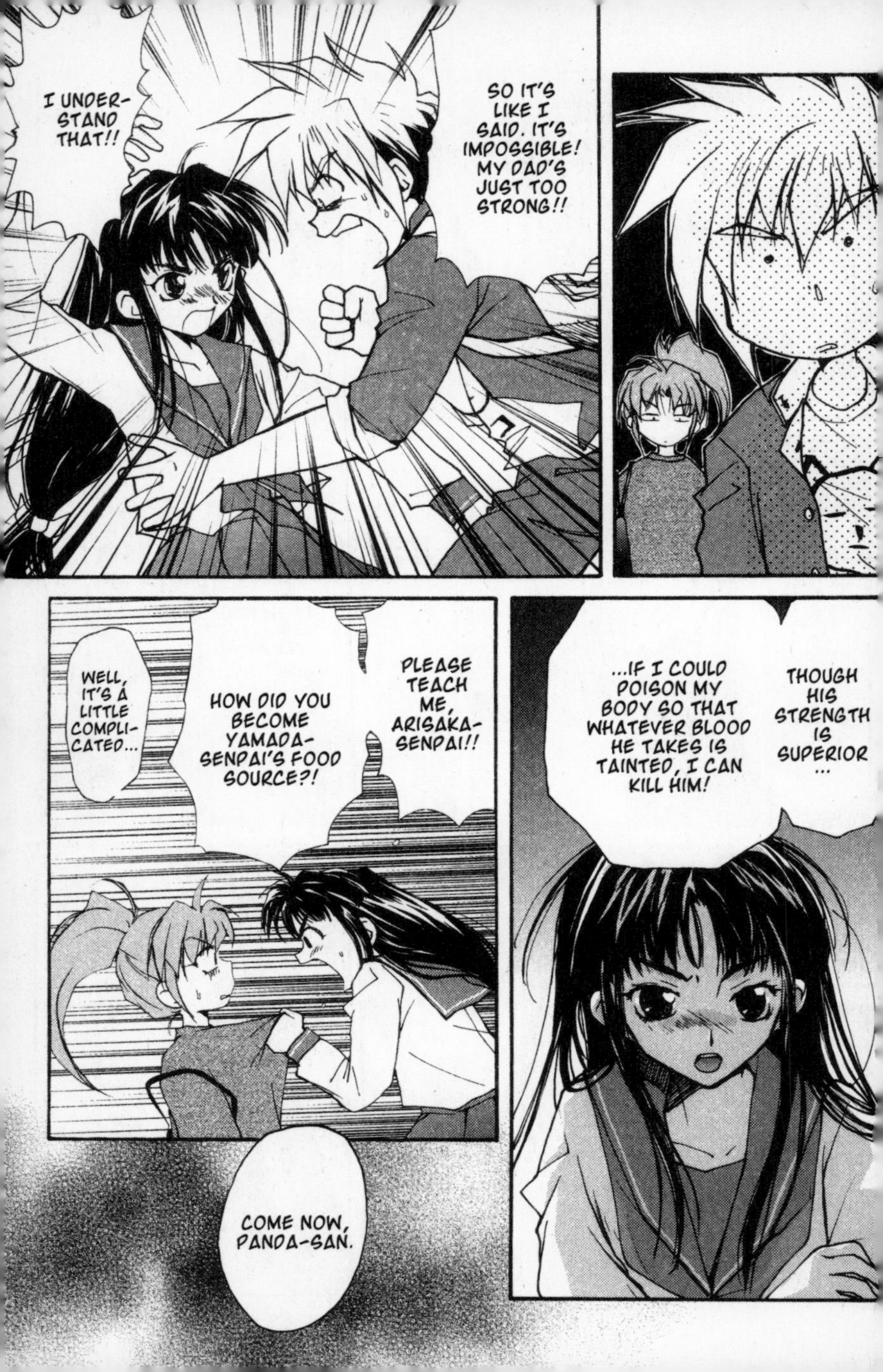
SO IT'S LIKE I SAID. IT'S IMPOSSIBLE! MY DAD'S JUST TOO STRONG!!
I UNDER-STAND THAT!!
THOUGH HIS STRENGTH IS SUPERIOR ...
...IF I COULD POISON MY BODY SO THAT WHATEVER BLOOD HE TAKES IS TAINTED, I CAN KILL HIM!
PLEASE TEACH ME, ARISAKA-SENPAI!!
HOW DID YOU BECOME YAMADA-SENPAI'S FOOD SOURCE?!
WELL, IT'S A LITTLE COMPLI-CATED...
COME NOW, PANDA-SAN.

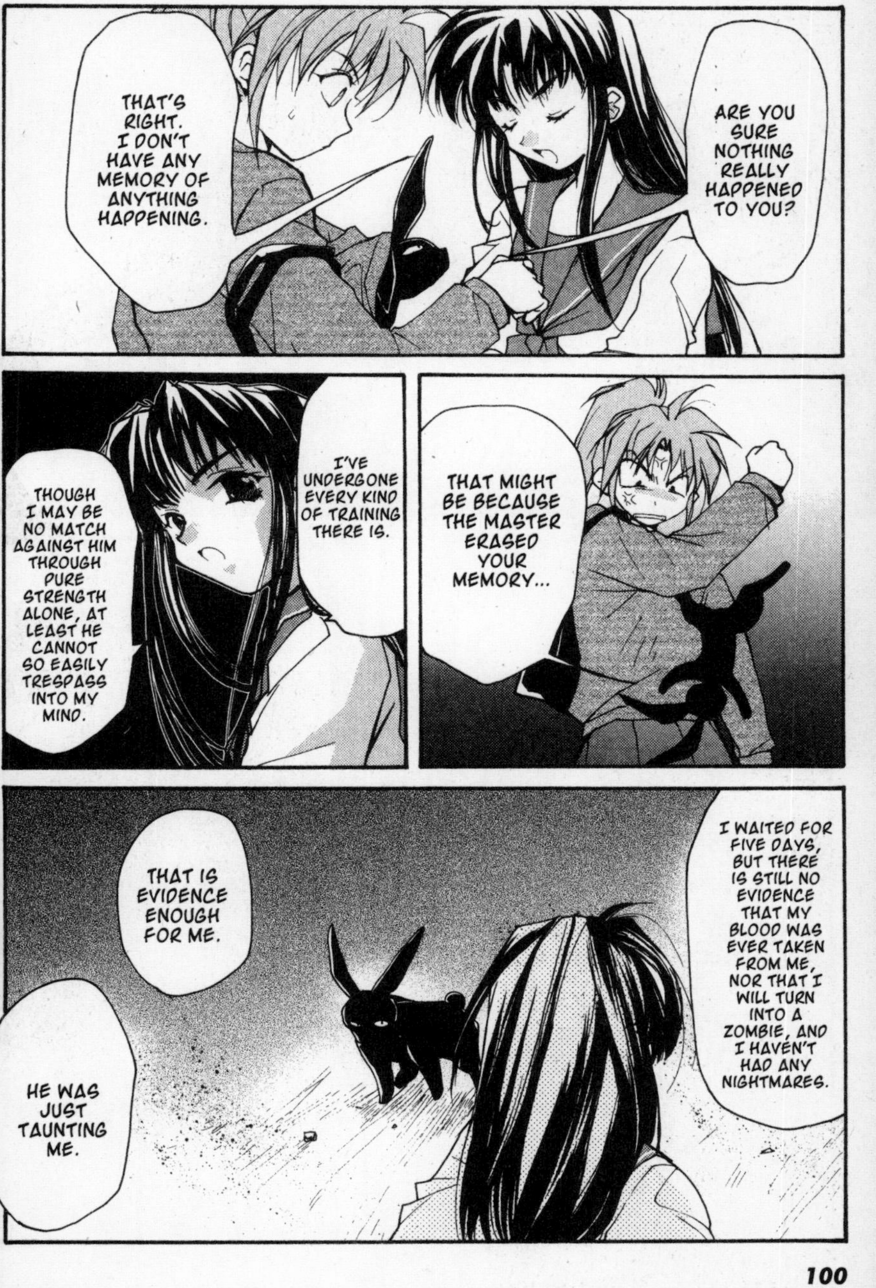
ARE YOU SURE NOTHING REALLY HAPPENED TO YOU?
THAT'S RIGHT. I DON'T HAVE ANY MEMORY OF ANYTHING HAPPENING.
THAT MIGHT BE BECAUSE THE MASTER ERASED YOUR MEMORY...
I'VE UNDERGONE EVERY KIND OF TRAINING THERE IS.
THOUGH I MAY BE NO MATCH AGAINST HIM THROUGH PURE STRENGTH ALONE, AT LEAST HE CANNOT SO EASILY TRESPASS INTO MY MIND.
I WAITED FOR FIVE DAYS, BUT THERE IS STILL NO EVIDENCE THAT MY BLOOD WAS EVER TAKEN FROM ME, NOR THAT I WILL TURN INTO A ZOMBIE, AND I HAVEN'T HAD ANY NIGHTMARES.
THAT IS EVIDENCE ENOUGH FOR ME.
HE WAS JUST TAUNTING ME.

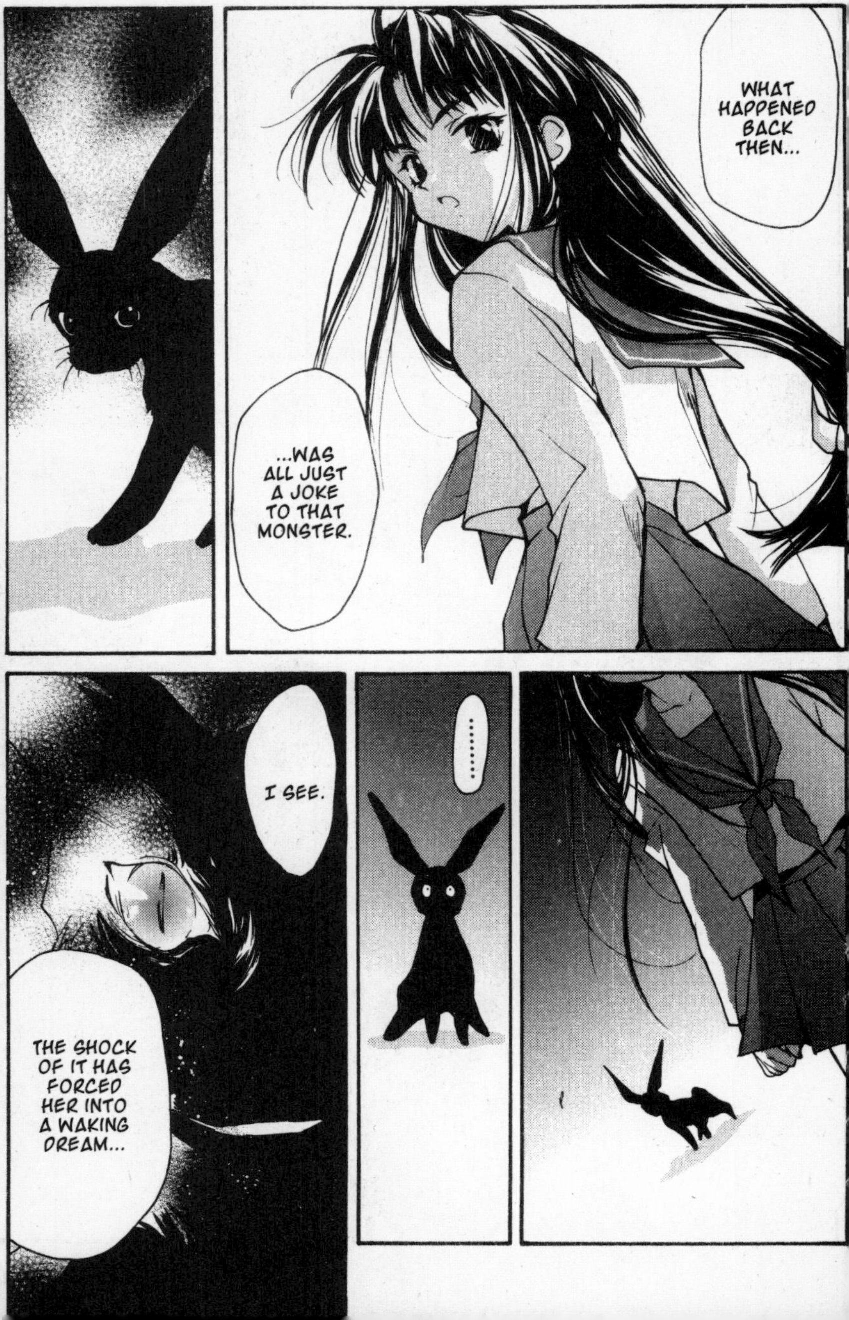
WHAT HAPPENED BACK THEN...
...WAS ALL JUST A JOKE TO THAT MONSTER.
......
I SEE.
THE SHOCK OF IT HAS FORCED HER INTO A WAKING DREAM...

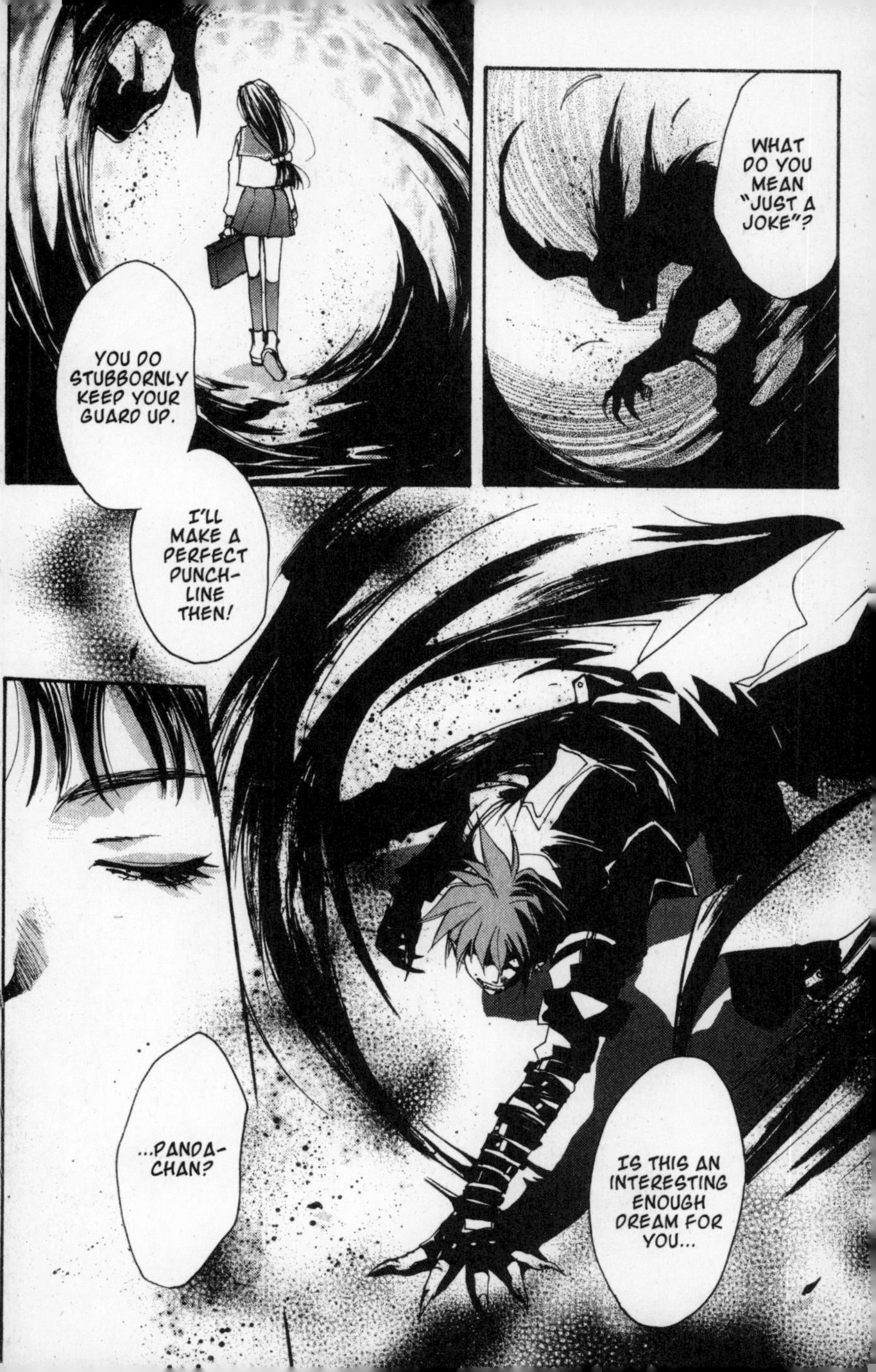
WHAT DO YOU MEAN "JUST A JOKE"?
YOU DO STUBBORNLY KEEP YOUR GUARD UP.
I'LL MAKE A PERFECT PUNCH-LINE THEN!
IS THIS AN INTERESTING ENOUGH DREAM FOR YOU...
...PANDA-CHAN?

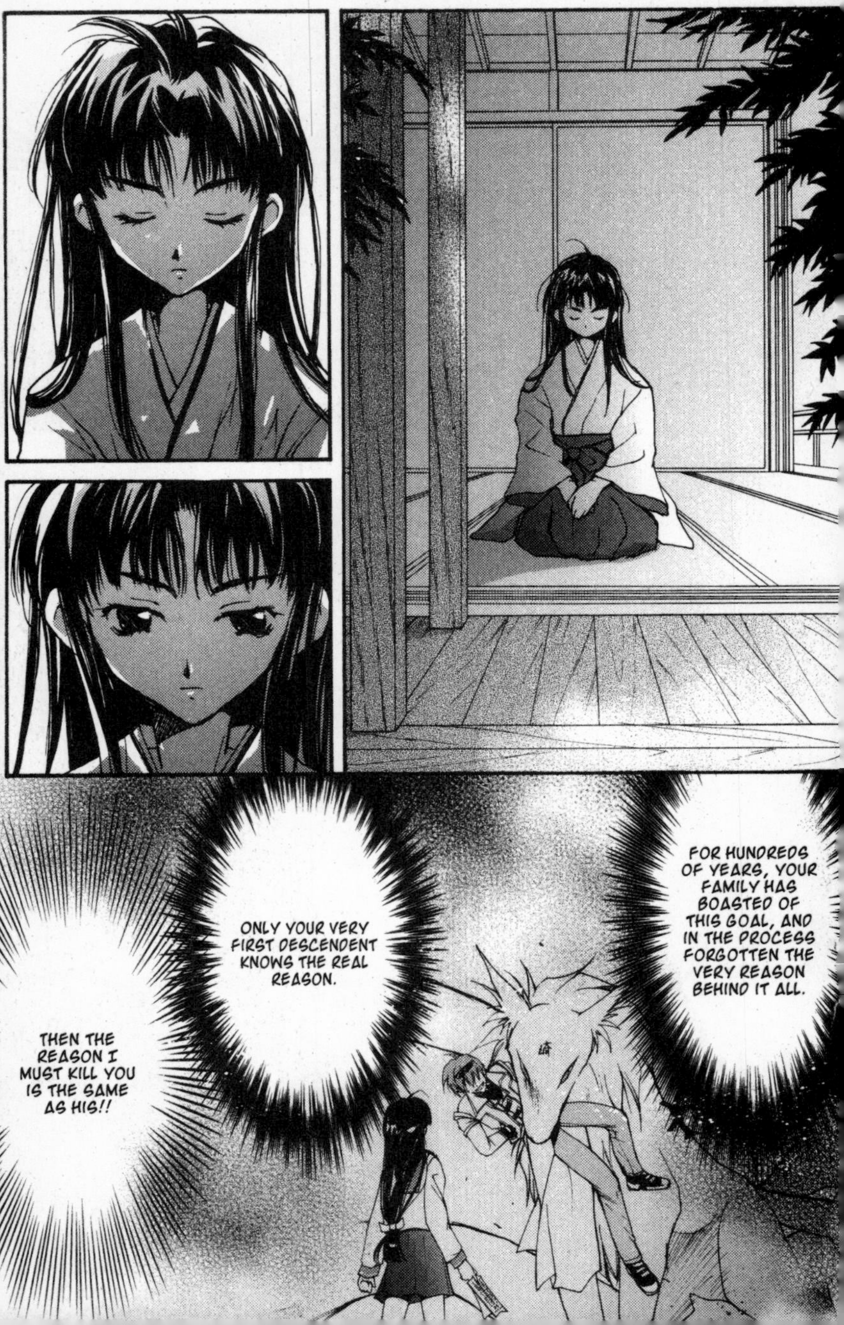
FOR HUNDREDS OF YEARS, YOUR FAMILY HAS BOASTED OF THIS GOAL, AND IN THE PROCESS FORGOTTEN THE VERY REASON BEHIND IT ALL.
ONLY YOUR VERY FIRST DESCENDENT KNOWS THE REAL REASON.
THEN THE REASON I MUST KILL YOU IS THE SAME AS HIS!!

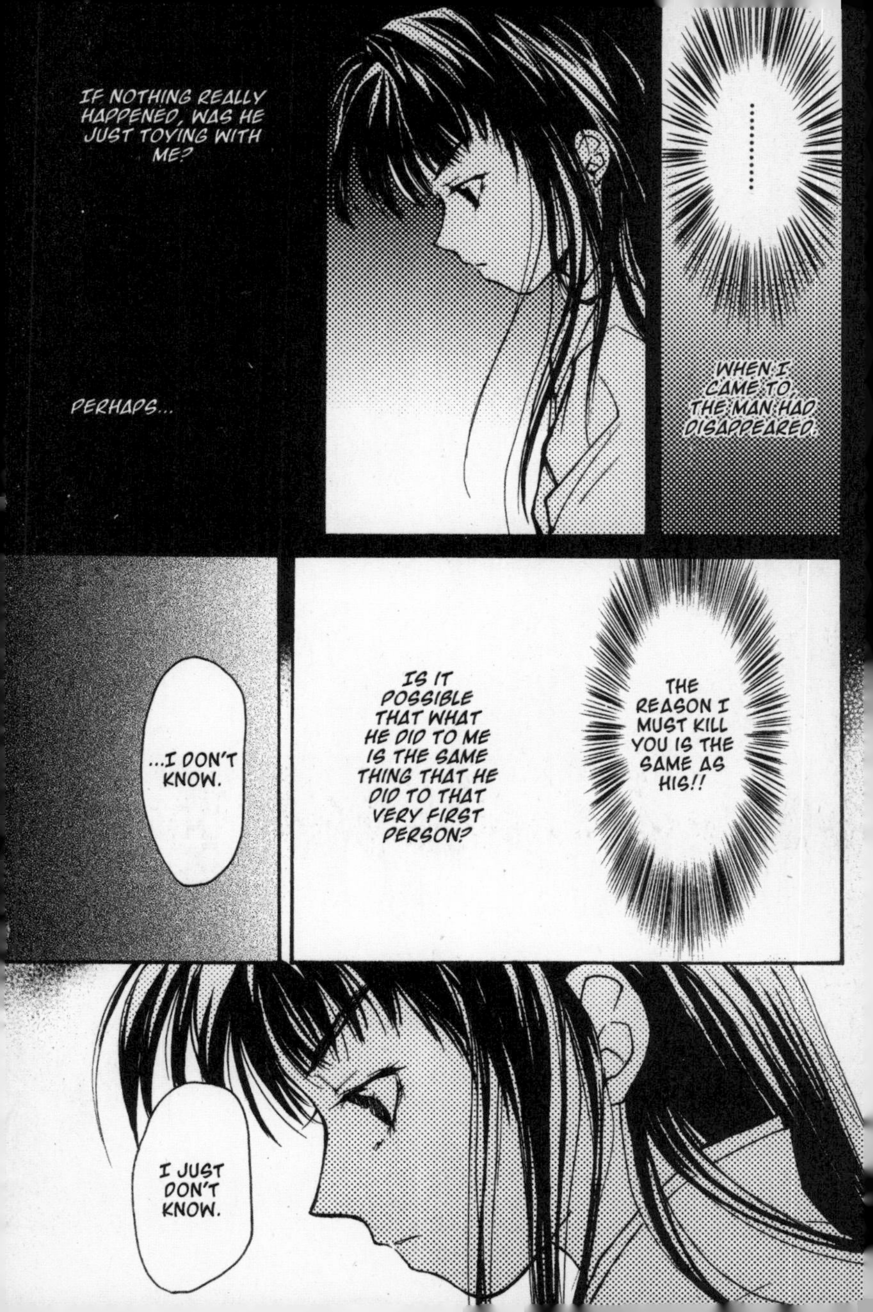
......
WHEN I CAME TO, THE MAN HAD DISAPPEARED.
IF NOTHING REALLY HAPPENED, WAS HE JUST TOYING WITH ME?
PERHAPS...
THE REASON I MUST KILL YOU IS THE SAME AS HIS!!
IS IT POSSIBLE THAT WHAT HE DID TO ME IS THE SAME THING THAT HE DID TO THAT VERY FIRST PERSON?
...I DON'T KNOW.
I JUST DON'T KNOW.

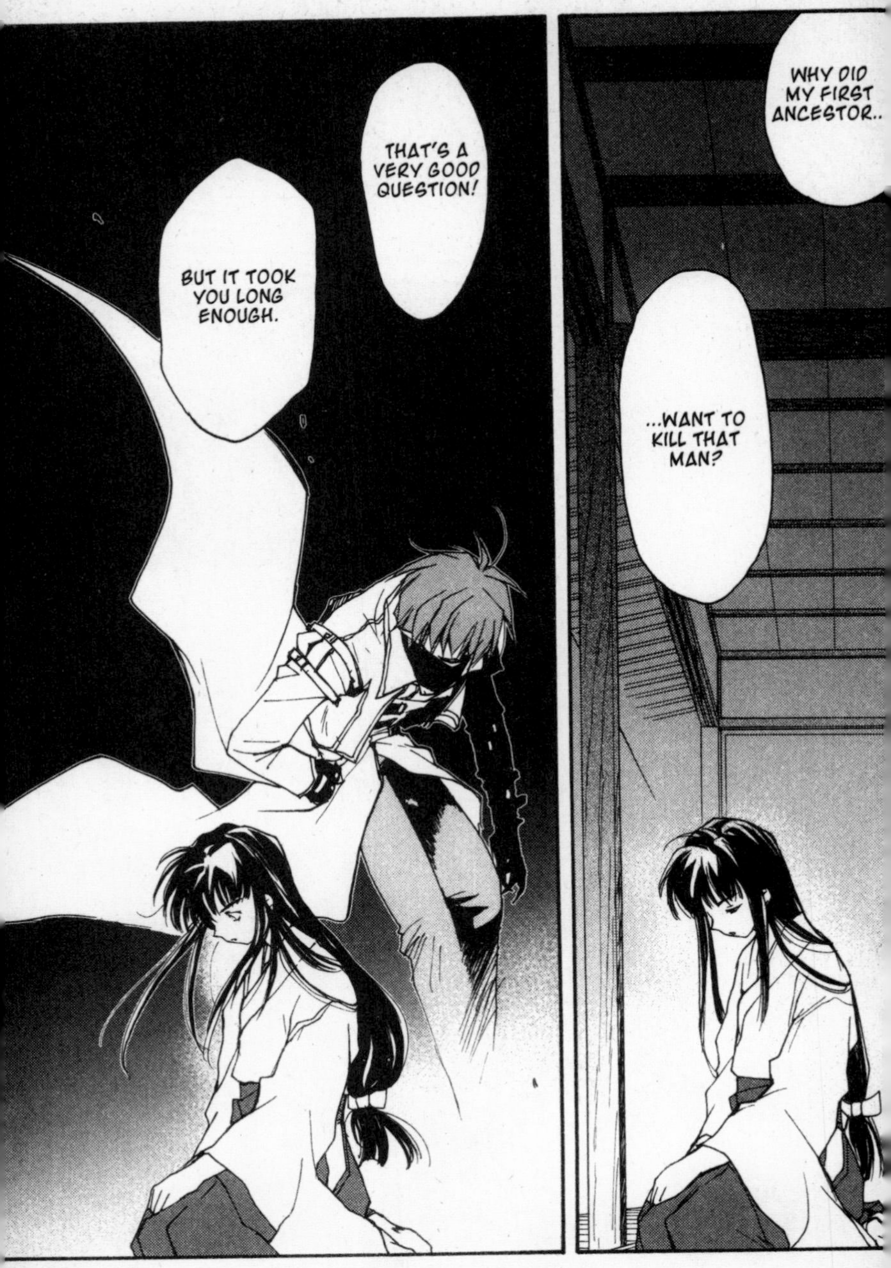
WHY DID MY FIRST ANCESTOR..
...WANT TO KILL THAT MAN?
THAT'S A VERY GOOD QUESTION!
BUT IT TOOK YOU LONG ENOUGH.

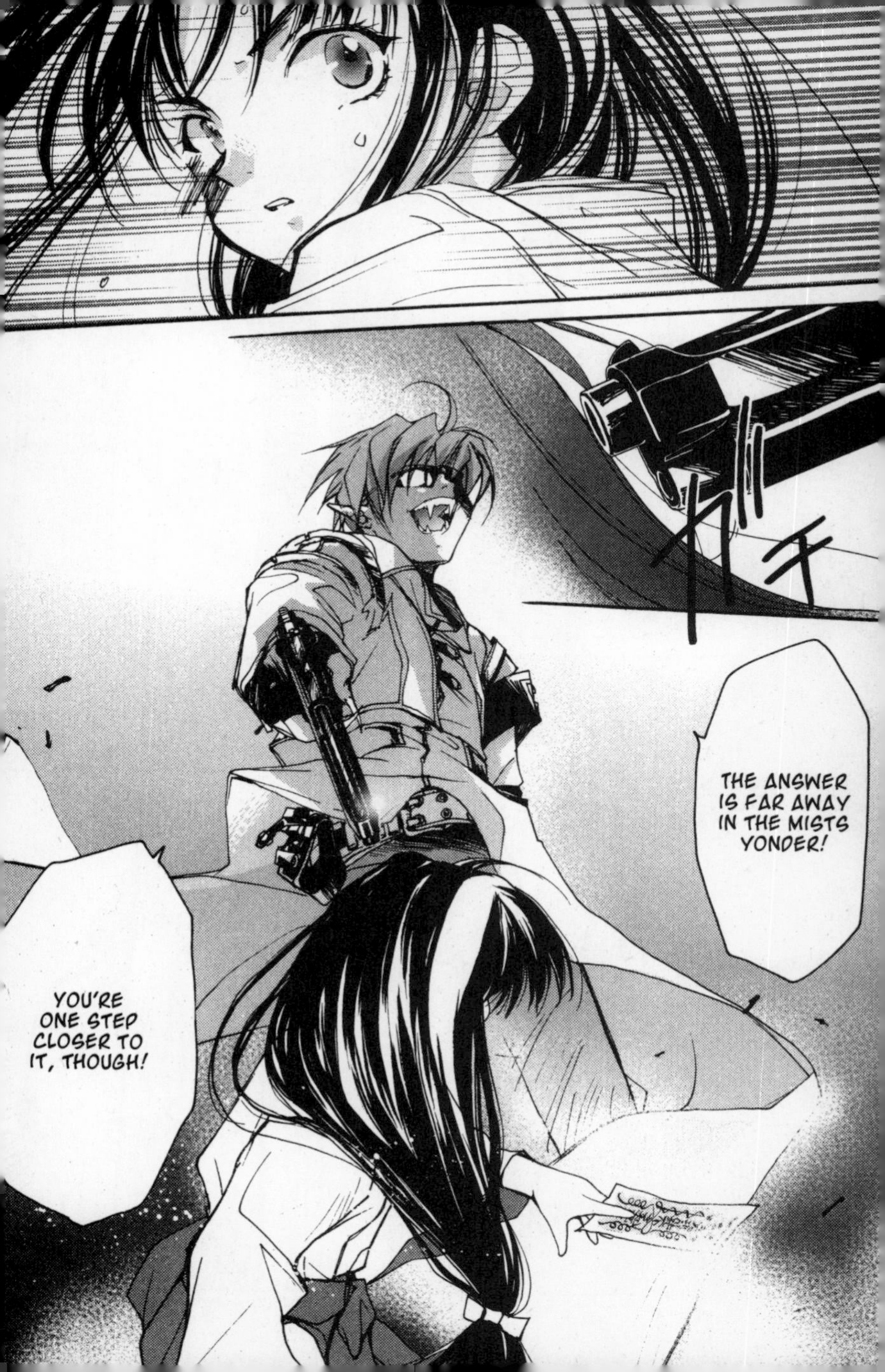
ガチ
THE ANSWER IS FAR AWAY IN THE MISTS YONDER!
YOU'RE ONE STEP CLOSER TO IT, THOUGH!

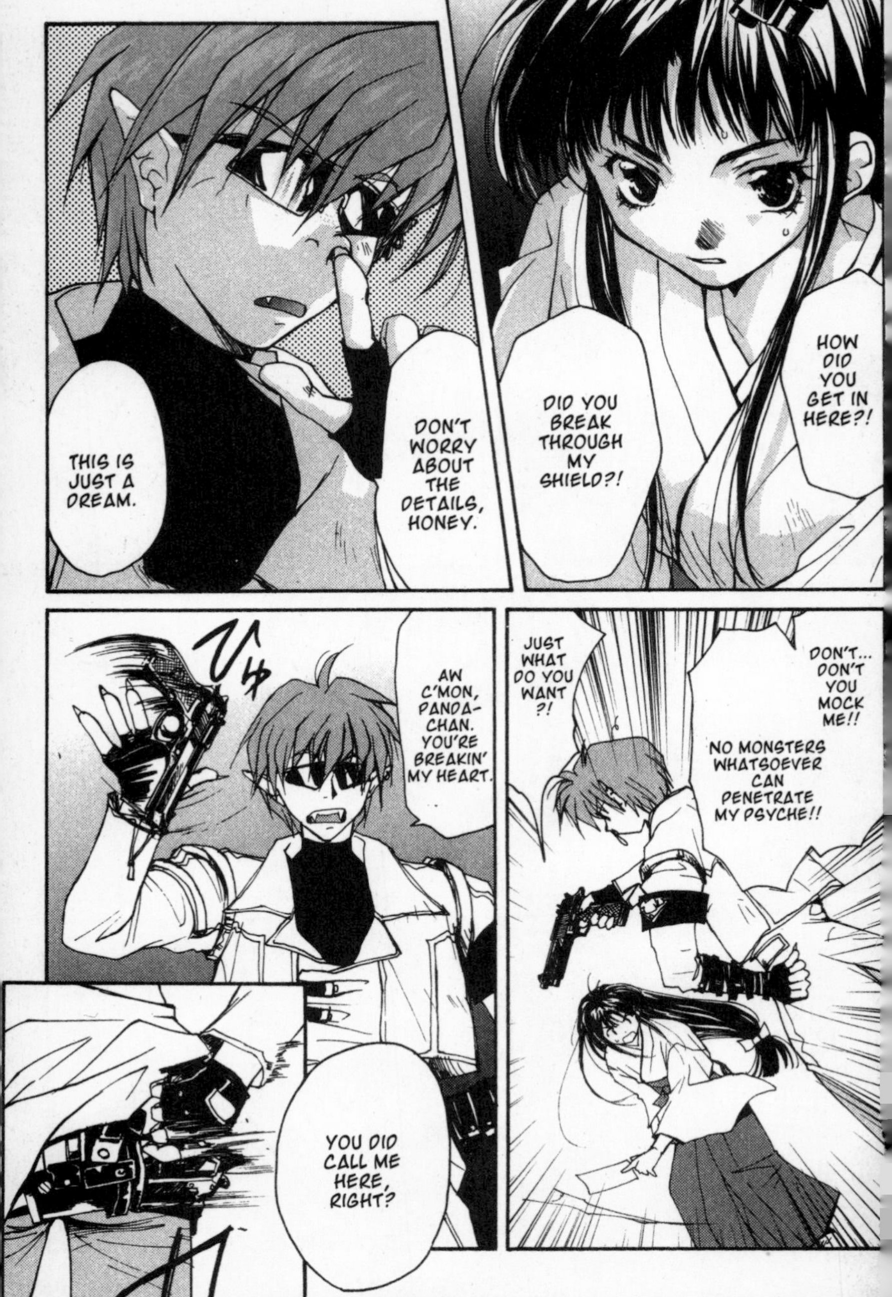
HOW DID YOU GET IN HERE?!
DID YOU BREAK THROUGH MY SHIELD?!
DON'T WORRY ABOUT THE DETAILS, HONEY.
THIS IS JUST A DREAM.
DON'T... DON'T YOU MOCK ME!!
JUST WHAT DO YOU WANT?!
NO MONSTERS WHATSOEVER CAN PENETRATE MY PSYCHE!!
AW C'MON, PANDA-CHAN. YOU'RE BREAKIN' MY HEART.
YOU DID CALL ME HERE, RIGHT?

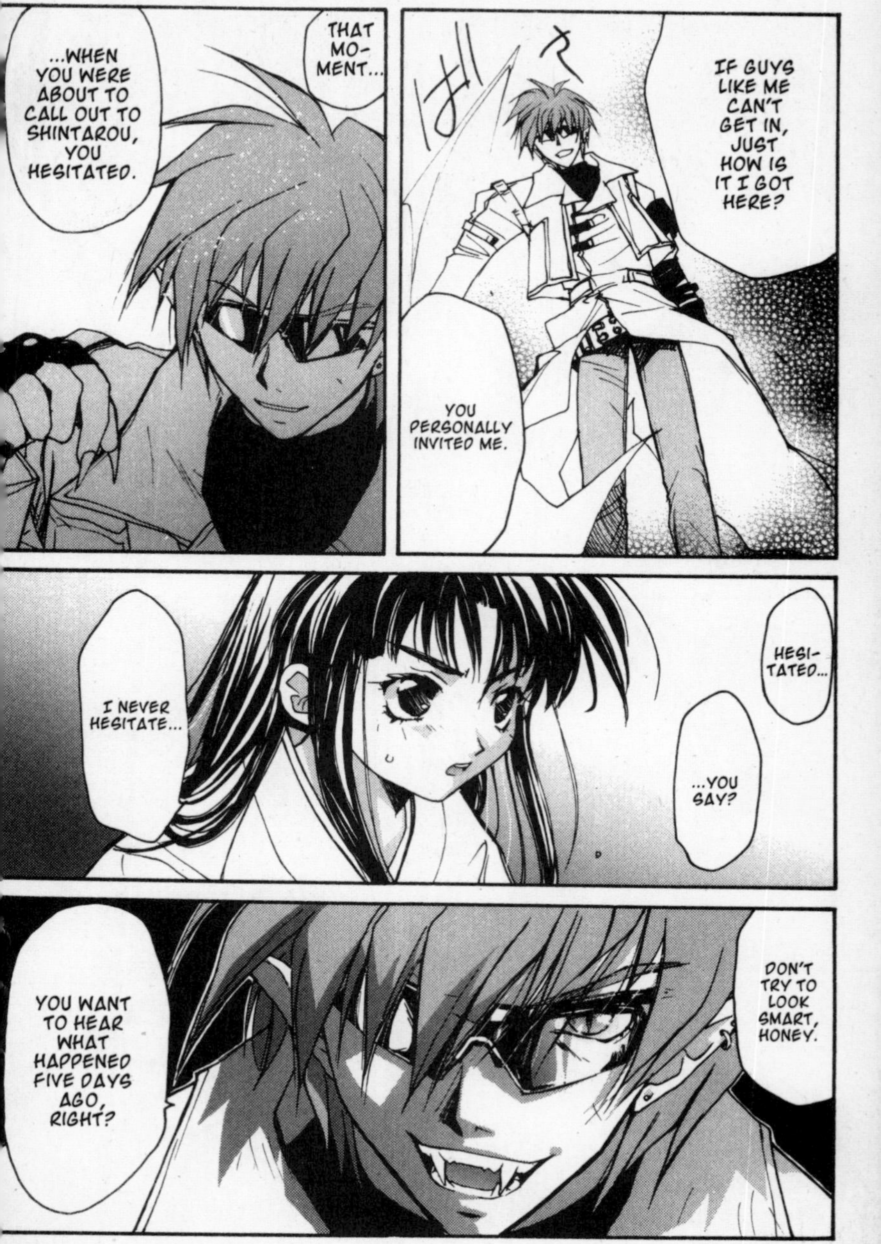

IF GUYS LIKE ME CAN'T GET IN, JUST HOW IS IT I GOT HERE?
YOU PERSONALLY INVITED ME.
THAT MO-MENT...
...WHEN YOU WERE ABOUT TO CALL OUT TO SHINTAROU, YOU HESITATED.
HESI-TATED...
...YOU SAY?
I NEVER HESITATE...
DON'T TRY TO LOOK SMART, HONEY.
YOU WANT TO HEAR WHAT HAPPENED FIVE DAYS AGO, RIGHT?

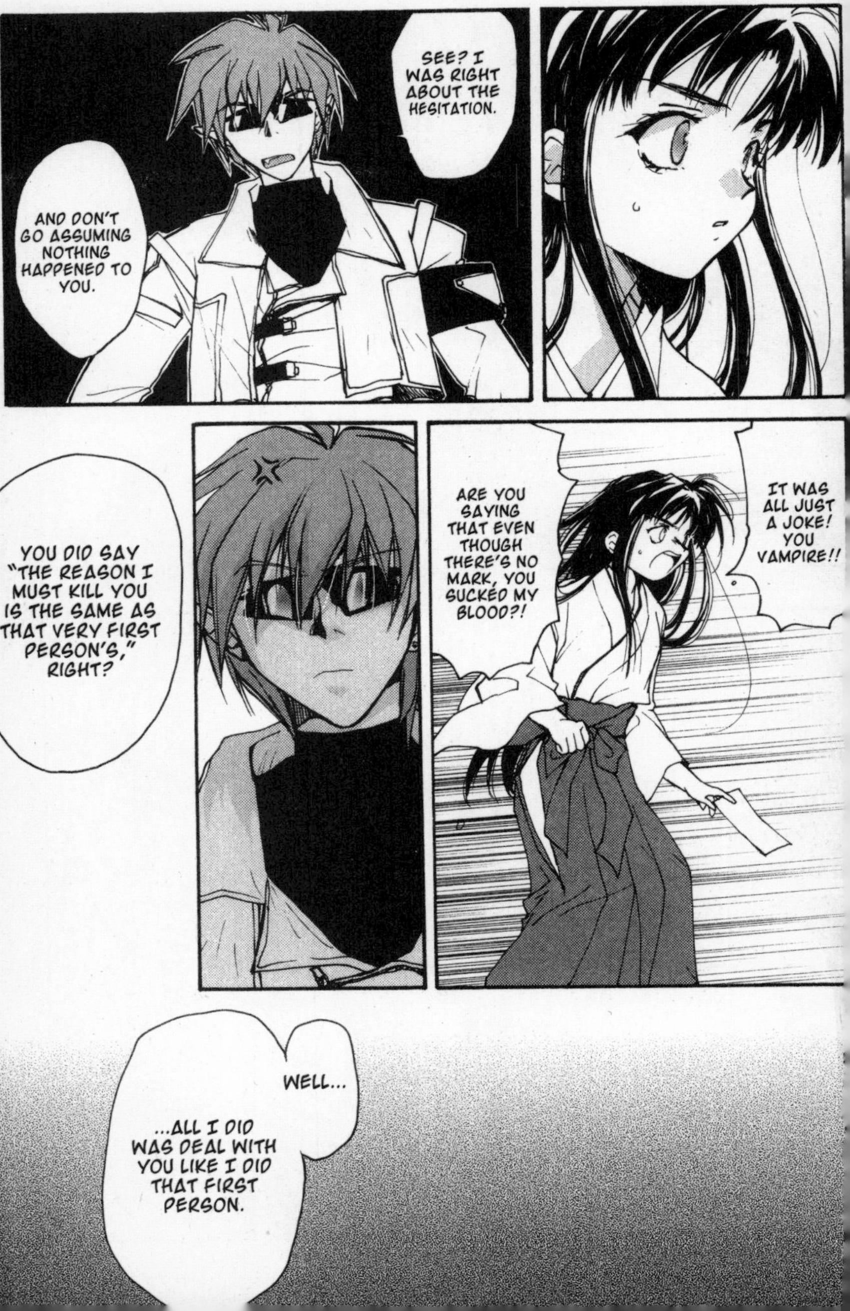
SEE? I WAS RIGHT ABOUT THE HESITATION.
AND DON'T GO ASSUMING NOTHING HAPPENED TO YOU.
IT WAS ALL JUST A JOKE! YOU VAMPIRE!!
ARE YOU SAYING THAT EVEN THOUGH THERE'S NO MARK, YOU SUCKED MY BLOOD?!
YOU DID SAY "THE REASON I MUST KILL YOU IS THE SAME AS THAT VERY FIRST PERSON'S," RIGHT?
WELL...
...ALL I DID WAS DEAL WITH YOU LIKE I DID THAT FIRST PERSON.

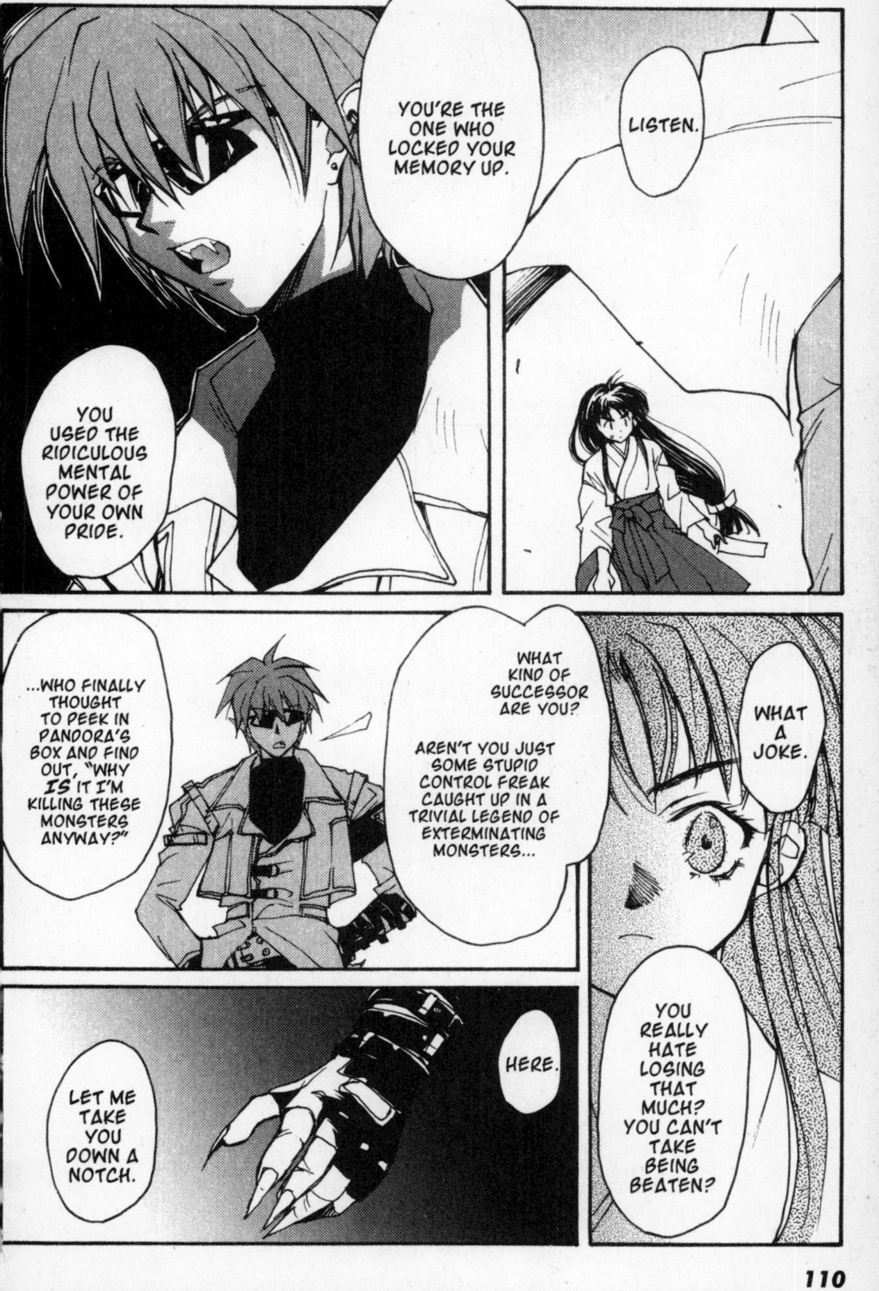

LISTEN.
YOU'RE THE ONE WHO LOCKED YOUR MEMORY UP.
YOU USED THE RIDICULOUS MENTAL POWER OF YOUR OWN PRIDE.
WHAT A JOKE.
YOU REALLY HATE LOSING THAT MUCH? YOU CAN'T TAKE BEING BEATEN?
WHAT KIND OF SUCCESSOR ARE YOU?
AREN'T YOU JUST SOME STUPID CONTROL FREAK CAUGHT UP IN A TRIVIAL LEGEND OF EXTERMINATING MONSTERS...
...WHO FINALLY THOUGHT TO PEEK IN PANDORA'S BOX AND FIND OUT, "WHY *IS* IT I'M KILLING THESE MONSTERS ANYWAY?"
HERE.
LET ME TAKE YOU DOWN A NOTCH.

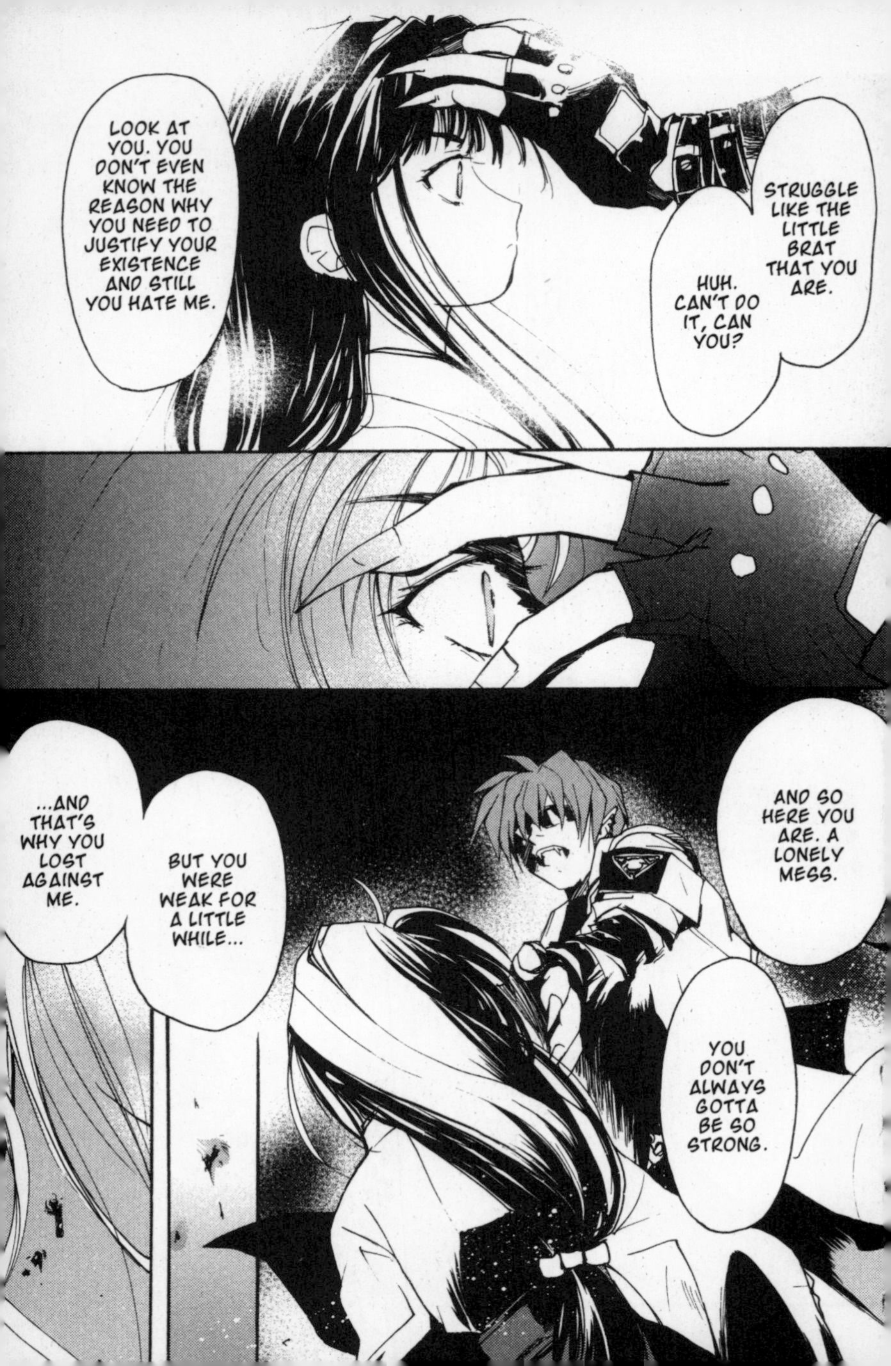
STRUGGLE LIKE THE LITTLE BRAT THAT YOU ARE.
HUH. CAN'T DO IT, CAN YOU?
LOOK AT YOU. YOU DON'T EVEN KNOW THE REASON WHY YOU NEED TO JUSTIFY YOUR EXISTENCE AND STILL YOU HATE ME.
AND SO HERE YOU ARE. A LONELY MESS.
YOU DON'T ALWAYS GOTTA BE SO STRONG.
BUT YOU WERE WEAK FOR A LITTLE WHILE...
...AND THAT'S WHY YOU LOST AGAINST ME.

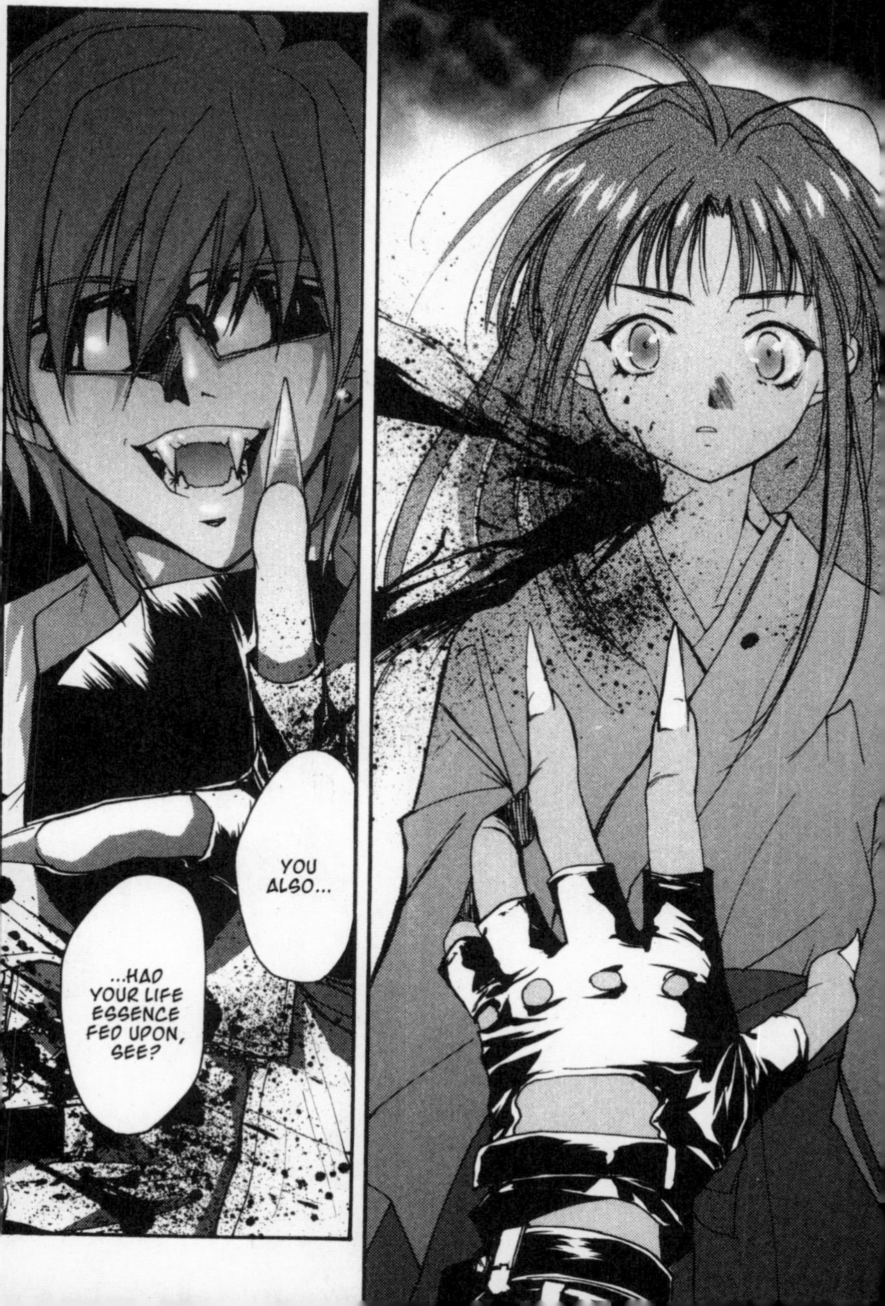
YOU ALSO...
...HAD YOUR LIFE ESSENCE FED UPON, SEE?

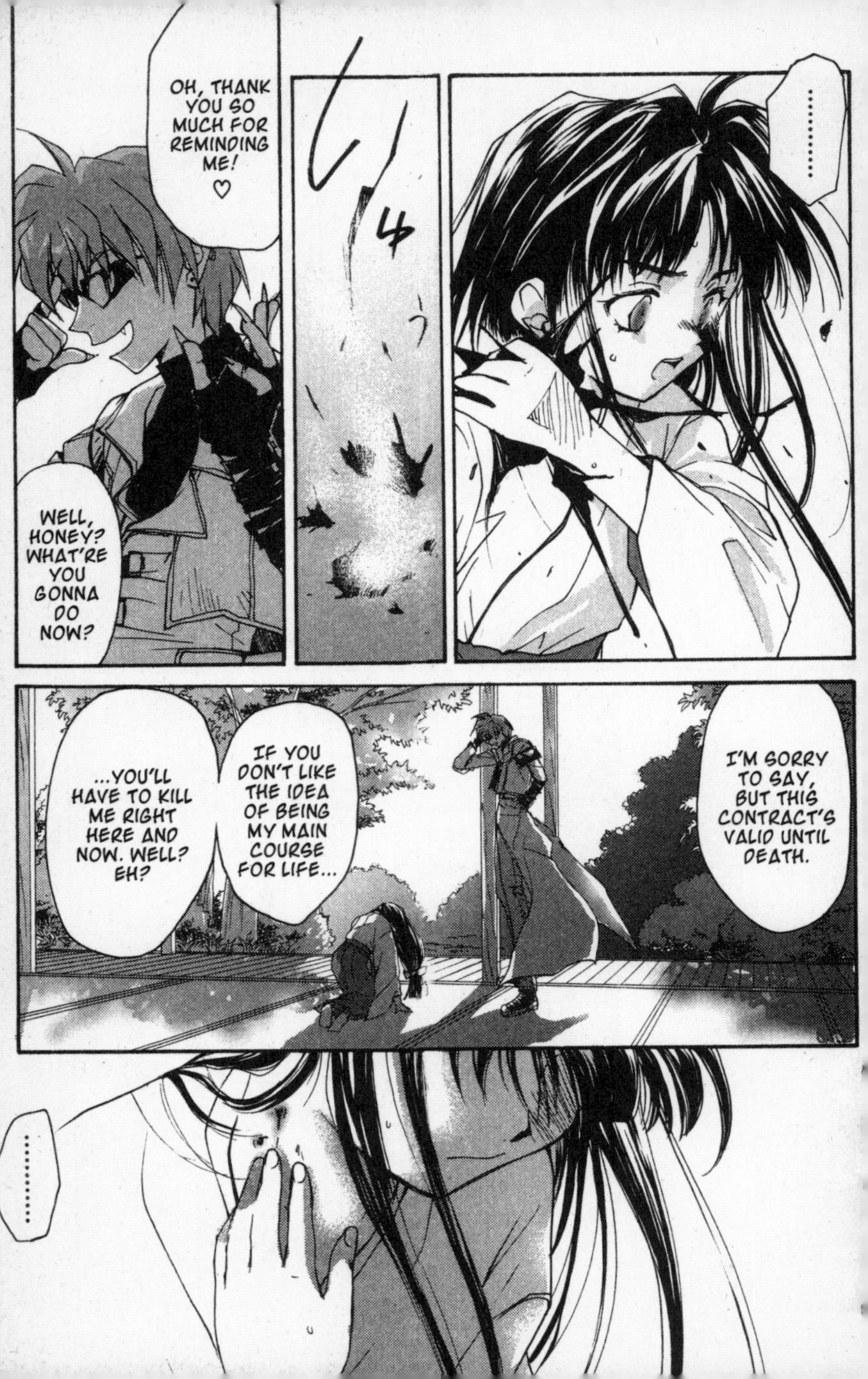
......
OH, THANK YOU SO MUCH FOR REMINDING ME! ♡
WELL, HONEY? WHAT'RE YOU GONNA DO NOW?
I'M SORRY TO SAY, BUT THIS CONTRACT'S VALID UNTIL DEATH.
IF YOU DON'T LIKE THE IDEA OF BEING MY MAIN COURSE FOR LIFE...
...YOU'LL HAVE TO KILL ME RIGHT HERE AND NOW. WELL? EH?
......

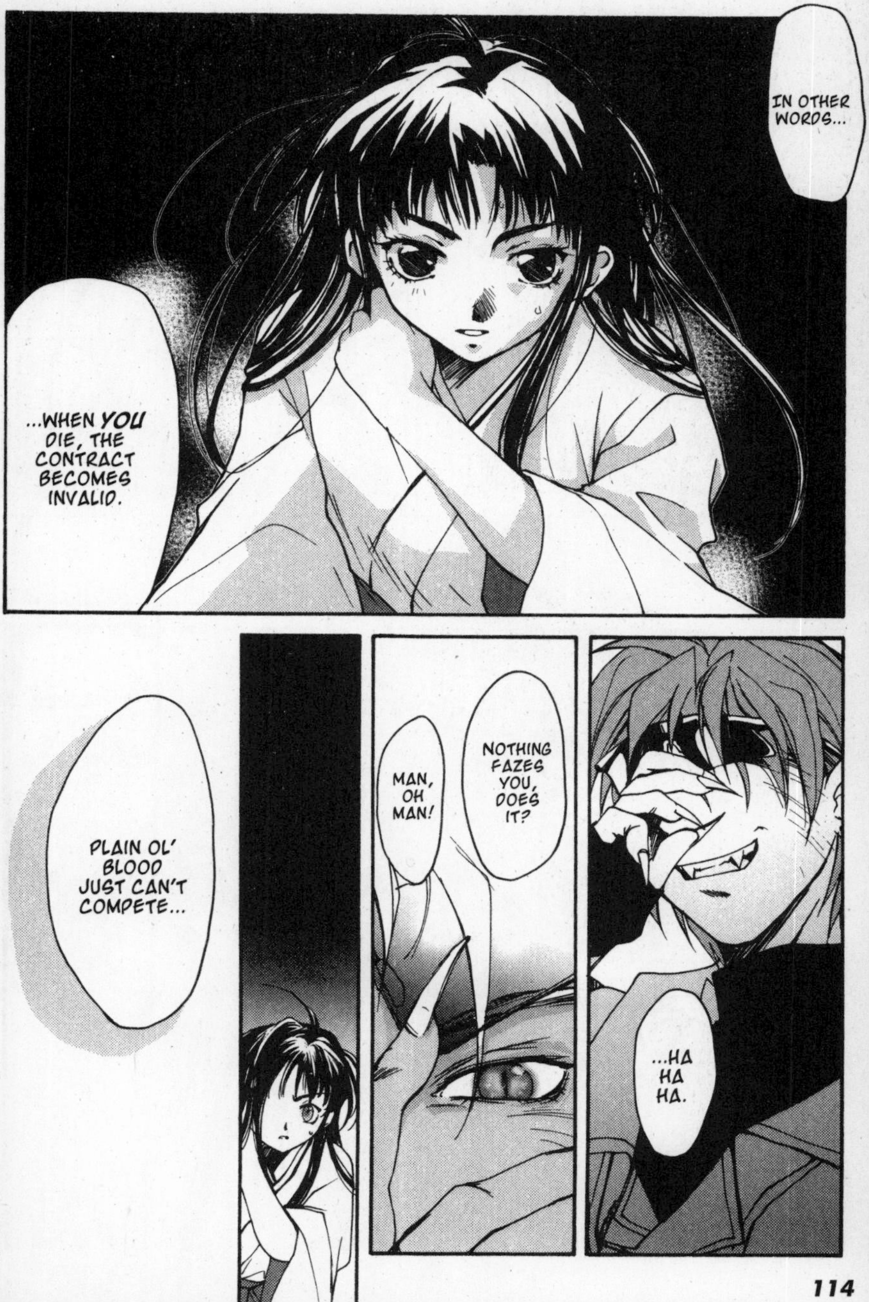
IN OTHER WORDS...
...WHEN YOU DIE, THE CONTRACT BECOMES INVALID.
...HA HA HA.
NOTHING FAZES YOU, DOES IT?
MAN, OH MAN!
PLAIN OL' BLOOD JUST CAN'T COMPETE...

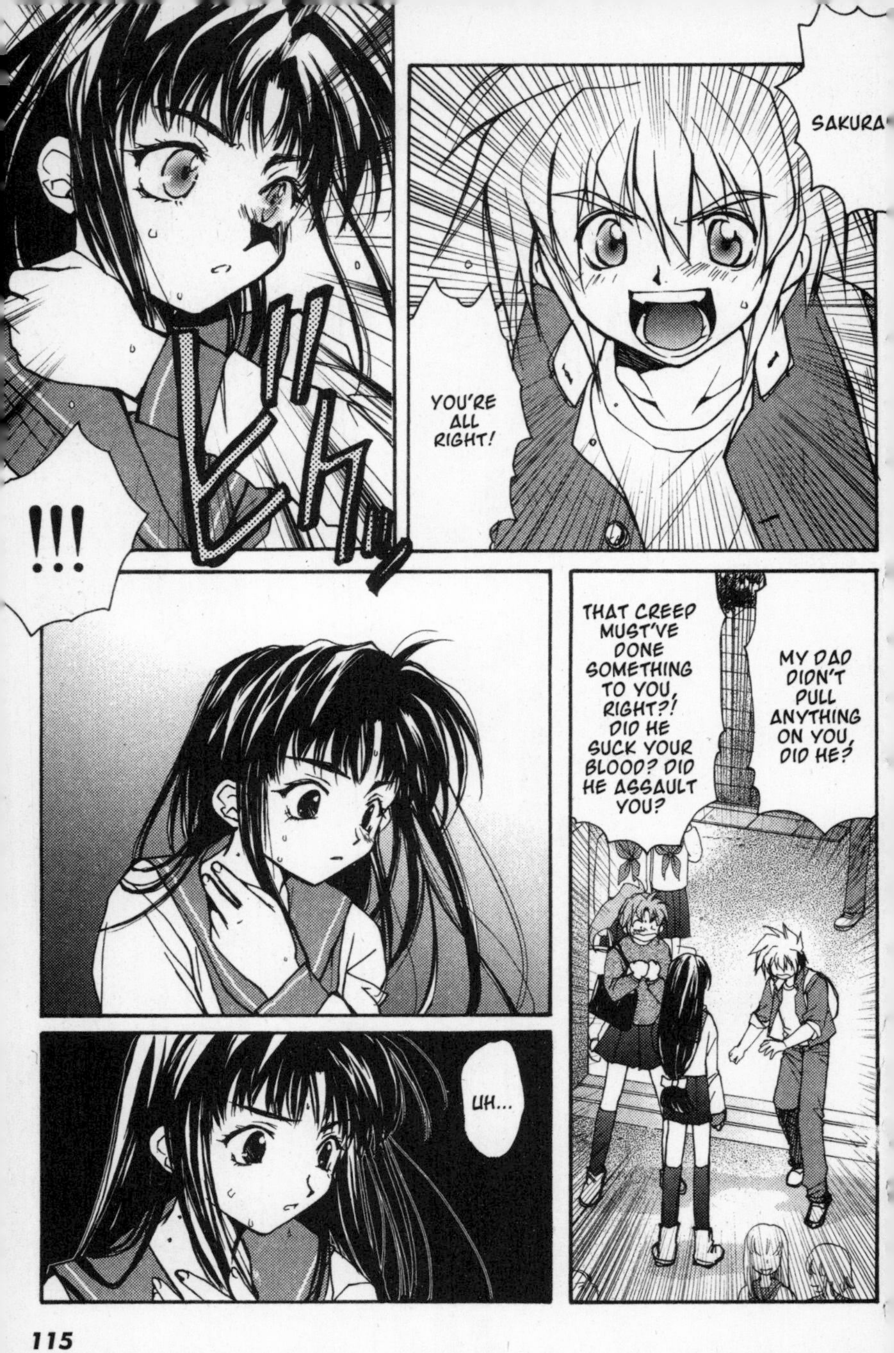
SAKURA
YOU'RE ALL RIGHT!
!!!
MY DAD DIDN'T PULL ANYTHING ON YOU, DID HE?
THAT CREEP MUST'VE DONE SOMETHING TO YOU, RIGHT?! DID HE SUCK YOUR BLOOD? DID HE ASSAULT YOU?
UH...

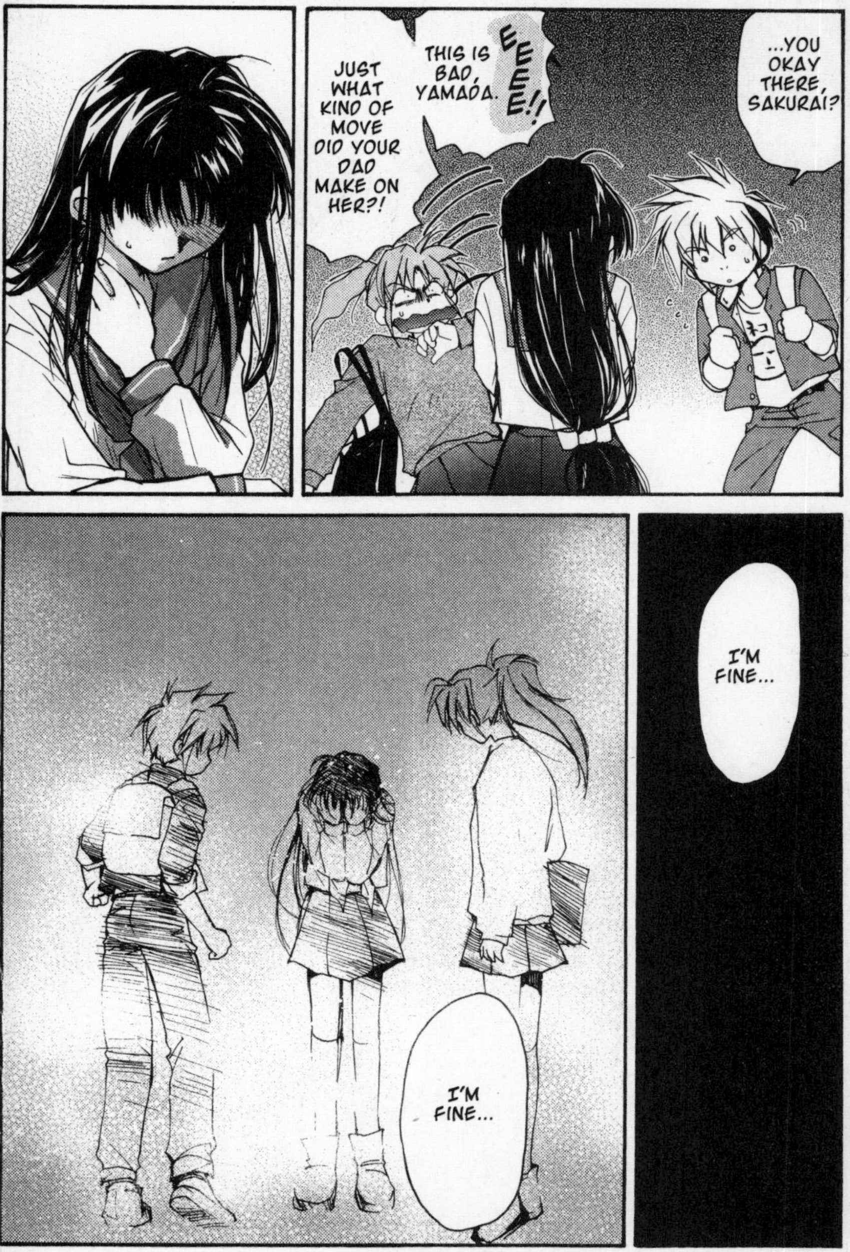
...YOU OKAY THERE, SAKURAI?
EEEEE!!
THIS IS BAD, YAMADA.
JUST WHAT KIND OF MOVE DID YOUR DAD MAKE ON HER?!
I'M FINE...
I'M FINE...

ACT 09 END

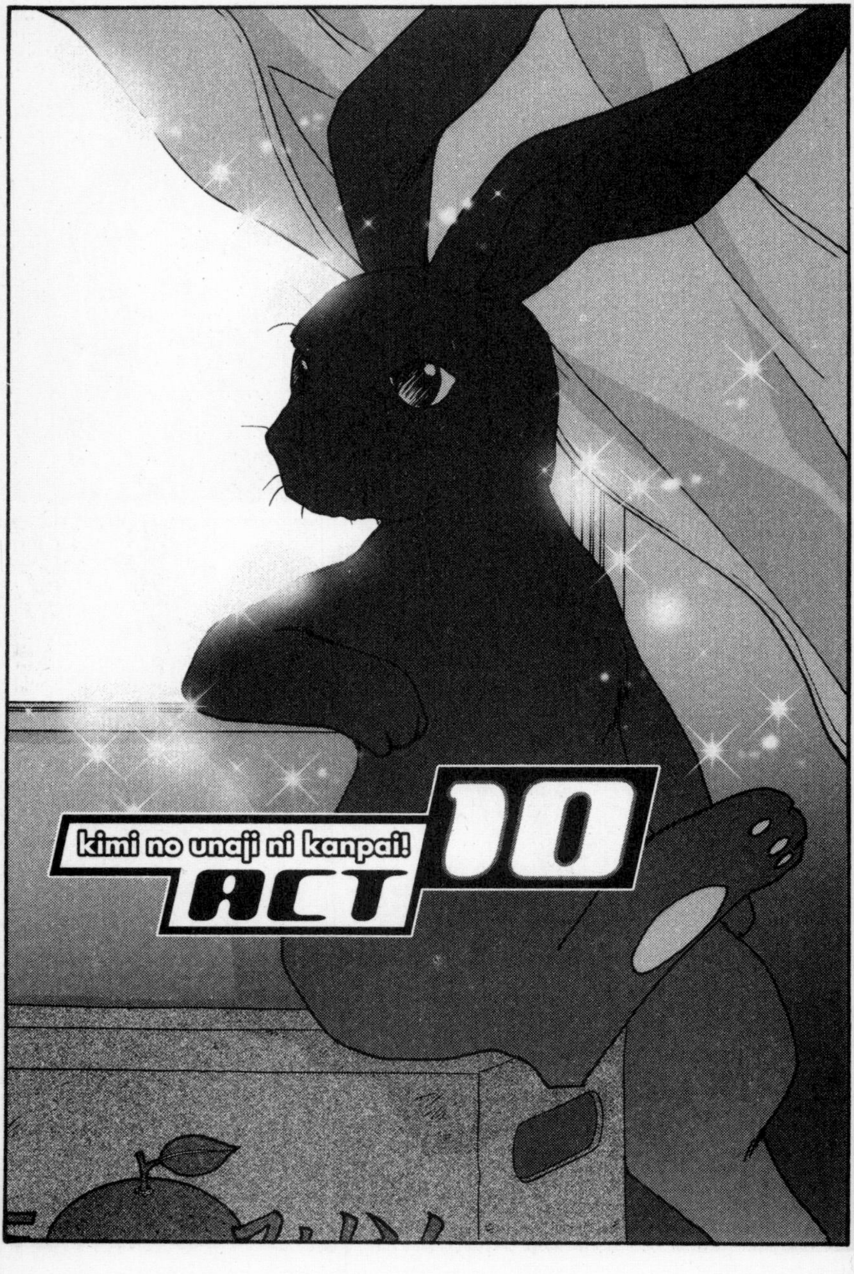
kimi no unaji ni kanpai!
ACT 10

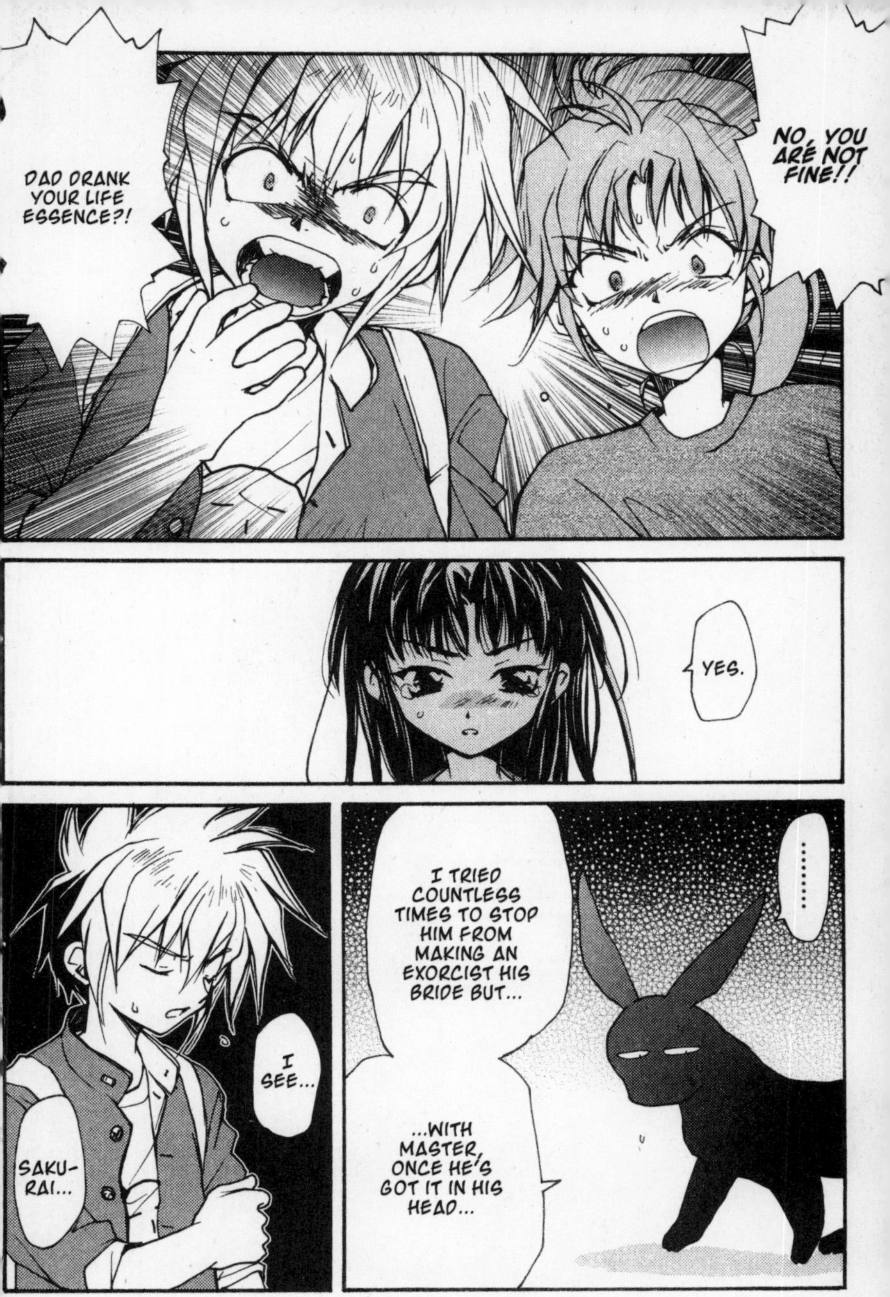
NO, YOU ARE NOT FINE!!
DAD DRANK YOUR LIFE ESSENCE?!
YES.
......
I TRIED COUNTLESS TIMES TO STOP HIM FROM MAKING AN EXORCIST HIS BRIDE BUT...
...WITH MASTER, ONCE HE'S GOT IT IN HIS HEAD...
I SEE...
SAKU-RAI...

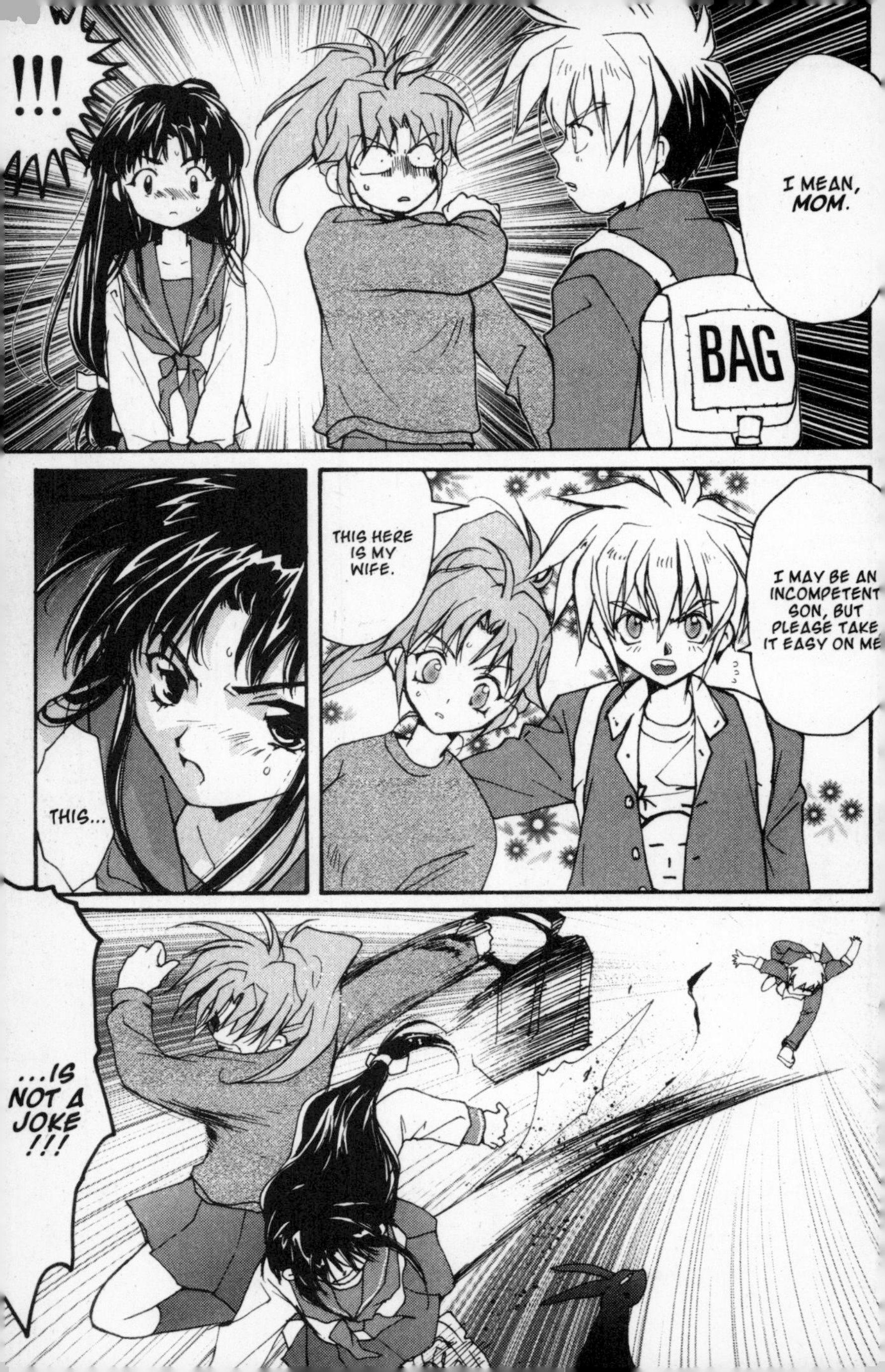
I MEAN, MOM.
BAG
!!!
I MAY BE AN INCOMPETENT SON, BUT PLEASE TAKE IT EASY ON ME
THIS HERE IS MY WIFE.
THIS...
...IS NOT A JOKE!!!

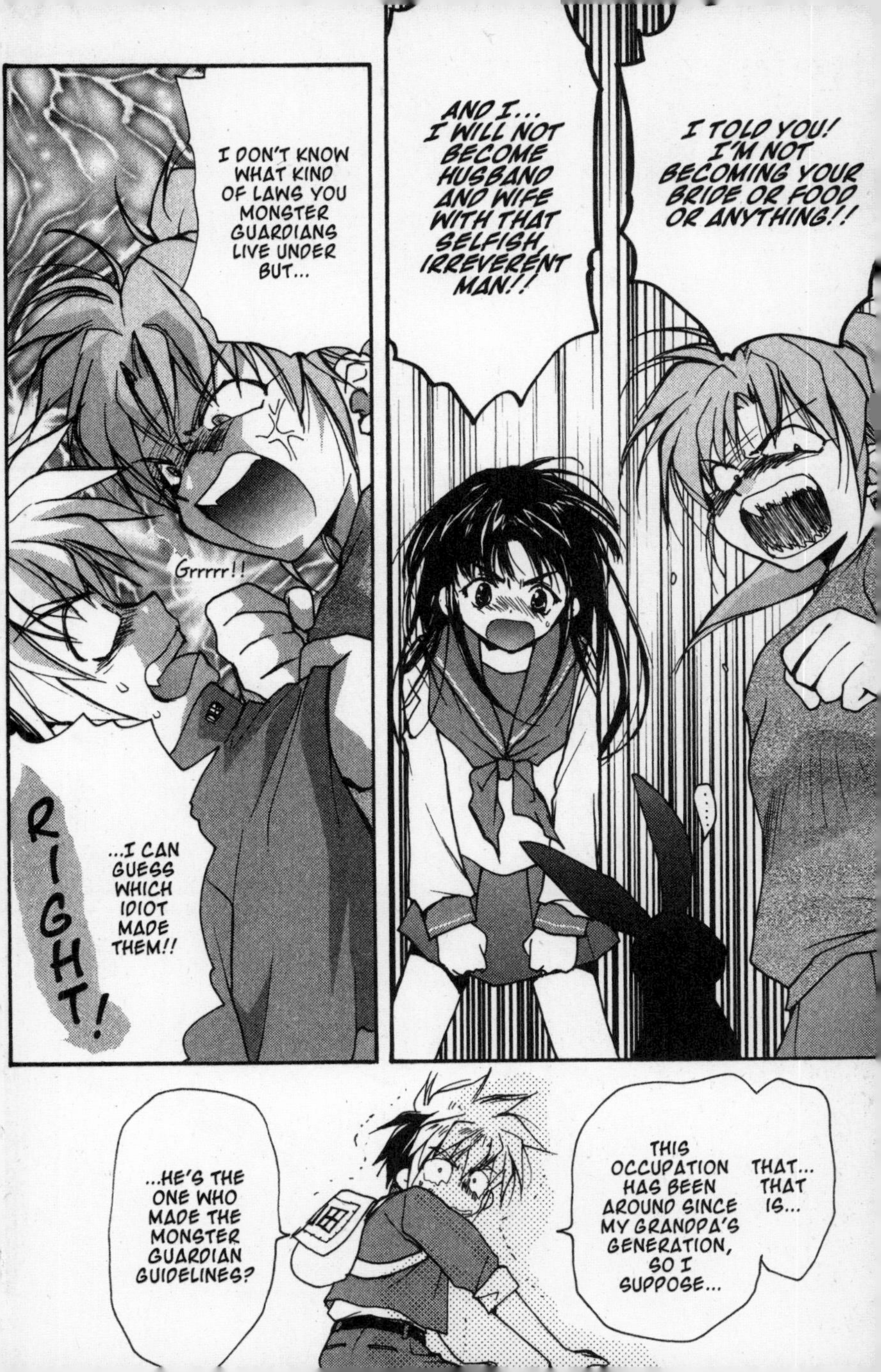
I TOLD YOU! I'M NOT BECOMING YOUR BRIDE OR FOOD OR ANYTHING!!
AND I... I WILL NOT BECOME HUSBAND AND WIFE WITH THAT SELFISH, IRREVERENT MAN!!
...
I DON'T KNOW WHAT KIND OF LAWS YOU MONSTER GUARDIANS LIVE UNDER BUT...
Grrrrr!!
...I CAN GUESS WHICH IDIOT MADE THEM!!
RIGHT!
THAT... THAT IS...
THIS OCCUPATION HAS BEEN AROUND SINCE MY GRANDPA'S GENERATION, SO I SUPPOSE...
...HE'S THE ONE WHO MADE THE MONSTER GUARDIAN GUIDELINES?

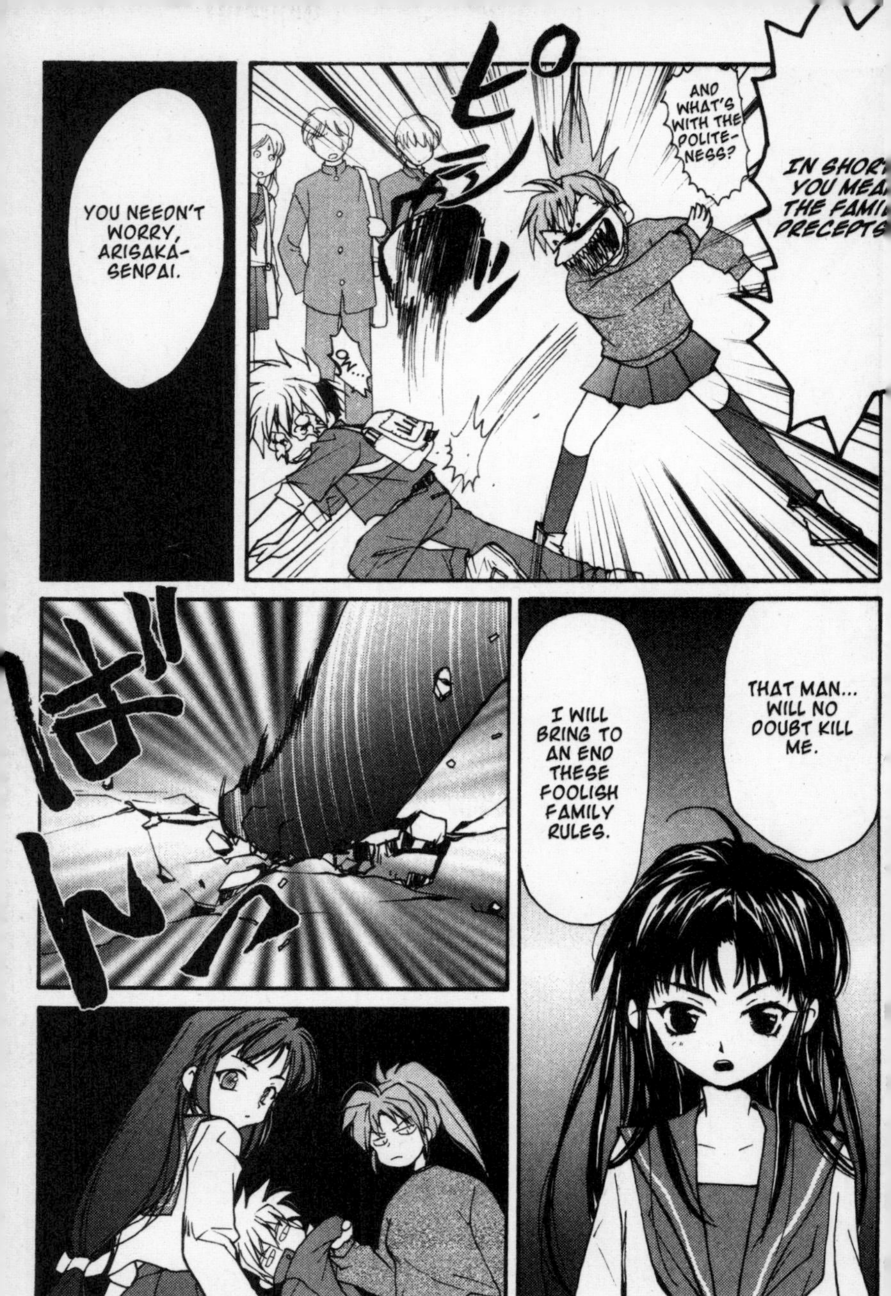
IN SHOR YOU MEA THE FAMI PRECEPTS
AND WHAT'S WITH THE POLITE-NESS?
OW...
YOU NEEDN'T WORRY, ARISAKA-SENPAI.
THAT MAN... WILL NO DOUBT KILL ME.
I WILL BRING TO AN END THESE FOOLISH FAMILY RULES.

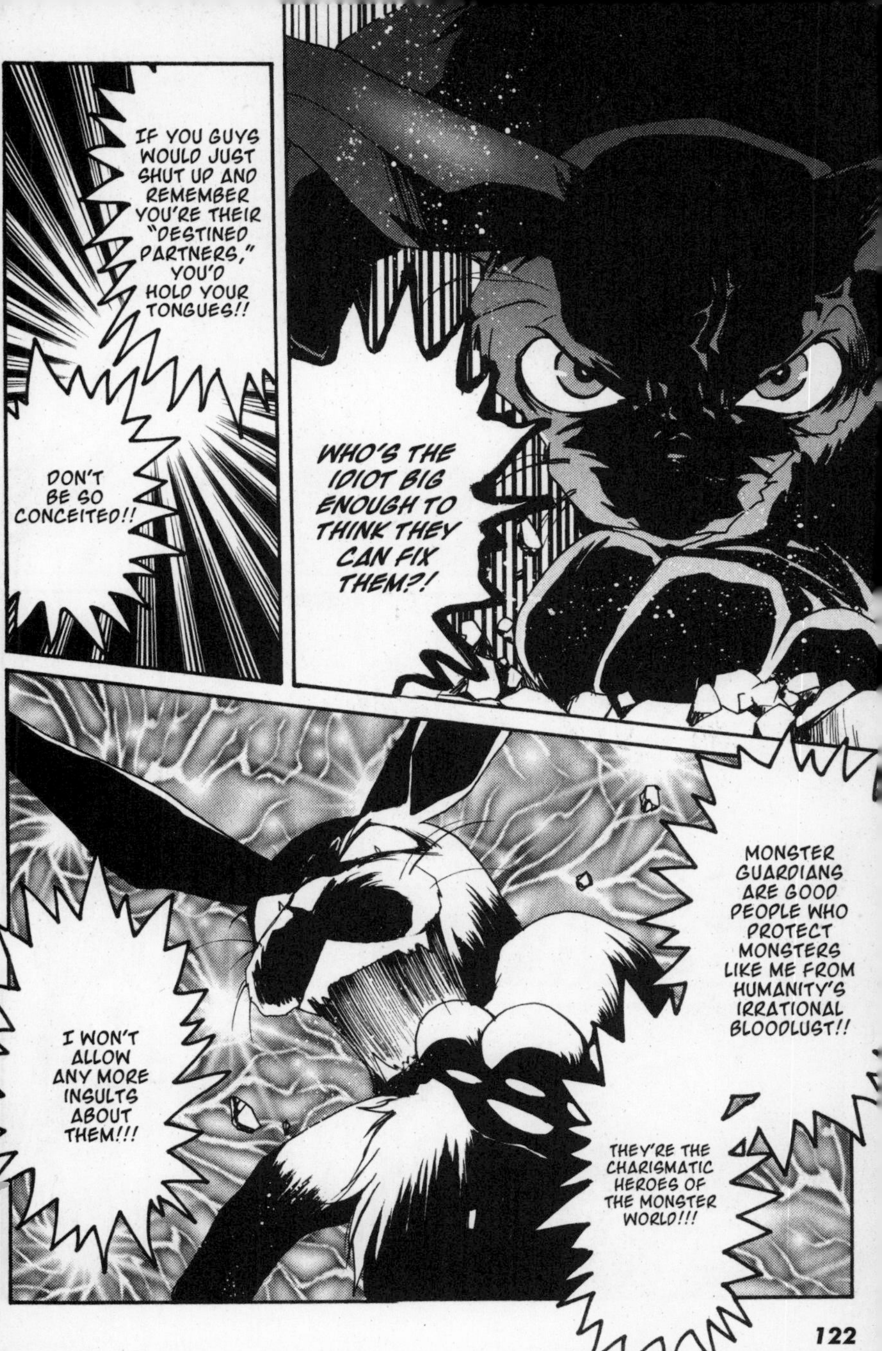
WHO'S THE IDIOT BIG ENOUGH TO THINK THEY CAN FIX THEM?!
IF YOU GUYS WOULD JUST SHUT UP AND REMEMBER YOU'RE THEIR "DESTINED PARTNERS," YOU'D HOLD YOUR TONGUES!!
DON'T BE SO CONCEITED!!
MONSTER GUARDIANS ARE GOOD PEOPLE WHO PROTECT MONSTERS LIKE ME FROM HUMANITY'S IRRATIONAL BLOODLUST!!
THEY'RE THE CHARISMATIC HEROES OF THE MONSTER WORLD!!!
I WON'T ALLOW ANY MORE INSULTS ABOUT THEM!!!

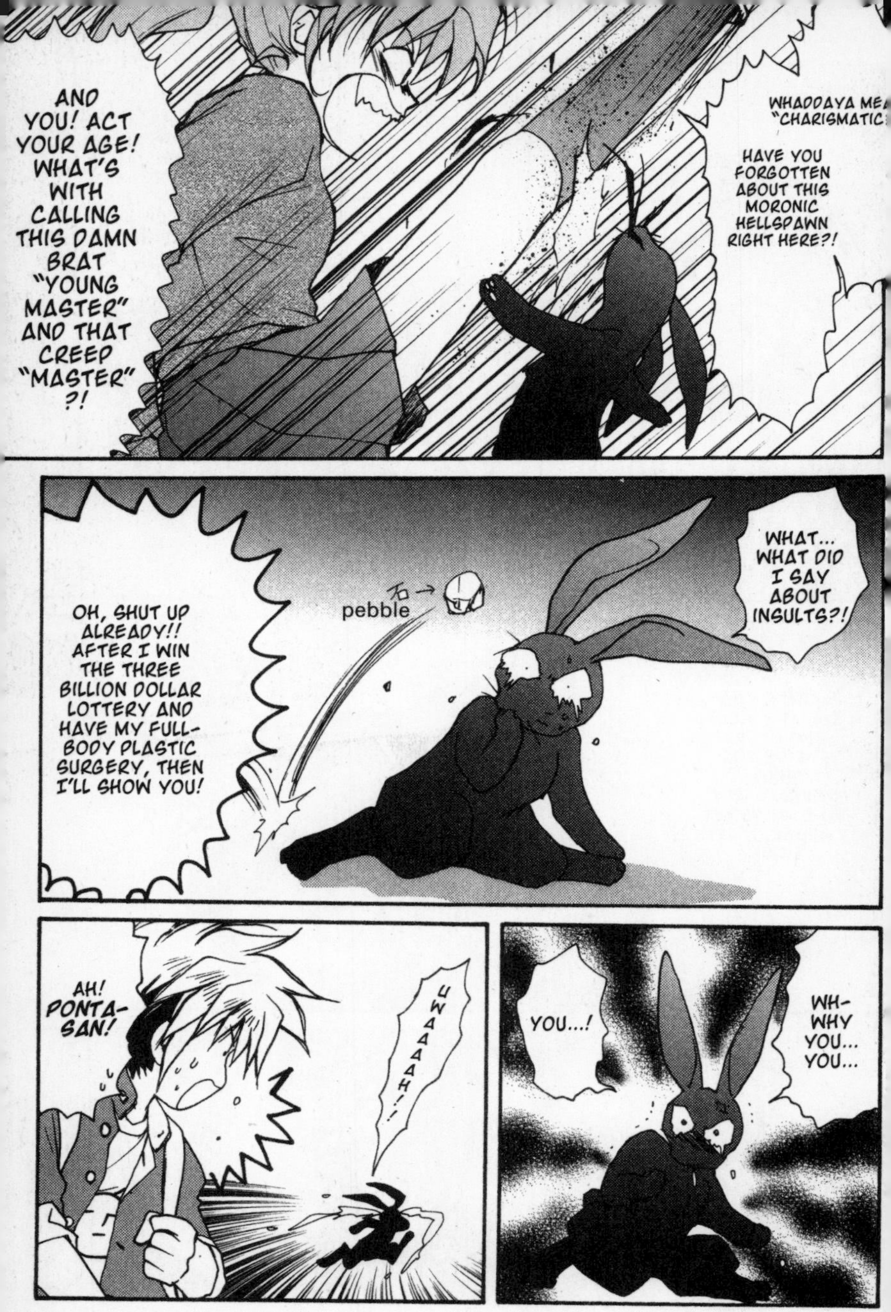
WHADDAYA MEA
"CHARISMATIC
HAVE YOU FORGOTTEN ABOUT THIS MORONIC HELLSPAWN RIGHT HERE?!
AND YOU! ACT YOUR AGE! WHAT'S WITH CALLING THIS DAMN BRAT "YOUNG MASTER" AND THAT CREEP "MASTER"?!
WHAT... WHAT DID I SAY ABOUT INSULTS?!
石→
pebble
OH, SHUT UP ALREADY!! AFTER I WIN THE THREE BILLION DOLLAR LOTTERY AND HAVE MY FULL-BODY PLASTIC SURGERY, THEN I'LL SHOW YOU!
WH- WHY YOU... YOU...
YOU...!
UWAAAAAH!!
AH! PONTA-SAN!

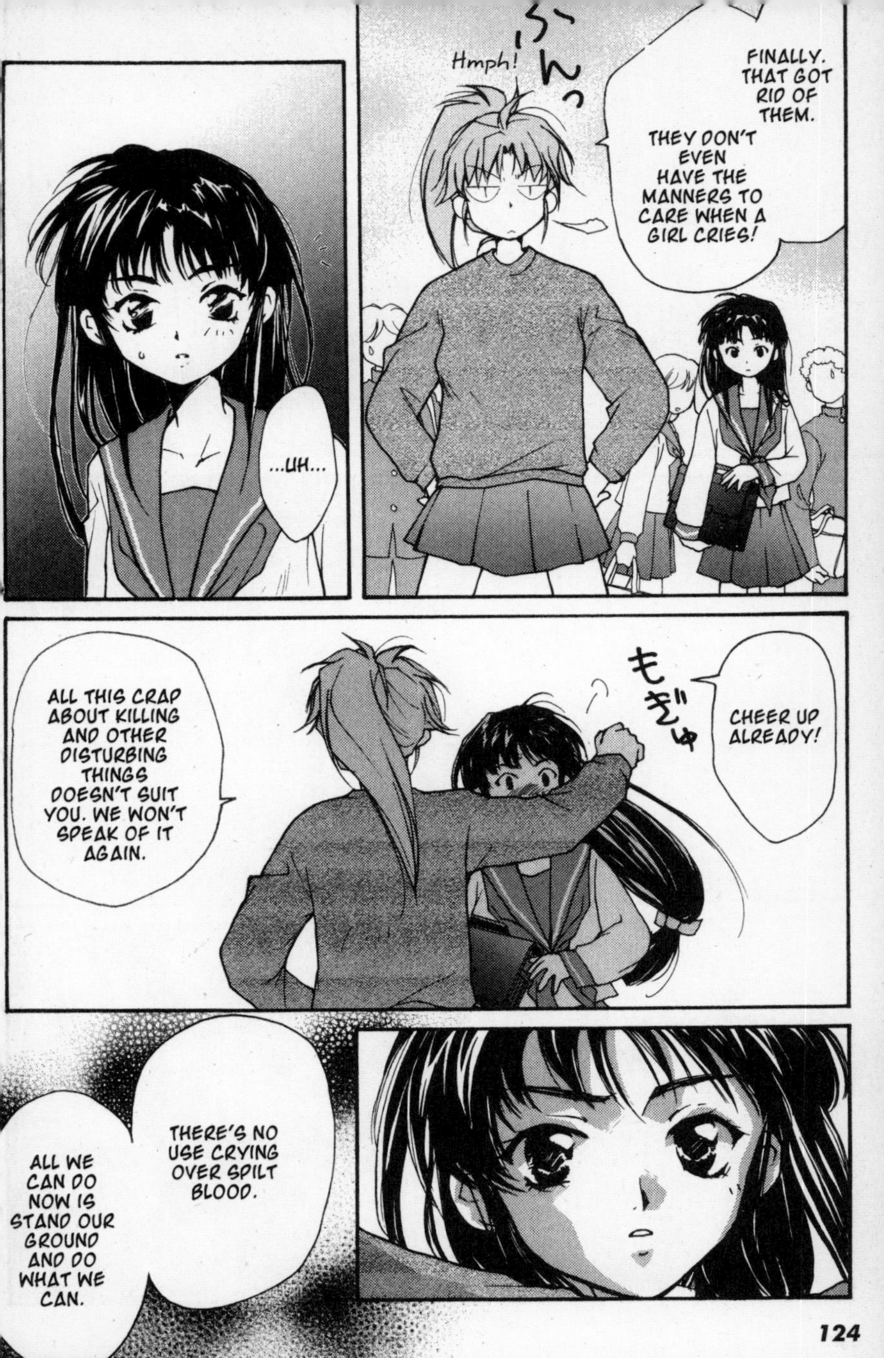
ふんっ
Hmph!
FINALLY. THAT GOT RID OF THEM.
THEY DON'T EVEN HAVE THE MANNERS TO CARE WHEN A GIRL CRIES!
...UH...
CHEER UP ALREADY!
もぎゅ
ALL THIS CRAP ABOUT KILLING AND OTHER DISTURBING THINGS DOESN'T SUIT YOU. WE WON'T SPEAK OF IT AGAIN.
THERE'S NO USE CRYING OVER SPILT BLOOD.
ALL WE CAN DO NOW IS STAND OUR GROUND AND DO WHAT WE CAN.

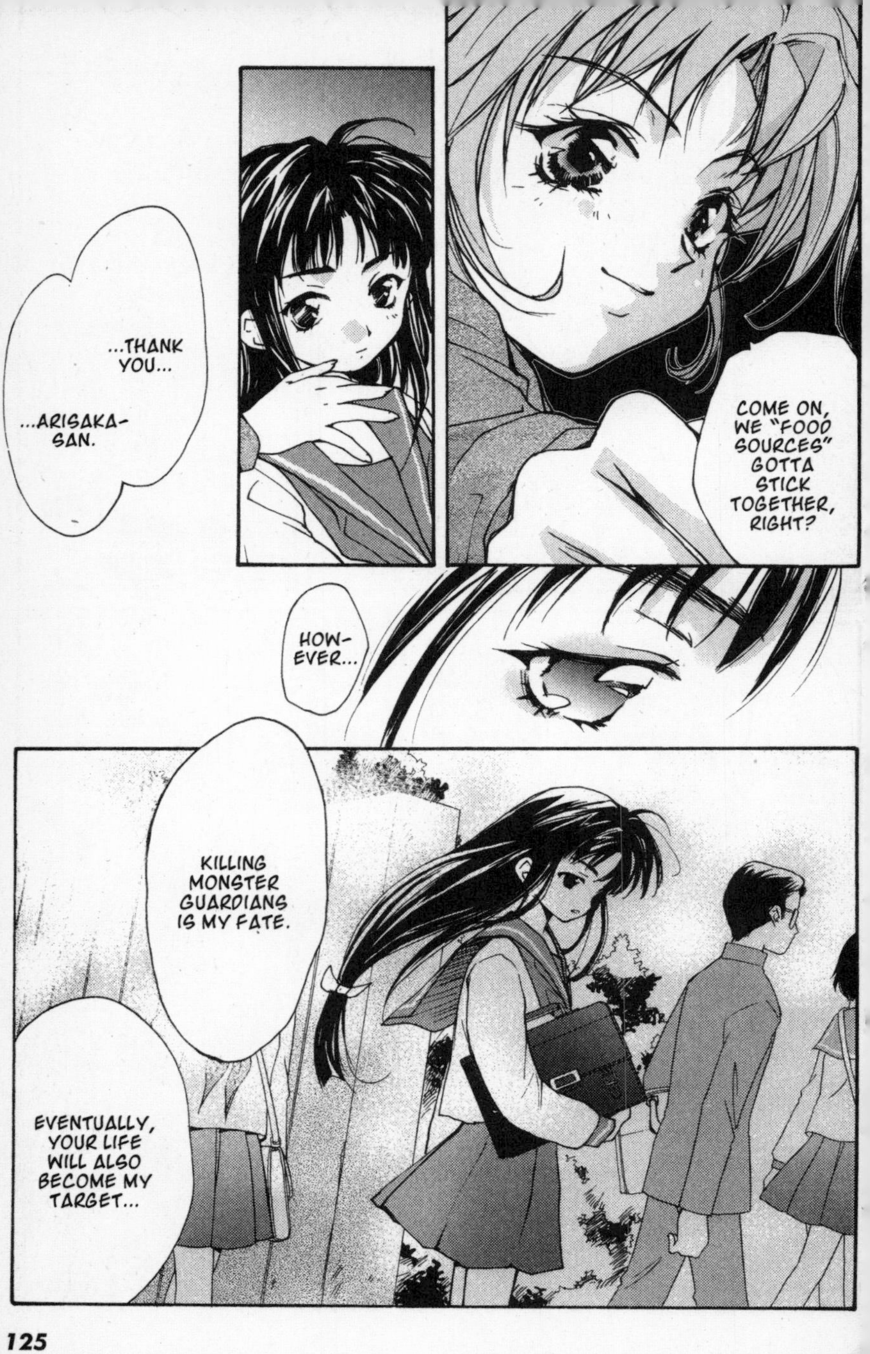
COME ON, WE "FOOD SOURCES" GOTTA STICK TOGETHER, RIGHT?
...THANK YOU...
...ARISAKA-SAN.
HOW-EVER...
KILLING MONSTER GUARDIANS IS MY FATE.
EVENTUALLY, YOUR LIFE WILL ALSO BECOME MY TARGET...

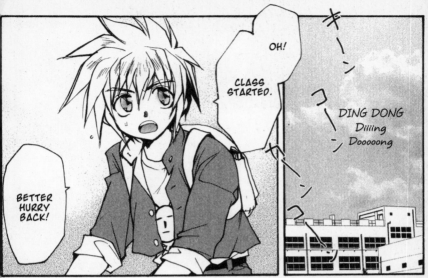

キーンコーンカーンコーン
DING DONG
Diiiing Doooong
OH!
CLASS STARTED.
BETTER HURRY BACK!
COME ON, PONTA-SAN, STOP CRYING.
SURE, NAO-CHAN WAS A LITTLE MEAN, BUT AT LEAST SHE WAS HONEST.
THAT ISN'T COMFORTING TO HEAR!!
JUST THINKING THAT MY PRECIOUS YOUNG MASTER IS PREY TO SUCH A RUDE GIRL LIKE THAT...!
Sniffle
YOUNG MASTER, WHOM I TENDERLY, CAREFULLY, WHOLE-HEARTEDLY RAISED!
ぐすぐす
SNIFFLE
NAO-CHAN MAY BE RUDE, BUT SHE'S A GOOD PERSON.
IN WHAT WAY?!

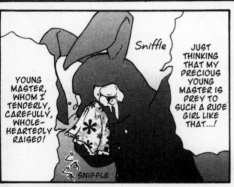

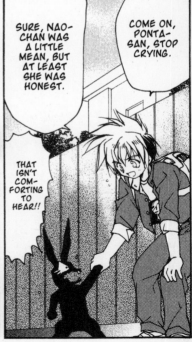

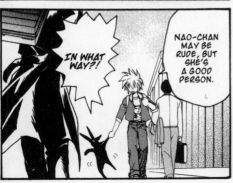

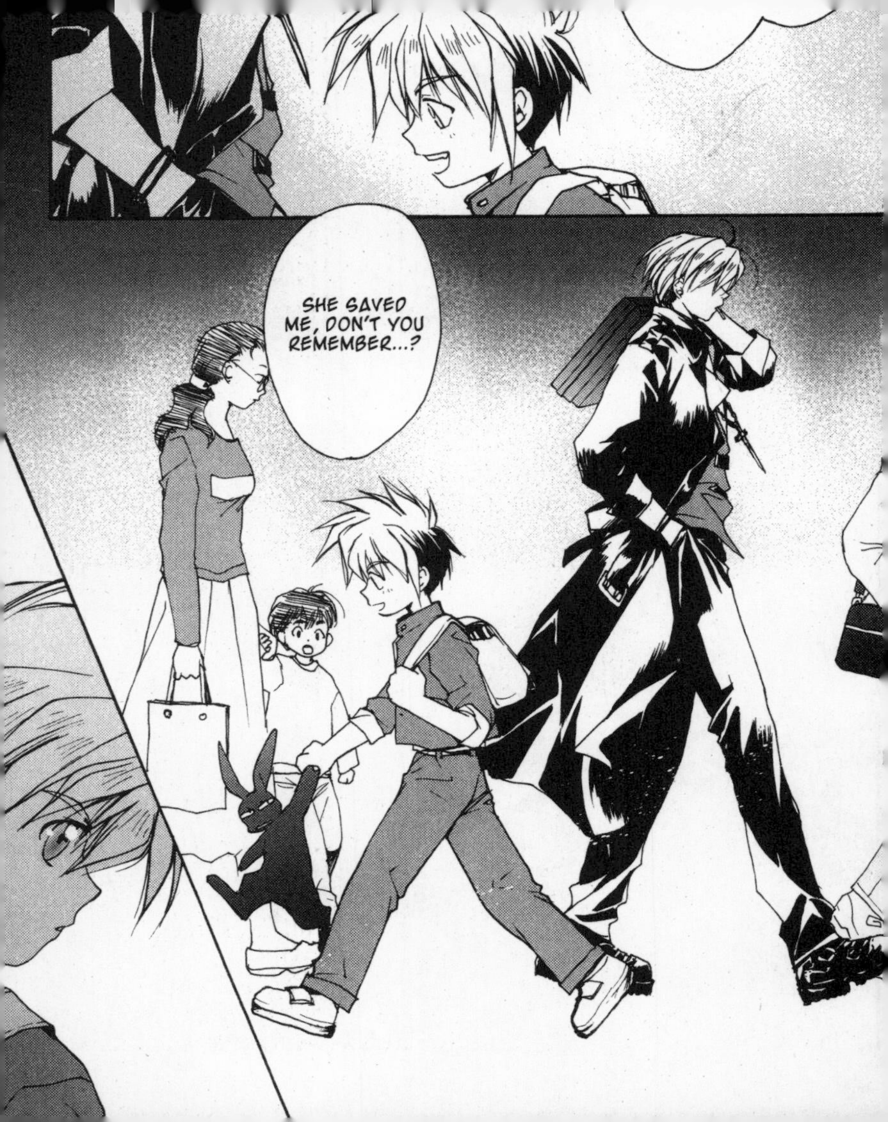
SHE SAVED ME, DON'T YOU REMEMBER...?

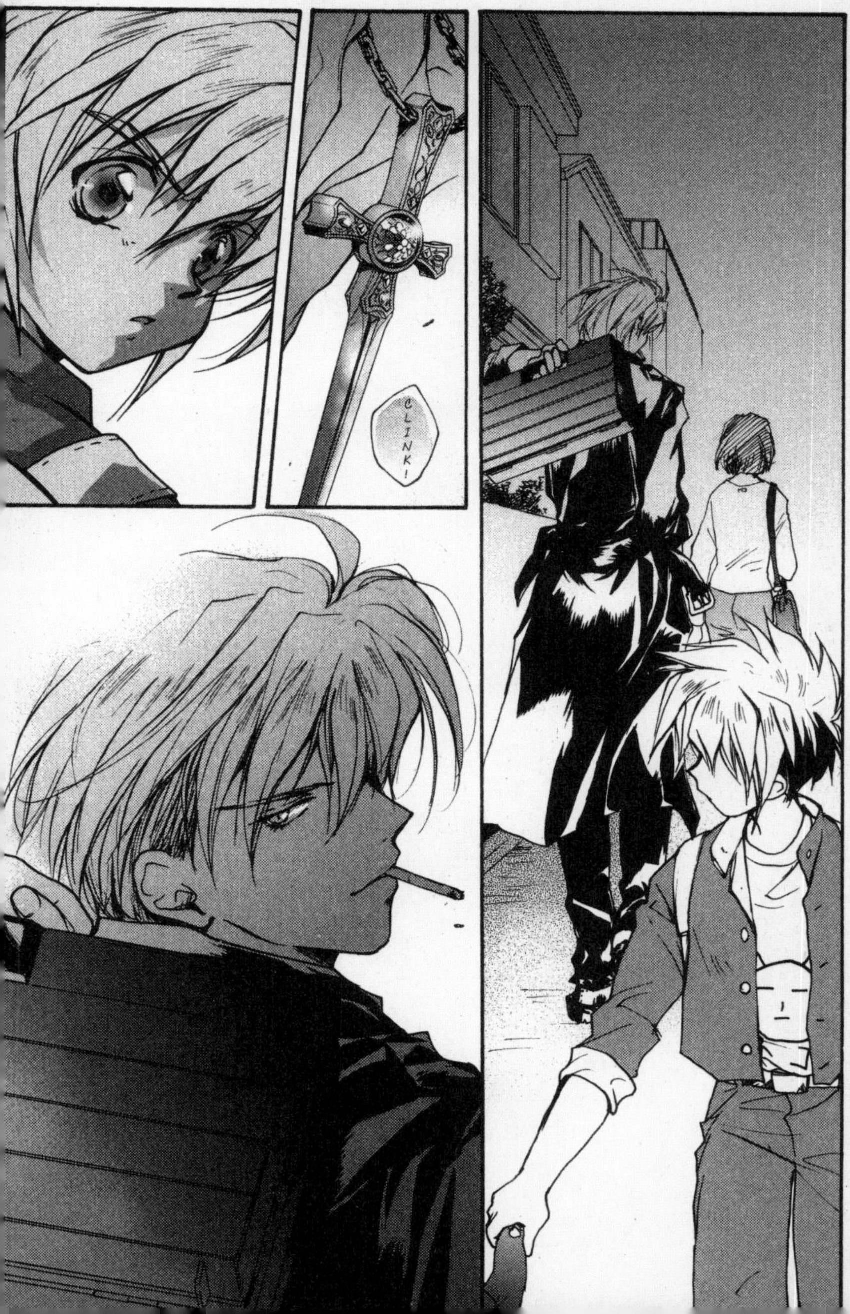
CLINK!

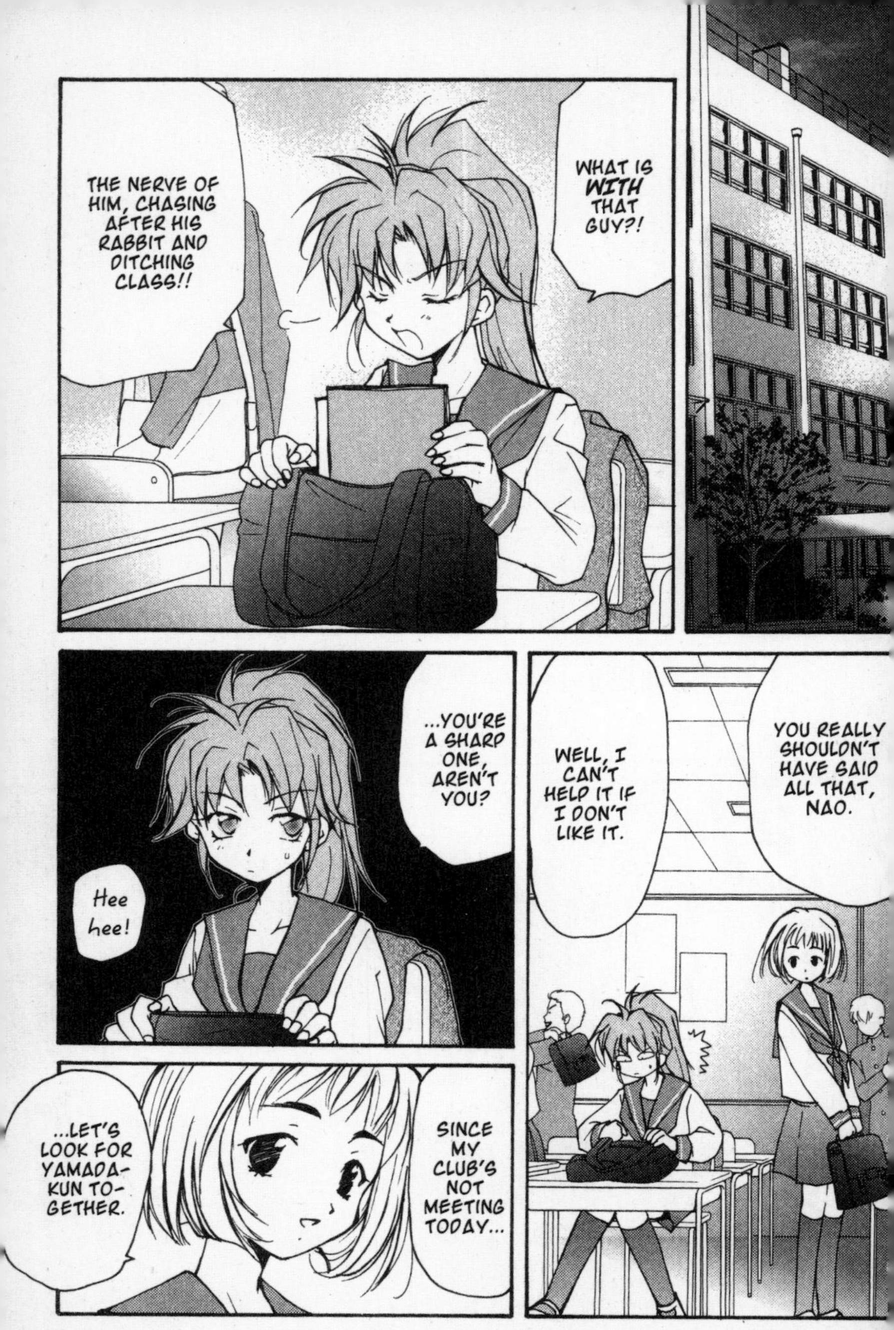
WHAT IS *WITH* THAT GUY?!
THE NERVE OF HIM, CHASING AFTER HIS RABBIT AND DITCHING CLASS!!
YOU REALLY SHOULDN'T HAVE SAID ALL THAT, NAO.
WELL, I CAN'T HELP IT IF I DON'T LIKE IT.
...YOU'RE A SHARP ONE, AREN'T YOU?
Hee hee!
SINCE MY CLUB'S NOT MEETING TODAY...
...LET'S LOOK FOR YAMADA-KUN TO-GETHER.

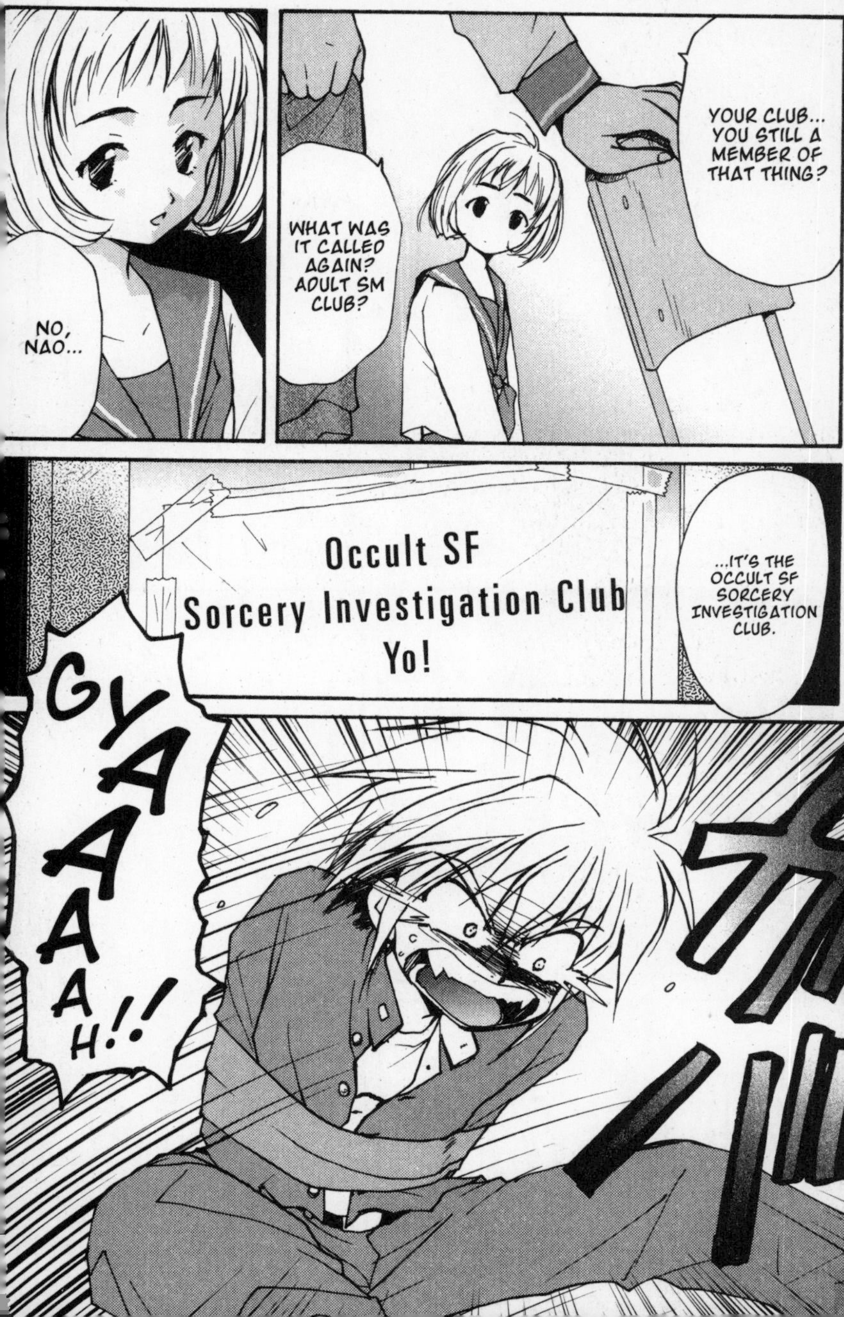
YOUR CLUB... YOU STILL A MEMBER OF THAT THING?
WHAT WAS IT CALLED AGAIN? ADULT SM CLUB?
NO, NAO...
...IT'S THE OCCULT SF SORCERY INVESTIGATION CLUB.
Occult SF Sorcery Investigation Club Yo!
GYAAAAAH!!!

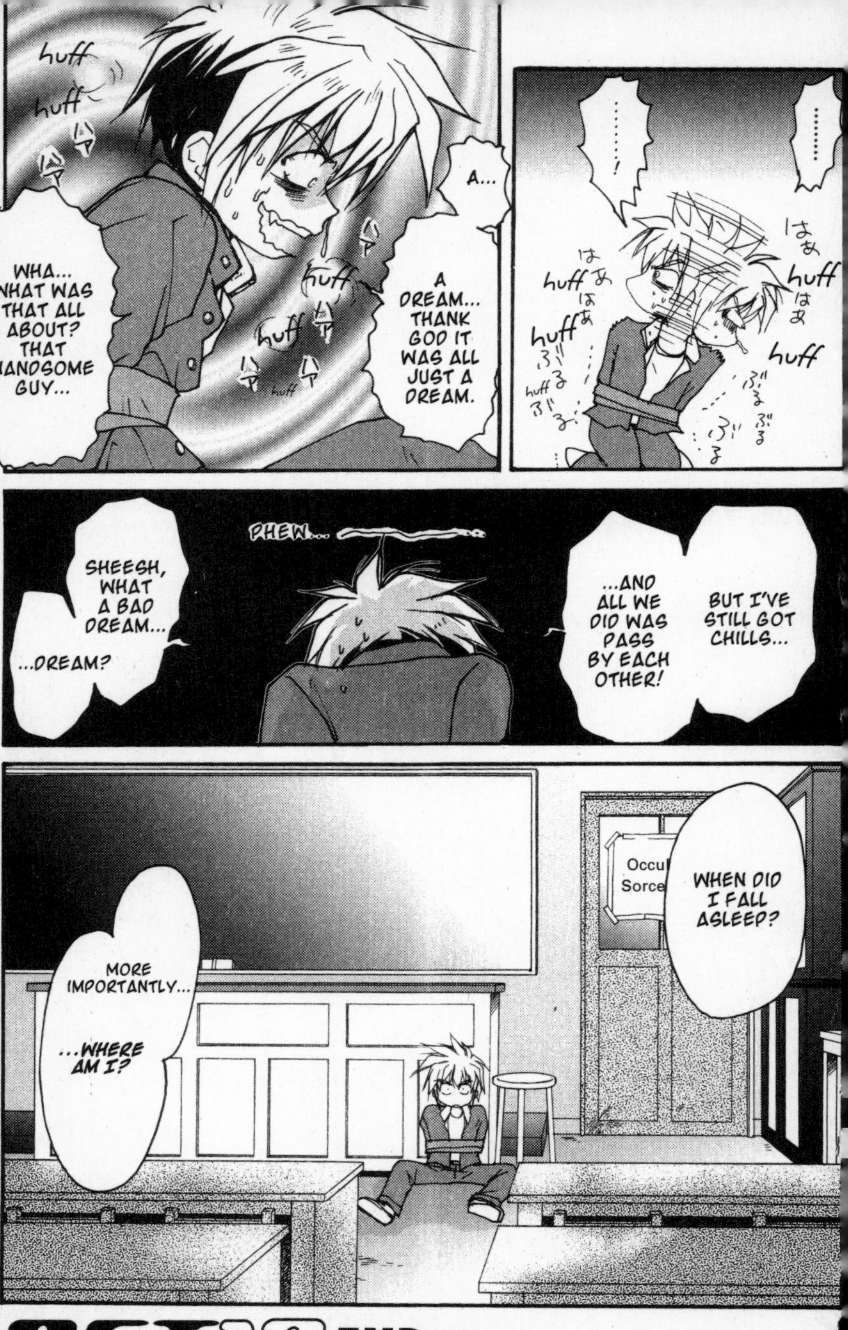
......
......!
huff
huff
huff
huff
A...
A DREAM... THANK GOD IT WAS ALL JUST A DREAM.
huff
huff
huff
huff
huff
WHA... WHAT WAS THAT ALL ABOUT? THAT HANDSOME GUY...
BUT I'VE STILL GOT CHILLS...
...AND ALL WE DID WAS PASS BY EACH OTHER!
PHEW...
SHEESH, WHAT A BAD DREAM...
...DREAM?
WHEN DID I FALL ASLEEP?
MORE IMPORTANTLY...
...WHERE AM I?

ACT 10 END

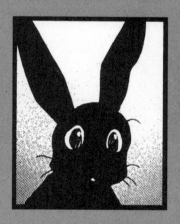

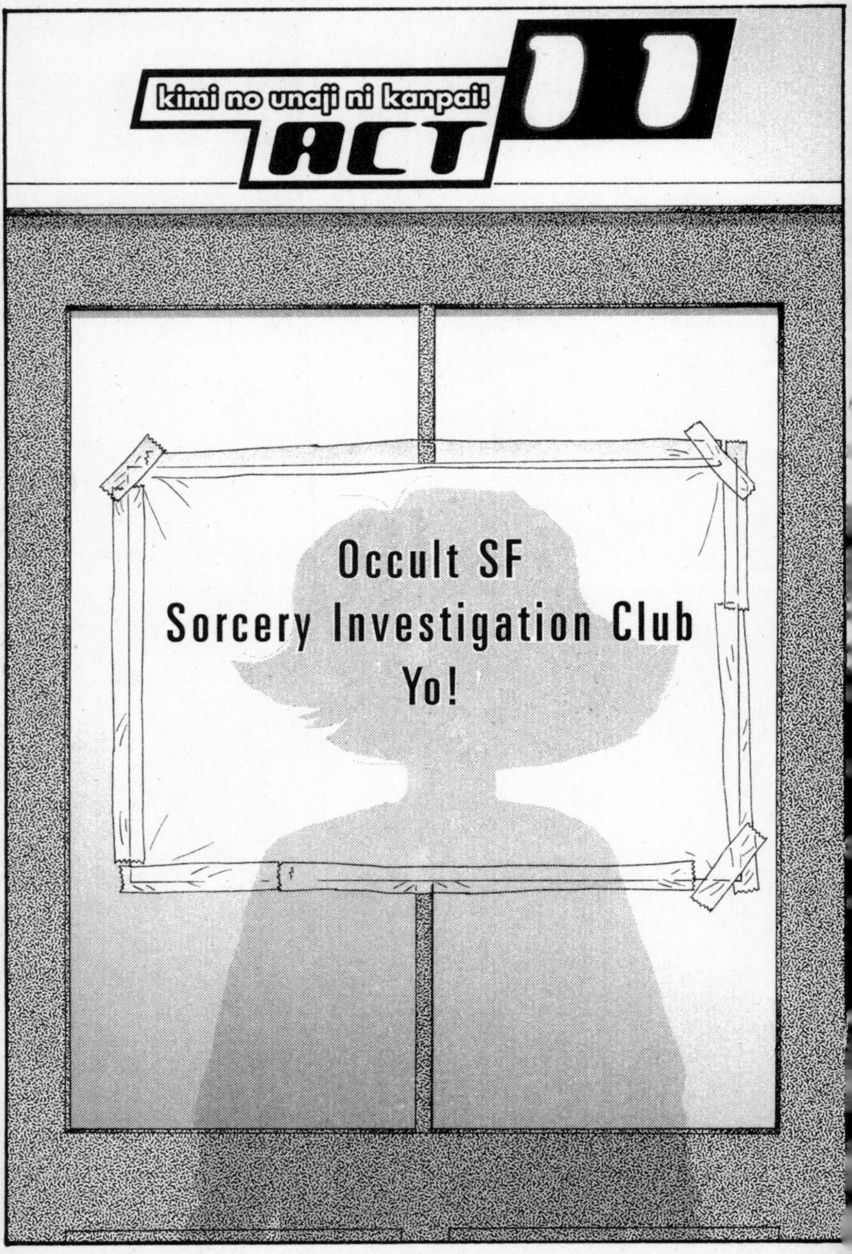
kimi no unaji ni kanpai!
ACT 11
Occult SF
Sorcery Investigation Club
Yo!

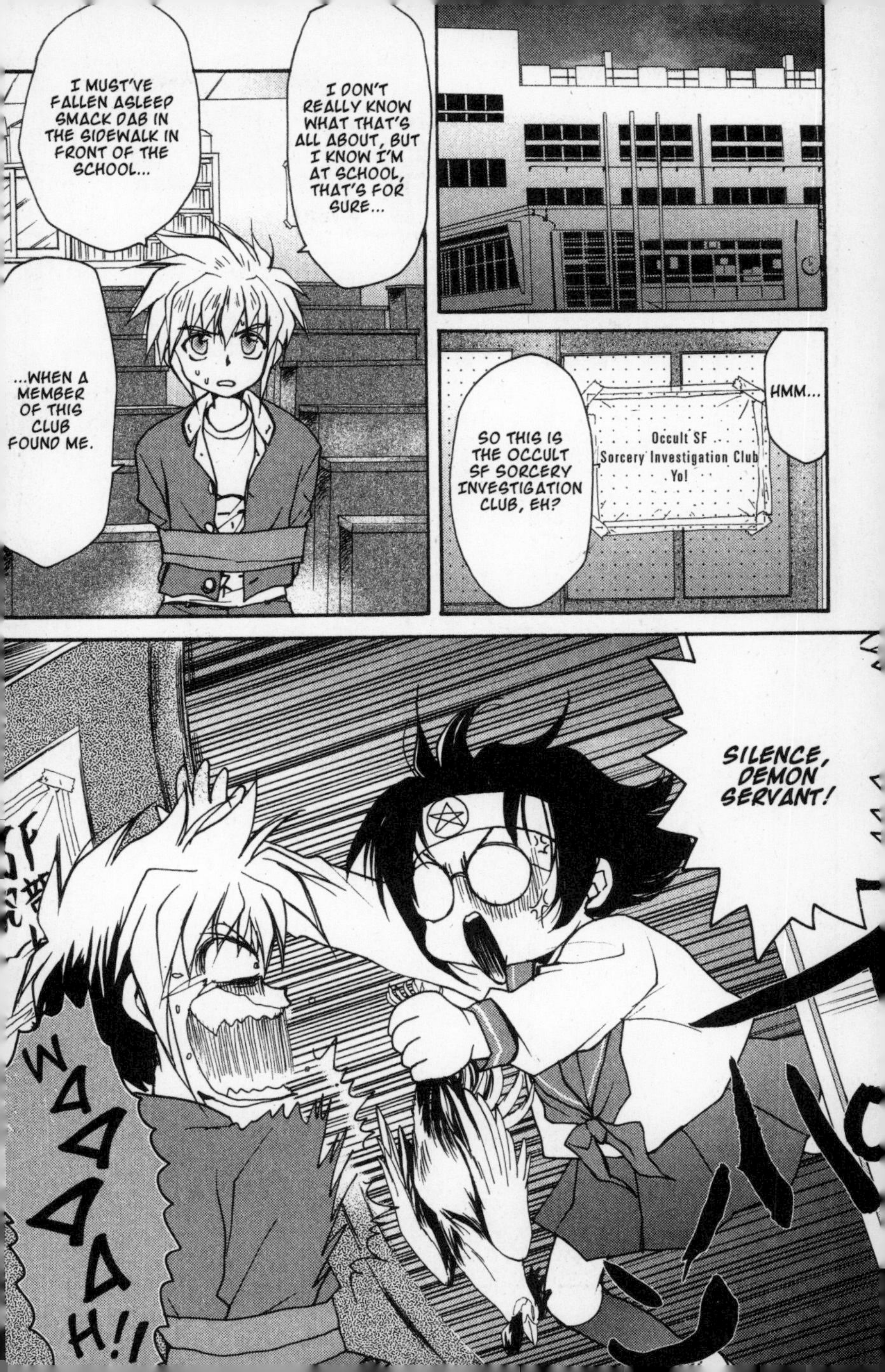
HMM...
Occult SF Sorcery Investigation Club Yo!
SO THIS IS THE OCCULT SF SORCERY INVESTIGATION CLUB, EH?
I DON'T REALLY KNOW WHAT THAT'S ALL ABOUT, BUT I KNOW I'M AT SCHOOL, THAT'S FOR SURE...
I MUST'VE FALLEN ASLEEP SMACK DAB IN THE SIDEWALK IN FRONT OF THE SCHOOL...
...WHEN A MEMBER OF THIS CLUB FOUND ME.
SILENCE, DEMON SERVANT!
WAAAAAH!!

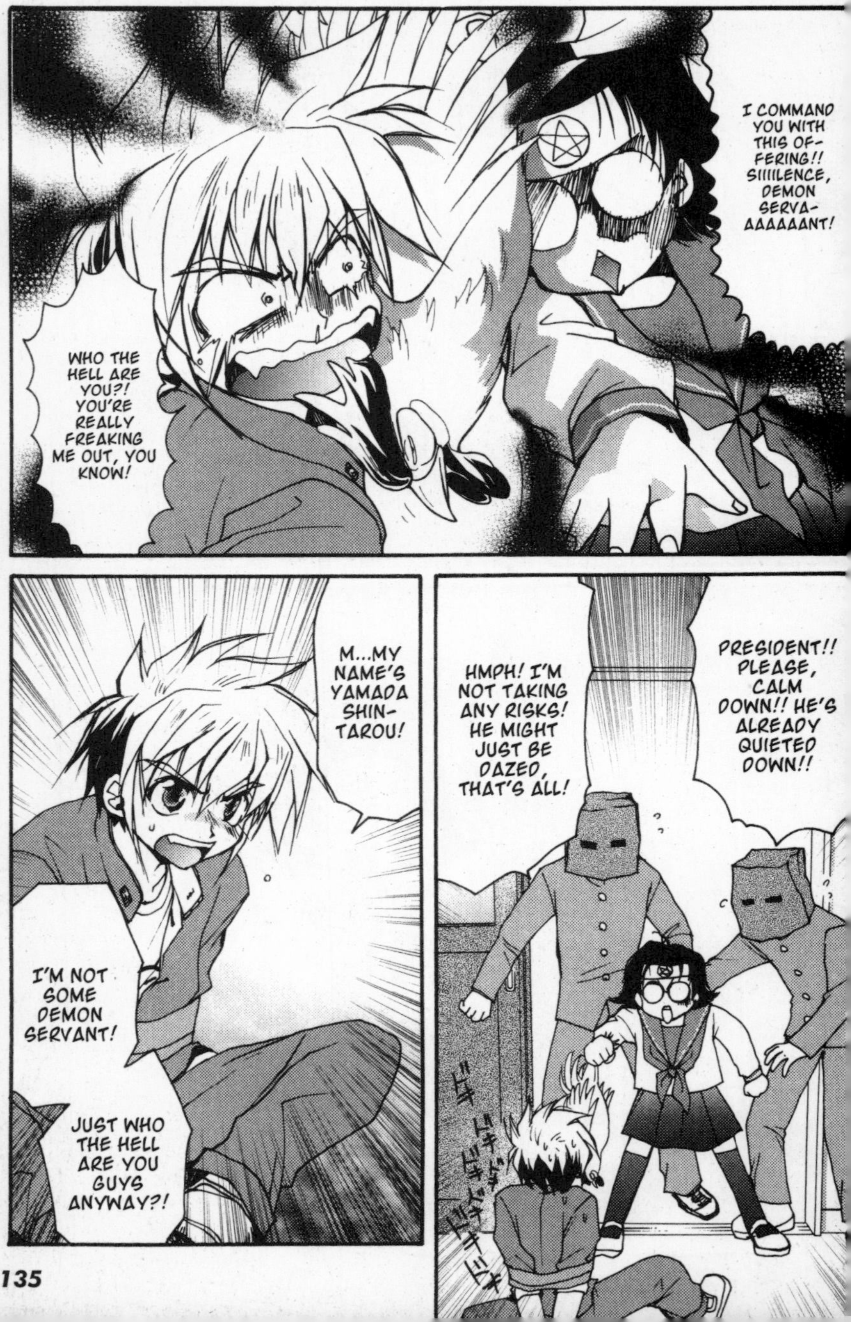
I COMMAND YOU WITH THIS OF-FERING!! SIIIILENCE, DEMON SERVA-AAAAAAANT!
WHO THE HELL ARE YOU?! YOU'RE REALLY FREAKING ME OUT, YOU KNOW!
PRESIDENT!! PLEASE, CALM DOWN!! HE'S ALREADY QUIETED DOWN!!
HMPH! I'M NOT TAKING ANY RISKS! HE MIGHT JUST BE DAZED, THAT'S ALL!
M...MY NAME'S YAMADA SHIN-TAROU!
I'M NOT SOME DEMON SERVANT!
JUST WHO THE HELL ARE YOU GUYS ANYWAY?!

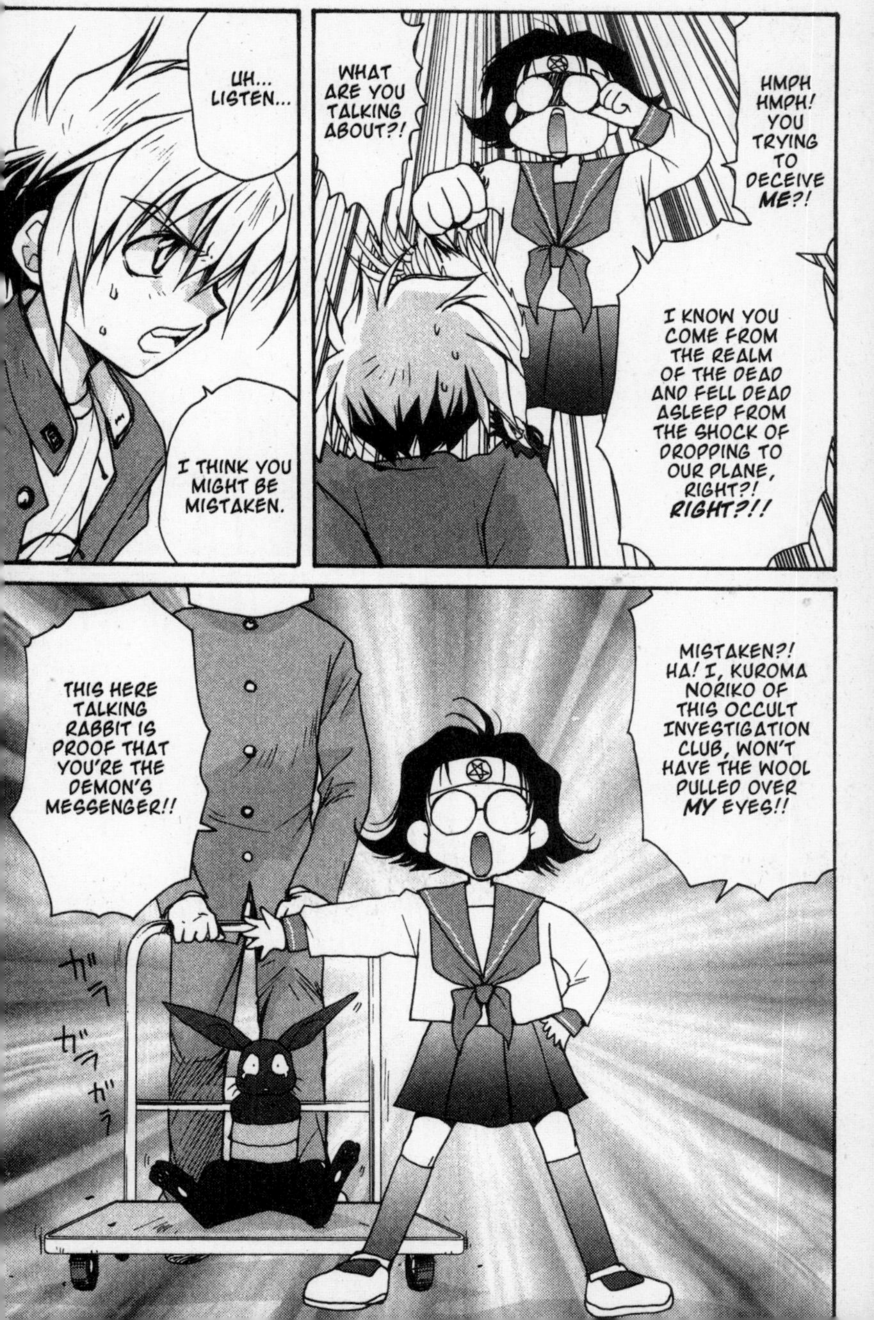
HMPH HMPH! YOU TRYING TO DECEIVE ME?!
WHAT ARE YOU TALKING ABOUT?!
I KNOW YOU COME FROM THE REALM OF THE DEAD AND FELL DEAD ASLEEP FROM THE SHOCK OF DROPPING TO OUR PLANE, RIGHT?! RIGHT?!!
UH... LISTEN...
I THINK YOU MIGHT BE MISTAKEN.
MISTAKEN?! HA! I, KUROMA NORIKO OF THIS OCCULT INVESTIGATION CLUB, WON'T HAVE THE WOOL PULLED OVER MY EYES!!
THIS HERE TALKING RABBIT IS PROOF THAT YOU'RE THE DEMON'S MESSENGER!!
ガラ
ガラガラ

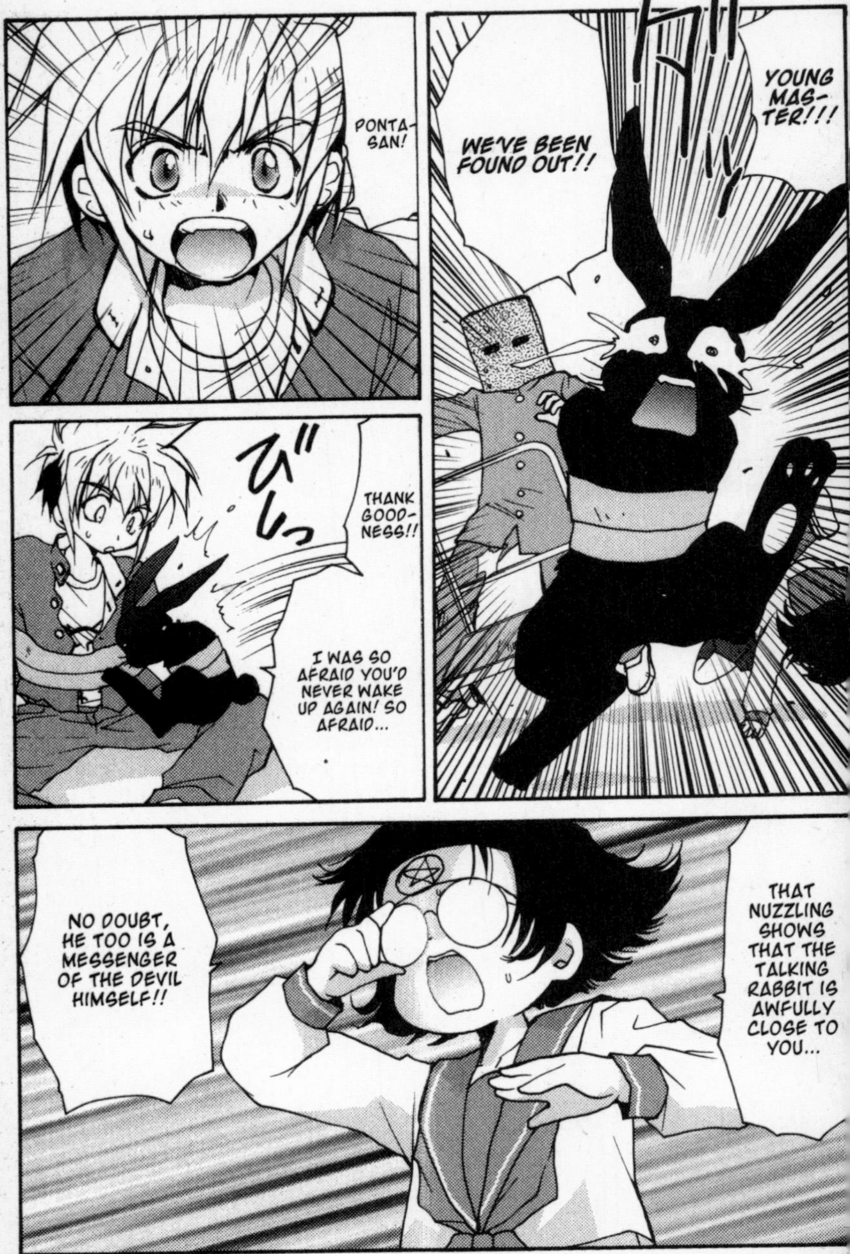
YOUNG MAS-TER!!!
WE'VE BEEN FOUND OUT!!
PONTA-SAN!
THANK GOOD-NESS!!
I WAS SO AFRAID YOU'D NEVER WAKE UP AGAIN! SO AFRAID...
THAT NUZZLING SHOWS THAT THE TALKING RABBIT IS AWFULLY CLOSE TO YOU...
NO DOUBT, HE TOO IS A MESSENGER OF THE DEVIL HIMSELF!!

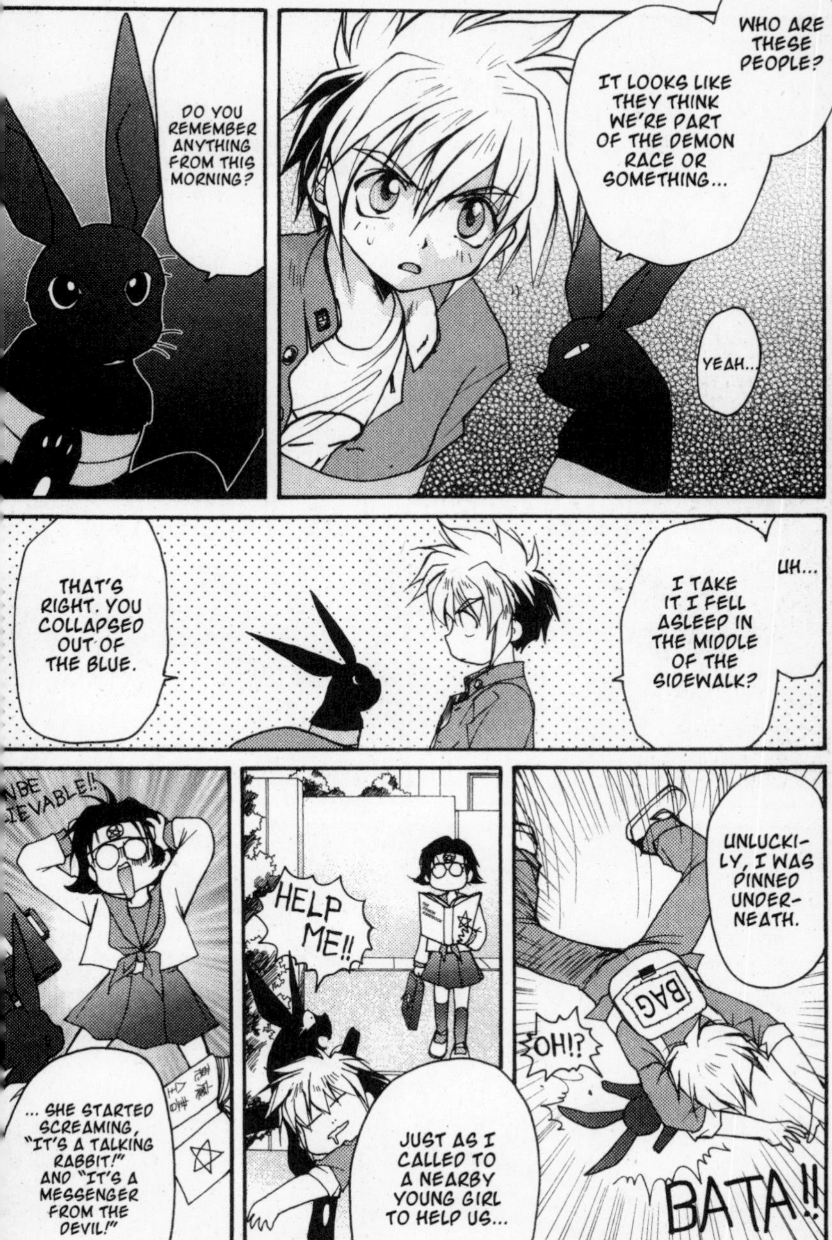
WHO ARE THESE PEOPLE?
IT LOOKS LIKE THEY THINK WE'RE PART OF THE DEMON RACE OR SOMETHING...
YEAH...
DO YOU REMEMBER ANYTHING FROM THIS MORNING?
UH...
I TAKE IT I FELL ASLEEP IN THE MIDDLE OF THE SIDEWALK?
THAT'S RIGHT. YOU COLLAPSED OUT OF THE BLUE.
UNLUCKILY, I WAS PINNED UNDERNEATH.
OH!?
BATA!!
BAG
JUST AS I CALLED TO A NEARBY YOUNG GIRL TO HELP US...
HELP ME!!
NBE IEVABLE!!
... SHE STARTED SCREAMING, "IT'S A TALKING RABBIT!" AND "IT'S A MESSENGER FROM THE DEVIL!"

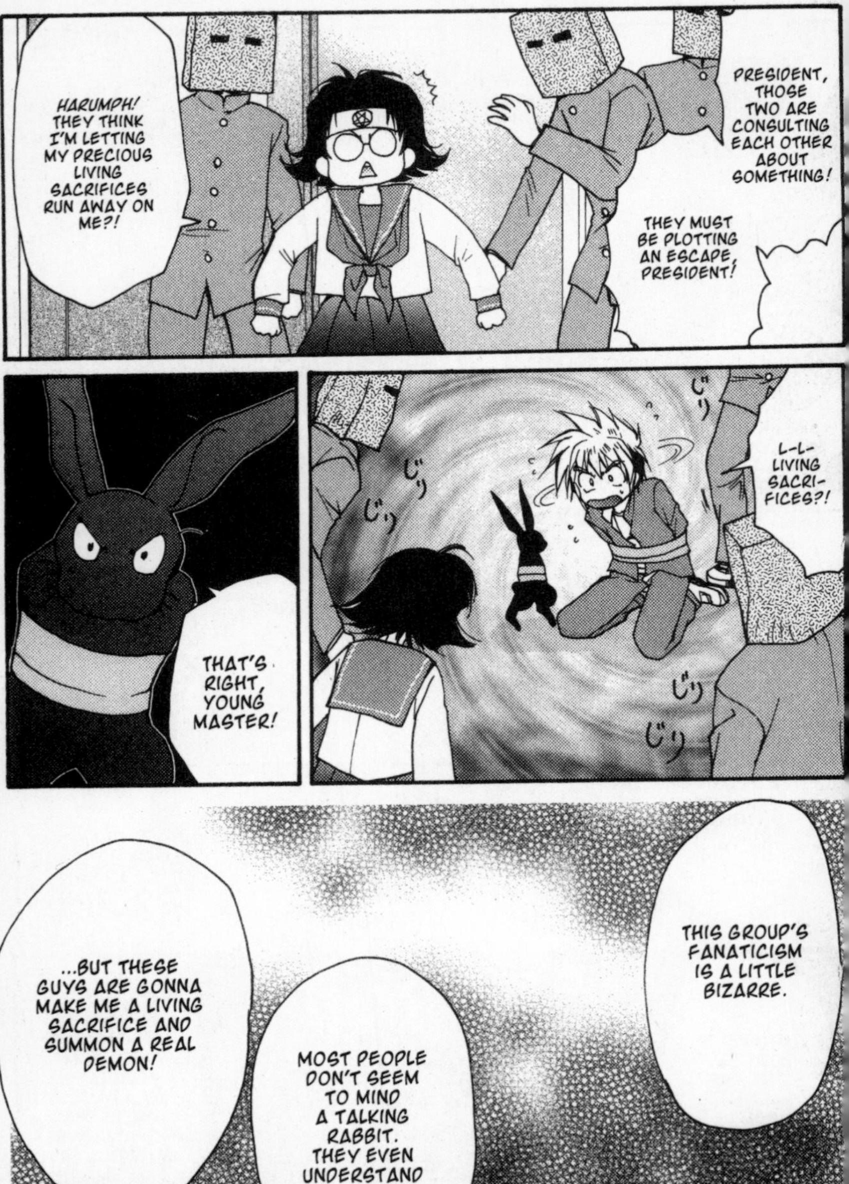
PRESIDENT, THOSE TWO ARE CONSULTING EACH OTHER ABOUT SOMETHING!
THEY MUST BE PLOTTING AN ESCAPE, PRESIDENT!
HARUMPH! THEY THINK I'M LETTING MY PRECIOUS LIVING SACRIFICES RUN AWAY ON ME?!
じり
L-L-LIVING SACRI-FICES?!
じり
じり
じり
じり
THAT'S RIGHT, YOUNG MASTER!
THIS GROUP'S FANATICISM IS A LITTLE BIZARRE.
MOST PEOPLE DON'T SEEM TO MIND A TALKING RABBIT. THEY EVEN UNDERSTAND ME...
...BUT THESE GUYS ARE GONNA MAKE ME A LIVING SACRIFICE AND SUMMON A REAL DEMON!

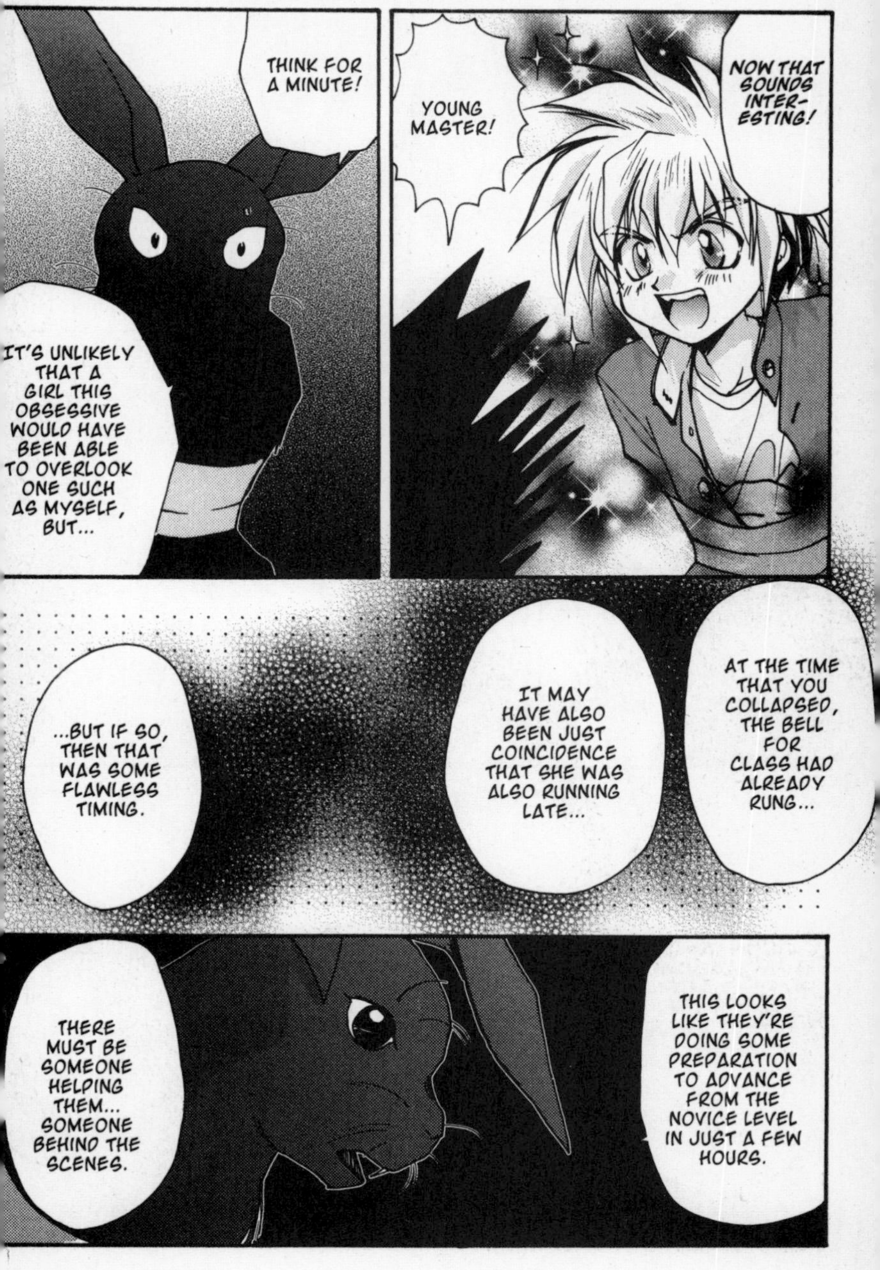
NOW THAT SOUNDS INTER-ESTING!
YOUNG MASTER!
THINK FOR A MINUTE!
IT'S UNLIKELY THAT A GIRL THIS OBSESSIVE WOULD HAVE BEEN ABLE TO OVERLOOK ONE SUCH AS MYSELF, BUT...
AT THE TIME THAT YOU COLLAPSED, THE BELL FOR CLASS HAD ALREADY RUNG...
IT MAY HAVE ALSO BEEN JUST COINCIDENCE THAT SHE WAS ALSO RUNNING LATE...
...BUT IF SO, THEN THAT WAS SOME FLAWLESS TIMING.
THIS LOOKS LIKE THEY'RE DOING SOME PREPARATION TO ADVANCE FROM THE NOVICE LEVEL IN JUST A FEW HOURS.
THERE MUST BE SOMEONE HELPING THEM... SOMEONE BEHIND THE SCENES.

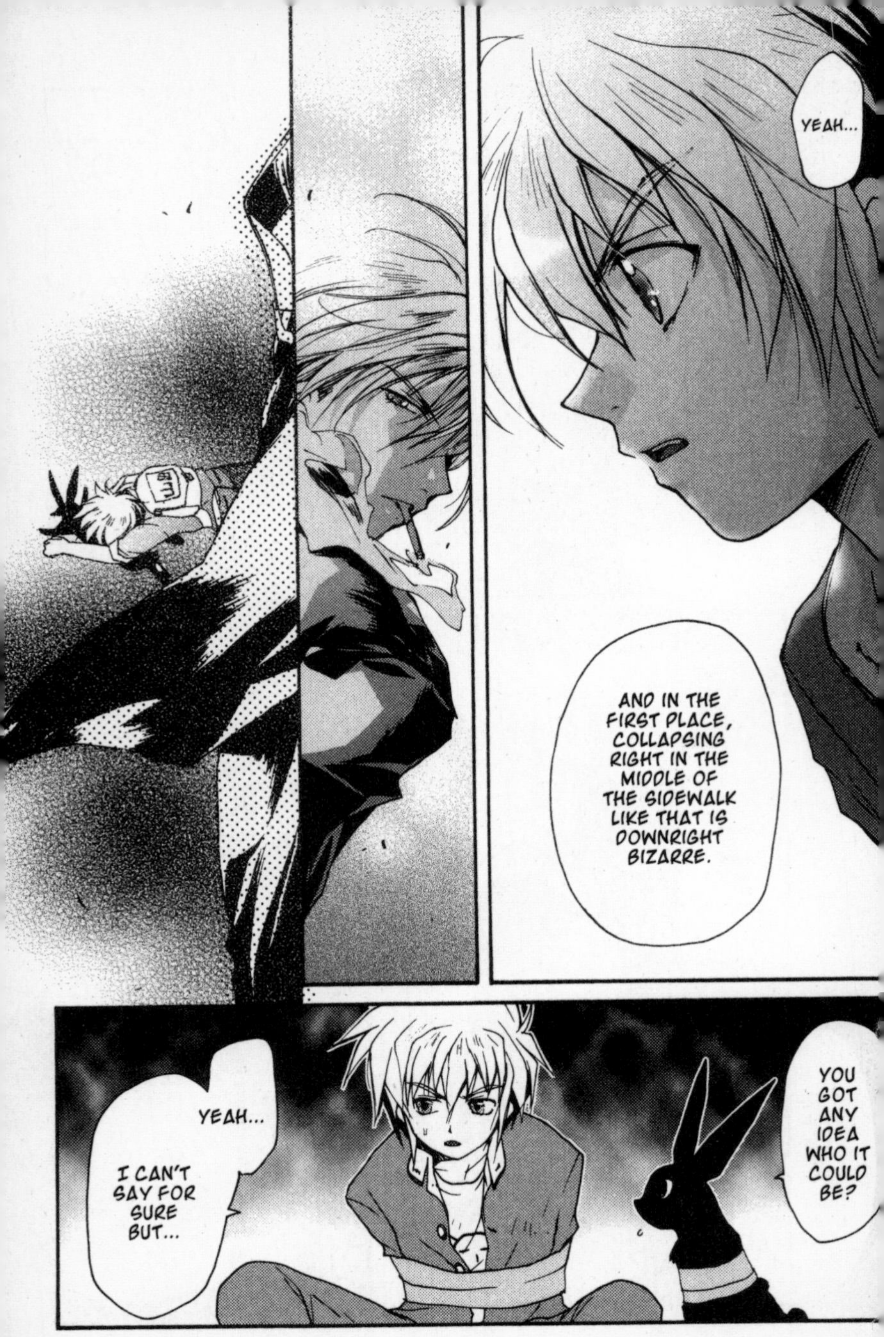
YEAH...
AND IN THE FIRST PLACE, COLLAPSING RIGHT IN THE MIDDLE OF THE SIDEWALK LIKE THAT IS DOWNRIGHT BIZARRE.
YOU GOT ANY IDEA WHO IT COULD BE?
YEAH...
I CAN'T SAY FOR SURE BUT...

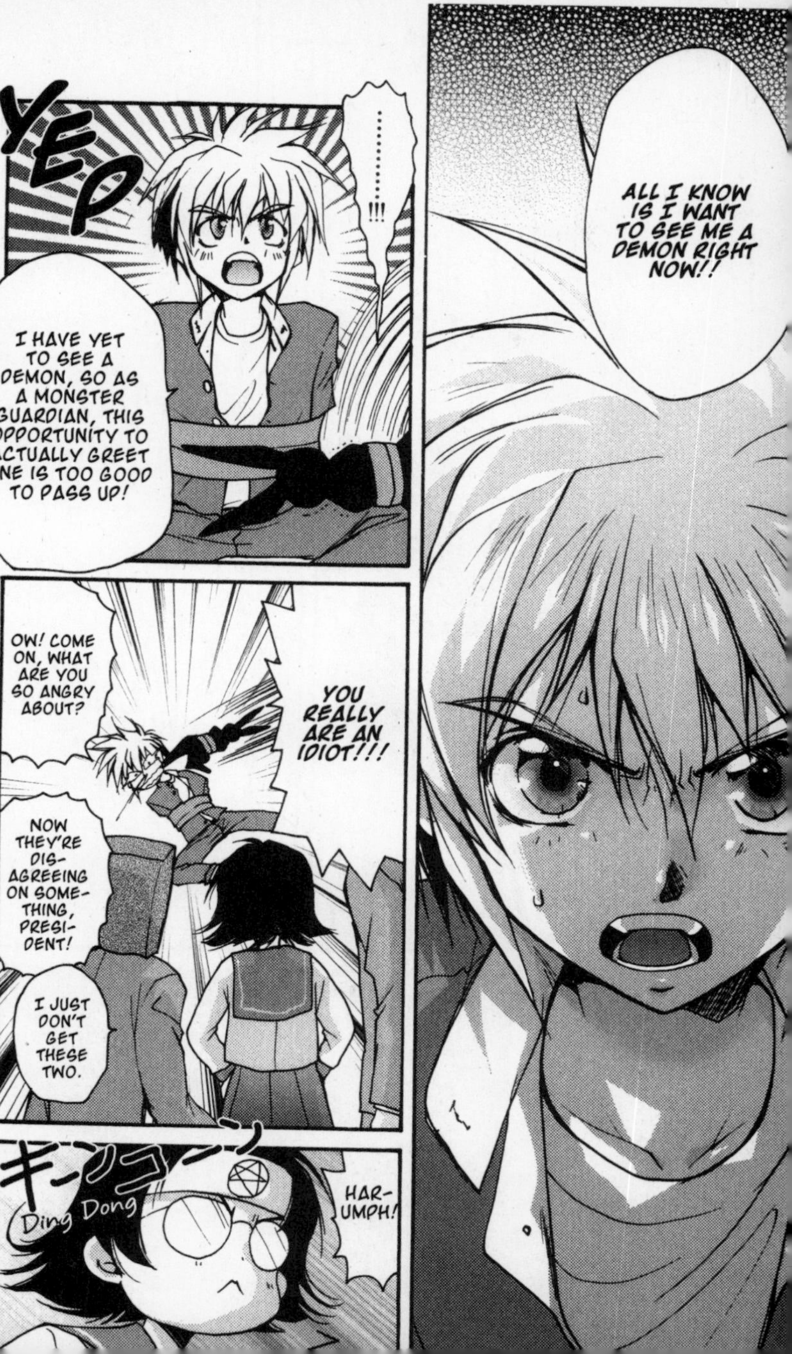
ALL I KNOW IS I WANT TO SEE ME A DEMON RIGHT NOW!!
......!!!
YEP
I HAVE YET TO SEE A DEMON, SO AS A MONSTER GUARDIAN, THIS OPPORTUNITY TO ACTUALLY GREET ONE IS TOO GOOD TO PASS UP!
YOU REALLY ARE AN IDIOT!!!
OW! COME ON, WHAT ARE YOU SO ANGRY ABOUT?
NOW THEY'RE DIS-AGREEING ON SOME-THING, PRESI-DENT!
I JUST DON'T GET THESE TWO.
HAR-UMPH!
キーンコーン
Ding Dong

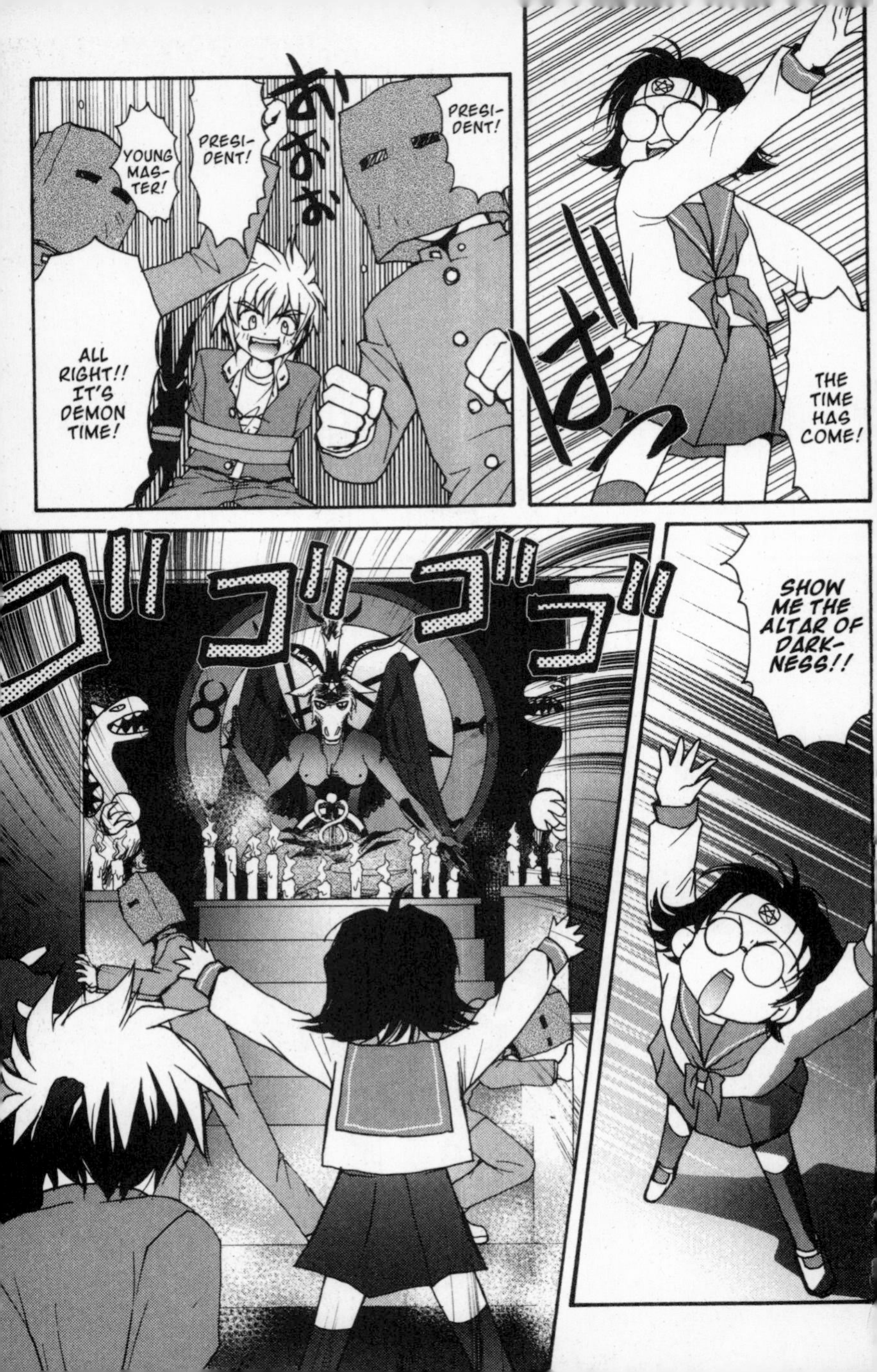
ばっ
THE TIME HAS COME!
PRESI-DENT!
おおぉ
PRESI-DENT!
YOUNG MAS-TER!
ALL RIGHT!! IT'S DEMON TIME!
SHOW ME THE ALTAR OF DARK-NESS!!
ゴゴゴゴ

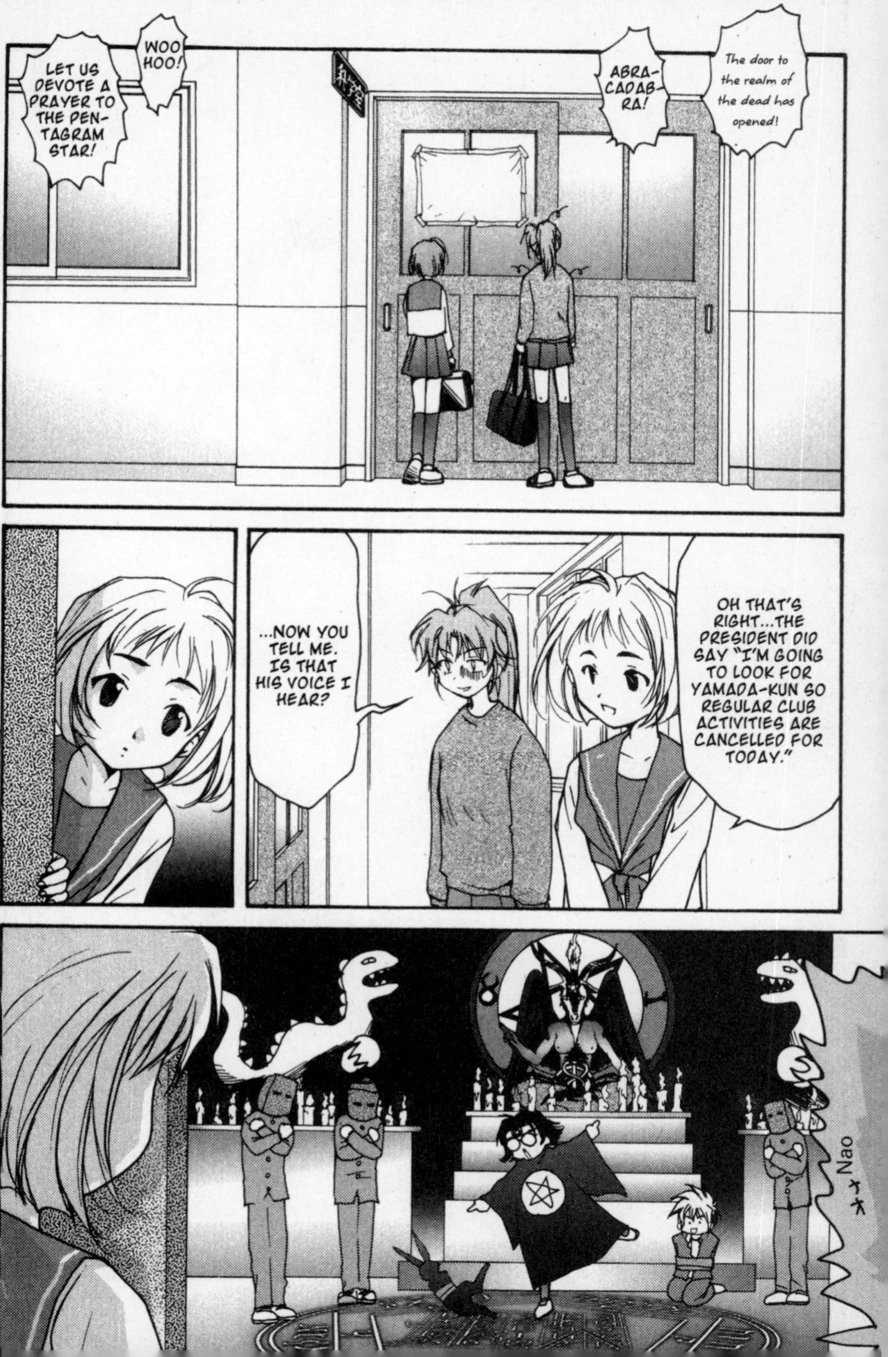

The door to the realm of the dead has opened!
ABRA-CADABRA!
WOO HOO!
LET US DEVOTE A PRAYER TO THE PEN-TAGRAM STAR!
OH THAT'S RIGHT...THE PRESIDENT DID SAY "I'M GOING TO LOOK FOR YAMADA-KUN SO REGULAR CLUB ACTIVITIES ARE CANCELLED FOR TODAY."
...NOW YOU TELL ME. IS THAT HIS VOICE I HEAR?
Nao

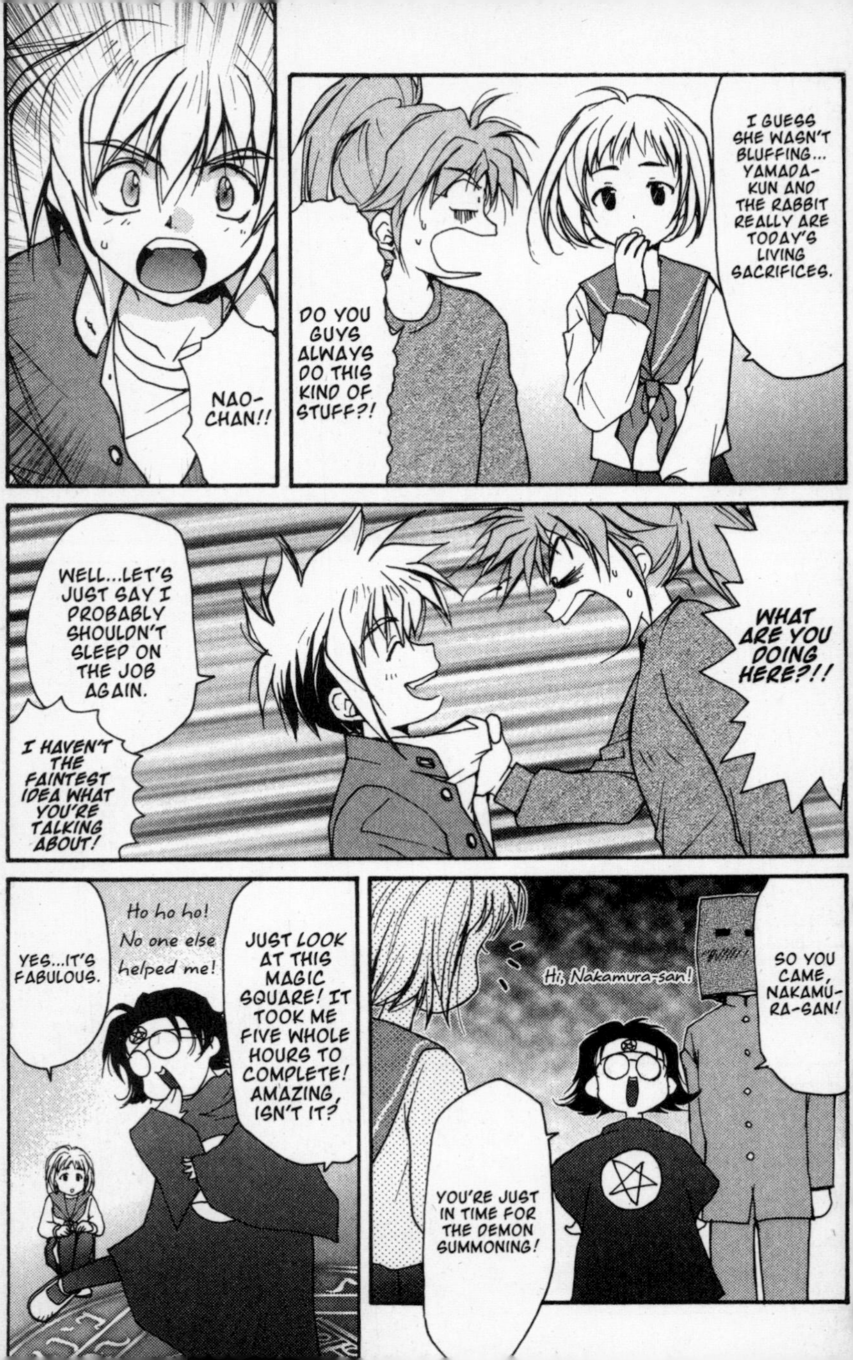
I GUESS SHE WASN'T BLUFFING... YAMADA-KUN AND THE RABBIT REALLY ARE TODAY'S LIVING SACRIFICES.
DO YOU GUYS ALWAYS DO THIS KIND OF STUFF?!
NAO-CHAN!!
WHAT ARE YOU DOING HERE?!!
WELL...LET'S JUST SAY I PROBABLY SHOULDN'T SLEEP ON THE JOB AGAIN.
I HAVEN'T THE FAINTEST IDEA WHAT YOU'RE TALKING ABOUT!
SO YOU CAME, NAKAMU-RA-SAN!
Hi, Nakamura-san!
YOU'RE JUST IN TIME FOR THE DEMON SUMMONING!
JUST LOOK AT THIS MAGIC SQUARE! IT TOOK ME FIVE WHOLE HOURS TO COMPLETE! AMAZING, ISN'T IT?
Ho ho ho! No one else helped me!
YES...IT'S FABULOUS.

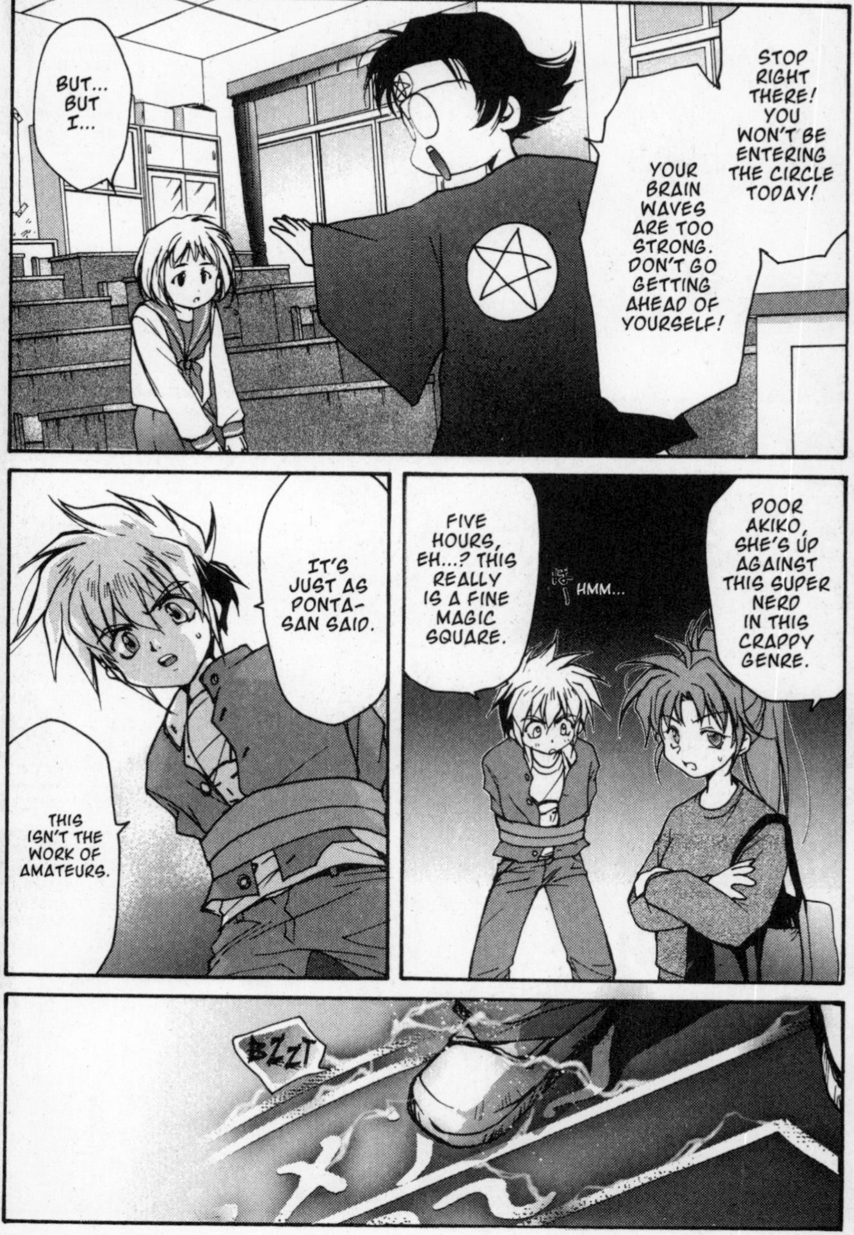
STOP RIGHT THERE! YOU WON'T BE ENTERING THE CIRCLE TODAY!
YOUR BRAIN WAVES ARE TOO STRONG. DON'T GO GETTING AHEAD OF YOURSELF!
BUT... BUT I...
POOR AKIKO, SHE'S UP AGAINST THIS SUPER NERD IN THIS CRAPPY GENRE.
HMM...
FIVE HOURS, EH...? THIS REALLY IS A FINE MAGIC SQUARE.
IT'S JUST AS PONTA-SAN SAID.
THIS ISN'T THE WORK OF AMATEURS.
BZZT

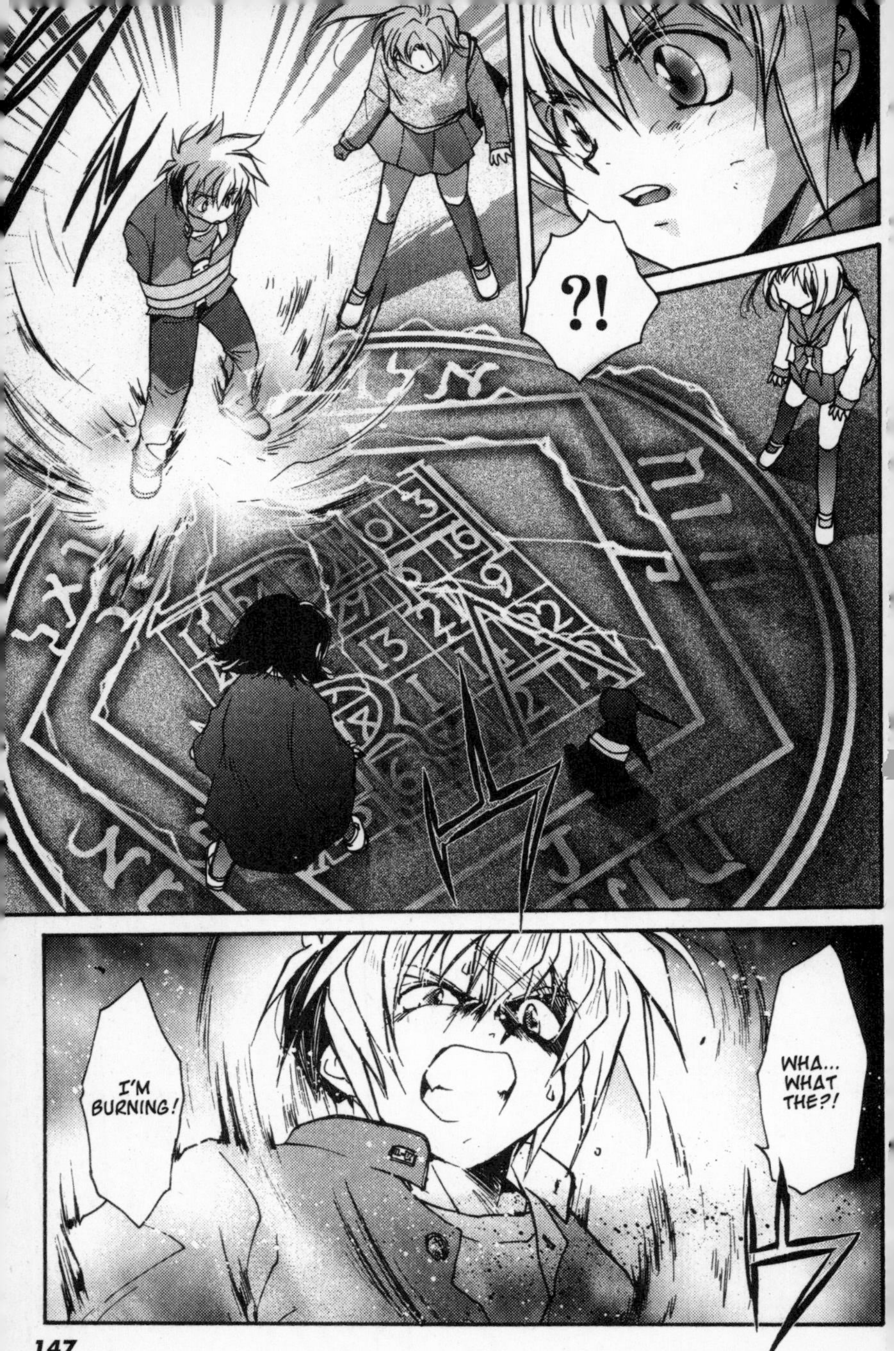
?!
WHA... WHAT THE?!
I'M BURNING!

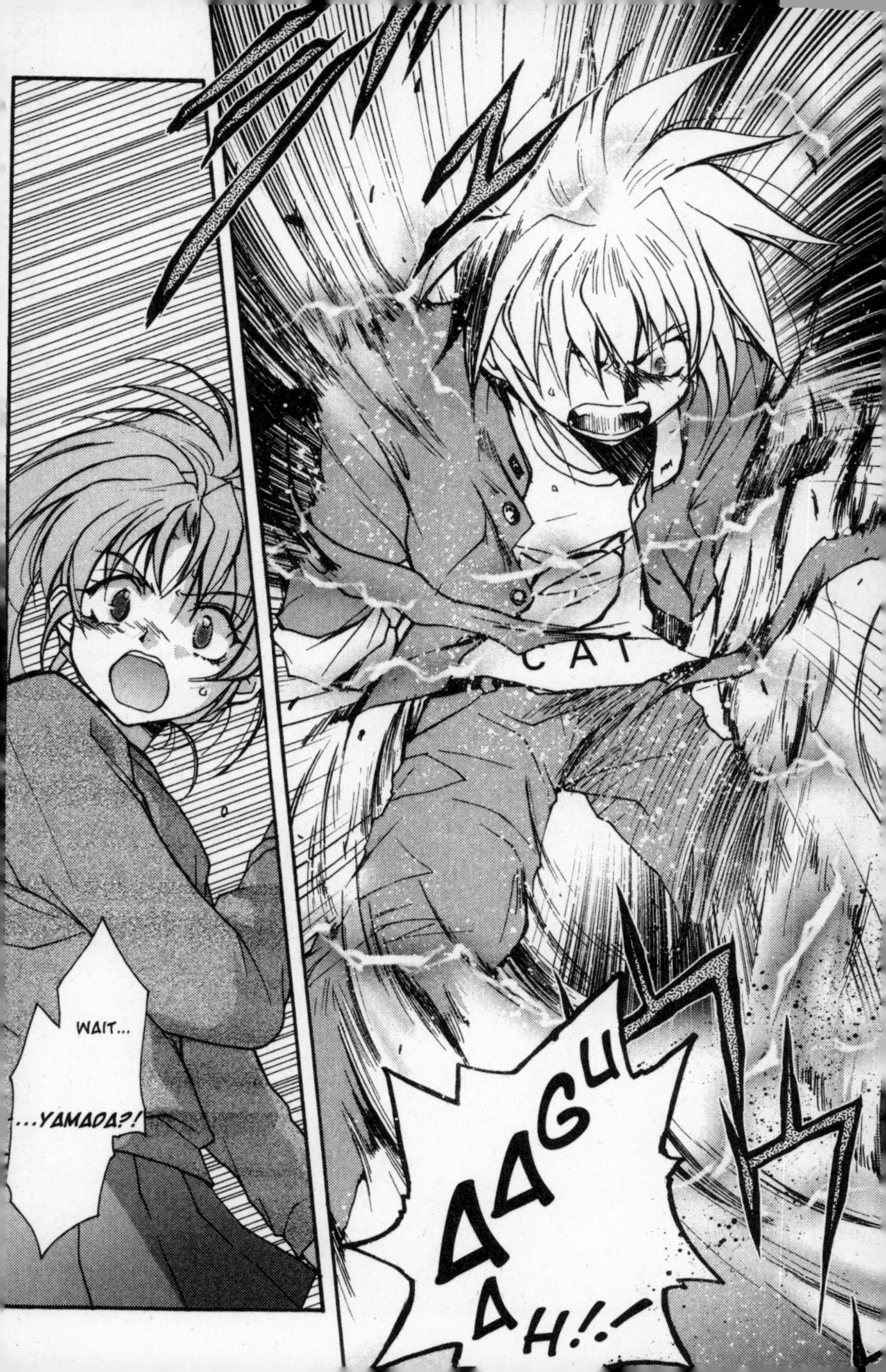
CAT
AAGUAH!!
WAIT...
...YAMADA?!

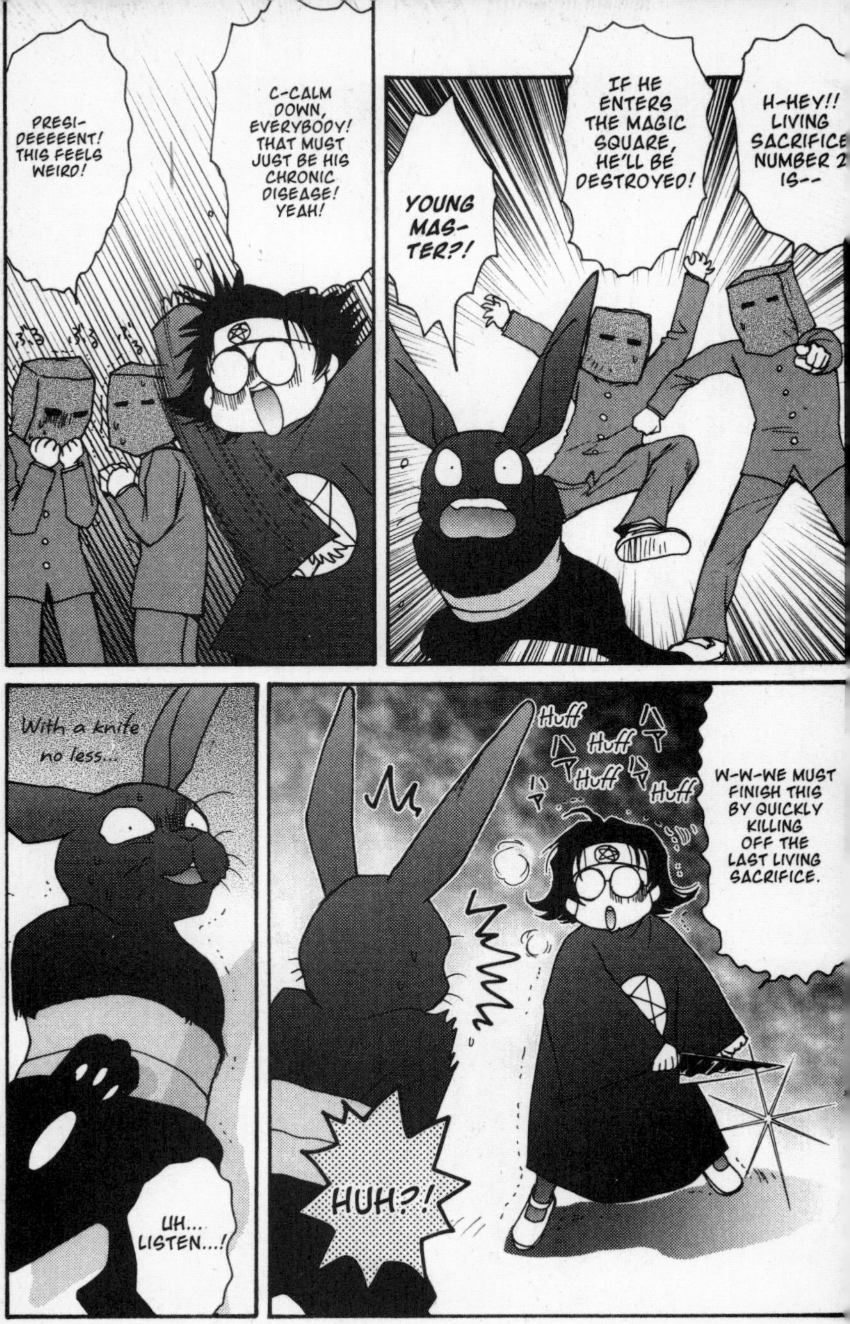
H-HEY!! LIVING SACRIFICE NUMBER 2 IS--
IF HE ENTERS THE MAGIC SQUARE, HE'LL BE DESTROYED!
YOUNG MAS-TER?!
C-CALM DOWN, EVERYBODY! THAT MUST JUST BE HIS CHRONIC DISEASE! YEAH!
PRESI-DEEEEENT! THIS FEELS WEIRD!
W-W-WE MUST FINISH THIS BY QUICKLY KILLING OFF THE LAST LIVING SACRIFICE.
Huff Huff Huff Huff
HUH?!
With a knife no less...
UH... LISTEN...!

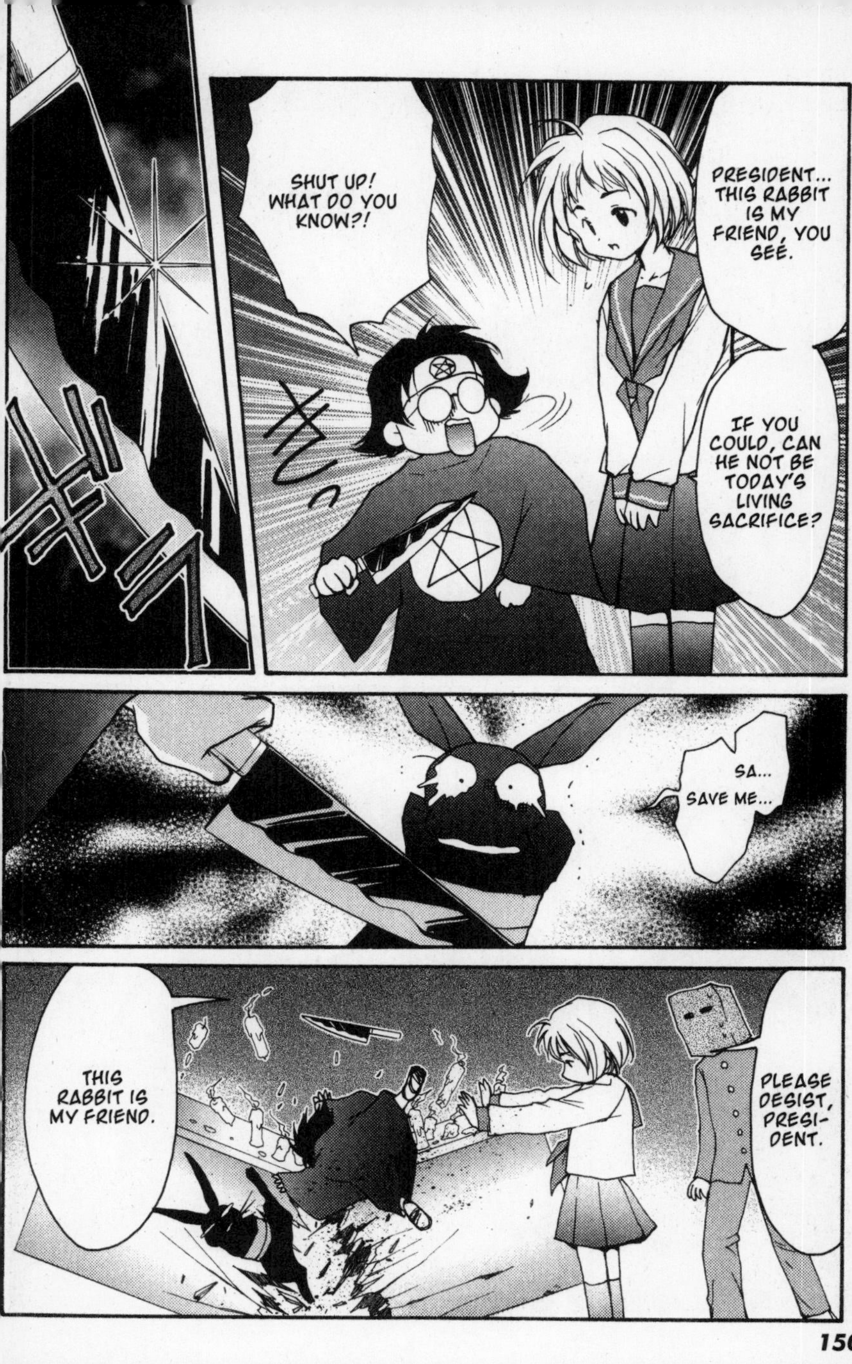
PRESIDENT... THIS RABBIT IS MY FRIEND, YOU SEE.
IF YOU COULD, CAN HE NOT BE TODAY'S LIVING SACRIFICE?
SHUT UP! WHAT DO YOU KNOW?!
SA... SAVE ME...
PLEASE DESIST, PRESIDENT.
THIS RABBIT IS MY FRIEND.

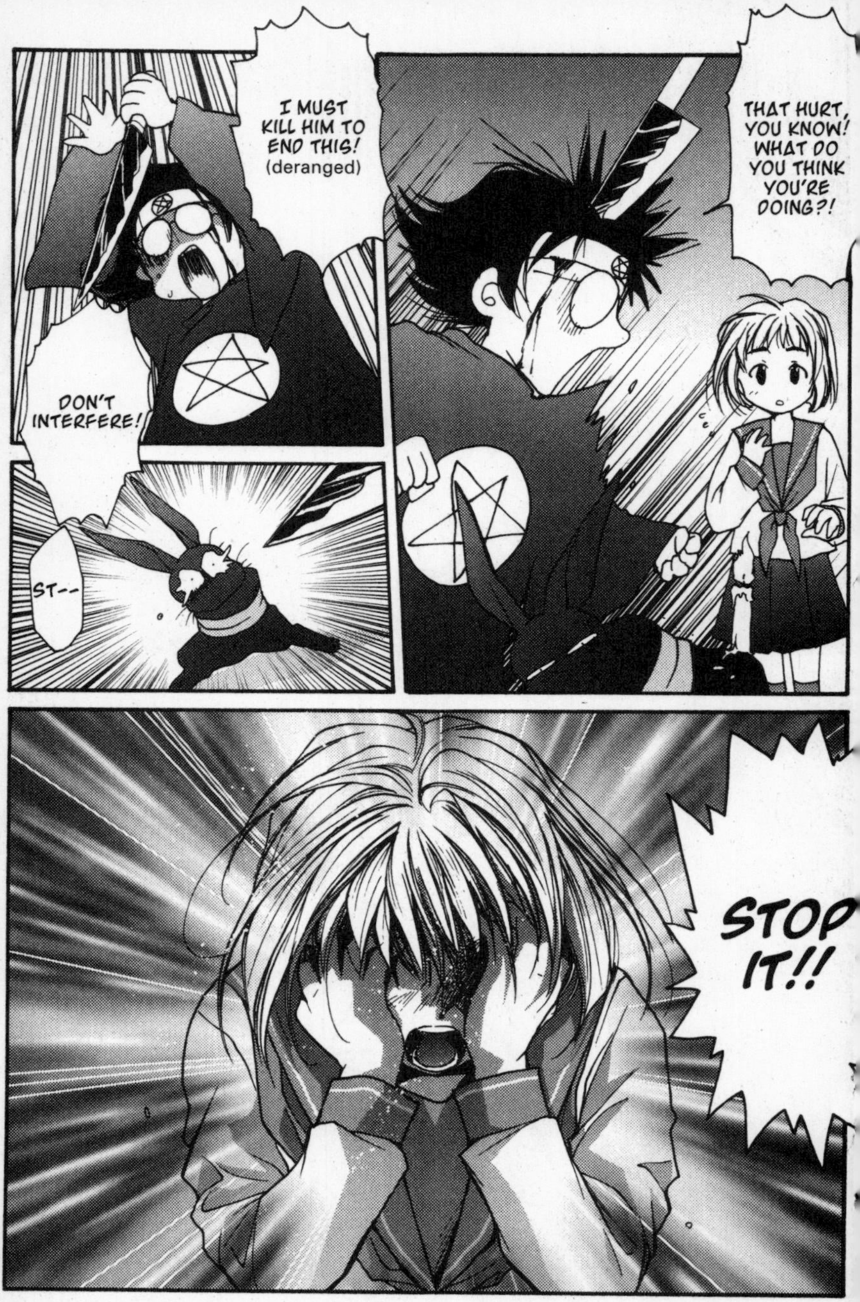
THAT HURT, YOU KNOW! WHAT DO YOU THINK YOU'RE DOING?!
I MUST KILL HIM TO END THIS! (deranged)
DON'T INTERFERE!
ST--
STOP IT!!

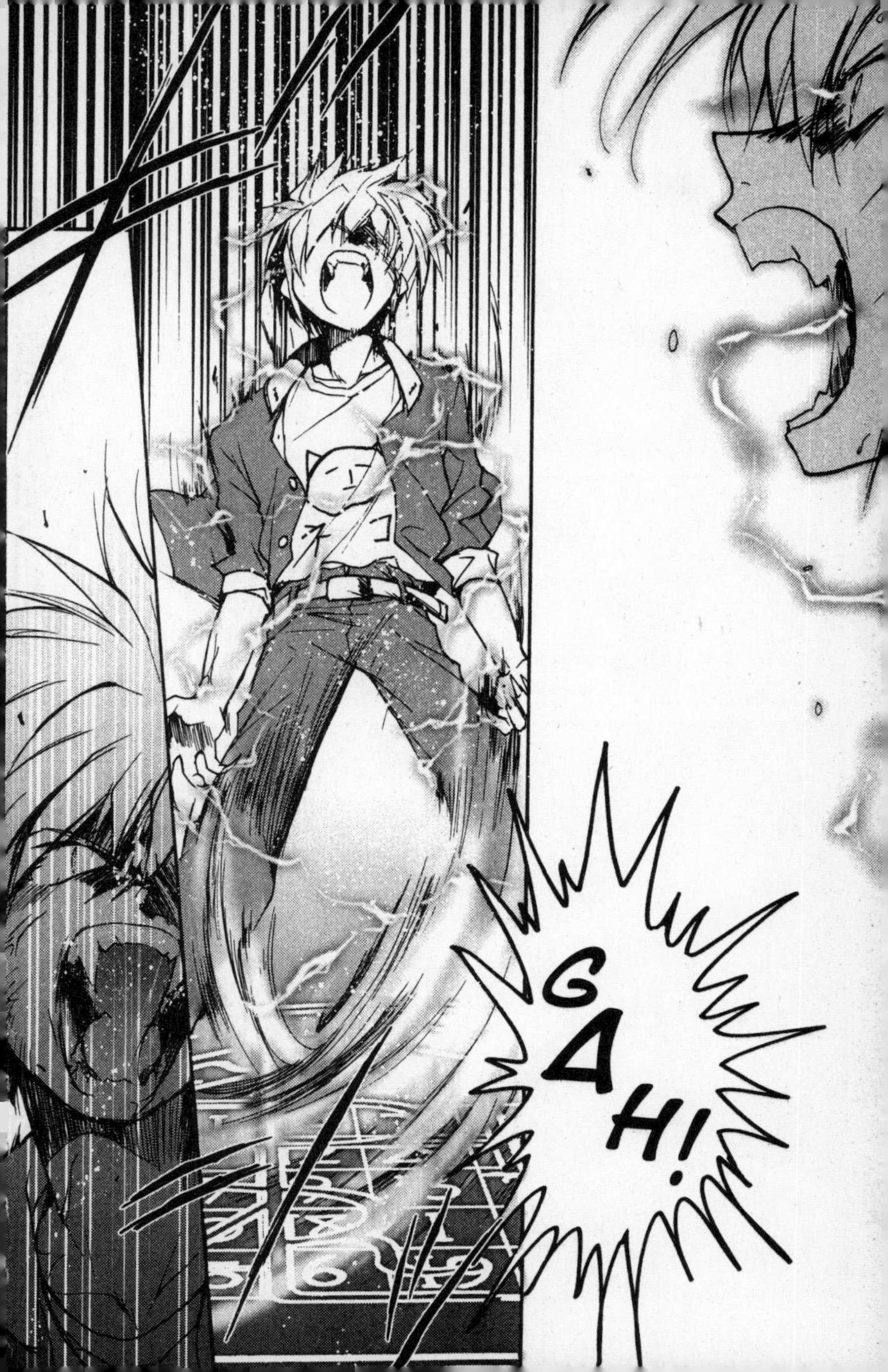
GAH!

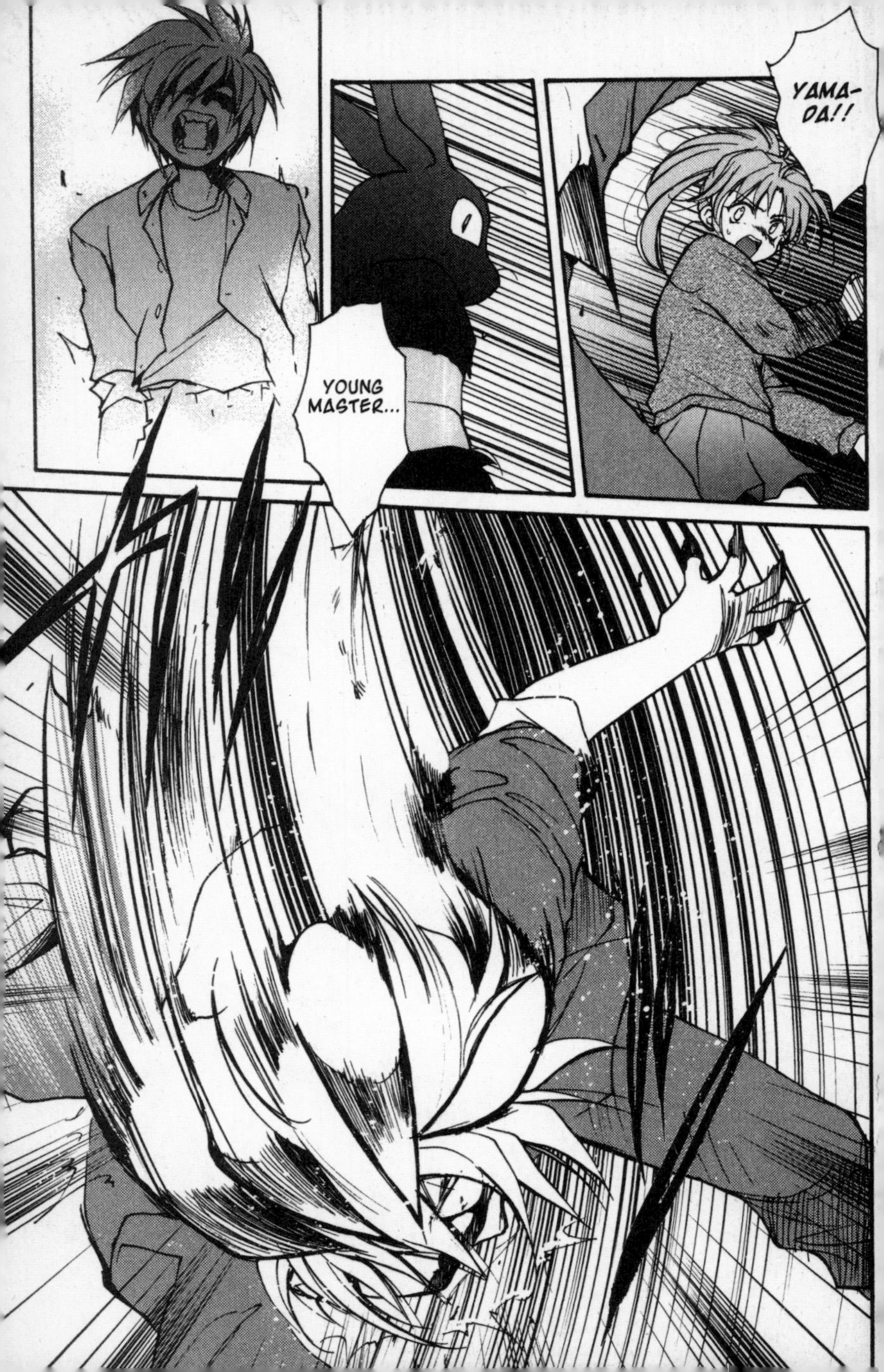
YAMA-DA!!
YOUNG MASTER...

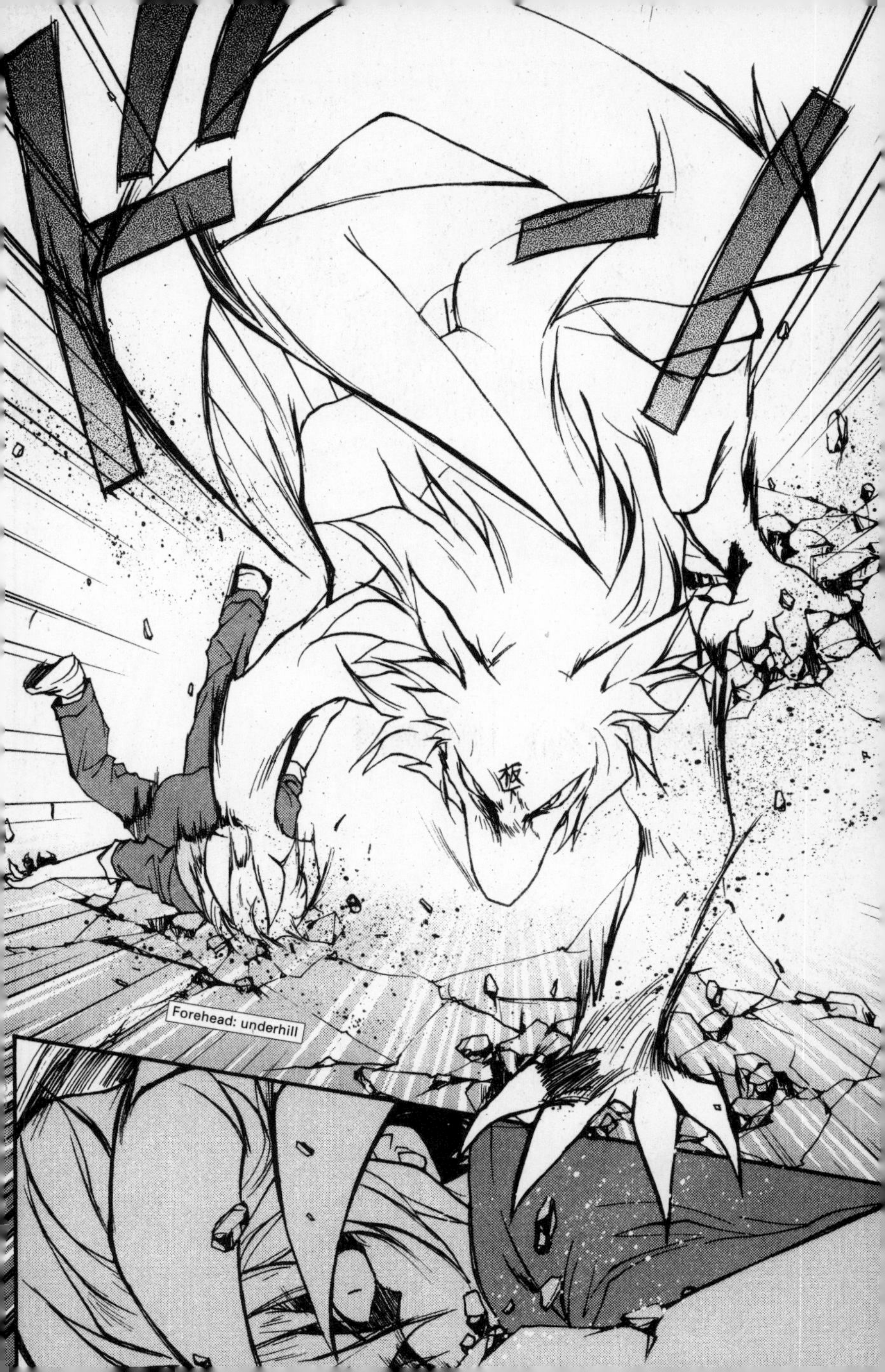
Forehead: underhill

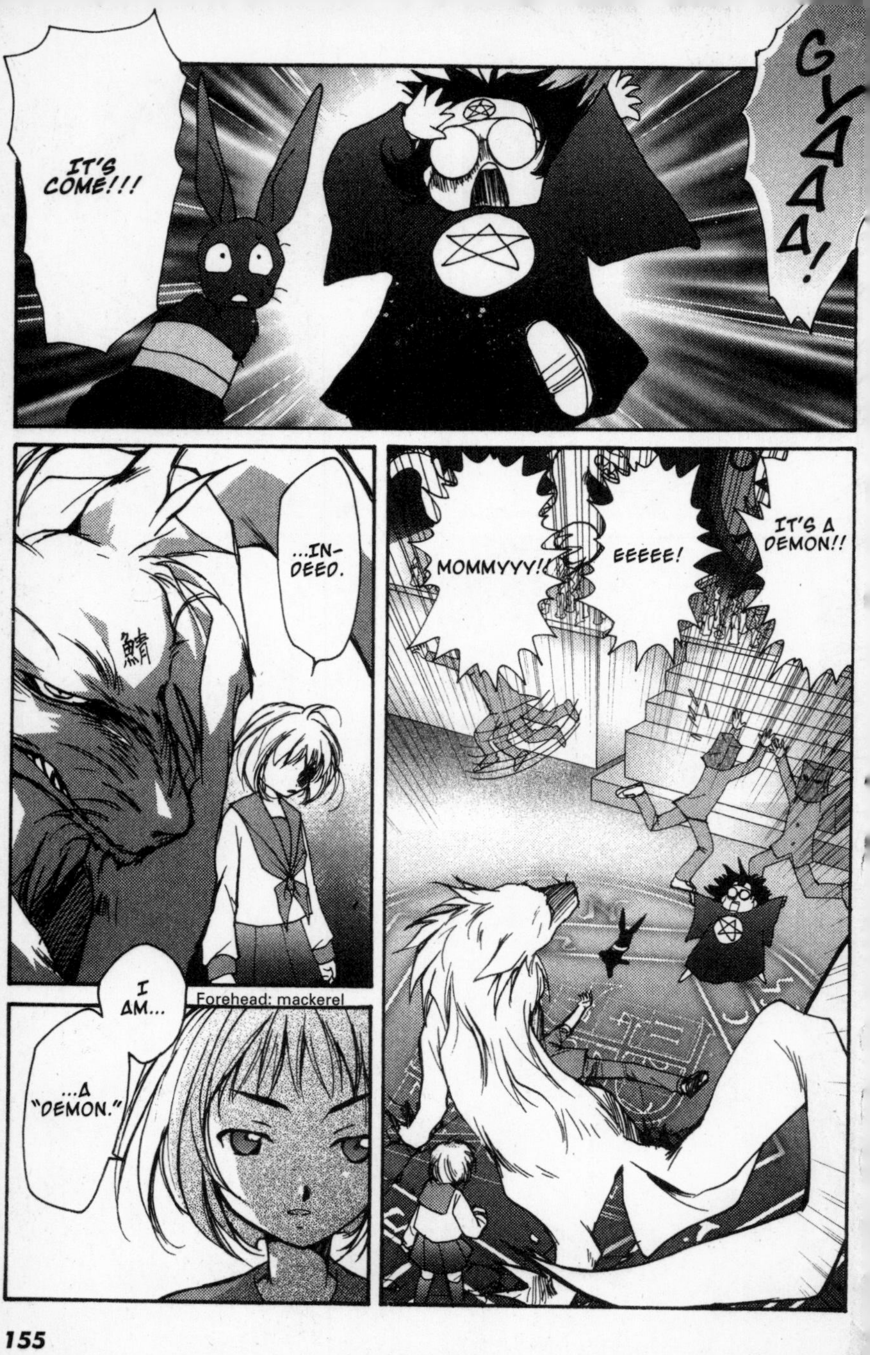
GYAAAA!
IT'S COME!!!
IT'S A DEMON!!
EEEEE!
MOMMYYY!!
...IN-DEED.
鯖
Forehead: mackerel
I AM...
...A "DEMON."

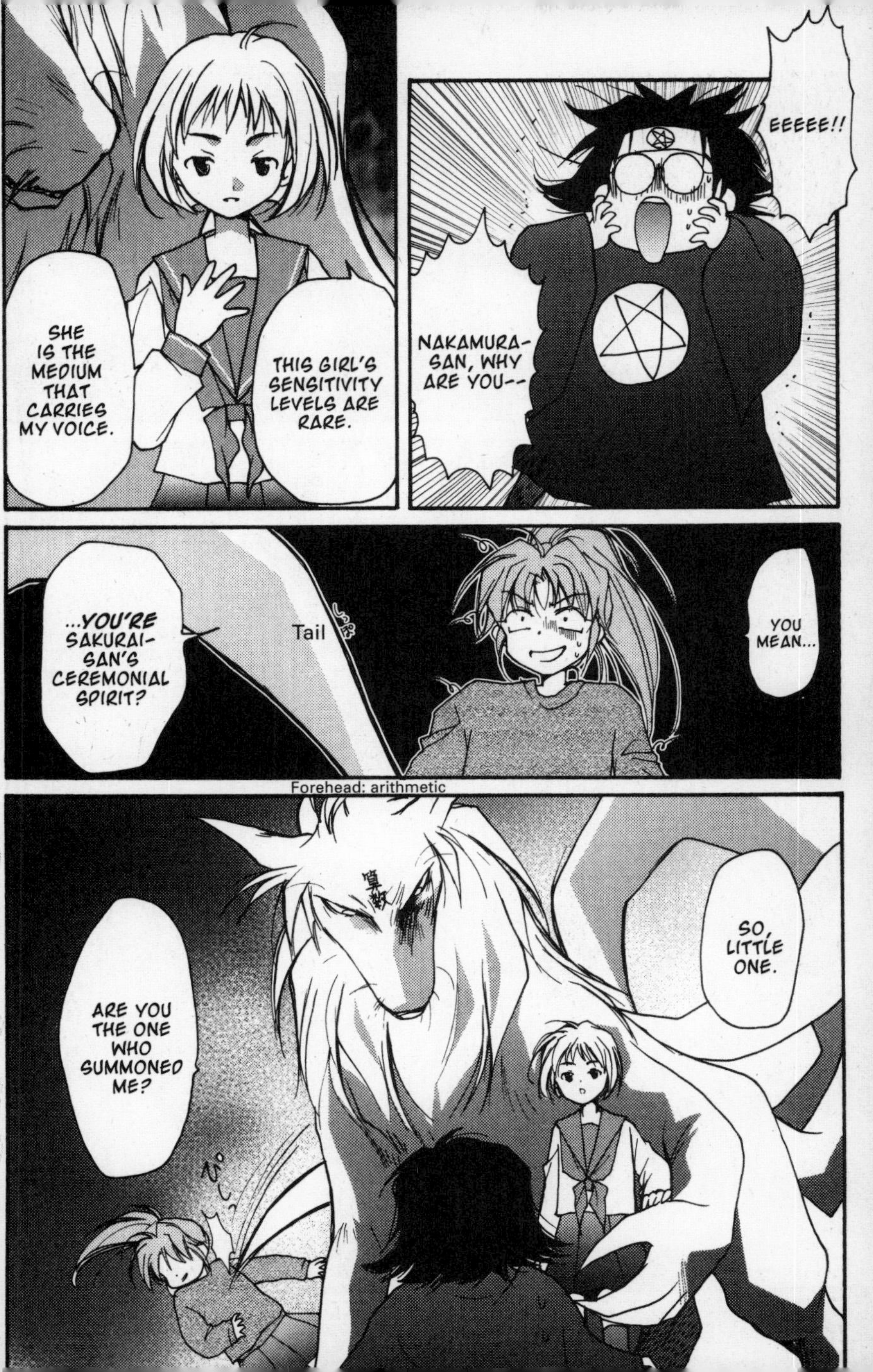
EEEEE!!
NAKAMURA-SAN, WHY ARE YOU--
THIS GIRL'S SENSITIVITY LEVELS ARE RARE.
SHE IS THE MEDIUM THAT CARRIES MY VOICE.
YOU MEAN...
Tail
...*YOU'RE* SAKURAI-SAN'S CEREMONIAL SPIRIT?
Forehead: arithmetic
算数
SO, LITTLE ONE.
ARE YOU THE ONE WHO SUMMONED ME?

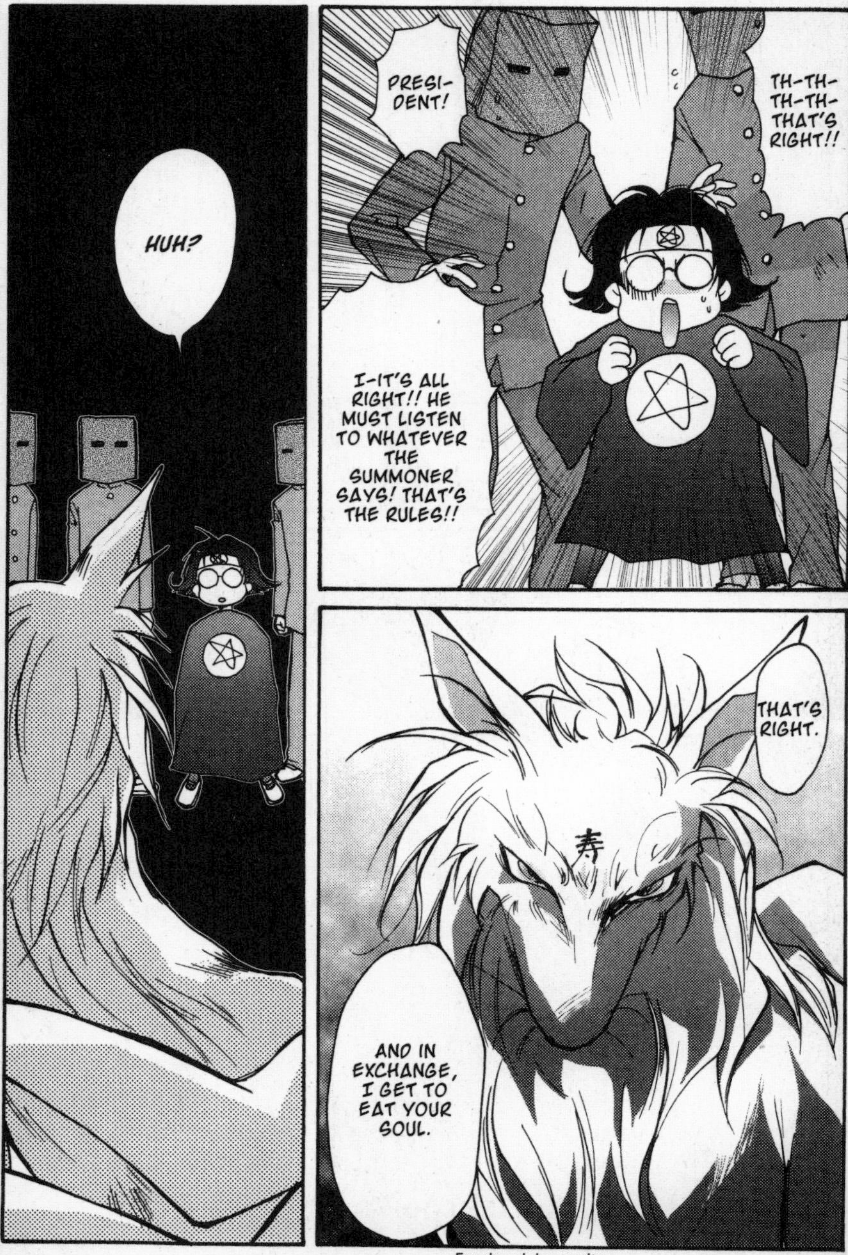
TH-TH-TH-TH-THAT'S RIGHT!!
PRESI-DENT!
I-IT'S ALL RIGHT!! HE MUST LISTEN TO WHATEVER THE SUMMONER SAYS! THAT'S THE RULES!!
THAT'S RIGHT.
AND IN EXCHANGE, I GET TO EAT YOUR SOUL.
寿
HUH?
Forehead: longevity

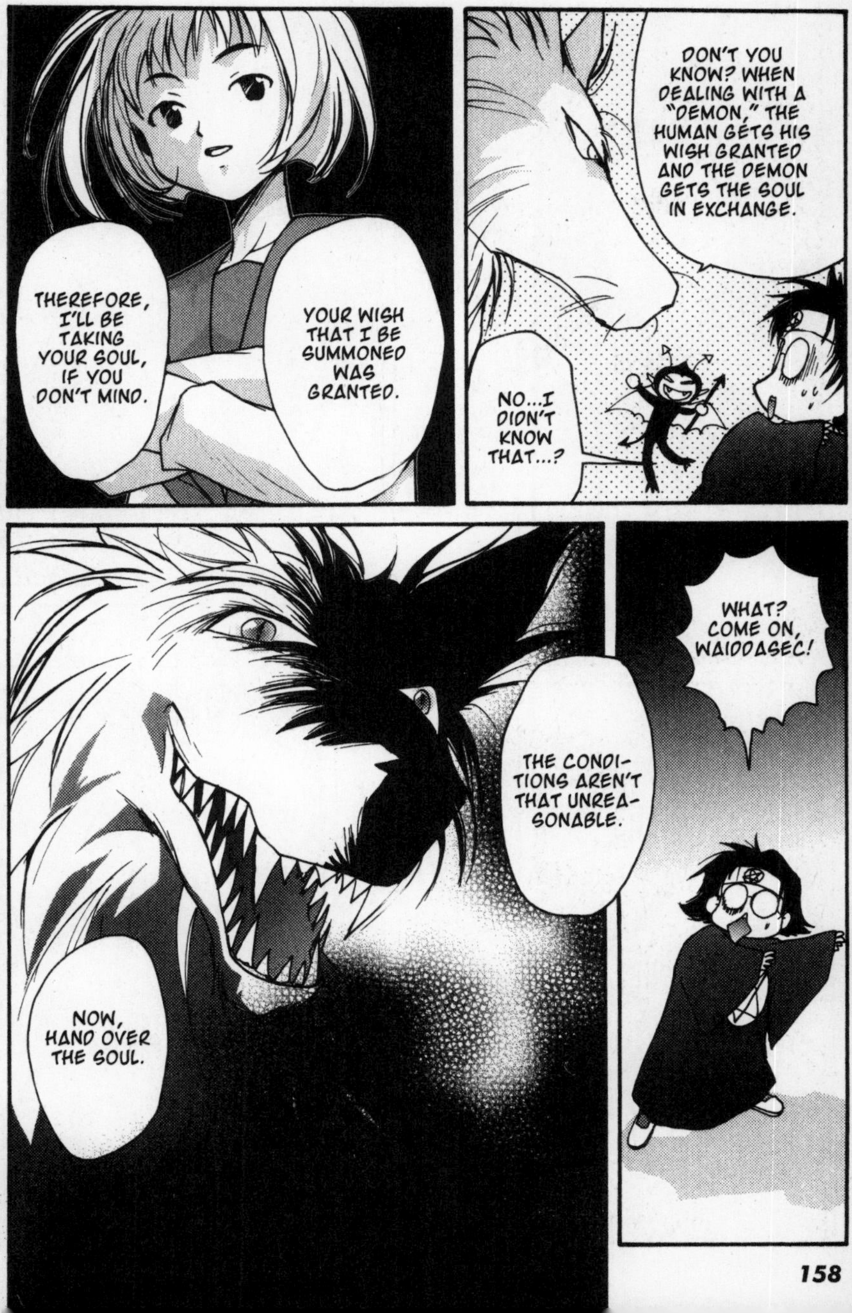
DON'T YOU KNOW? WHEN DEALING WITH A "DEMON," THE HUMAN GETS HIS WISH GRANTED AND THE DEMON GETS THE SOUL IN EXCHANGE.
NO...I DIDN'T KNOW THAT...?
YOUR WISH THAT I BE SUMMONED WAS GRANTED.
THEREFORE, I'LL BE TAKING YOUR SOUL, IF YOU DON'T MIND.
WHAT? COME ON, WAIDDASEĆ!
THE CONDITIONS AREN'T THAT UNREASONABLE.
NOW, HAND OVER THE SOUL.

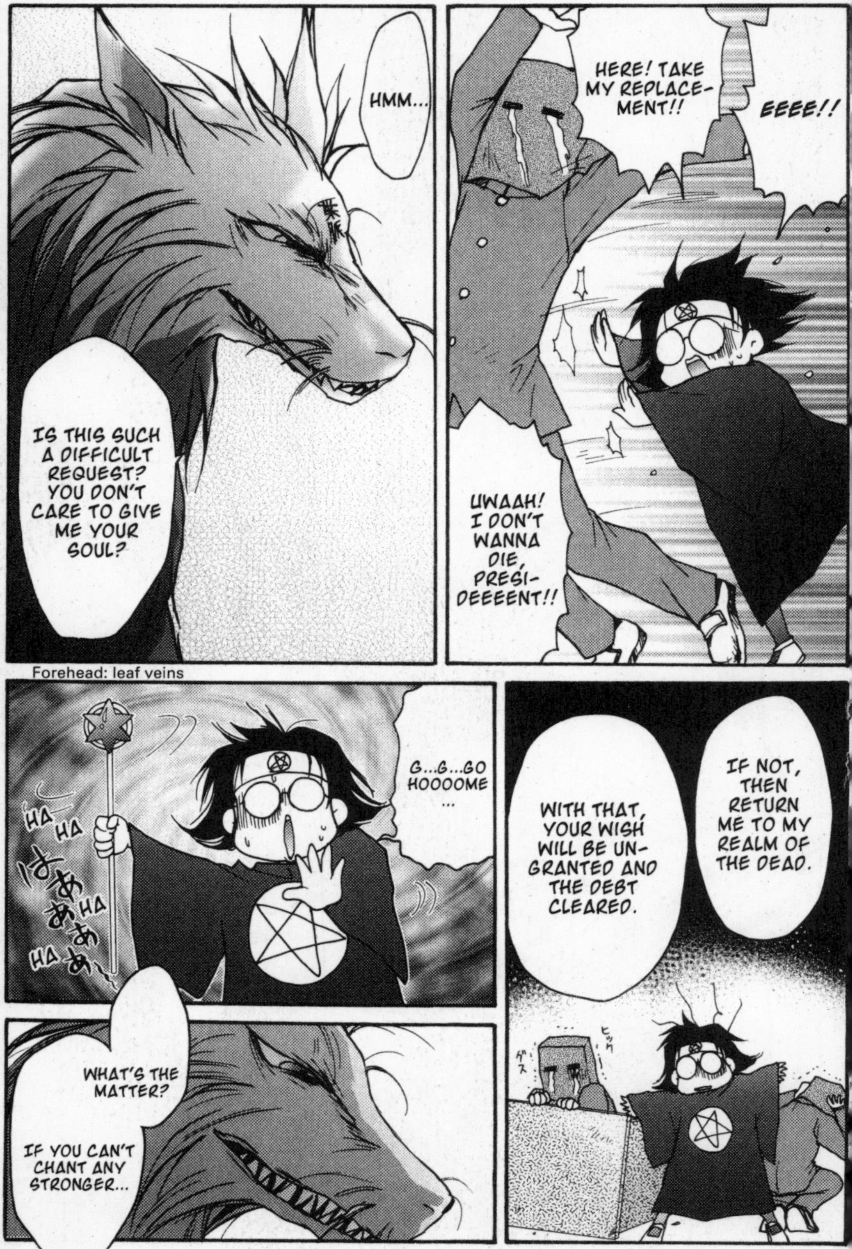
HERE! TAKE MY REPLACEMENT!!
EEEE!!
UWAAH! I DON'T WANNA DIE, PRESI-DEEEENT!!
HMM...
IS THIS SUCH A DIFFICULT REQUEST? YOU DON'T CARE TO GIVE ME YOUR SOUL?
IF NOT, THEN RETURN ME TO MY REALM OF THE DEAD.
WITH THAT, YOUR WISH WILL BE UN-GRANTED AND THE DEBT CLEARED.
G...G...GO HOOOOME...
HA HA HA HA
WHAT'S THE MATTER?
IF YOU CAN'T CHANT ANY STRONGER...

Forehead: leaf veins

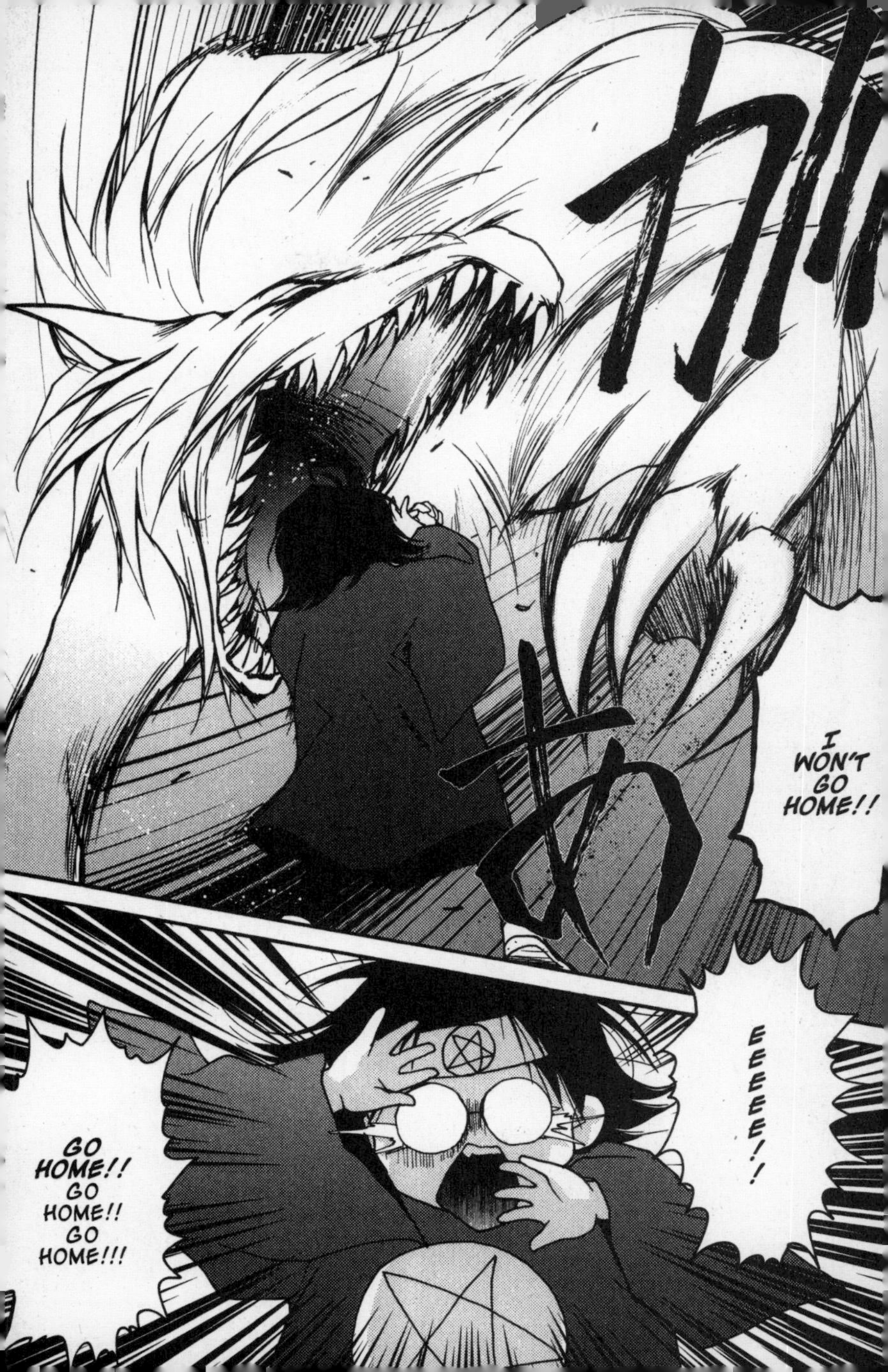
I WON'T GO HOME!!
EEEEE!!
GO HOME!! GO HOME!! GO HOME!!!

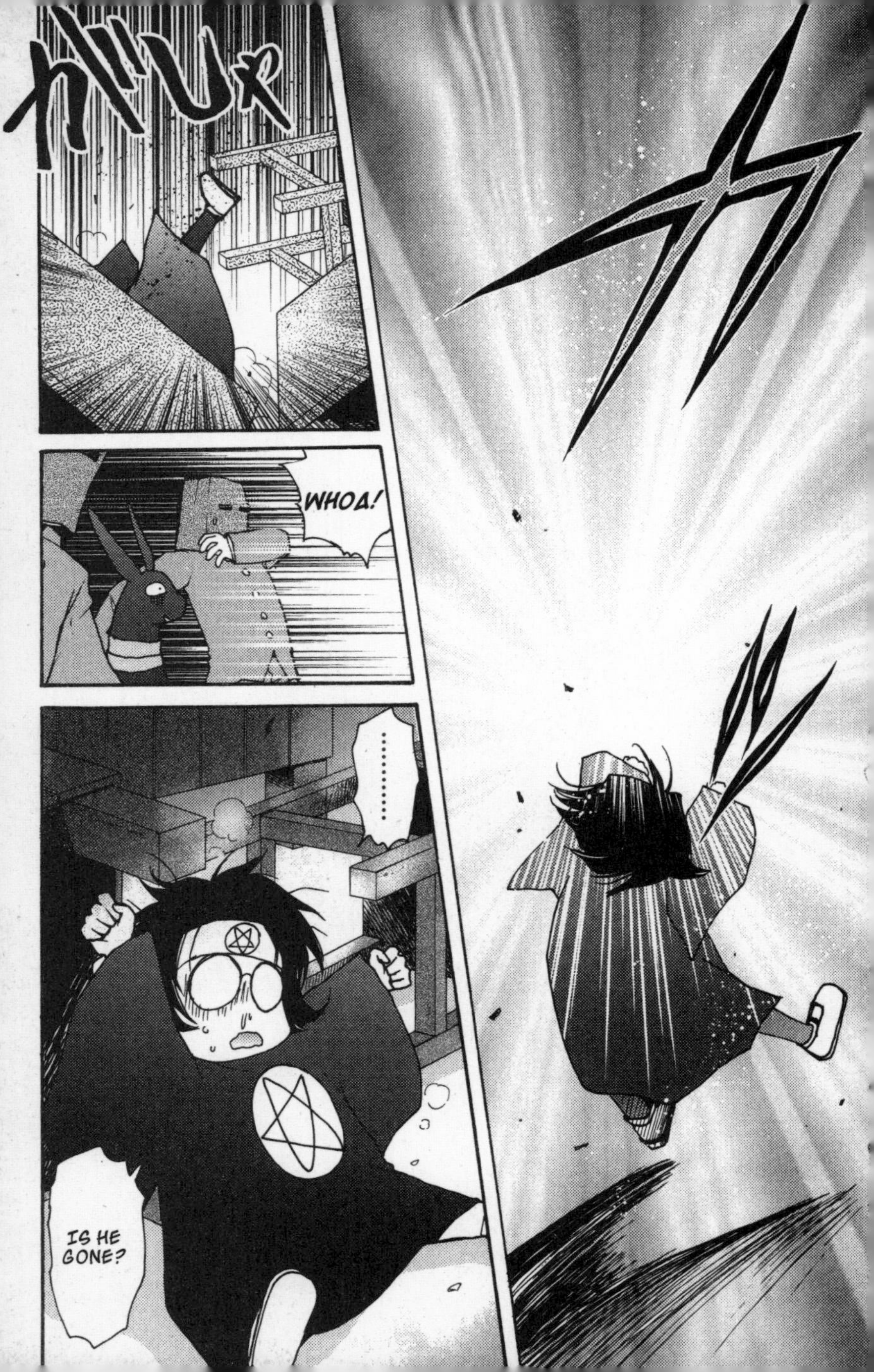
WHOA!
......
IS HE GONE?

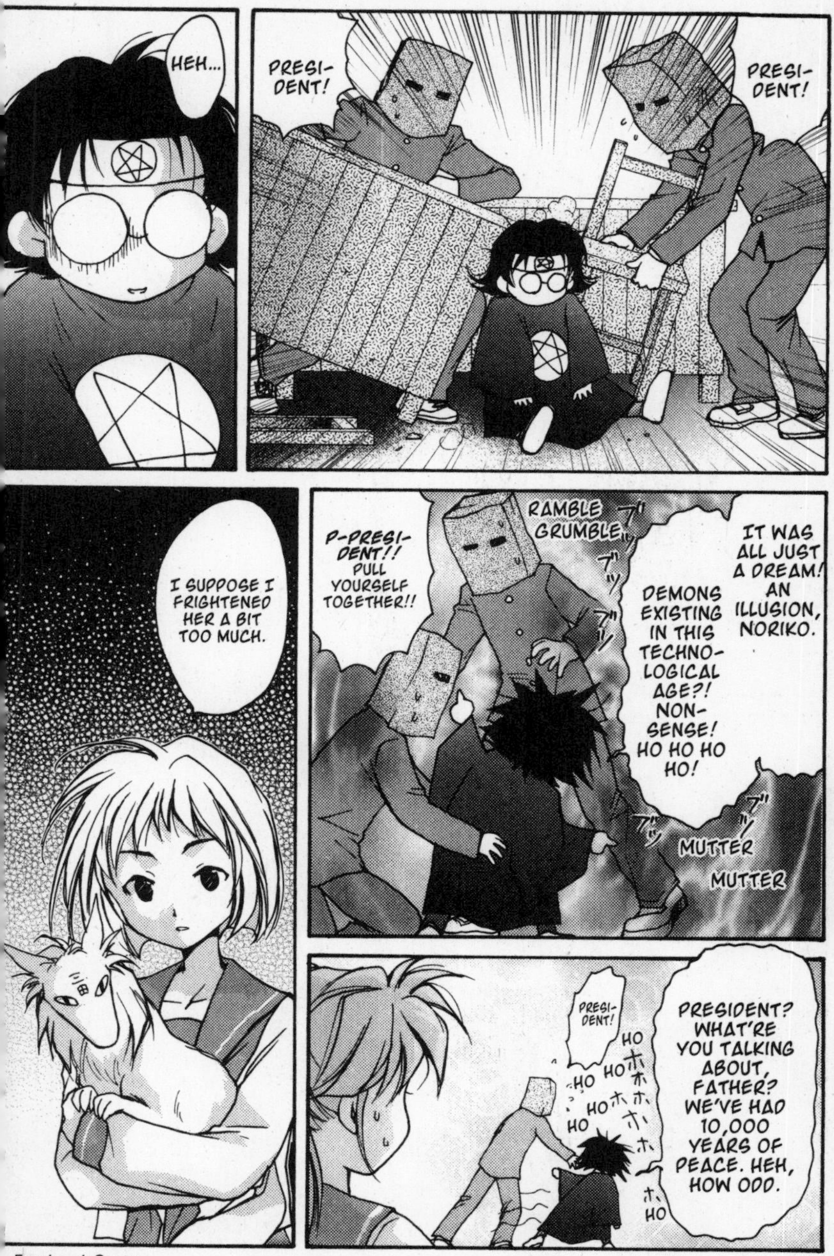
PRESI-DENT!
PRESI-DENT!
HEH...
IT WAS ALL JUST A DREAM! AN ILLUSION, NORIKO.
DEMONS EXISTING IN THIS TECHNO-LOGICAL AGE?! NON-SENSE! HO HO HO HO!
RAMBLE GRUMBLE
P-PRESI-DENT!! PULL YOURSELF TOGETHER!!
MUTTER
MUTTER
PRESIDENT? WHAT'RE YOU TALKING ABOUT, FATHER? WE'VE HAD 10,000 YEARS OF PEACE. HEH, HOW ODD.
PRESI-DENT!
HO HO HO HO HO HO
I SUPPOSE I FRIGHTENED HER A BIT TOO MUCH.

Forehead: Santa

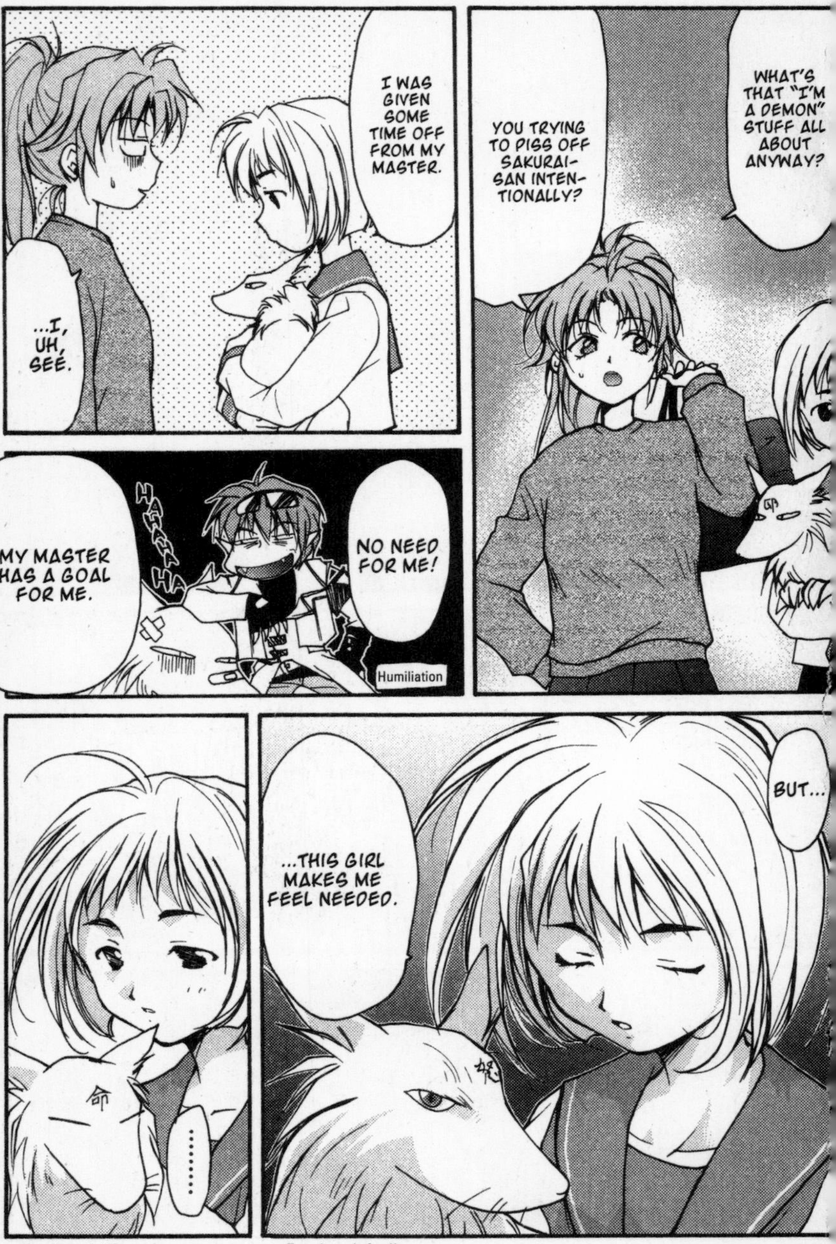
WHAT'S THAT "I'M A DEMON" STUFF ALL ABOUT ANYWAY?
YOU TRYING TO PISS OFF SAKURAI-SAN INTENTIONALLY?
I WAS GIVEN SOME TIME OFF FROM MY MASTER.
...I, UH, SEE.
NO NEED FOR ME!
HAHAHAHA
Humiliation
MY MASTER HAS A GOAL FOR ME.
BUT...
...THIS GIRL MAKES ME FEEL NEEDED.
......

Forehead: feelings

Forehead: life

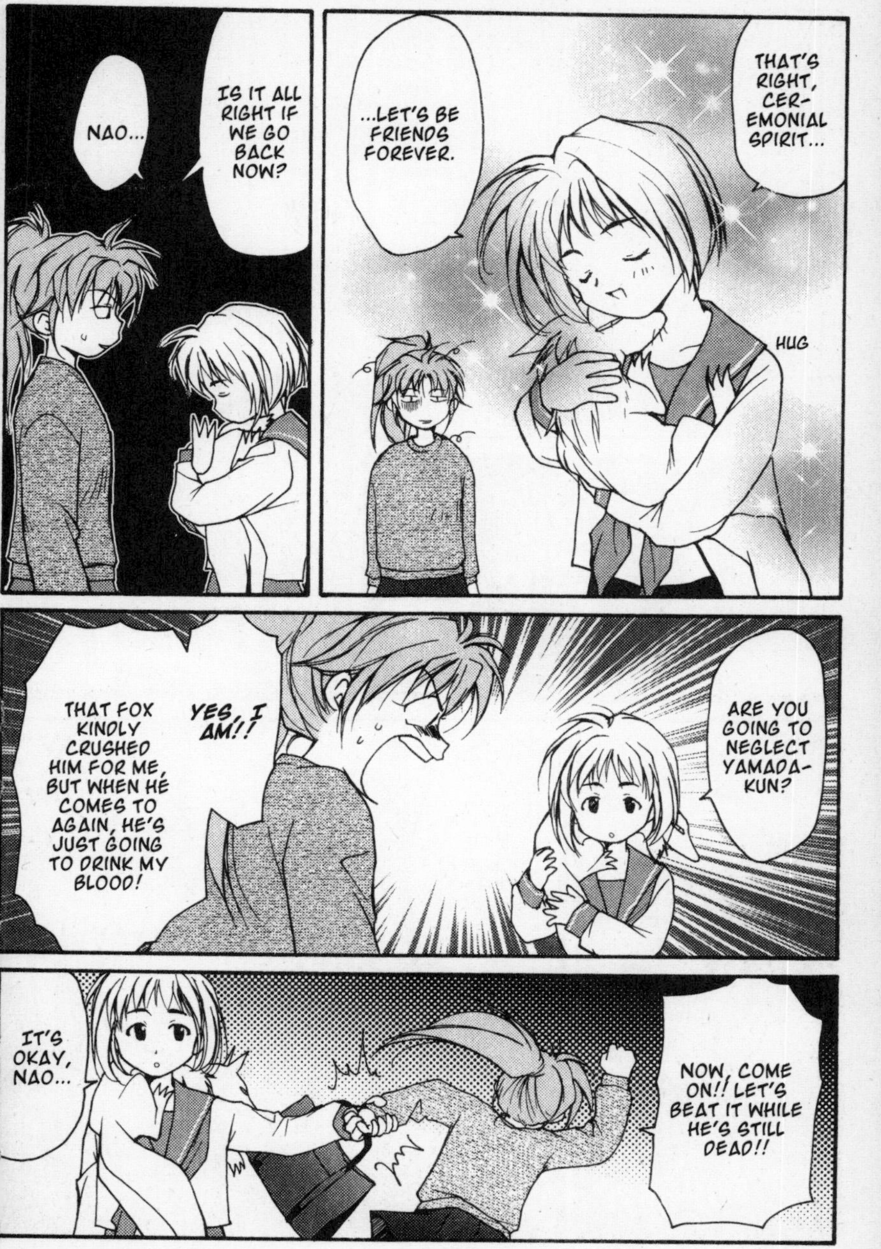

THAT'S RIGHT, CER-EMONIAL SPIRIT...
HUG
...LET'S BE FRIENDS FOREVER.
IS IT ALL RIGHT IF WE GO BACK NOW?
NAO...
ARE YOU GOING TO NEGLECT YAMADA-KUN?
YES, I AM!!
THAT FOX KINDLY CRUSHED HIM FOR ME, BUT WHEN HE COMES TO AGAIN, HE'S JUST GOING TO DRINK MY BLOOD!
NOW, COME ON!! LET'S BEAT IT WHILE HE'S STILL DEAD!!
IT'S OKAY, NAO...

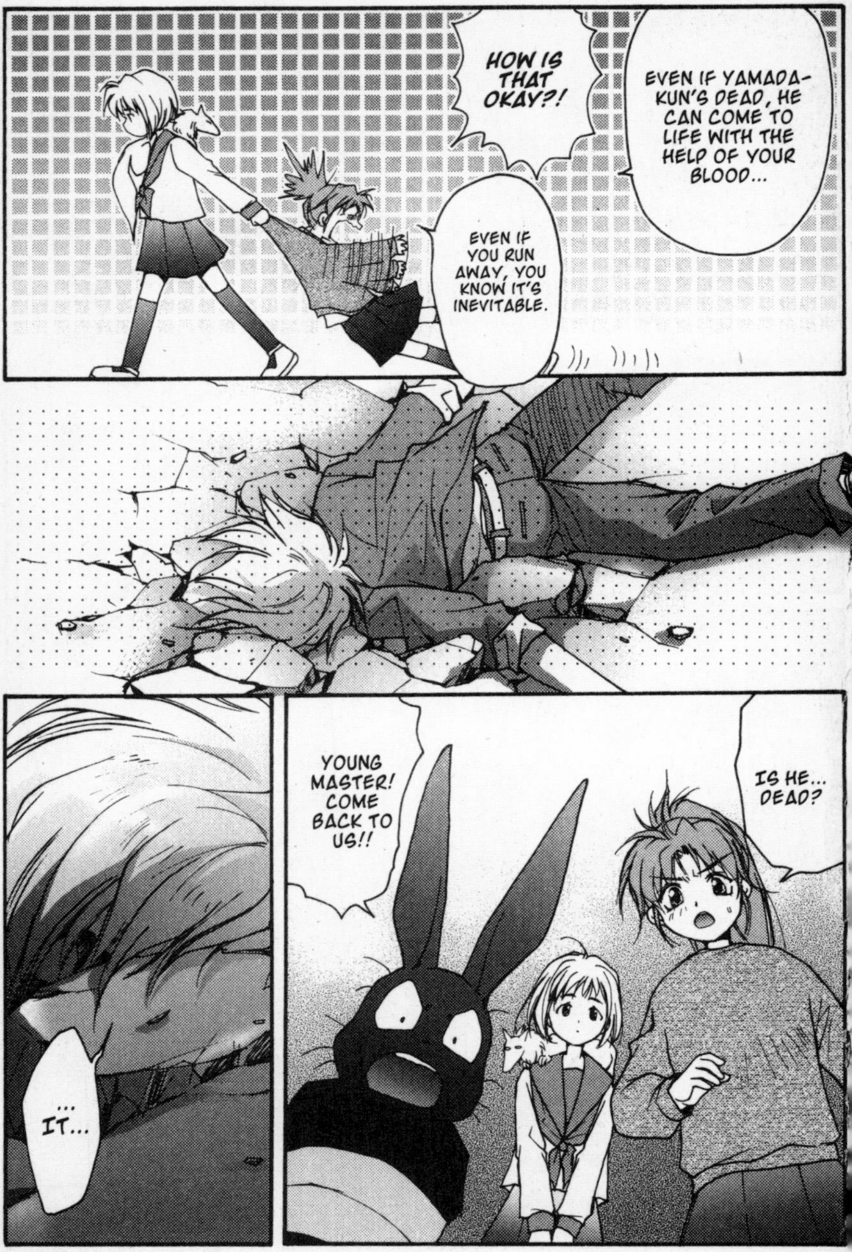
EVEN IF YAMADA-KUN'S DEAD, HE CAN COME TO LIFE WITH THE HELP OF YOUR BLOOD...
HOW IS THAT OKAY?!
EVEN IF YOU RUN AWAY, YOU KNOW IT'S INEVITABLE.
IS HE... DEAD?
YOUNG MASTER! COME BACK TO US!!
... IT...

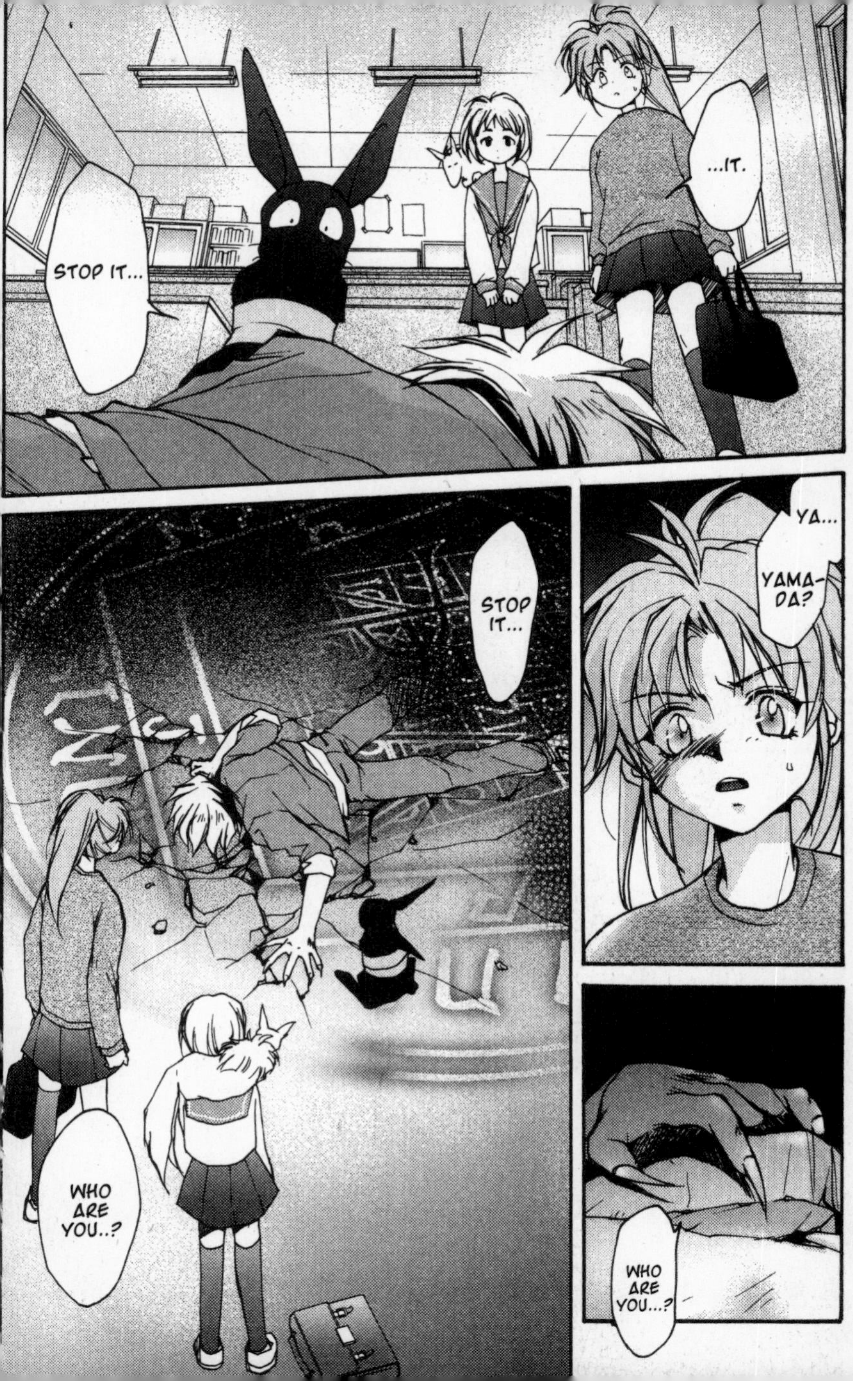
...IT.
STOP IT...
YA...
YAMA-DA?
WHO ARE YOU...?
STOP IT...
WHO ARE YOU..?

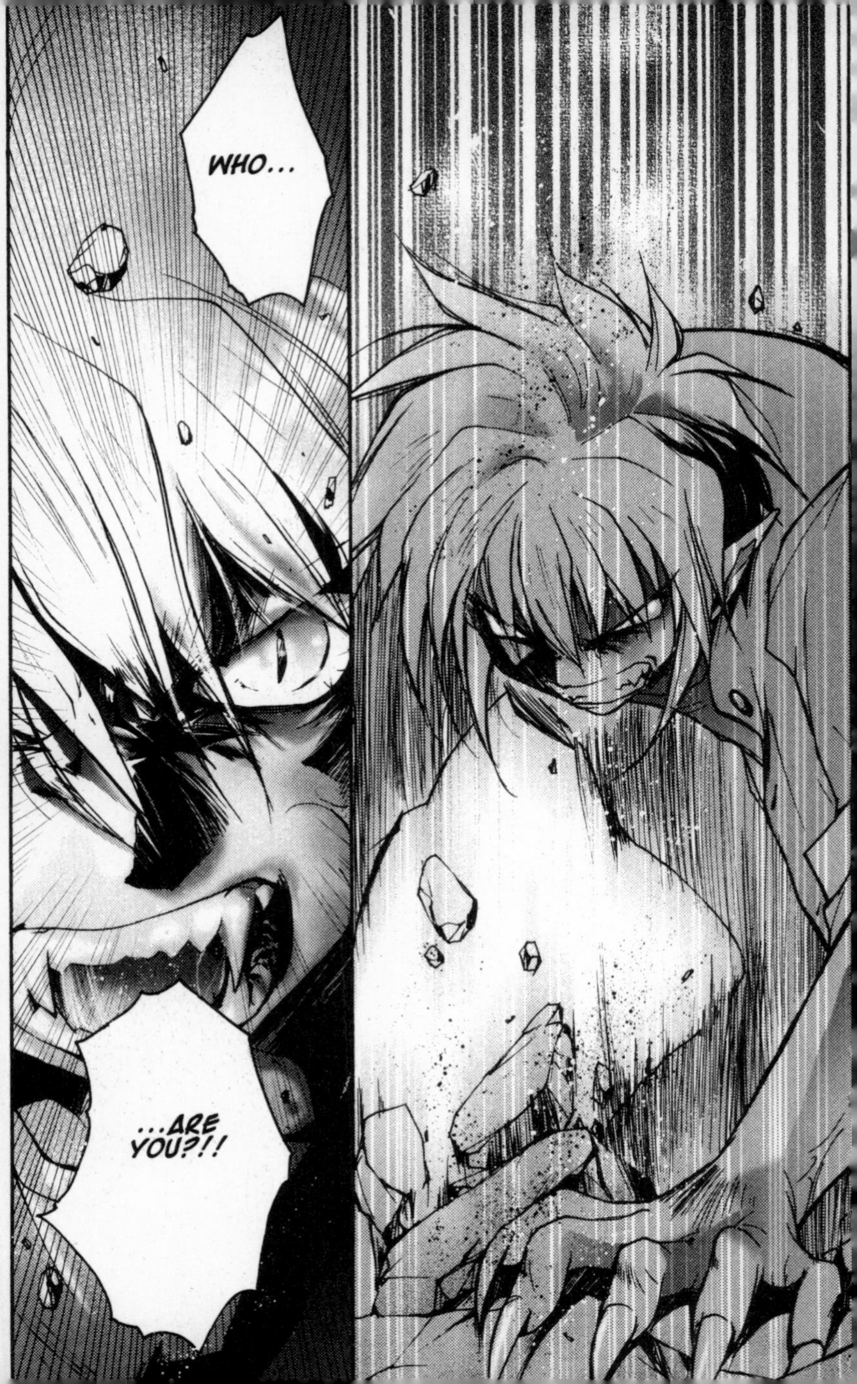
WHO...
...ARE YOU?!!

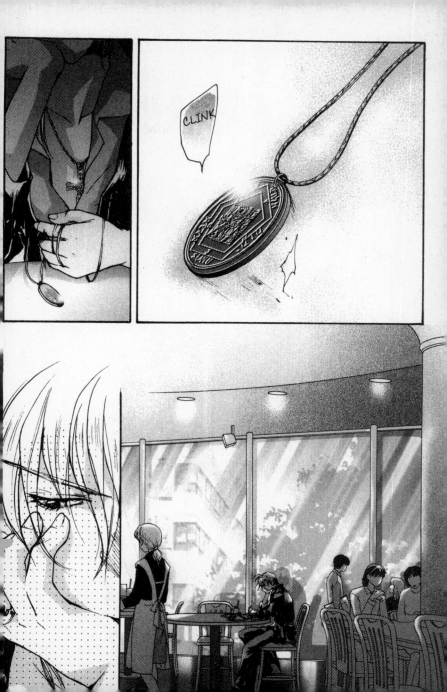

CLINK

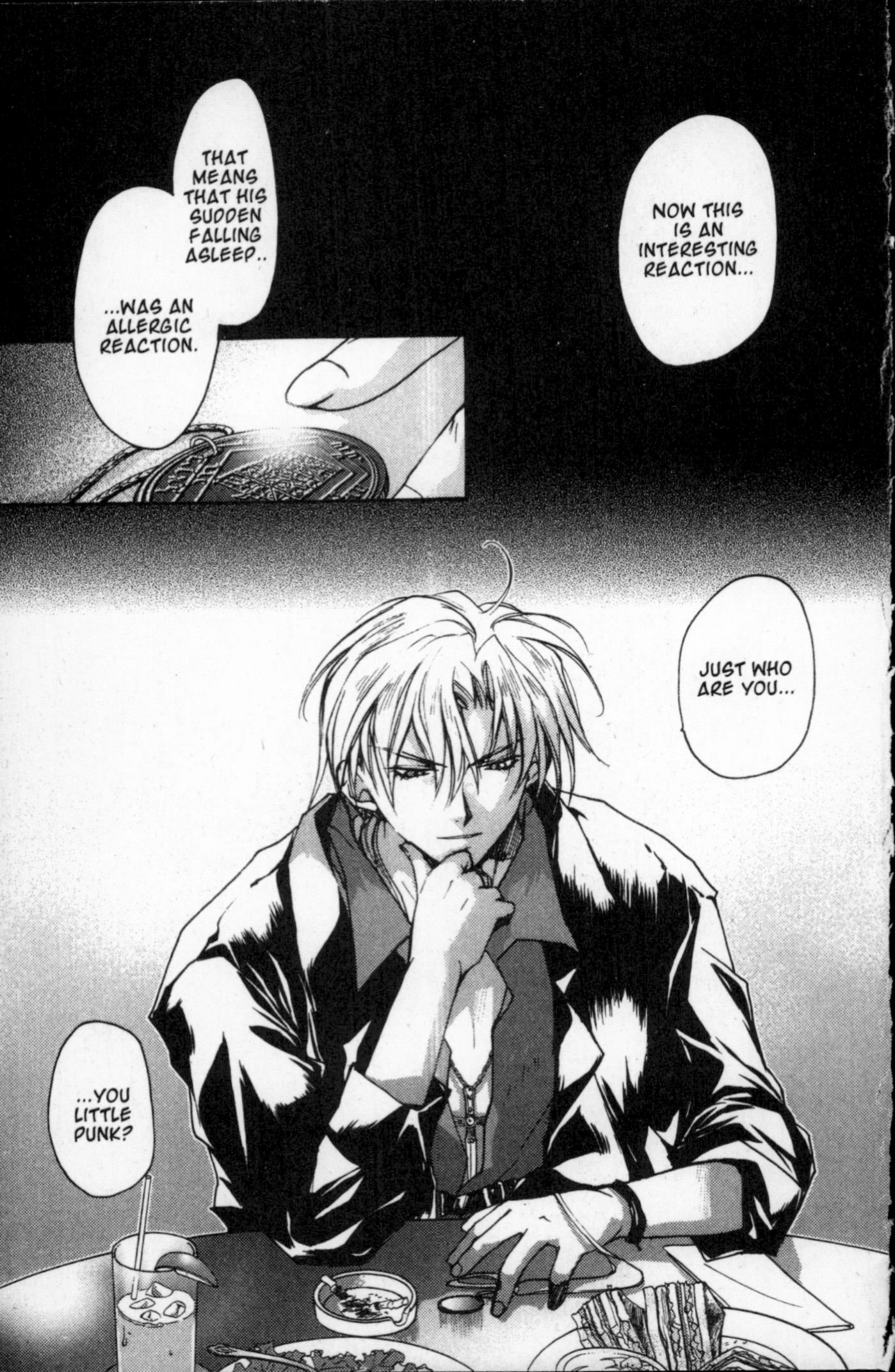
NOW THIS IS AN INTERESTING REACTION...
THAT MEANS THAT HIS SUDDEN FALLING ASLEEP..
...WAS AN ALLERGIC REACTION.
JUST WHO ARE YOU...
...YOU LITTLE PUNK?

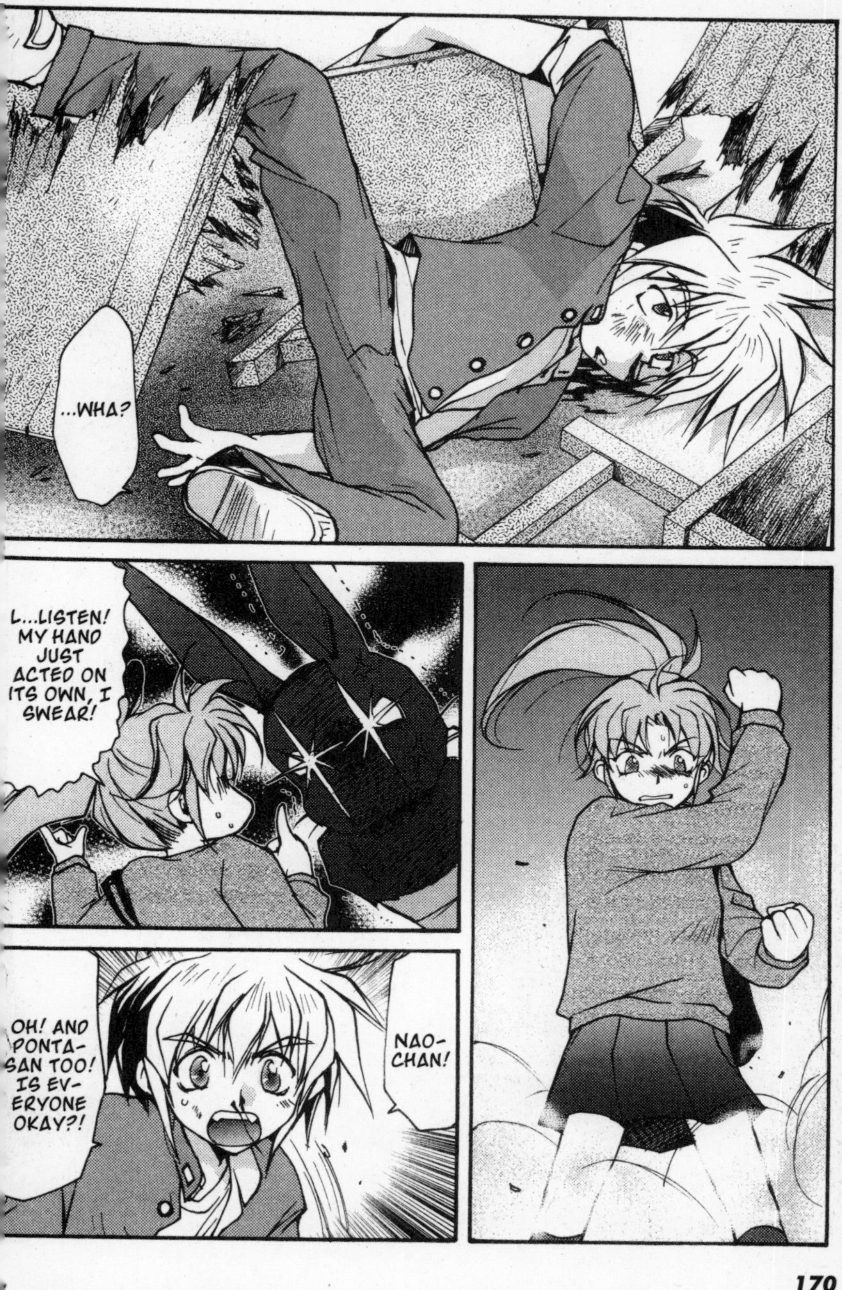
...WHA?
L...LISTEN! MY HAND JUST ACTED ON ITS OWN, I SWEAR!
NAO-CHAN!
OH! AND PONTA-SAN TOO! IS EV-ERYONE OKAY?!

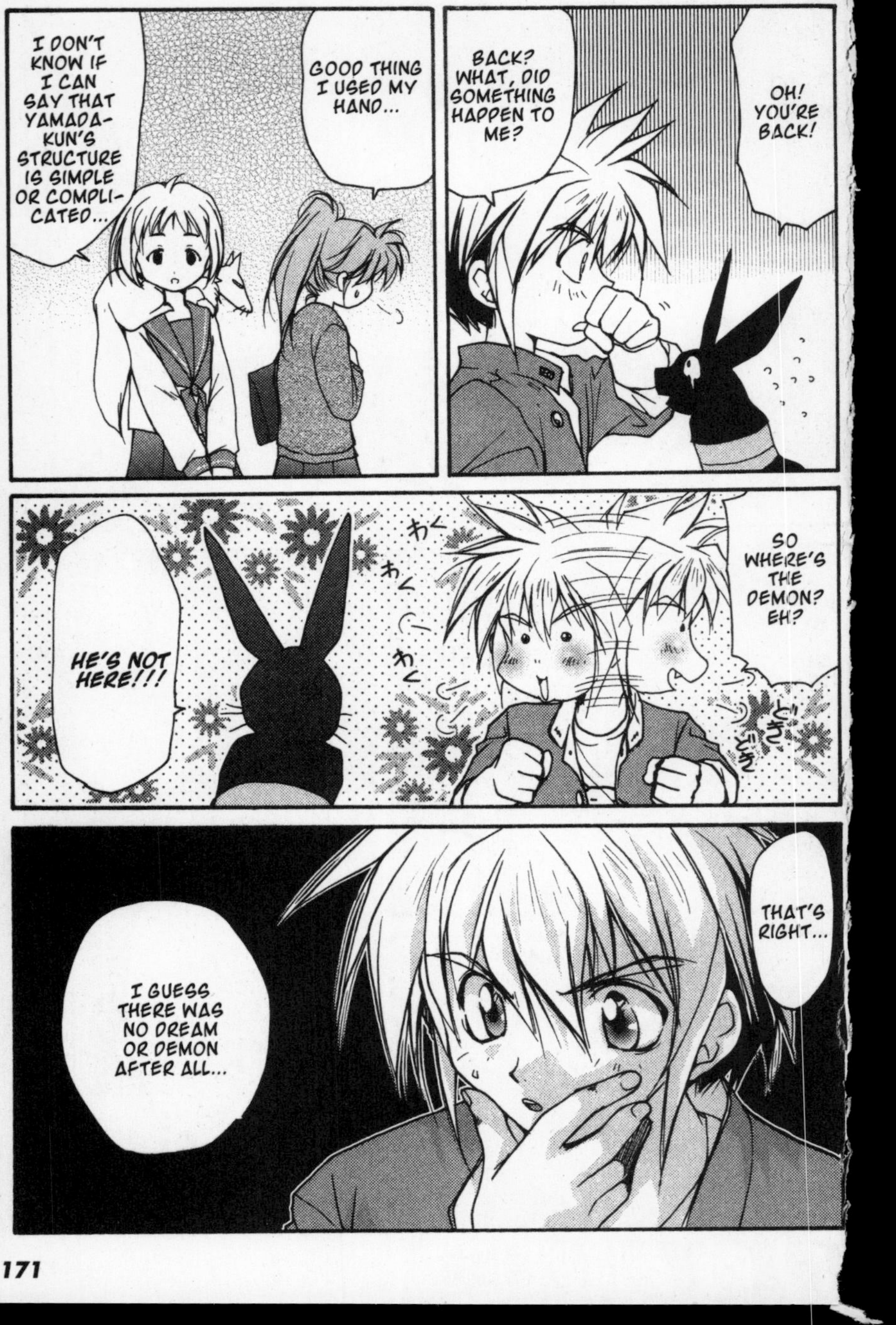
OH! YOU'RE BACK!
BACK? WHAT, DID SOMETHING HAPPEN TO ME?
GOOD THING I USED MY HAND...
I DON'T KNOW IF I CAN SAY THAT YAMADA-KUN'S STRUCTURE IS SIMPLE OR COMPLI-CATED...
SO WHERE'S THE DEMON? EH?
どきどき
わく
わく
わく
HE'S NOT HERE!!!
THAT'S RIGHT...
I GUESS THERE WAS NO DREAM OR DEMON AFTER ALL...

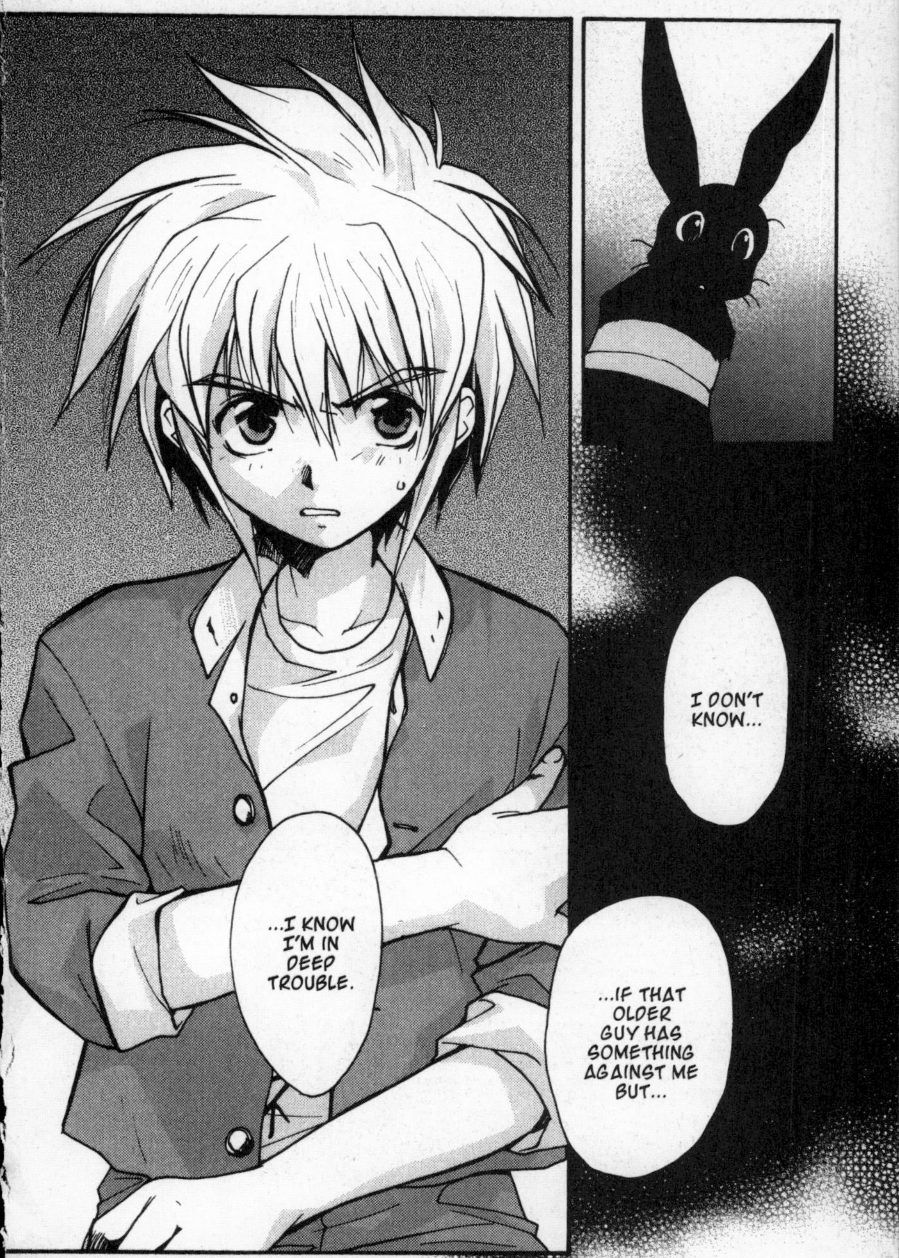
I DON'T KNOW...
...IF THAT OLDER GUY HAS SOMETHING AGAINST ME BUT...
...I KNOW I'M IN DEEP TROUBLE.

ACT 00 END

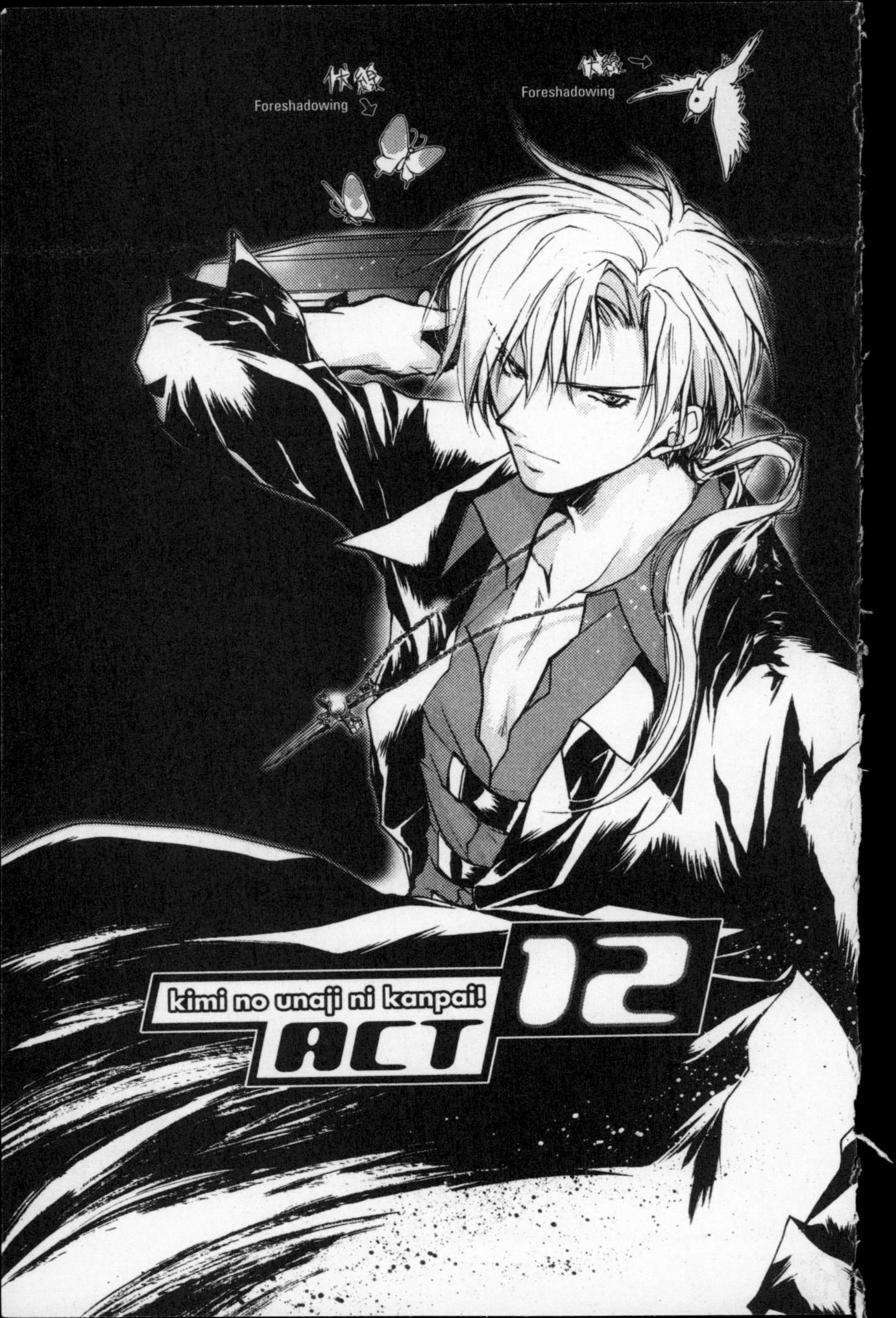

伏線
Foreshadowing
伏線
Foreshadowing
kimi no unaji ni kanpai!
ACT 12

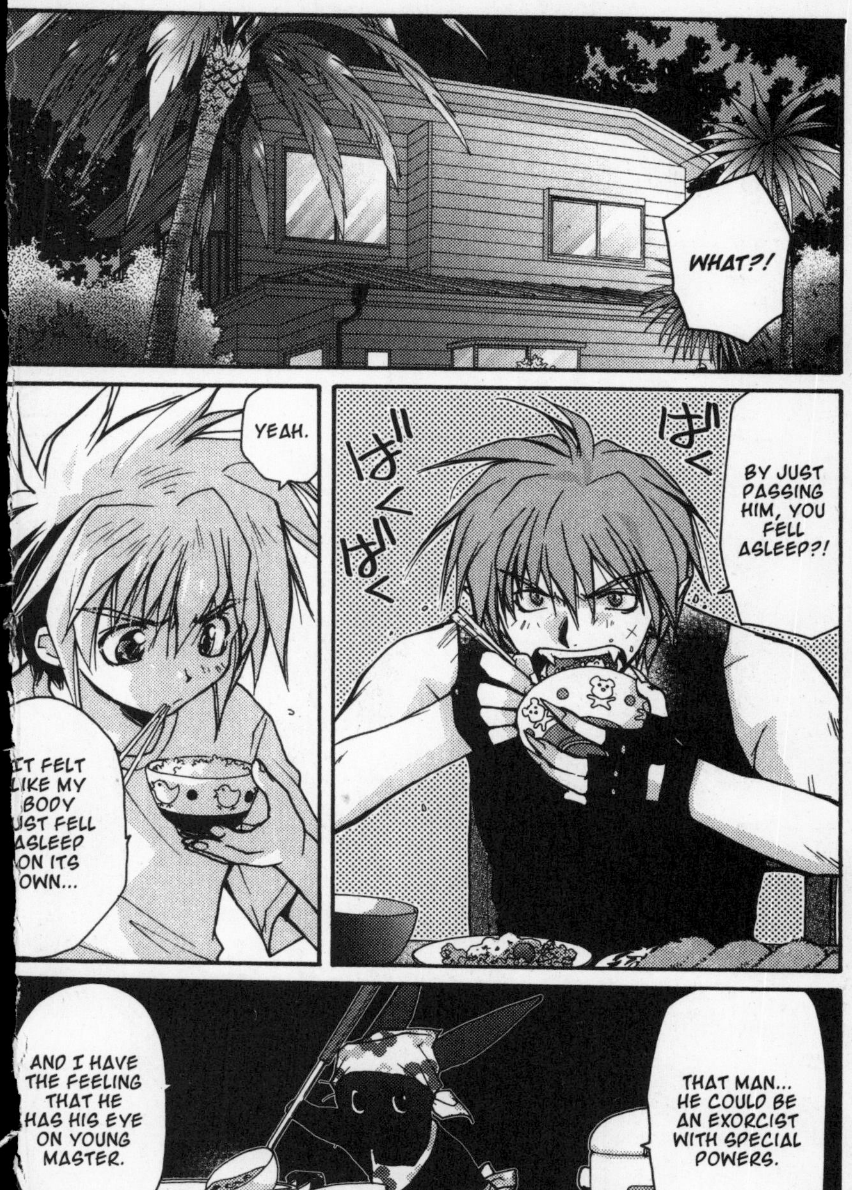
WHAT?!
ばく
BY JUST PASSING HIM, YOU FELL ASLEEP?!
ばくばく
YEAH.
IT FELT LIKE MY BODY JUST FELL ASLEEP ON ITS OWN...
THAT MAN... HE COULD BE AN EXORCIST WITH SPECIAL POWERS.
AND I HAVE THE FEELING THAT HE HAS HIS EYE ON YOUNG MASTER.

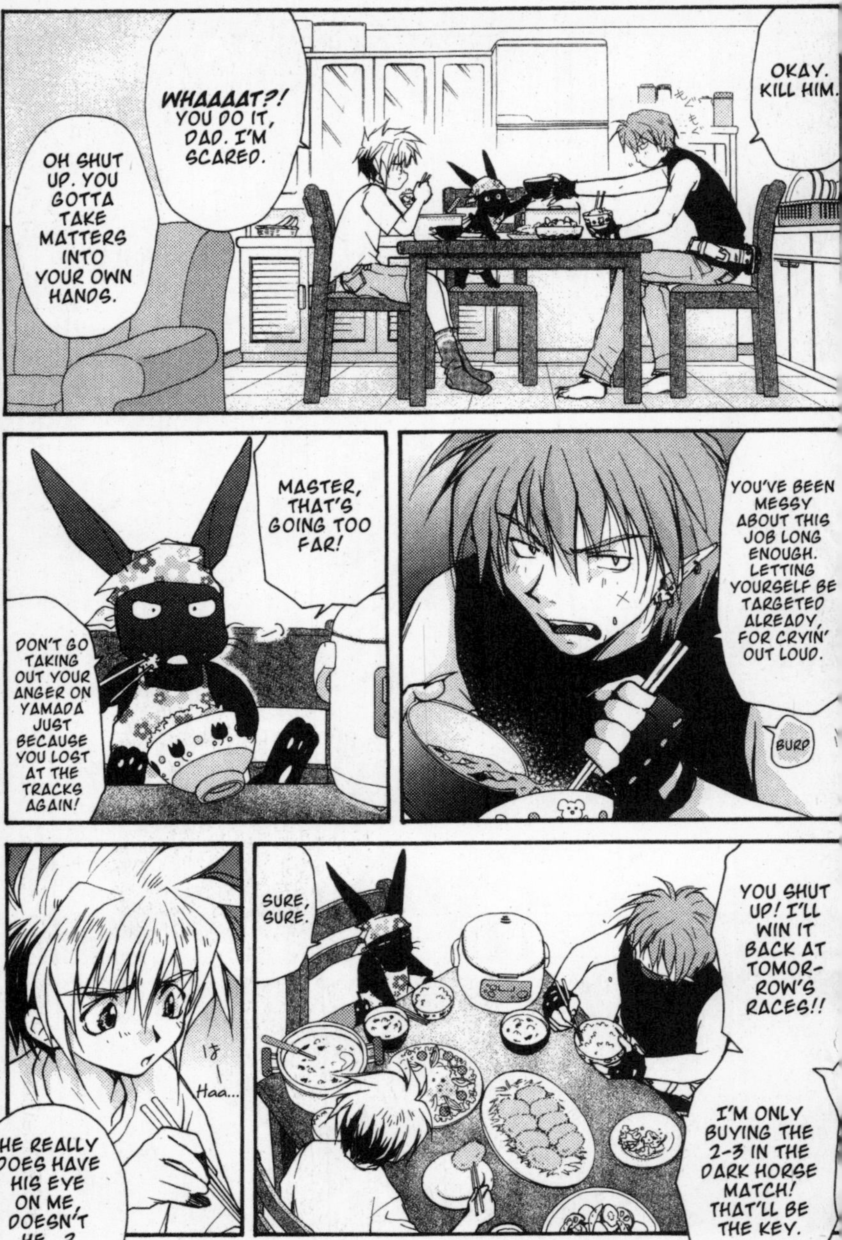
OKAY. KILL HIM.
WHAAAAT?! YOU DO IT, DAD. I'M SCARED.
OH SHUT UP. YOU GOTTA TAKE MATTERS INTO YOUR OWN HANDS.
YOU'VE BEEN MESSY ABOUT THIS JOB LONG ENOUGH. LETTING YOURSELF BE TARGETED ALREADY, FOR CRYIN' OUT LOUD.
BURP
MASTER, THAT'S GOING TOO FAR!
DON'T GO TAKING OUT YOUR ANGER ON YAMADA JUST BECAUSE YOU LOST AT THE TRACKS AGAIN!
YOU SHUT UP! I'LL WIN IT BACK AT TOMORROW'S RACES!!
SURE, SURE.
I'M ONLY BUYING THE 2-3 IN THE DARK HORSE MATCH! THAT'LL BE THE KEY.
は
Haa...
HE REALLY DOES HAVE HIS EYE ON ME, DOESN'T HE...?

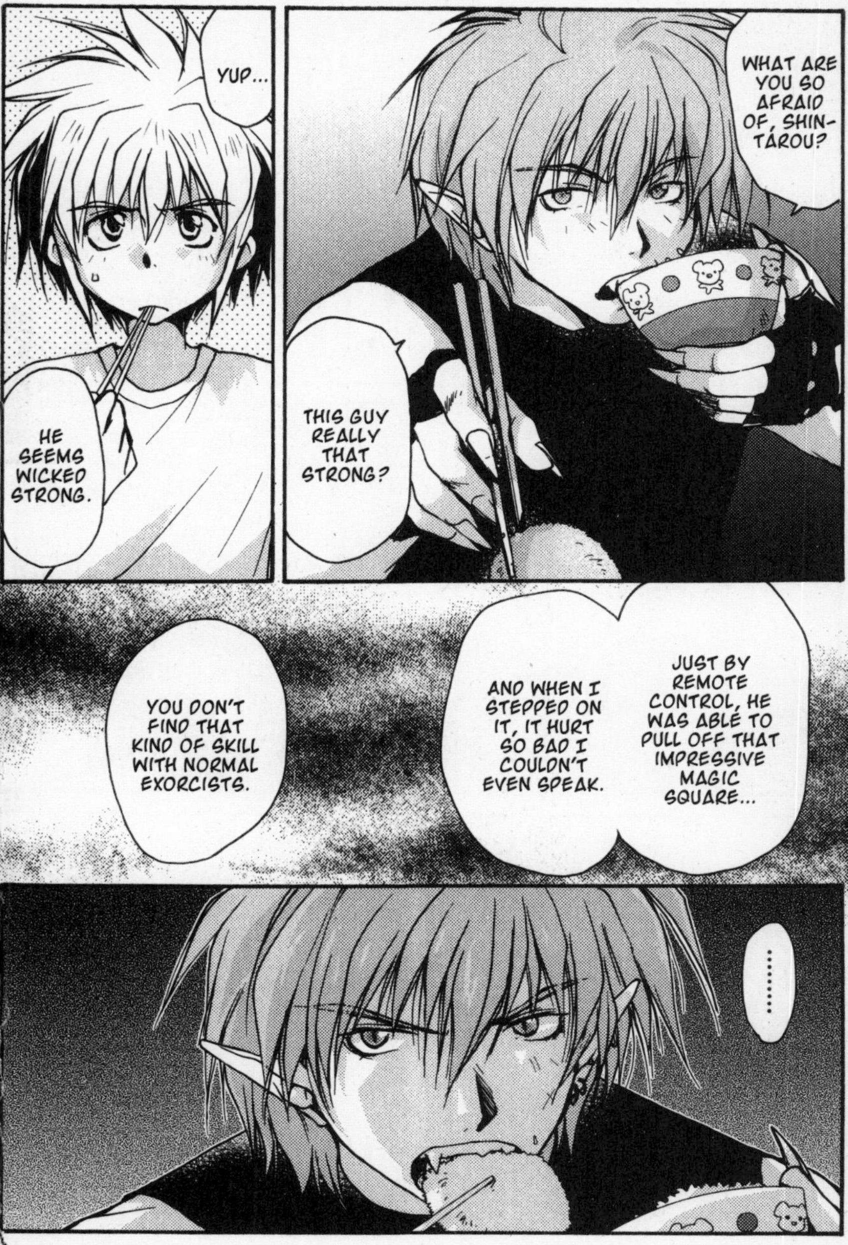
WHAT ARE YOU SO AFRAID OF, SHIN-TAROU?
THIS GUY REALLY THAT STRONG?
YUP...
HE SEEMS WICKED STRONG.
JUST BY REMOTE CONTROL, HE WAS ABLE TO PULL OFF THAT IMPRESSIVE MAGIC SQUARE...
AND WHEN I STEPPED ON IT, IT HURT SO BAD I COULDN'T EVEN SPEAK.
YOU DON'T FIND THAT KIND OF SKILL WITH NORMAL EXORCISTS.
....

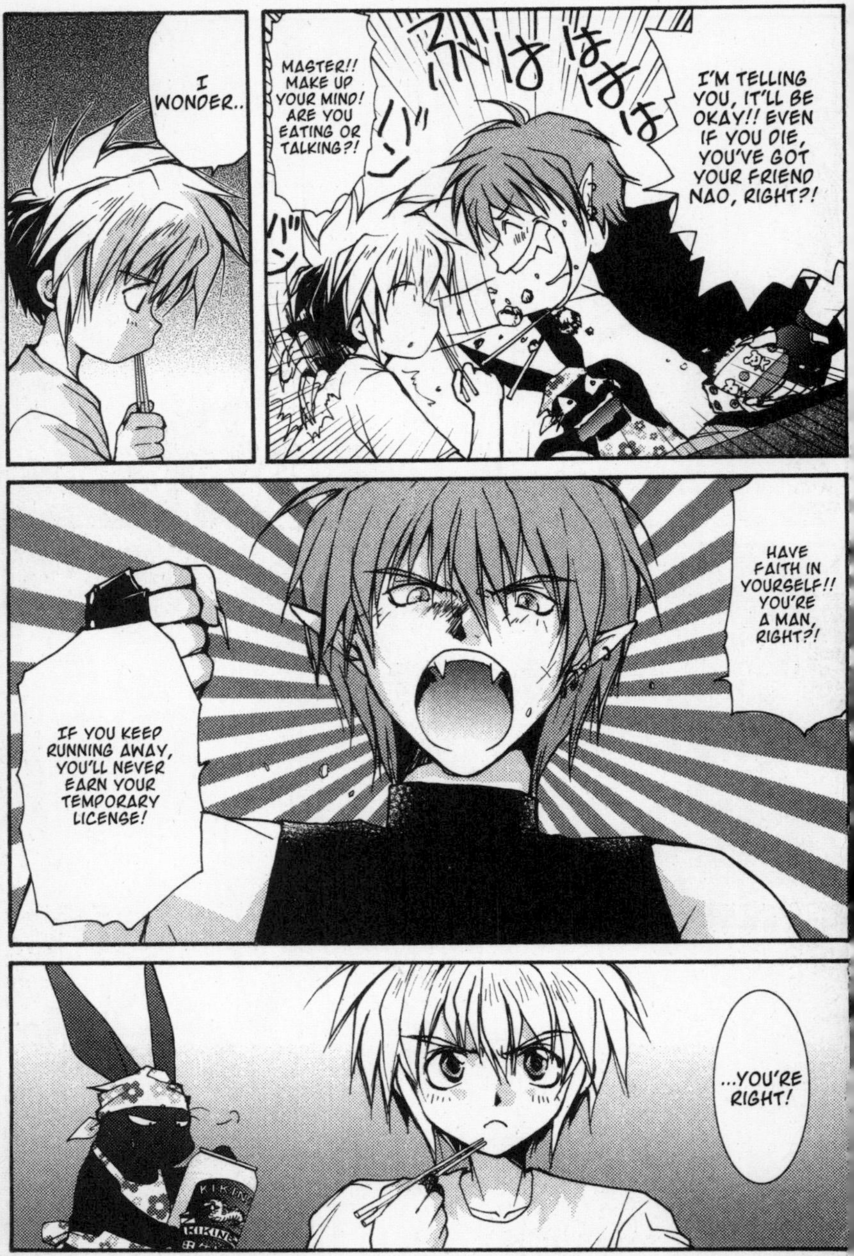
I'M TELLING YOU, IT'LL BE OKAY!! EVEN IF YOU DIE, YOU'VE GOT YOUR FRIEND NAO, RIGHT?!
ぶはははは
MASTER!! MAKE UP YOUR MIND! ARE YOU EATING OR TALKING?!
I WONDER..
HAVE FAITH IN YOURSELF!! YOU'RE A MAN, RIGHT?!
IF YOU KEEP RUNNING AWAY, YOU'LL NEVER EARN YOUR TEMPORARY LICENSE!
...YOU'RE RIGHT!

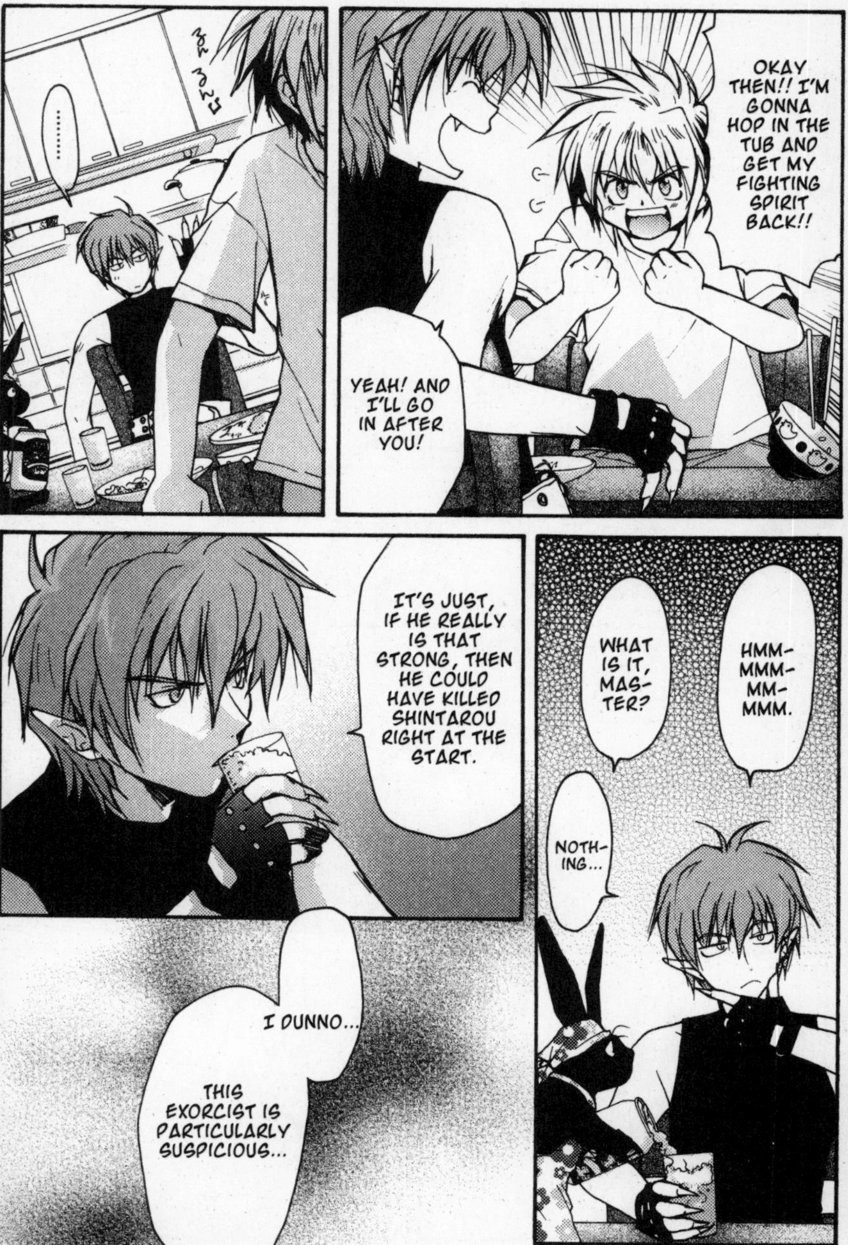
OKAY THEN!! I'M GONNA HOP IN THE TUB AND GET MY FIGHTING SPIRIT BACK!!
YEAH! AND I'LL GO IN AFTER YOU!
......
HMM-MMM-MM-MMM.
WHAT IS IT, MASTER?
NOTHING...
IT'S JUST, IF HE REALLY IS THAT STRONG, THEN HE COULD HAVE KILLED SHINTAROU RIGHT AT THE START.
I DUNNO...
THIS EXORCIST IS PARTICULARLY SUSPICIOUS...

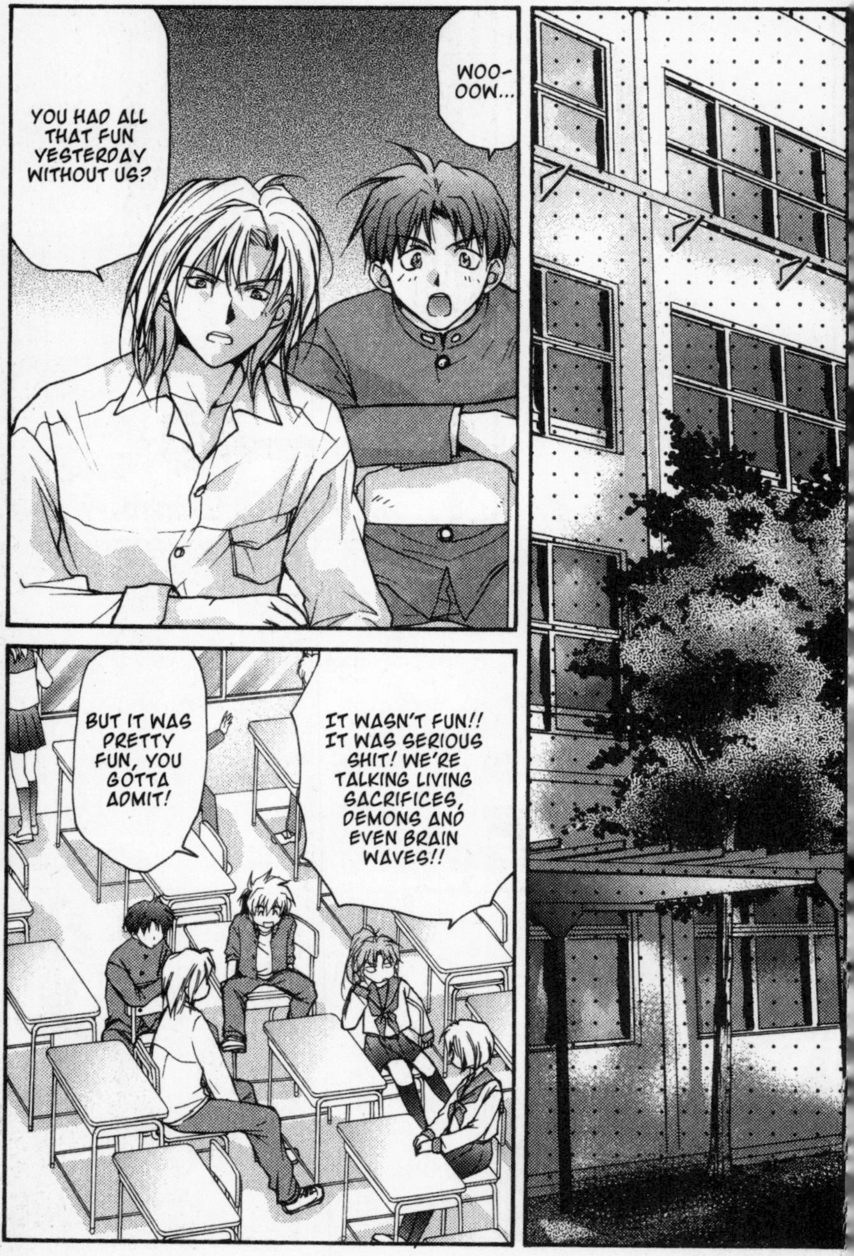
WOO-OOW...
YOU HAD ALL THAT FUN YESTERDAY WITHOUT US?
IT WASN'T FUN!! IT WAS SERIOUS SHIT! WE'RE TALKING LIVING SACRIFICES, DEMONS AND EVEN BRAIN WAVES!!
BUT IT WAS PRETTY FUN, YOU GOTTA ADMIT!

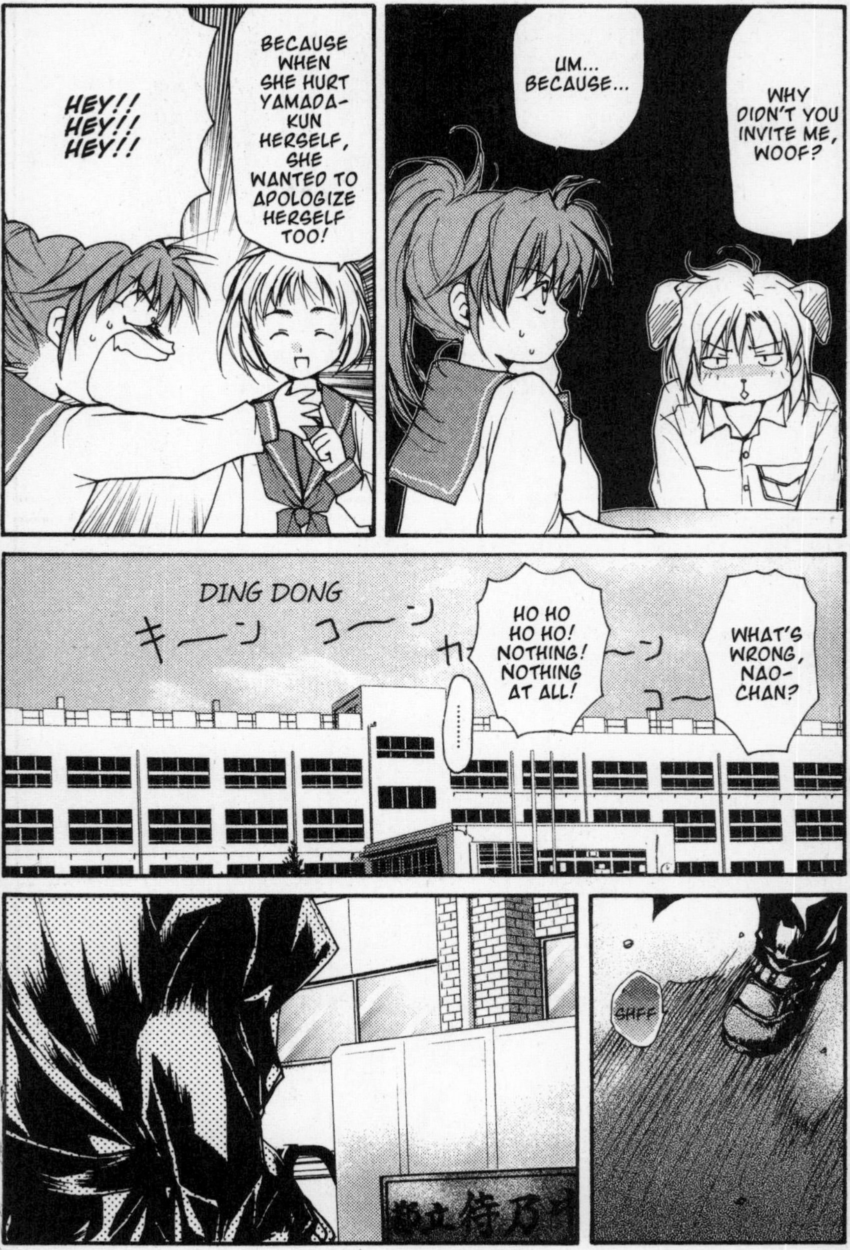
WHY DIDN'T YOU INVITE ME, WOOF?
UM... BECAUSE...
BECAUSE WHEN SHE HURT YAMADA-KUN HERSELF, SHE WANTED TO APOLOGIZE HERSELF TOO!
HEY!! HEY!! HEY!!
WHAT'S WRONG, NAO-CHAN?
HO HO HO HO! NOTHING! NOTHING AT ALL!
....
DING DONG
キーン
コーン
SHFF

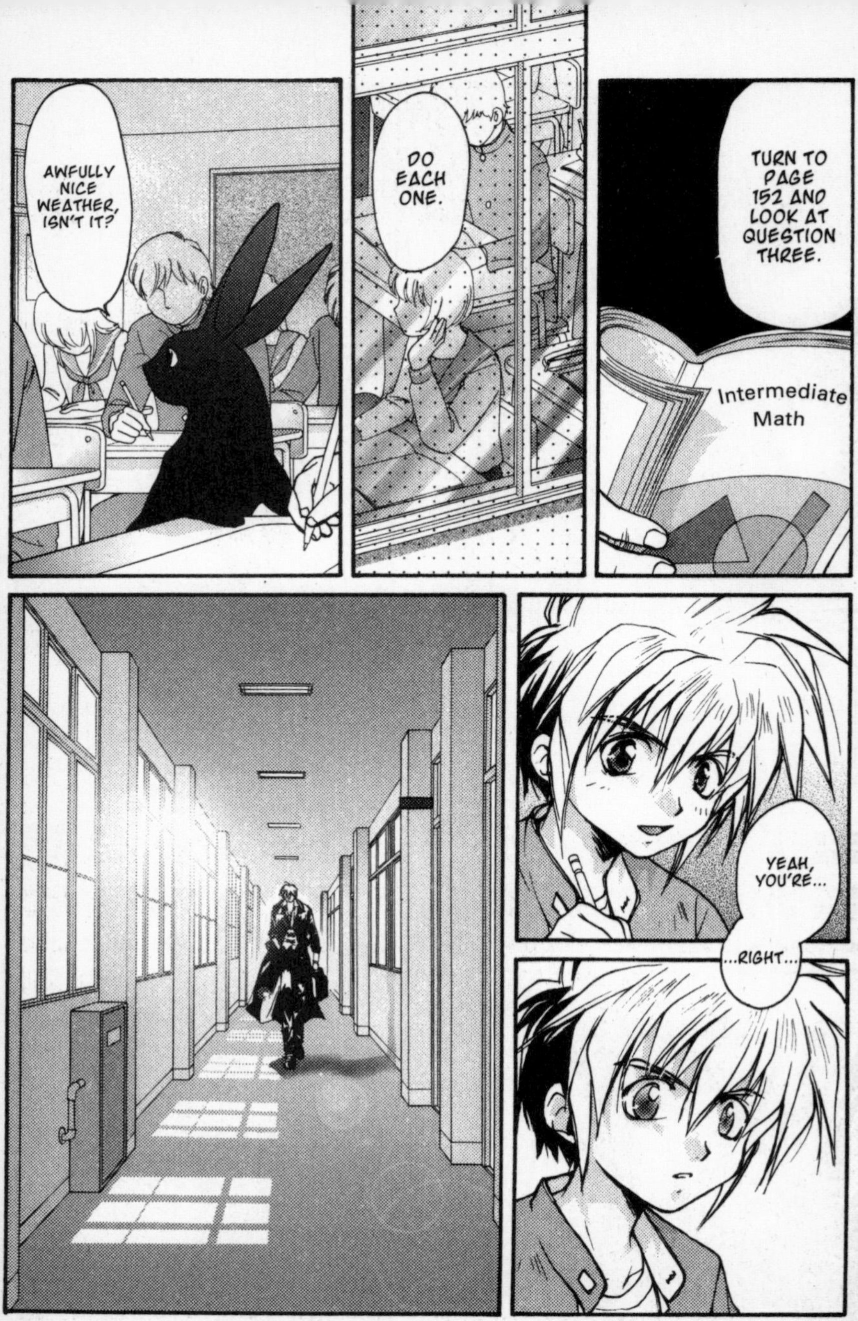
TURN TO PAGE 152 AND LOOK AT QUESTION THREE.
Intermediate Math
DO EACH ONE.
AWFULLY NICE WEATHER, ISN'T IT?
YEAH, YOU'RE...
...RIGHT...

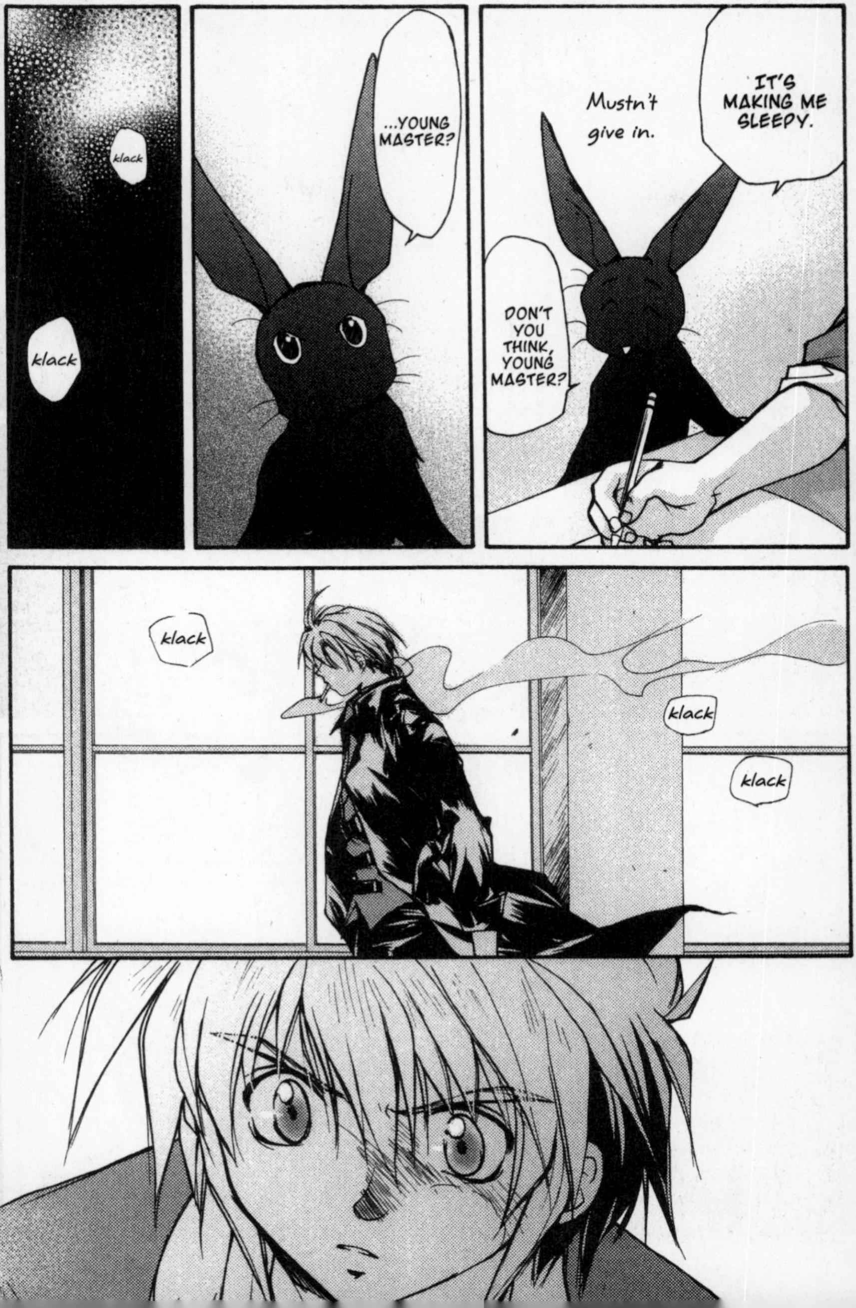

IT'S MAKING ME SLEEPY.
Mustn't give in.
DON'T YOU THINK, YOUNG MASTER?
...YOUNG MASTER?
klack
klack
klack
klack
klack

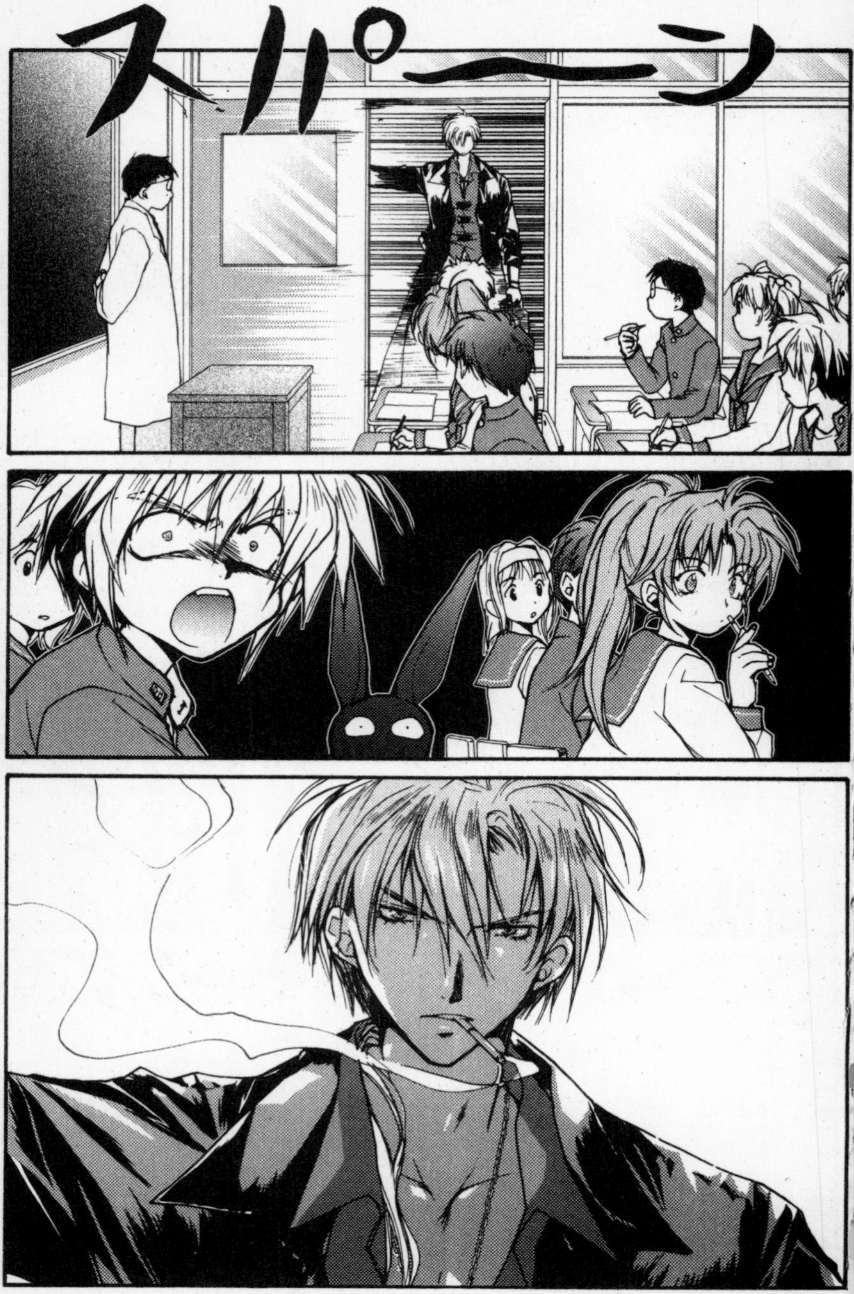
スパーーン

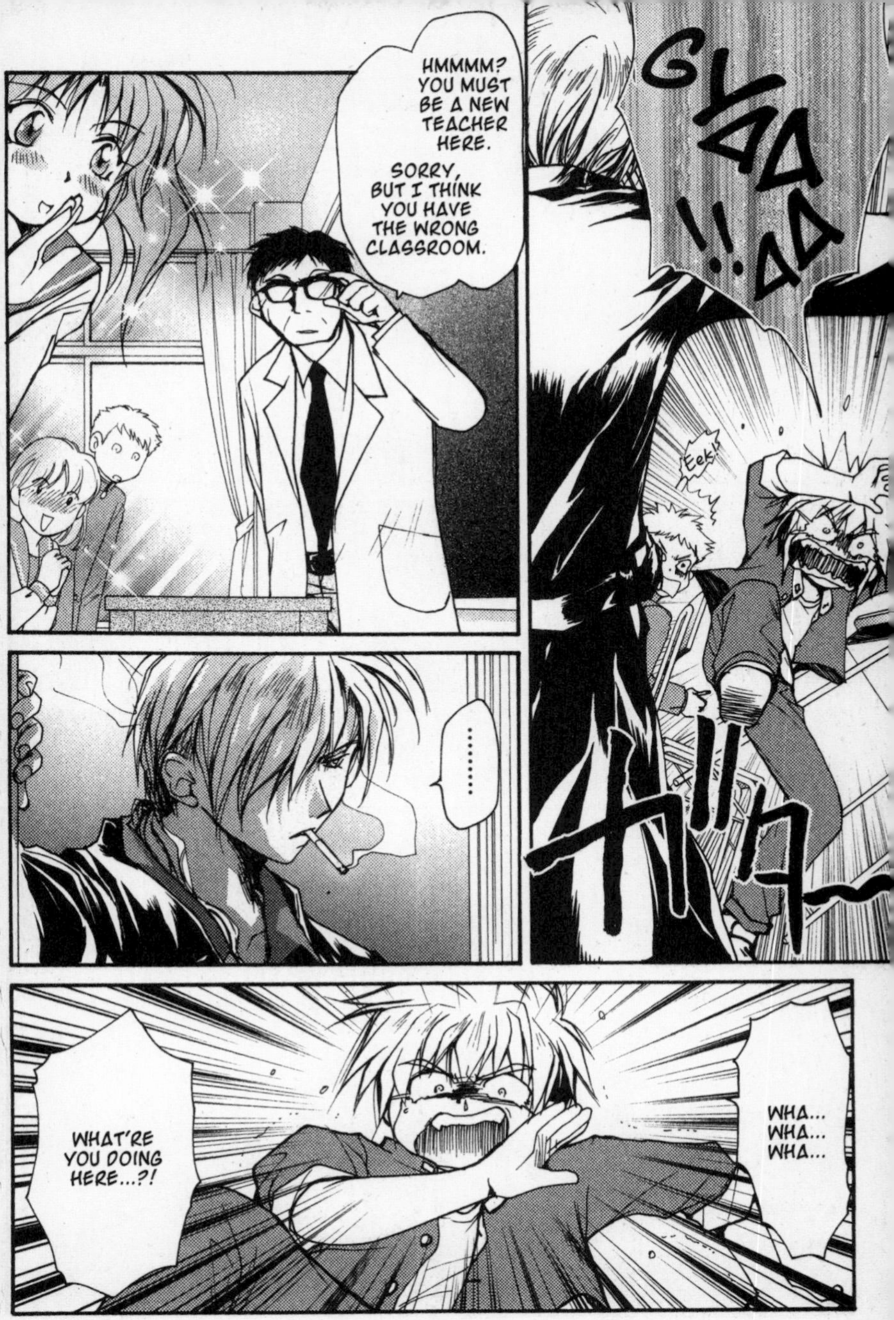
GYAA!!AA
Eek!
ガタ〜
HMMMM? YOU MUST BE A NEW TEACHER HERE.
SORRY, BUT I THINK YOU HAVE THE WRONG CLASSROOM.
....
WHA... WHA... WHA...
WHAT'RE YOU DOING HERE...?!

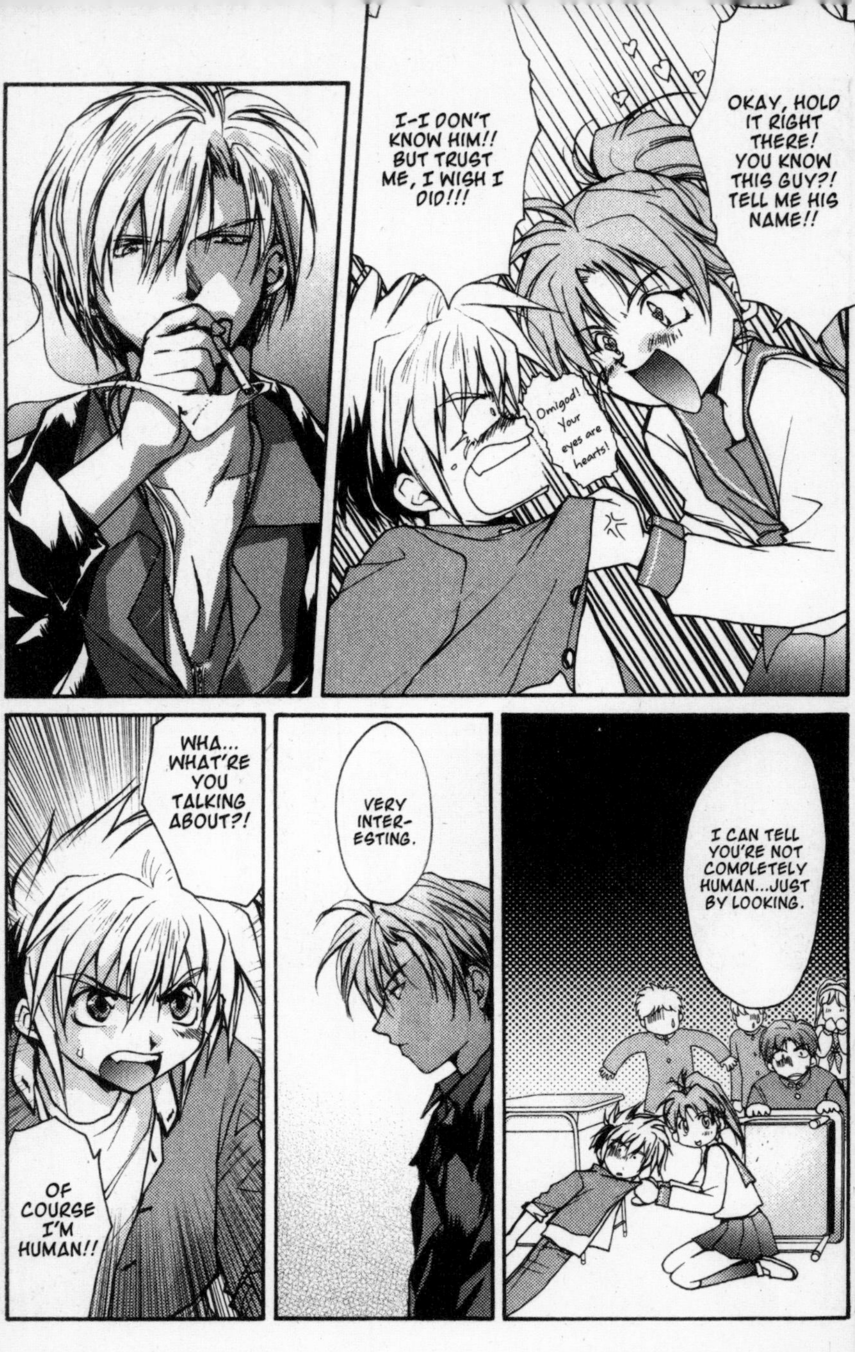
OKAY, HOLD IT RIGHT THERE! YOU KNOW THIS GUY?! TELL ME HIS NAME!!
I-I DON'T KNOW HIM!! BUT TRUST ME, I WISH I DID!!!
Omigod! Your eyes are hearts!
I CAN TELL YOU'RE NOT COMPLETELY HUMAN...JUST BY LOOKING.
VERY INTER-ESTING.
WHA... WHAT'RE YOU TALKING ABOUT?!
OF COURSE I'M HUMAN!!

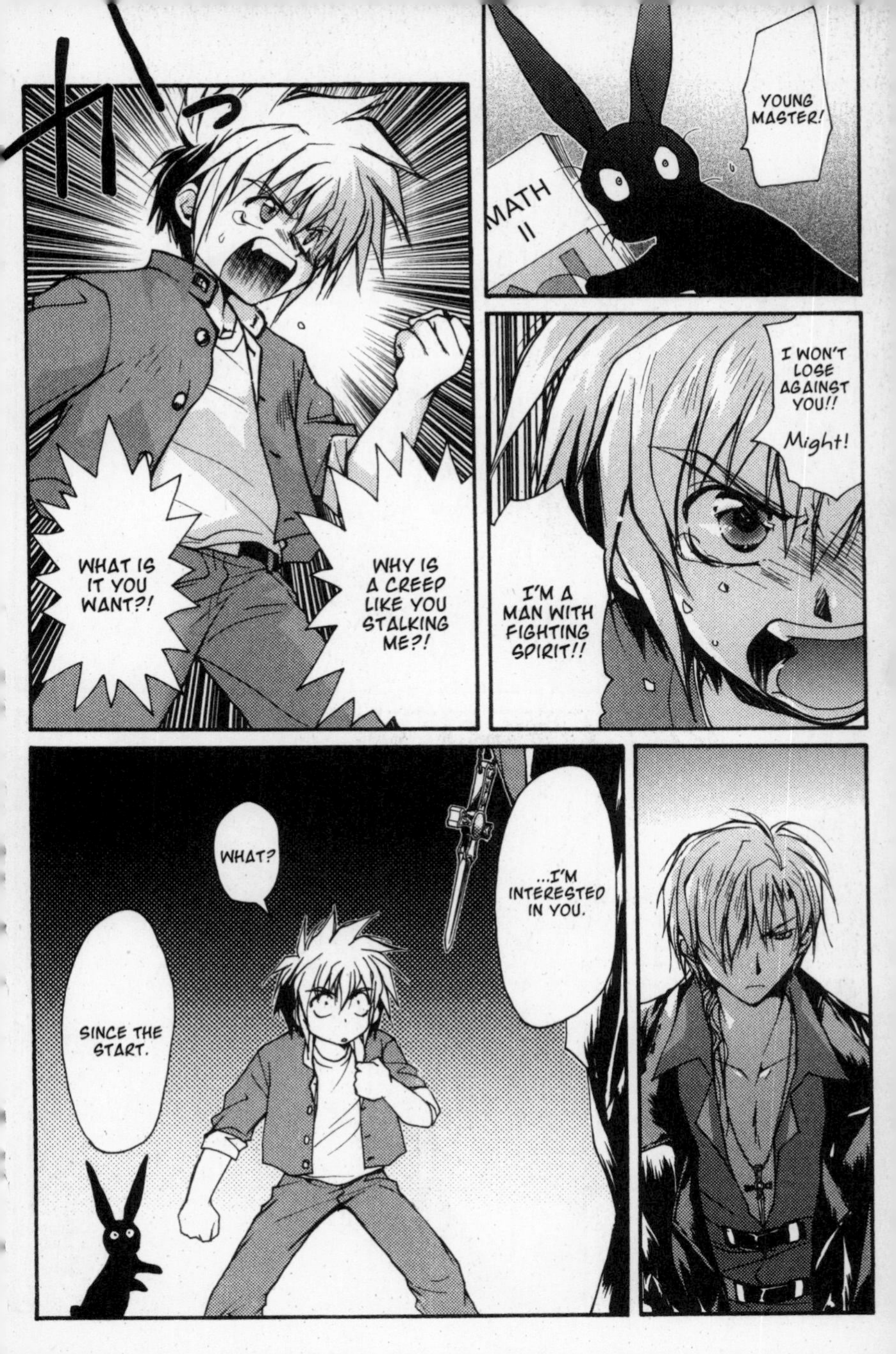
YOUNG MASTER!
MATH II
I WON'T LOSE AGAINST YOU!!
Might!
I'M A MAN WITH FIGHTING SPIRIT!!
カッ
WHY IS A CREEP LIKE YOU STALKING ME?!
WHAT IS IT YOU WANT?!
...I'M INTERESTED IN YOU.
WHAT?
SINCE THE START.

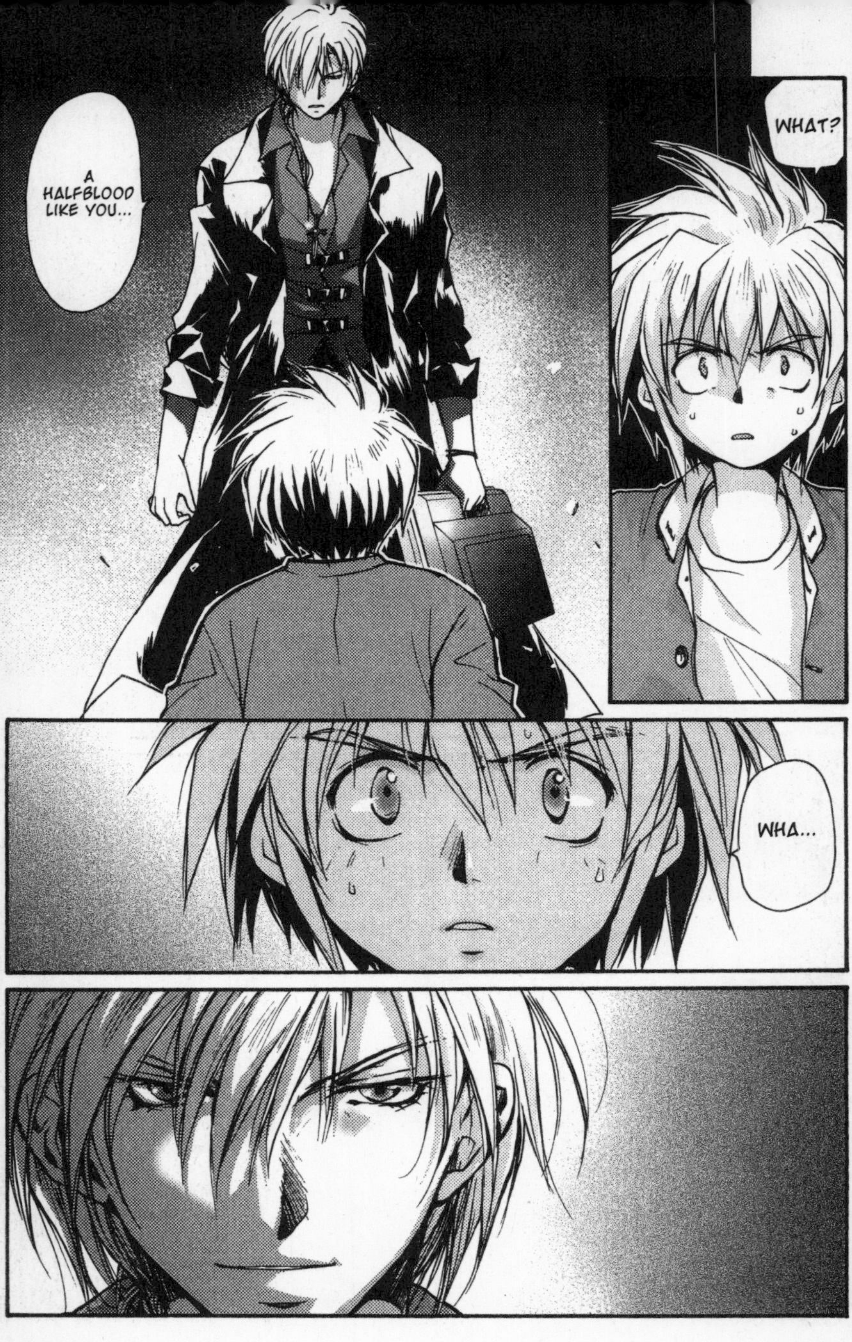
WHAT?
A HALFBLOOD LIKE YOU...
WHA...

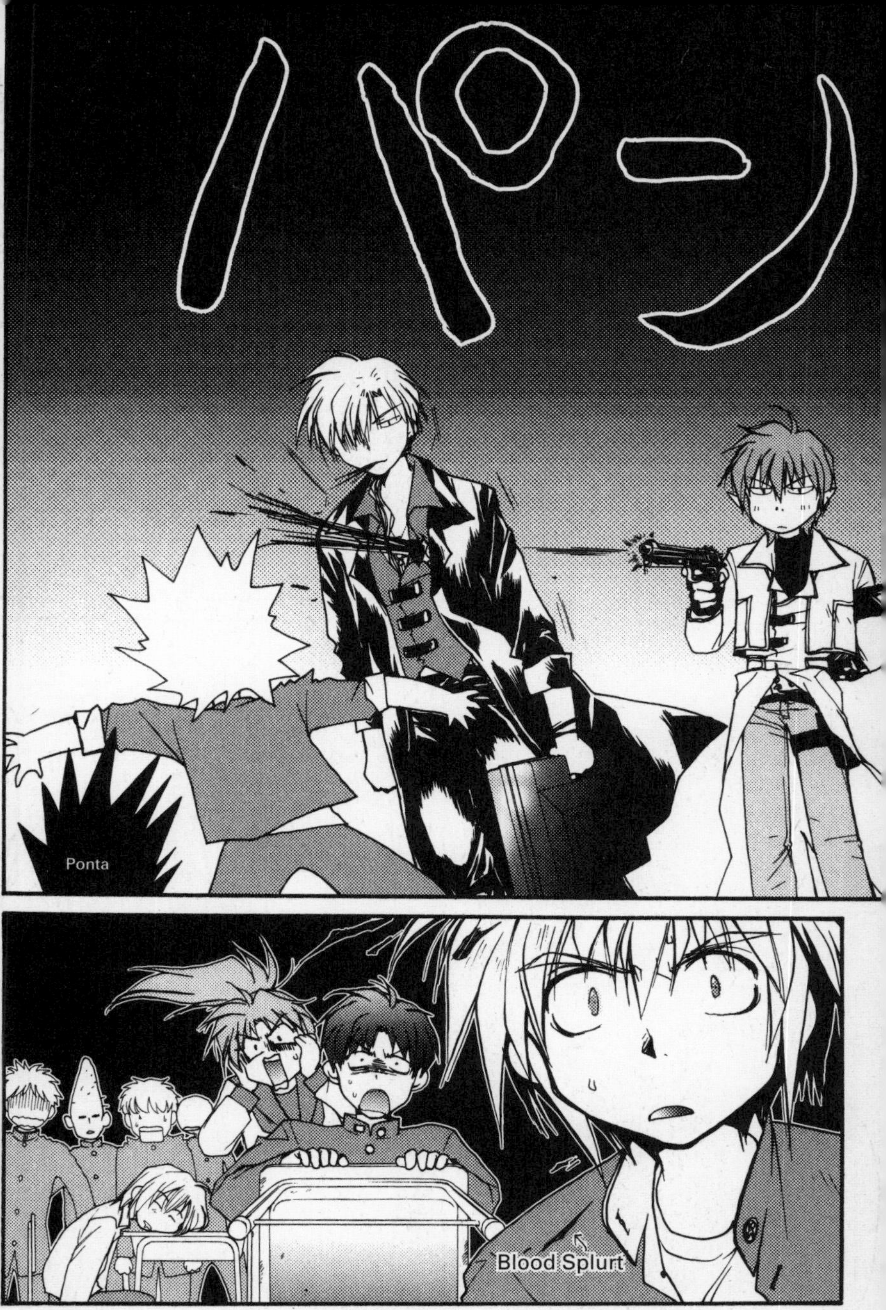
パーン
Ponta
Blood Splurt

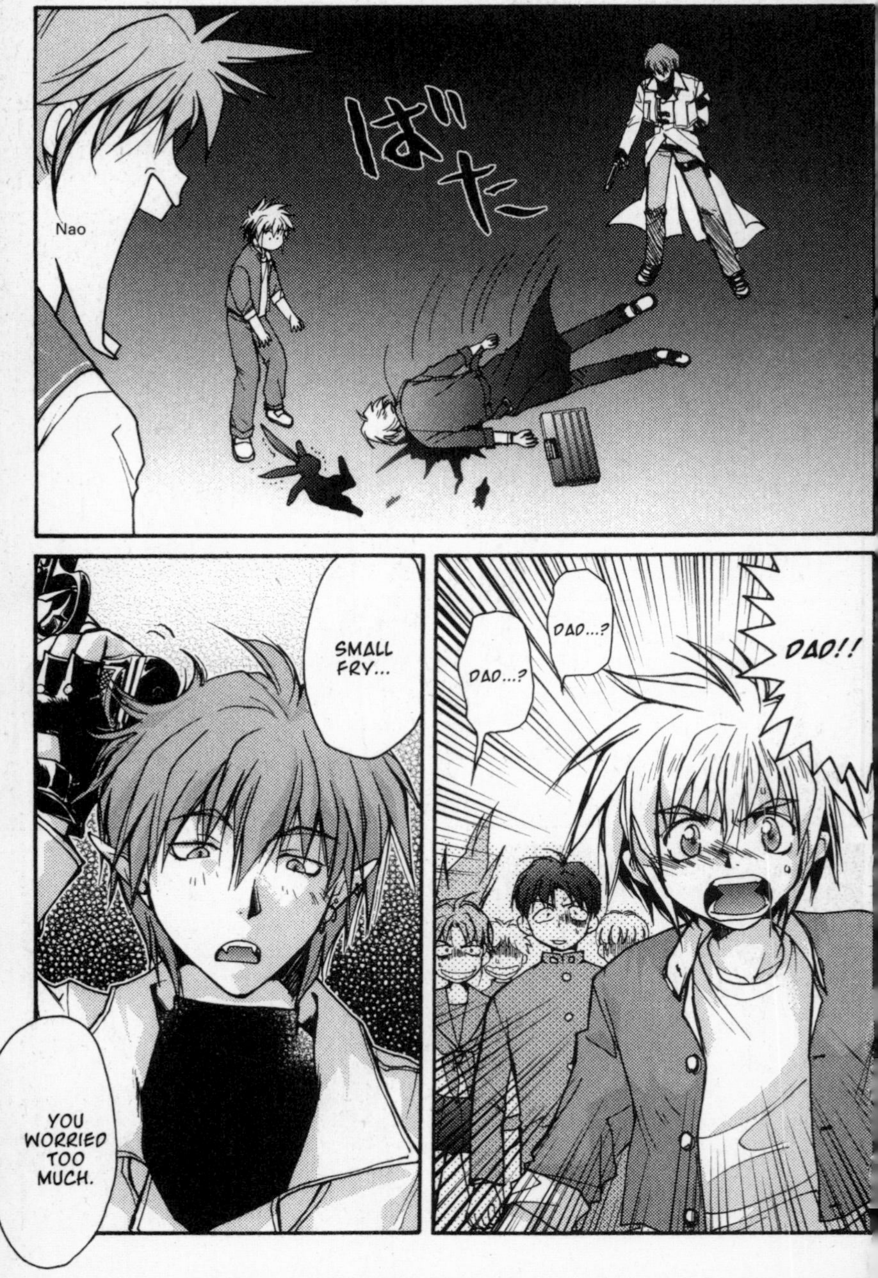
ばいた～
Nao
DAD!!
DAD...?
DAD...?
SMALL FRY...
YOU WORRIED TOO MUCH.

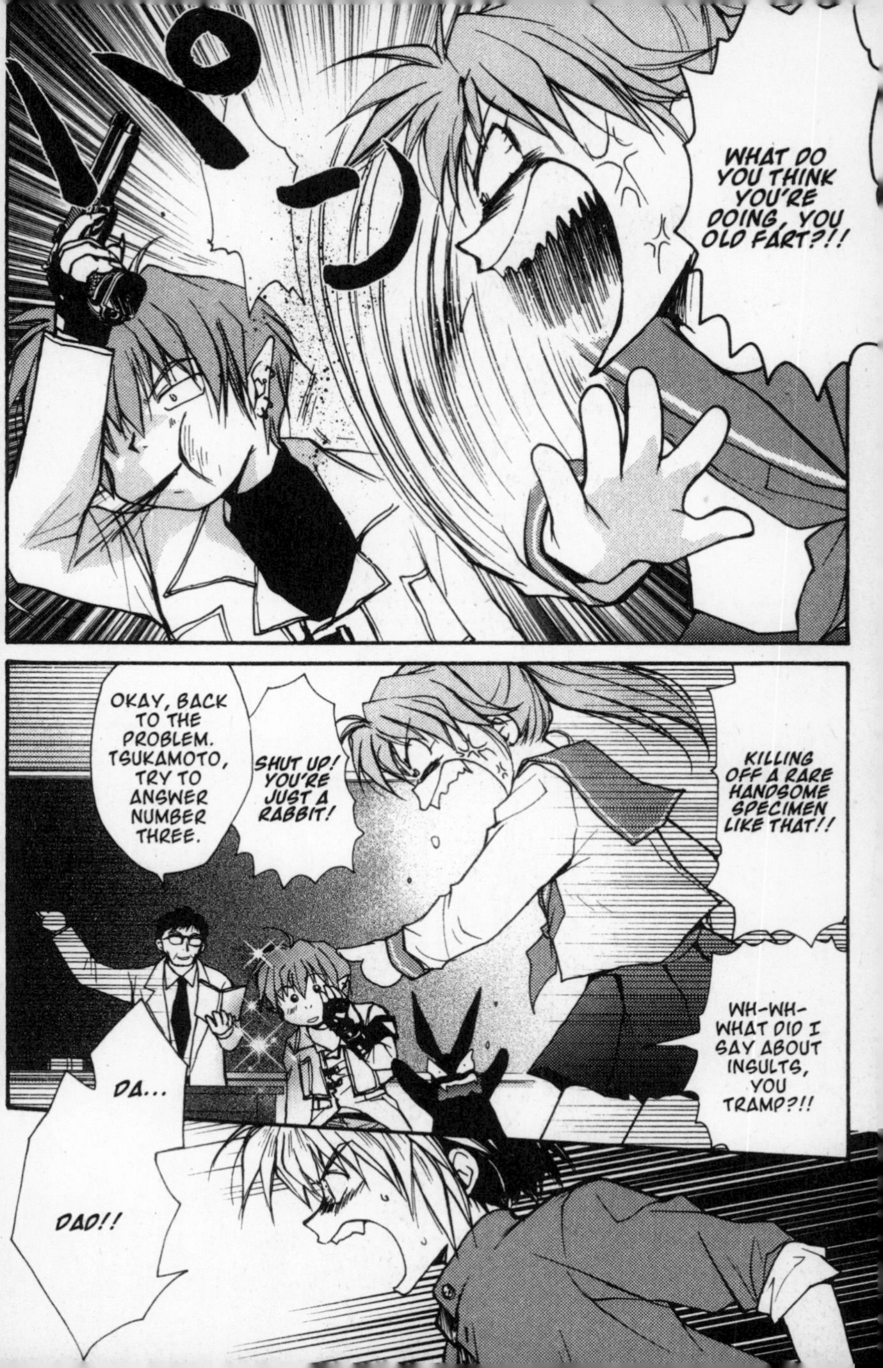
WHAT DO YOU THINK YOU'RE DOING, YOU OLD FART?!!
KILLING OFF A RARE HANDSOME SPECIMEN LIKE THAT!!
SHUT UP! YOU'RE JUST A RABBIT!
OKAY, BACK TO THE PROBLEM. TSUKAMOTO, TRY TO ANSWER NUMBER THREE.
WH-WH-WHAT DID I SAY ABOUT INSULTS, YOU TRAMP?!!
DA...
DAD!!

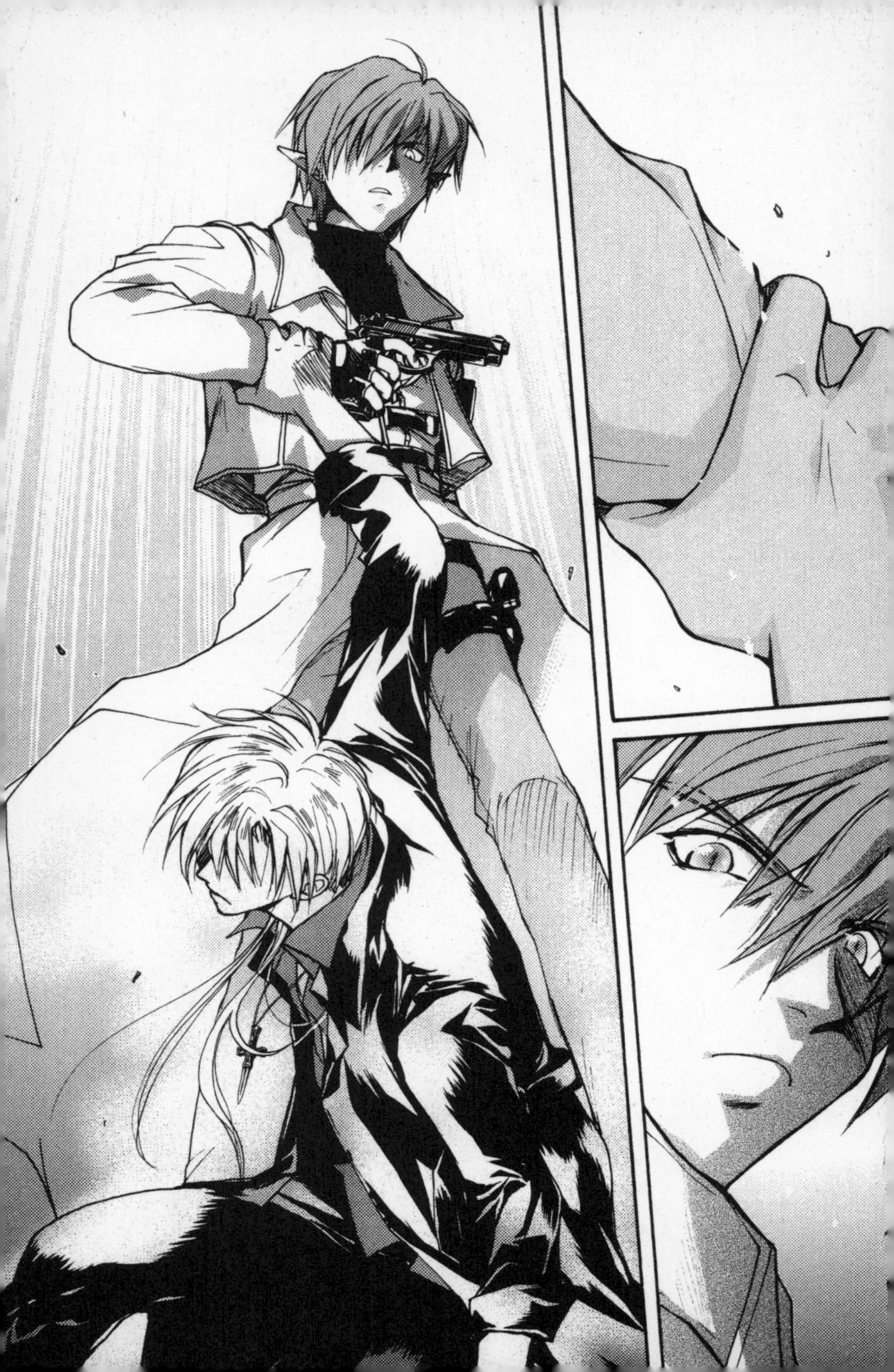

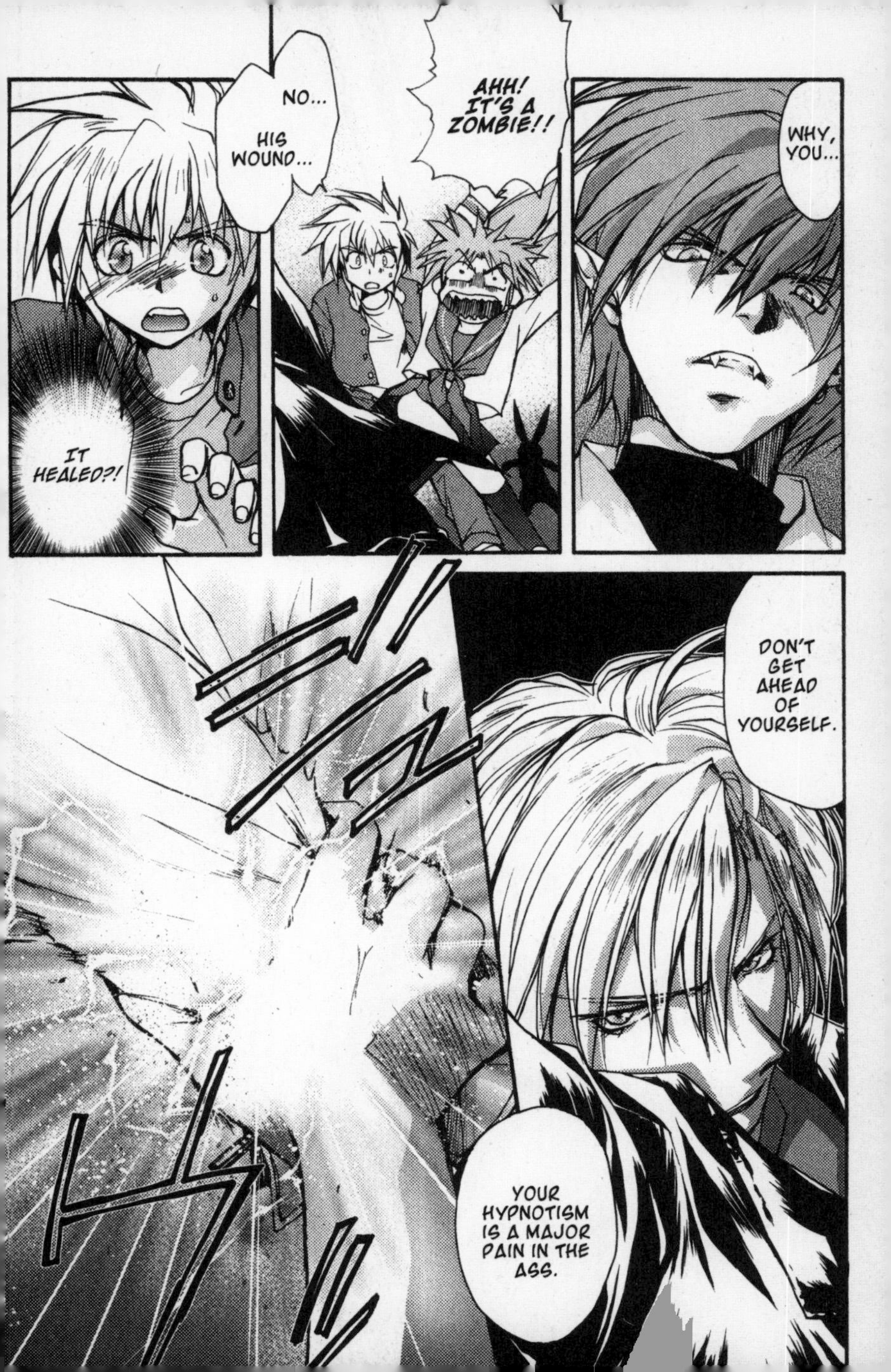
WHY, YOU...
AHH! IT'S A ZOMBIE!!
NO... HIS WOUND...
IT HEALED?!
DON'T GET AHEAD OF YOURSELF.
YOUR HYPNOTISM IS A MAJOR PAIN IN THE ASS.

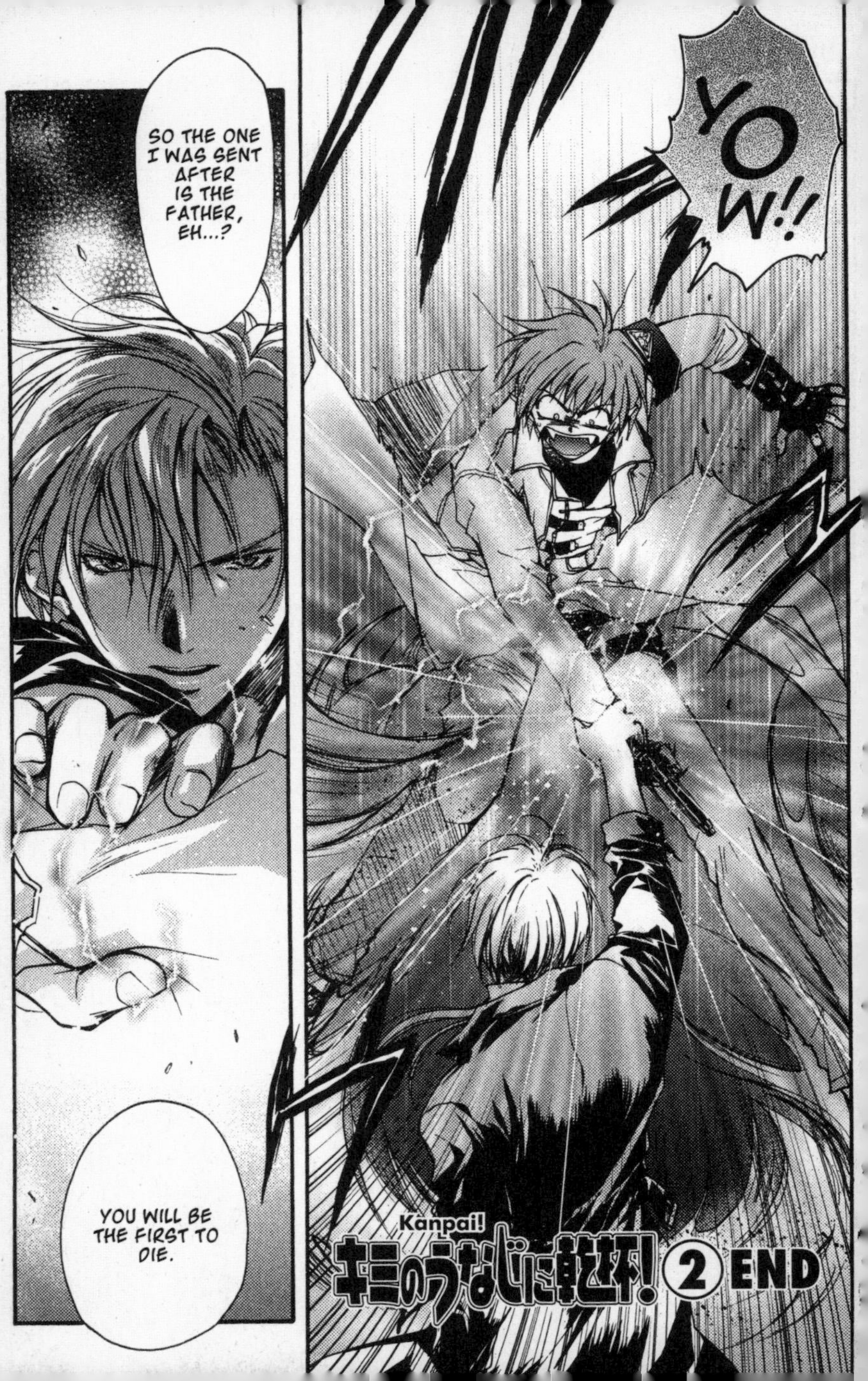
YOW!!
Kanpai!
キミのうなじに乾杯! 2 END
SO THE ONE I WAS SENT AFTER IS THE FATHER, EH...?
YOU WILL BE THE FIRST TO DIE.

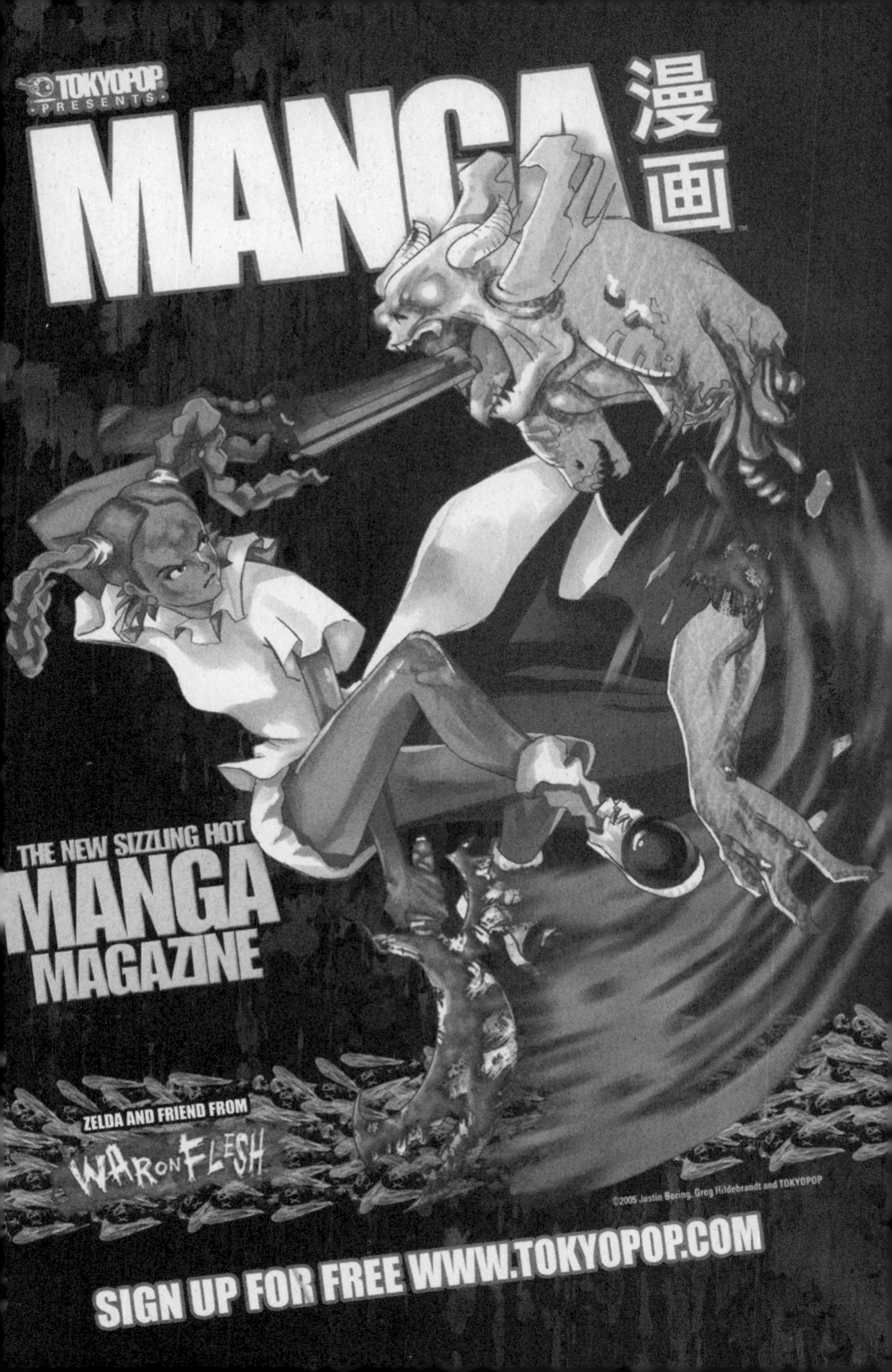

TOKYOPOP PRESENTS
MANGA 漫画
THE NEW SIZZLING HOT
MANGA
MAGAZINE
ZELDA AND FRIEND FROM
WAR ON FLESH
©2005 Justin Boring, Greg Hildebrandt and TOKYOPOP
SIGN UP FOR FREE WWW.TOKYOPOP.COM

TOKYOPOP SHOP

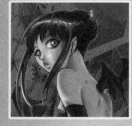
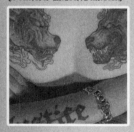

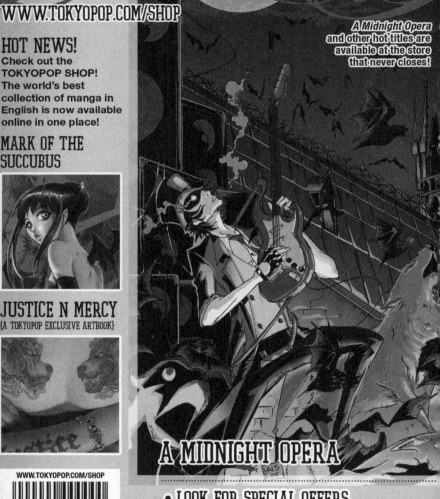

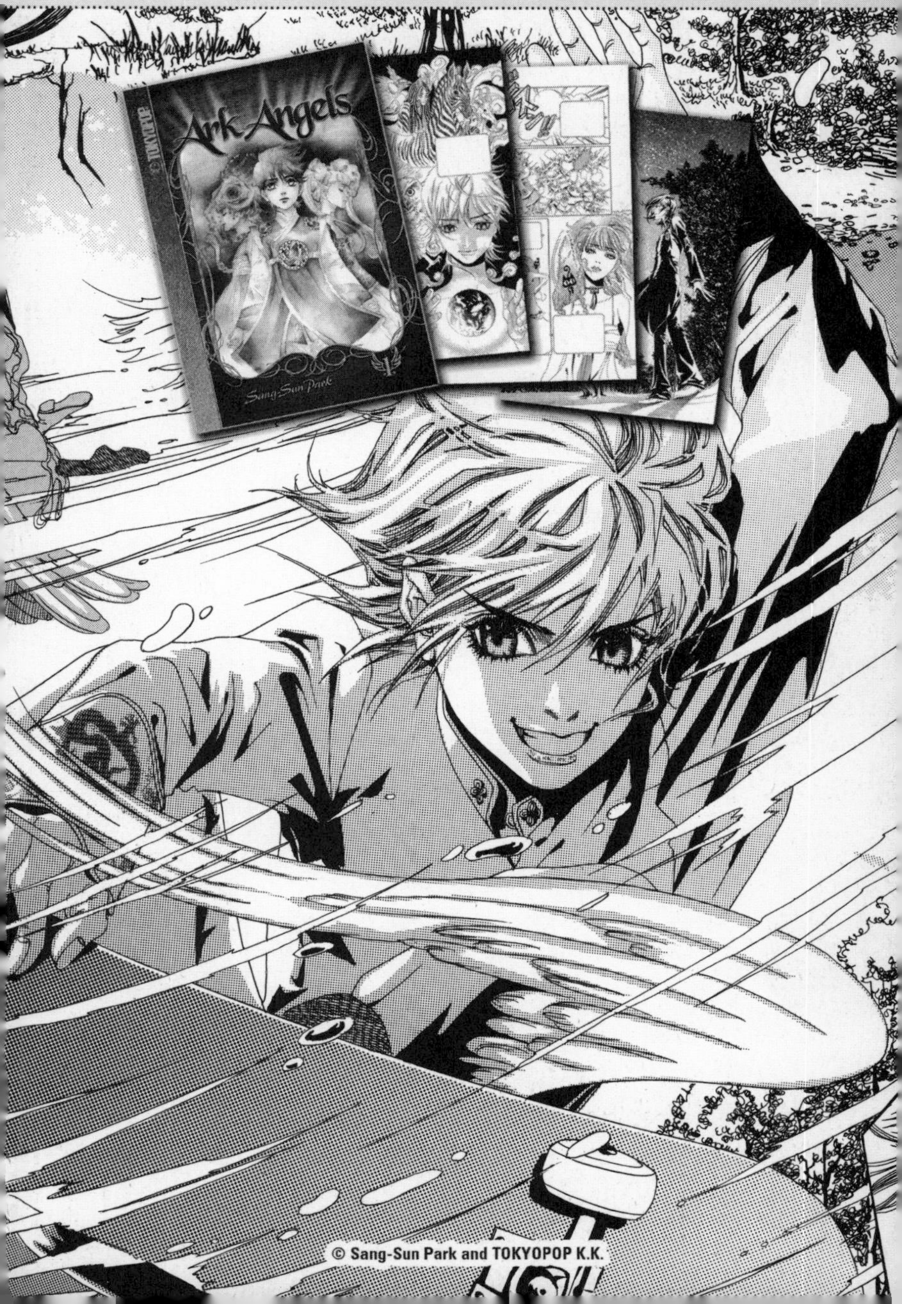
Ark Angels
TOKYOPOP
1
Sang-Sun Park

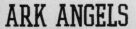

Ark Angels

Girls just wanna have fun—while saving the world.

From a small lake nestled in a secluded forest far from the edge of town, something strange has emerged: Three young girls—Shem, Hamu and Japheth—who are sisters from another world. Equipped with magical powers, they are charged with saving all the creatures of Earth from extinction. However, there is someone or something sinister trying to stop them. And on top of trying to save our world, these sisters have to live like normal human girls: They go to school, work at a flower shop, hang out with friends and even fall in love!

FROM THE CREATOR OF THE TAROT CAFÉ!

SPOTLIGHT

TOKYOPOP MANGA SUPPLEMENT

THE DREAMING

BY QUEENIE CHAN

T
TEEN
AGE 13+
TOKYOPOP
the dreaming
I
Queenie Chan
THE DORMS ARE ON THE SECOND FLOOR.
THIS WAY!
LIGHTS OUT AT TEN - BUT YOU CAN READ IN BED.
SU...
...AND WHAT'S BEHIND THAT DOOR ANYWAY?
WHAT THE---

ALL OF THEM VANISHED...WITHOUT A TRACE.

When twin sisters Amber and Jeanie enroll in an Australian boarding school, they soon uncover a dark, unexplained secret: Students have been known to walk off into the surrounding bushlands, where they have vanished completely! Few know how the girls disappeared...fewer yet know why. Amber and Jeanie soon realize that the key to unlocking a secret that has been hidden for years may lie in the world of their dreams!

SUSPENSE-HORROR SHOJO FROM THE CREATOR OF THE HIT WEB MANGA *BLOCK G.*

FOR MORE INFORMATION VISIT: WWW.TOKYOPOP.COM/THEDREAMING

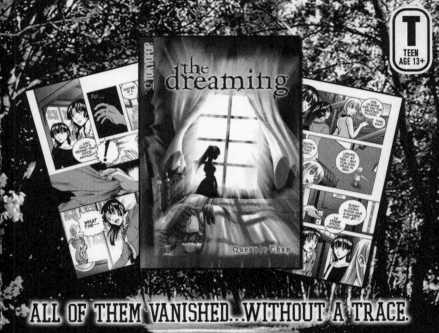

e frontier

MANGA STUDIO™ 3.0

WHAT WILL *YOU* CREATE?

The Best Software For Digital Manga Creation

e frontier's Manga Studio lets you draw, ink, tone and letter your manga in the computer. A library of **1800 digital tones** uses vector technology for moiré-free results. Automated drawing tools speed the process of creating your sequential art. Twelve types of layers keep your work organized and easy to edit. Scan in existing artwork and finish it in the computer, saving time and money on materials. Manga Studio's 1200-dpi resolution ensures professional-quality files that can be saved in several popular formats.

For more information or to purchase, visit:
www.e-frontier.com/go/tokyopop

SPECIAL INTRODUCTORY PRICE FOR MANGA STUDIO 3.0 DEBUT:
$49.99

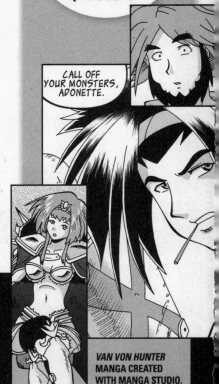

CALL OFF YOUR MONSTERS, ADONETTE.

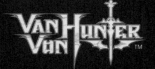

VAN VON HUNTER™

Copyright © 2005 e frontier America, Inc. and © 2003-2005 CelSys, Inc. Manga images from Van Von Hunter © 2005 Pseudomé Studio LLC. TOKYOPOP is a registered trademark and Van Von Hunter is a trademark of TOKYOPOP Inc. All other logos, product names and company names are trademarks or registered trademarks of their respective owners.

VAN VON HUNTER MANGA CREATED WITH MANGA STUDIO.

S0-ASI-959

STOP!

This is the back of the book.
You wouldn't want to spoil a great ending!

This book is printed "manga-style," in the authentic Japanese right-to-left format. Since none of the artwork has been flipped or altered, readers get to experience the story just as the creator intended. You've been asking for it, so TOKYOPOP® delivered: authentic, hot-off-the-press, and far more fun!

DIRECTIONS

If this is your first time reading manga-style, here's a quick guide to help you understand how it works.

It's easy... just start in the top right panel and follow the numbers. Have fun, and look for more 100% authentic manga from TOKYOPOP®!

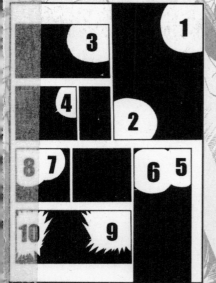

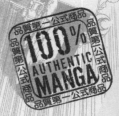